ASIA IN WASHINGTON

ASIA IN WASHINGTON

Exploring the Penumbra of Transnational Power

KENT E. CALDER

BROOKINGS INSTITUTION PRESS
Washington, D.C.

Copyright © 2014
THE BROOKINGS INSTITUTION
1775 Massachusetts Avenue, N.W., Washington, DC 20036
www.brookings.edu

The Brookings Institution is a private nonprofit organization devoted
to research, education, and publication on important issues of domestic
and foreign policy. Its principal purpose is to bring the highest quality
independent research and analysis to bear on current and emerging policy
problems. Interpretations or conclusions in Brookings publications
should be understood to be solely those of the authors.

Library of Congress Cataloging-in-Publication data
Calder, Kent E.
  Asia in Washington : exploring the penumbra of transnational power /
Kent E. Calder.
      pages   cm
  Includes bibliographical references and index.
  ISBN 978-0-8157-2538-1 (pbk. : alk. paper) 1. Globalization—Politcal
aspect—Asia. 2. Globalization—Political aspects—Washington (D.C.)
3. Asia—Foreign relations—21st century. 4. Asia—Foreign relations—United
States. 5. United States—Foreign relations—Asia. I. Title.
  JZ1318.C25 2014
  327.7305—dc23   2014000178

9 8 7 6 5 4 3 2 1

Printed on acid-free paper

Typeset in Sabon

Composition by Cynthia Stock
Silver Spring, Maryland

To the memory of
SPEAKER THOMAS S. FOLEY
Statesman, Diplomat,
and Builder of True Trans-Pacific Partnership

Contents

Appendixes

List of Figures
and Tables

Figures

Tables

List of Abbreviations

AAAF	Asian American Action Fund
ADB	Asian Development Bank
AEI	American Enterprise Institute
ASEAN	Association of Southeast Asian Nations
CCNA	Coordination Council for North American Affairs (China/Taiwan)
CCTV	China Central Television
CFIUS	Committee on Foreign Investment in the United States
CFR	Council on Foreign Relations
CIA	Central Intelligence Agency
CII	Confederation of Indian Industry
CRS	Catholic Relief Services
CSIS	Center for Strategic and International Studies
CSCC	Committee on Scholarly Communication with China
FAPA	Formosan Association for Public Affairs
FARA	Foreign Agents Registration Act
FTA	Free trade agreement
IMF	International Monetary Fund
IALI	Indian American Leadership Initiative
INGO	International non-governmental organization
JASW	Japan America Society of Washington, D.C.
JCAW	Japanese Commerce Association of Washington, D.C.

JETRO	Japan External Trade Organization
JICC	Japan Information and Cultural Center
KAVC	Korean American Voters' Council
KEI	Korea Economic Institute
KMT	Kuomintang (China/Taiwan)
KORUS	Korea-US (as in KORUS Free Trade Agreement)
KOTRA	Korea Trade-Investment Promotion Agency
METI	Ministry of Economics, Trade, and Industry (Japan)
MOF	Ministry of Finance (Japan)
MOFA	Ministry of Foreign Affairs (Japan)
NASA	National Aeronautics and Space Administration
NASSCOM	National Association of Software and Service Companies (India)
NCGUB	National Coalition Government of the Union of Burma
NCUSCR	National Committee on United States–China Relations
NFTC	National Foreign Trade Council
NKAL	Network of Korean American Leaders
NGO	Nongovernmental organization
NSA	National Security Agency
PRC	People's Republic of China
SAIS	School of Advanced International Studies (Johns Hopkins University)
SLORC	State Law and Order Restoration Council (Burma)
TECRO	Taipei Economic and Cultural Representative Office
USCBC	U.S.-China Business Council
USCPF	U.S.-China Policy Foundation
USIBC	U.S.-India Business Council
USINDO	United States–Indonesia Society
USINPAC	United States India Political Action Committee
USJC	U.S.-Japan Council
USSFTA	United States–Singapore Free Trade Agreement

Preface and Acknowledgments

Americans, like people of virtually all nations, reflexively view the world through the perspective of their nation-state. The doings of the president make front-page news almost daily, and the White House stands among our preeminent national symbols. The vital details of the nation's birth and growth are commonplace to our schoolchildren, and the nation's capital is a symbolic arena that we visit and revisit, vicariously at least, almost every day.

Yet the actual details of everyday political life in Washington, and how America's capital really does interact with the world, remain remarkably obscure. Neither I nor, I suppose, the reader has ever shaken hands with a nation-state. Yet we have no better concept to help us interpret life in the nation's capital or to understand how it actually relates to the broader world.

My personal fascination with Washington and its meaning for the broader world began early in my junior high school career, as I raptly listened to John F. Kennedy's inaugural address being piped into my seventh-grade classroom. Having just returned from Southeast Asia, where my father had been working with the Ford Foundation on development projects, I empathized with the globalism embodied in Kennedy's words and was mesmerized with the solemn symbolism of that statecentric, presidential-succession event. Washington seemed to me to be a place where the world could be changed, through the application of American ideas and power, and I vowed to understand it, somehow, someday.

My first chance came nearly a decade later, in my undergraduate years, when I served as a congressional intern with the House of Representatives' Banking and Currency Committee. Over the ensuing four decades and more, I have come back to Washington in many incarnations—as a researcher with the U.S. Federal Trade Commission; to testify before various congressional committees; as Japan chair at the Center for Strategic and International Studies; and as a fresh Schedule C State Department appointee, en route to Tokyo to assist the U.S. ambassador to Japan. For the past decade I have taught at SAIS/Johns Hopkins University and headed the Reischauer Center for East Asian Studies there.

Viewing Washington from these multiple angles over nearly half a century has convinced me that the statecentric paradigm cannot adequately explain either the way Washington really operates or its impact on the broader world. I have come to realize that one needs to start with the trees in the forest—the individual decisionmakers, working in law firms, universities, think tanks, media organizations, and multilateral institutions, as well as the U.S. government. One also needs to understand the personal networks that connect all these bodies, and the various social communities that they form, to grasp how the U.S. capital actually works. Equally, one also has to be conscious of the rapid, however imperceptible, pace of recent change in the nation's capital. Today's Washington is profoundly different from the town where I worked as a congressional student intern during the Vietnam War.

The direction of Washington's incessant, continuing change is instructional and was a principal motive for my writing this book. Washington is growing at once more pluralistic, especially outside the government, and also more global. It is rapidly developing a shadowy "penumbra of power"—a diverse web of nongovernmental institutions with significant government contacts and access—that is mediating a deepening relationship between official Washington and the broader world. Even as the American nation-state has become geopolitically preeminent since the collapse of the Soviet Union, the broad Washington sociopolitical community has also become more interdependent with external actors and agenda-setting efforts. And no one has been more vigorous in striving to influence the course of Washington than the nations of Asia, together with related transnational networks of both Asian and American origin.

Both economic and security impulses propel the countries of Asia to influence America's capital in its varied official and unofficial dimensions, although their effectiveness varies, as we shall see.

The research presented here began nearly eight years ago when I asked my student research assistant at SAIS, Erin Murphy, to put together a list of recent think tank activities relating to various nations of Asia. It gathered unique momentum through the efforts, beginning soon thereafter, of Mariko de Freytas, a previous student of mine at Princeton, who felicitously reappeared in Washington and agreed to join the Reischauer Center. Mariko, whose father is a native Washingtonian, shared with me a fascination with the slow emergence of a "strategic information complex" of global scope before our very eyes along Massachusetts Avenue in the heart of Washington; she continued as my key research assistant for more than four years. I owe Mariko my deepest thanks, especially for the painstaking work she did in documenting the emergence of Washington as a global political city, presented in chapters 1 and 2.

Another key source of inspiration over the past six years of research has been my graduate seminar at SAIS on Asia in Washington, inaugurated in the fall of 2007. Through innumerable visits over the ensuing years to Capitol Hill, the State Department, think tank offices, embassies, and even seminars in a Georgetown Chinese teahouse or two, I have gained a much more refined sense of Washington agenda setting, and I thank both students and our hosts for that deeper perspective. Along parallel lines, a seminar and research project on Washington's idea industry, generously supported by the Center for Global Partnership of the Japan Foundation, has recently allowed us to bring in outside speakers and do supplementary research to deepen collective insights. I particularly appreciate the special assistance that Junichi Chano, a Reischauer Center Visiting Fellow during the 2013–14 academic year, provided in organizing, supporting, and contributing intellectually to that project.

Over the years I have completed eleven books, with eight publishers, so the production process has grown somewhat routine. I have been pleasantly impressed, however, with the speed, cooperative attitude, and scholarly sensitivity of the Brookings Institution Press, and must say a special word of thanks to them. Chris Kelaher, Janet Walker, and copy editor Diane Hammond, as well as my superb graphic designer, Bill Nelson, have been wonderful to work with.

Finally, I would be remiss not to mention the key role that our growing Reischauer Center research community has provided in making this book a reality. At the latter stages of research—fact checking, graphics, and invaluable overall assistance—Megan Dick has provided selfless and highly efficient help. Narae Choi, Alison Evans, Gyung Hee Kim, Lisa Hanson, Hiro Hasegawa, Junya Hashimoto, Haillee Lee, Zongyuan Liu, Yimian Li, Sumiyo Nishizaki, James Pai, Shin Shoji, Yanan Wang, and Yukie Yoshikawa have all likewise contributed significantly. I am also indebted to Donald Abelson, Daniel Bob, Bill Brooks, Paul Choi, Rust Deming, Ronna Freiberg, Francis Fukuyama, John Harrington, Andrew Horvats, Karl Jackson, Marc Knapper, David Lampton, Eunjung Lim, Satu Limaye, Arthur Lord, Michael Mandelbaum, James McGann, Walter Mondale, Vali Nasr, Don Oberdorfer, Skipp Orr, John Roos, Saskia Sassen, David Shear, Kurt Tong, Stephen Walt, Bill Wise, Quangsheng Zhao, and many other colleagues in the academic and policy communities for their insights and perspectives. And of course I am grateful to my family, for their support and for their gentle proddings that this project be completed swiftly. Responsibility for any failings and mistakes, of which many no doubt remain, must remain mine alone.

Introduction:
Toward a New Paradigm for International Relations

For three and a half centuries and more, international relations has been seen as a matter of ties among nation-states: France, China, Russia, Japan, and, preeminently over the past two decades, the United States of America. Yet in a globalizing system of rising complexity, that view has grown too simple. It is time for a new paradigm.

To be sure, America has the strongest military in the world. Despite persistent U.S. domestic controversy over fiscal policy, the dollar continues to prevail as the global key currency. In many ways the United States still remains, as Secretary of State Madeleine Albright often self-confidently put it in the late 1990s, the "indispensable nation."[1]

Yet there is much that such rhetoric does not, in the early twenty-first century, adequately explain about international affairs. Why does the "indispensable nation" acquiesce to trade and financial policies that blunt its growth, and why does it not work harder to configure the rules of the game? Why does it oscillate so strikingly over time in the dynamism of its response to the world? Why does it pay so much attention to some small countries, often not highly strategic, and ignore other large ones, some among the most consequential in the world?

The Problem for Analysis

Much, in the final analysis, proves obscure when the focus is only on nations. Instead, the conceptual net needs to be cast more widely, to encompass a broader range of international actors. On an ever more

1

complex global chessboard, leaders and their publics interact across protean dimensions. To comprehend that reality, and to foretell the future, those multiple dimensions of public affairs need to be grasped and their role in the complex interactions that now configure the world better conceptualized.

Subnational actors, to be sure, have gotten significant attention in international relations theory for over two decades. They were a concern of classic works, such as Robert Keohane and Joseph Nye's *Power and Interdependence,* in the late 1970s.[2] Subnational analyses, however, have generally focused on transnational actors, such as multinational corporations and global religious organizations, rather than on geographically defined units such as cities. Yet cities are a crucial—perhaps *the* crucial—dimension of the subnational universe, which is growing ever more important in global affairs. Throughout the Middle Ages— indeed, until the Peace of Westphalia in 1648—cities were key actors in international relations. And they are becoming so once again, as the reality of global localism grows ever more salient.[3]

An extensive and useful literature has evolved concerning the notion of the global city.[4] This notion has been applied, however, mainly in the economic realm. New York and London have been examined in detail, as quintessential expressions, with the notion being applied to Tokyo also.[5] Surprisingly, however, the concept of the global city has rarely been applied to political affairs.[6]

For many years, that failure to include predominantly political towns within the rubric of *global city* was apt. These cities were, in truth, parochial, with little international dimension. Their overriding concern was domestic politics, with a focus on the local legislature. Washington, D.C., itself was dominated by parochial congressional politics throughout the first two-thirds (1800–1950 or so) of its existence (see chapter 1).

Yet global politics is changing profoundly, and diplomats ignore that historic transformation at their peril. Telecommunications and transportation are much faster and more efficient than they have ever been before, while economic relations are more intimate and interactive, creating an increasingly tangible new global political-economic community. Global political cities, rising within this broader configuration, are distinguished not by their agglomeration of CEOs or their intensity of financial trading but rather by their remarkable influence (as sophisticated, yet often nongovernmental, communities interactive with government) over policy decisions and by their amassing of strategic intelligence on topics that range from national policy trends to geopolitical risk.

Why Asia in Washington?

Washington is a particularly interesting focal point of research on global political cities for several reasons. Most important, of course, it is the geographical seat of the world's most powerful national government. Almost as vital, however, it is one of the world's most significant centers of multilateral policy activity, with the headquarters of the World Bank, the International Monetary Fund, the Inter-American Development ment Bank, and the Organization of American States, just to name a few major resident organizations located within its confines. It also hosts one of the world's most vigorous NGO communities, housing groups such as the World Wildlife Fund and InterAction as well as major activities of Amnesty International and the International Red Cross. Building on but transcending the capabilities of the U.S. government, Washington also houses a formidable information analysis complex, including the world's most influential think tanks.

As a consequence of the foregoing, enhanced by the soft-power legitimacy of American society and values in a global world, Greater Washington has emerged in the Internet age as a preeminent agenda-setting center. It has done so even on issues—ranging from the massacre of Armenians by Turkey during World War I, to the ill treatment of "comfort women" in East Asia during World War II, to ethnic cleansing in Darfur today—that are virtually unrelated to America's conventional bilateral relations with the world or, indeed, even to the United States as a geopolitical entity at all.

Within Washington, the role of Asia, as opposed to other global regions, is an especially important subject for research, particularly as a topic in contemporary international political economy. Again, one can distinguish several reasons. Substantively, Asia represents the core of the non-Western industrialized world; its political-economic prospects determine the capacity of non-Western nations to challenge the long-standing preeminence of the West. More abstractly, Asia's rapid socioeconomic rise raises the important conceptual question of how economic power and geopolitical influence are related in today's world, if indeed they are related at all. In addition, since Asian people are mainly non-Caucasian, the role of Asia in Washington implicitly raises the delicate and troublesome issue of how race matters in international global governance.

U.S.-Asian relations are uniquely configured, being both highly asymmetric along many dimensions and also characterized by large gaps in mutual understanding. They thus present important cases in the study of both misperception and the impact of cognitive distortions on international relations. Finally, since Asia has been late developing compared to the West, its changing role in Washington raises major issues regarding how rising powers assimilate themselves into global governance structures. These are no doubt more starkly posed in the drama of what I call Asia in Washington than in any other world region's relationships with the U.S. national capital.

Conceptual Ambitions

Together with its substantive promise as a vehicle for deepening our understanding of the world around us, *Asia in Washington* can also make important contributions to ongoing theoretical debates in both domestic politics and international political economy. It promises to contribute in seven major areas: a critique of realist theory, an illustration that domestic structure matters, an explication of the subnational factors that shape international relations, an explication of how crisis affects policy outcomes, an elaboration of how bandwagoning operates, an argument against empire theorists, and a contribution to understanding global governance

—*Critique of realist theory.* Realist formulations of international interactions have been under attack intermittently for at least half a century.[7] Yet how the behavior of sociopolitical communities at the subnational level actually inhibits or redirects national power projection has rarely been examined in detail. This volume demonstrates through concrete comparative case studies of foreign governmental interaction with Washington that influence does not flow only from conventional power characteristics, such as GDP, military strength, and geographical scale, but also from subnational sociopolitical traits.

—*Illustration that domestic structure matters.* The past decades have brought persistent admonitions to "bring the state back in."[8] Yet states are by no means homogeneous, and their configuration profoundly influences policy outcomes. All too little concrete analysis of just when and how state structure matters has been undertaken. By showing contrasts between the open character of the Washington political community, with its extensive extragovernmental penumbra of power, and the more closed sociopolitical character of many other global political cities, this research strives to make the importance of domestic social structure for policy clear.

—*Explication of subnational factors that shape international relations.* Subnational political-economic factors, apart from state structure, have been identified as generally important in international relations.[9] As yet there has not been much work done on the concrete causal processes through which subnational forces influence nation-state behavior. This research strives to help fill that gap by showing concretely the relationship between embassies and local ethnic communities, for example, or degrees of interministerial conflict within national governments.

—*Explication of how crisis affects policy outcomes.* Social science theory has increasingly recognized that political-economic crisis moves policymaking forward.[10] Yet views remain unsettled on precisely how crisis influences policy content or decisionmaking search processes.[11] By exploring how Washington expands under crisis conditions, such as civil war, world war, security crisis (as 9/11), and financial crisis (as 2008), this book examines the impact of crisis itself on the sociopolitical fabric of global cities.

—*Elaboration of how bandwagoning operates.* As Stephen Walt and others note, bandwagoning appears to be salient in the foreign policy of smaller nations dealing with the United States in the post–cold war world.[12] *Asia in Washington* considers how such countries—especially those that are upwardly mobile in international affairs, like the nations of Asia—curry favor with a dominant power, such as the United States, and thus compromise the hegemonic influence of such a power.

—*Argument against empire theorists.* The past decade has witnessed an explosion of literature regarding the political economy of empire, much of it presenting the post–cold war United States as a modern hegemon.[13] *Asia in Washington* explores the formidable problems that even leaders of a nation with overwhelming military power experience in shaping global policy agendas, when transnational actors have extensive access in a global political city like Washington. The book also considers how those transnational actors work to shape superpower agendas.

—*Contribution to understanding global governance.* As worldwide political-economic interdependence has risen, the importance of strengthened global-governance institutions has been ever more keenly recognized.[14] Clearly nation-states alone cannot, in the post–cold war world, unilaterally determine the parameters within which the global system should operate. Yet they do have some influence. This volume strives to show how transnational interactions in the capital of the world's most powerful nation—the home to so many important multilateral institutions as well—shapes the emergence of global norms and governing institutions, with a special focus on the interaction of the American and Asian actors in that process.

About the Book

This volume explores how Washington, as a sociopolitical community with important global functions transcending the U.S. government, is influenced by its interaction with Asia and what that interaction means for world affairs more generally. The chapters address four aspects. The first discussion develops the concept of the global political city and identifies the unique features of Washington within that context. These passages note that Washington has changed greatly as a sociopolitical community over the past thirty years. In particular, the American capital has developed a pronounced penumbra of power outside the U.S. government, which engages in intense interaction with the broader world—and that is gaining an ever more influential role in setting global agendas.

The second group of chapters contrasts the functional importance of Washington for Asia, and conversely of Asia for Washington, as those general transpacific relationships have evolved since the early days of the American republic around the dawn of the nineteenth century. These chapters point out that the transpacific equation has shifted substantially since World War II, with Washington growing increasingly important for Asia—but with the converse not nearly as true. This discussion shows the broad incentives that drive Asian nations to work so hard at cultivating relations with Washington and the skewed patterns of interest and indifference with which they must contend in their dealings with official Washington. It thus clarifies the nature of the structural problem that Asian actors confront as they operate within Washington itself.

The third group of chapters examines comparatively the sociopolitical approaches of major Asian nations to Washington—how they articulate their interests and publicize their national agendas. This discussion points out that large nations, powerful in economic and political-military terms, are surprisingly ineffective in achieving their desired ends in Washington. To the contrary, smaller states, such as Singapore, appear to more efficiently achieve their objectives in the U.S. national capital.

The final discussion examines the global implications of Asia's distinctive patterns of interaction with the Washington sociopolitical community, both within and beyond the U.S. government. It suggests that Washington's relatively open penumbra of power—universities, think tanks, mass media, lobbyists, and other opinion makers—operates to constrain the dominance of what is often postulated to be a globally dominant American hegemon. It does so particularly by moderating and recalibrating the role of the formal American policy process in global agenda setting. Asian nations are especially active in monitoring and moderating Washington in the economic area, where their role in the U.S. capital is a major force in creating a more balanced and multilateral pattern of global governance than has generally been recognized to exist.

The pages to follow thus tell a counterintuitive story, one that is of major significance in understanding world affairs both today and in the foreseeable future. Even as U.S. preeminence in the conventional calculus of global power begins to wane, the international influence of Washington as a global agenda-setting community continues to grow, as we shall see in the coming pages.

1

Washington as a Global Political City

For well over three hundred and fifty years, since the 1648 Peace of Westphalia, states have been the central actors of the international system. Since the end of the Thirty Years' War, it has been states, after all, that decide matters of war and peace, conduct diplomacy, and fight wars. In domestic affairs it is they that have generally guaranteed civil order, received and collected taxes, erected public works, and provided for the general welfare. And the state's role grew markedly greater, in both domestic and international affairs, across the course of the twentieth century, galvanized by leaders as varied in their roles and persuasions as Franklin D. Roosevelt, Joseph Stalin, Adolf Hitler, and Willy Brandt.

In theory, as in practice, the state has traditionally been dominant for centuries. Thomas Hobbes and Jean Bodin developed the classical rationale for state power four hundred years ago, just as the classical nation-state itself was emerging in the France of Louis XIV and the Britain of Henry VIII.[1] Since then, the nation-state has been the central concept in the emerging discipline of political science. When scholars have strayed toward more society-based perspectives, political sociologists like Theda Skocpol and Margaret Weir have insisted on "bringing the state back in."[2] And in international relations theory—the outward-looking face of government—the state also has been conceptually central for a long and illustrious line of political thinkers, beginning with Hobbes and continuing through Hans Morgenthau, Kenneth Waltz, John Mearsheimer, and other scholars of the realist tradition in particular.[3]

The Underdeveloped Analysis of Cities
in Their Broader Political Context

Amid this emphasis on the role of the state in both domestic and international affairs, the study of cities and their broader political-economic functions has been neglected. To be sure, the vigorous interdisciplinary field of urban studies has emerged since the 1960s, bringing urban planners, architects, sociologists, criminologists, anthropologists, philosophers, and even a few political scientists together to consider how cities operate, evolve, and relate to the higher domestic layers of government—states, prefectures, and nations—in which they are embedded.[4] Yet for many years little work was done on the role of cities in the international system.

Such analysis of the global role of cities has been inhibited both by the insignificance of the role that cities played and by the dominance of the realist, state-centric paradigm in international relations. For two millennia and more, a few cities have figured importantly in international politics. The significant early municipal players were imperial capital cities—Thebes, Babylon, Persepolis, Alexandria, Rome, and Constantinople, to name a few. There were also city-states, which combined national and municipal characteristics—Athens and Sparta in the classic age and Venice, Genoa, and the members of the Hanseatic League during the Middle Ages.

The functions of these communities as cities—their interest-group configurations, the way services were provided, and even their physical layout—materially affected how the broader nations in which they were embedded functioned. Yet little research has been undertaken on these linkages between the anatomy of cities and the functioning of the nations and empires of which they were a part. And such studies as did emerge—including those of factionalism in classic Rome and its implications for imperial stability—were generally limited to a single case and not systematically comparative.

Over the past decade, the serious comparative study of cities in their global context has at last begun to emerge. Leading this effort has been the sociologist Saskia Sassen.[5] In a series of seminal volumes she has articulated the concept of the global city, clearly distinguishing it from the notion of the world city, which in her terminology denotes a great metropolis of the past.[6] She has undertaken serious empirical work on the emerging international economic roles of New York and London and the impact of such developments on local urban life, as global financial markets become more and more deeply integrated. Rejecting the notion that globalization disperses production and diffuses a city's economic power, Sassen argues that globalization leads to the concentration of financial, technological, and other highly specialized services. Cities become increasingly strategic as their capacity for producing global control expands, she contends. Yet Sassen does not probe in detail the systemic implications of the increasing dynamism of cities for global political affairs.

Building on Sassen's general notion of the global city, a school of comparative research has grown up that evaluates and ranks cities in terms of their importance and efficiency in discharging broader international functions—including, to a limited degree, politics.[7] A. T. Kearney, the Chicago Council on Global Affairs, and *Foreign Policy* magazine have collaborated on one influential comparative study. They considered the global role of major cities along five dimensions—business activity, human capital, information exchange, cultural experience, and political engagement. Based on values assumed in these dimensions, they constructed an aggregate index.[8]

Although important advances have been made over the past decade in the comparative assessment of global cities in their social and economic dimensions, systematic analysis of their political functions still remains underdeveloped. Conspicuously lacking, in particular, is an assessment of how local structures and their evolution influence international politics. Analysts simply have not given much thought to how the institutional configuration of city governments, the interest group profiles prevailing in urban communities, or the linkages of local communities with one another affect the broader political systems in which they are embedded. The international political role of cities is another particularly neglected realm, despite the long-standing international importance of cities within the context of empire, as noted above; the emergence of dynamic new mayoral networks like the C-40 illustrates this increasingly important trend.[9] The converse issue—how international politics affects sociopolitical life in key global cities—is even less explored.

Toward a Political Analysis of Cities in the Global Context

In this volume I develop the concept of the global political city and document in a preliminary way the functions of such cities in international affairs. I define a global political city as one that manifests the broad characteristics of a global city as conceptualized by Sassen but one that also serves as a microsetting for global political transactions, which she does not consider in detail. In a global political city, policies of multiple jurisdictions are shaped, and can be influenced, not only by the local national government but also by foreign governments and transnational actors. Key elements of global political cities include the following:

—A policy hub, exercising disproportionate influence on global policy debates.

—A political-diplomatic community, with dense networks of official and nonofficial actors shaping global affairs.

—A strategic information complex, within which flows important political, military, and country-risk information with global portent.

A few cities, as we have seen, have previously held major political-economic importance in international affairs. Most of these, however, were imperial capitals (Rome, Baghdad, Khanbalik, Paris, Vienna, St. Petersburg, London), in which nation-state influence traditionally loomed large.[10] Such metropolitan centers held unusual international significance due to the strength and wealth of the empires over which they ruled, and imperial interests largely dominated their civic life. A few trading centers that were not imperial capitals, such as New York, Rotterdam, and Singapore, have also been functionally important for the global economy, with their significance magnified during periods of broad international economic integration, such as the early twentieth century and the post–World War II period.

Conceptually speaking, it is useful to regard global cities with political-economic functions as being arrayed on a fourfold table that distinguishes political and economic functions (figure 1-1). On the one axis is a given city's political role—generally expressed historically through its formal imperial functions, although this pattern is likely changing. On the other axis is the global city's role as an economic center. The graphic locations presented here along economic and political

Figure 1-1. *Conceptualizing the Global Political-Economic Role of Cities*

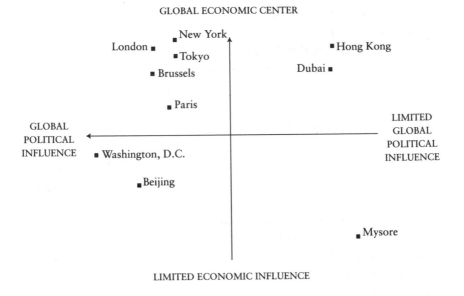

dimensions are broadly consistent with values assigned by the "2012 Global Cities Index."[11]

The position of a given city in such a political-economic matrix can, of course, easily change over time—and in fact often does so—as its global significance in a given area waxes and wanes. New York City, for example, was briefly once the capital of the United States, with important political functions—George Washington, for instance, was inaugurated there in 1789, as first president under the U.S. Constitution. New York was eclipsed politically by Washington, D.C., after 1800, however, and even for a time by Albany, the New York state capital. Still, it revived on the multinational stage in the early 1950s, when it became the permanent headquarters of the United Nations in 1952. And its global role was enhanced further by the activities of Mayor Michael Bloomberg, as chairman of the C-40 global association of mayors during the early 2010s.

Brussels is another case in point—both as a global city with clear political functions and as one whose global transnational functions have come to decisively eclipse and grow distinct from those of the nation-state within which it is geographically embedded. Brussels had some international political standing, to be sure, as the formal colonial master of the mineral-rich Belgian Congo (1908–60).[12] Further back, Brussels was a relatively important city even in the 1430s as the capital of Burgundy, although its political importance depended entirely on the whims of the European rulers of the time. By the 1830s, with the onset of the Enlightenment, Brussels assumed a broader informal role than that of a mere national capital. The city's relative freedom from censorship, in contrast to Paris, made it a refuge for such libertarian thinkers as Baudelaire and Hugo.

Emigrés such as the Polish organizers of the failed 1830 November Insurrection, or Karl Marx and the Young Hegelians, intensified the revolutionary spirit of Brussels, enhancing its transnational political influence. By the 1850s Brussels was also the confluence of "the three great wire services that were revolutionizing journalism: Reuters of Britain, Havas of France, and Wolff of Germany."[13] This strategic intellectual position within Europe allowed Brussels a further role in the dissemination of ideological journalism, enabling the city to become influential in the formation and spread of revolutionary movements across the entire continent.[14] And since 1958 Brussels's transnational political standing has been sharply enhanced because the city serves not only as the headquarters of an increasingly cohesive and powerful European Community but also the headquarters of NATO since 1967. It is also the headquarters of some internationally prominent NGOs, such as the International Crisis Group. Growing in both local cohesion and global political-economic importance, the position of Brussels has hence been moving up and to the left in figure 1-1.

The historical evolution of Brussels shows clearly the potential for dynamic change in the political-economic role of cities over time, in a fashion distinct from that of the nation-states of which they are geographically part. The Belgian parliament is clearly of declining relative importance in a world of deepening European and global integration.[15] Yet Brussels as a strategic venue for global transactions is retaining its importance—not only as Belgium's capital but also as a locus for international institutions.

Even such a simple typological framework as presented in figure 1-1 generates important empirical puzzles both for comparative political

Figure 1-2. *State, Community, and the Evolution of Global Political Cities*

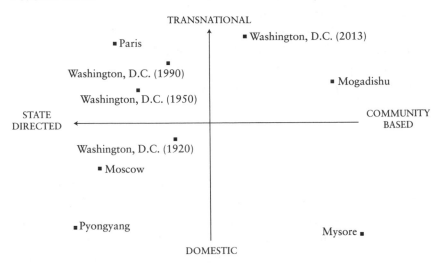

research and for international political economy. How, for example, does the political-economic importance of individual cities like Brussels and New York in international affairs change over time, and what factors drive such transitions? Conversely, how do such changing roles—the emergence of Brussels as the EU capital, for example—affect the prosperity and politics of cities themselves, and with what feedback effects on the national and international systems?

In the real world, political cities of course vary considerably in the degree to which they are dominated by the nation-state in which they are geographically embedded. In extreme cases, like Kim Jong-un's Pyongyang and Stalin's Moscow, there is little civil community even moderately detached from the state. Conversely, in cities like Gaza and Mogadishu, vigorous—indeed, anarchic and destructive—political communities exist in social environments where state power is virtually nonexistent. These distinctions are represented along the horizontal axis of figure 1-2, which also shows how the character of Washington as a global political city has evolved over the past century.

Political communities—as distinct from the nation-states in which they are embedded—have a second dimension of critical relevance in applying the global political city concept: the degree to which they are geographically limited by national political boundaries. Pyongyang and Stalin's Moscow stand, in their isolation, at one pole, as suggested in figure 1-2, while contemporary Washington, in its cosmopolitanism, clearly stands at the other.

The typologies presented in figures 1-1 and 1-2, when applied to concrete cases, suggest that cities characteristically shift their positioning over time. Washington certainly has done so. Major global political cities in Western democracies are typically growing at once both more transnational and less state dominated in the post–cold war world, making the distinction between state and global political city, as defined here, increasingly important. A parallel trend is discernible in nondemocratic and non-Western societies also, although the pace of divergence between state and societal dynamics is less rapid. Thus, the importance of the global political city appears to be growing worldwide, with cities like Washington and Brussels in the vanguard of a broader trend.

Washington as a Global Political City

Washington is no doubt the most important global political city in the world, and its significance is closely related to the global political influence of the American nation-state. Yet Washington as a complex of sociopolitical institutions is far from being a straightforward agent of American geopolitical power, as crude state-centric analyses of international relations might assume. To the contrary, Washington as a vibrant global political city has a discrete importance as a microsetting for global transactions that is separate from and sometimes in tension with American state power. This informal role moderates the American state, transforms its expressed interests, and opens the U.S. policy process as a whole to information and influences from elsewhere in the world. Indeed, Washington's role as a global political city, transcending the limitations and interests of the American nation-state, converts the United States into a power much more responsive to broad global concerns, on issues ranging from trade to human rights, than it would otherwise be, forcing heavy qualifications on recently fashionable notions of American empire.[16]

Washington's character as a generally open, decentralized political community does not necessarily imply a neutral orientation in international affairs. For complex sociopolitical reasons, many of them historically embedded, there is considerable variation in the access that different nations actually enjoy there.[17] Britain, for example, enjoys unusual entrée, due to linguistic ties and long-standing sociopolitical relationships. Washington's distinctive sociopolitical structure does, however, create at least the potential for broad, moderating access if a sufficiently wide range of groups avail themselves of this opportunity.

Washington's paradoxical receptivity to transnational influences, despite the manifest power of the nation-state within which it is geographically embedded, is rooted in its distinctive history. In contrast to London, Paris, Rome, Madrid, and Lisbon, Washington was never a major imperial capital in its formative years. Imperial capitals had the powerful state institutions that an imperial role naturally generated (and even narrow colonial interests, such as the Caribbean slave owners and rum merchants of eighteenth-century London). The United States did, to be sure, acquire a few overseas possessions, most notably the Philippines, in the early twentieth century.[18] Yet America acquired those possessions relatively late; they provided few economic benefits for the metropole and generated only marginal sociopolitical changes in Washington itself. One exception was the sugar lobby, related to American corporate interests in the Philippines and Hawaii, which gave an anomalous protectionist cast to American trade policies in that area, even when broader U.S. trade policy was more free-trade oriented.[19]

Imperial standing thus failed to transform Washington politically, socially, or economically as substantially as it had major European capitals. And imperial standing, such as it was, did not make Washington a major diplomatic center either. Other factors ultimately propelled its rise.

This absence of early American empire and international standing, combined with Washington's character as an artifact of sudden political decision, meant that the new U.S. capital evolved, for the first century and more of its existence, without a sophisticated, embedded, domestic foreign policy structure. There were no permanent diplomatic establishments at all in Washington, for example, until after the Civil War.[20] And when envoys did arrive in person, in the early nineteenth century, they quickly departed, finding Washington a "hardship post" and "uncivilized."[21]

Indeed, Washington was so tiny and unsophisticated that it did not even have street numbering until 1854.[22] Until World War II the State and War Departments were housed in a single building next to the White House. Elaborate, large-scale foreign policy institutions, including today's State Department, Pentagon, and Central Intelligence Agency, began to evolve in Washington during the momentous, turbulent decade spanning World War II and the Korean War.

Yet as those bodies finally emerged, their roles developed in counterintuitive ways within a distinctive political-economic context, best captured through citycentric comparative analysis that distinguishes between formal governmental structures, on the one hand, and broader notions of community, on the other. Most important, Washington emerged as a global political city, with sophisticated formal and informal mechanisms for managing global affairs within a weak, decentralized, yet rapidly expanding American state. The Washington that first confronted the world as America became a great power thus lacked entrenched state institutions as well as embedded interests.

Lacking international exposure, Washington was, however, parochial in another way. The trajectory and sequencing of its evolution, relative to that of the American nation-state, gave birth to a sprawling, yet remarkably decentralized and permeable process of U.S. policymaking, generally devoid of embedded institutions and interests. This pattern continues to give foreign actors in Washington significantly more points of access than is common in many of the centralized imperial capitals of Europe and Asia, most notably Paris, Moscow, and Beijing. Those complex seats of former empires—so different in their local sociopolitical configuration—are Washington's major counterparts today in international affairs.

Washington, as noted earlier, was never a major imperial capital, in contrast to the classic world cities of strong states in Europe and Asia.[23] And it lacked a large-scale foreign policy apparatus until World War II. This distinctive historical-institutional heritage has three major long-term implications for American foreign policymaking. First, the embassies of major counterpart nations—Britain, France, Japan, and even Soviet Russia—established themselves in Washington during a period when the State Department and other major U.S. foreign policy institutions were still undeveloped. This reality gave those early embassies entrée to American foreign policymaking—most pronounced in the case of the British, who were America's first diplomatic interlocutors. These British envoys got to know senior American diplomats informally and established traditions of detailed advance consultation, allowing them to significantly influence American policy even as their national power dramatically waned, relative to that of the United States, after World War II. This easy entrée, which the British and to a lesser degree other foreign diplomats enjoyed in Washington, contrasted to the much lower degree of transparency prevailing in major European capitals—or indeed in Asia.

Parochial domestic institutions—Congress, domestic bureaucracies, and even domestic lobbies, such as those of early K Street—evolved before the major U.S. foreign policy institutions did. This development rendered diplomacy more vulnerable to parochial pressures and lobbying influence in the United States than in many other parts of the world. Additionally, American business interests did not rapidly move to Washington, making them relatively remote from the foreign policy process—epitomized in the classic detachment of Washington from America's automobile industry, based in Detroit. Early Washington, after all, did not have the entrenched, colonially related commercial interests, highly complicit with government, characteristic of such imperial capitals as Paris, London, Lisbon, and historic Brussels. Yankee entrepreneurs like Henry Ford wanted distance from government—not intimacy.

Indeed, Ford deeply mistrusted Franklin D. Roosevelt, considering the president's intervention in business-employee relations as meddling. As a classic entrepreneur, Ford had an abiding faith in American business itself, hoping that "American industrialists would just forget these alphabet schemes and take hold of their industries and run them with good, sound American business sense."[24] Ford's alternative corporate welfare approach provided his employees with social services, such as hygiene counseling, and created a legal department to help employees who were seeking to own their homes.[25] Ford, however, feared unionization and resisted Roosevelt, refusing to abide by the National Industrial Recovery Act (NIRA) in 1933, even at the cost of being excluded from bidding for government business.[26]

Indeed, Ford was openly critical of government, "whose particular genius is to try to run other people's business."[27] This government-skeptic worldview did not propel either Ford or his successors into an easy embrace of Washington, either in the Great Depression or in a lesser extremity like the financial crisis of 2008.

While it has had an uneasy relationship with entrepreneurs, Washington has long housed a vigorous NGO community, notably adapted to influencing the open, decentralized American foreign policy process, with its many, highly visible pressure points. This relationship with NGOs began evolving in the aftermath of World War I. The American Federation of Labor, which moved to 901 Massachusetts Avenue in 1916, created a publicity bureau in 1921 after conferring with domestic and international labor unions.[28] That same year, the Red Cross established itself on the National Mall, within a five-minute walk of the White House. The Vatican representation moved soon thereafter opposite what would become the vice president's residence near the Naval Observatory on upper Massachusetts Avenue.

Many other religious bodies, including Orthodox Judaism, the Mennonite Church, the Unitarian Universalist Association, and the Roman Catholic Church, also established an early official lobbying presence in Washington.[29] The oldest and largest of these religious offices, the United Methodist Church's General Board of Church and Society, traces its history to the Prohibition era (1919–33).[30] Mainline Protestant churches, such as the Episcopal and the Evangelical Lutheran Church of America, have maintained lobbying offices in the District since the 1950s, playing a substantial role thereafter in the civil rights movement and in opposition to the Vietnam War.[31]

Religious NGOs such as Caritas, based in Alexandria, Virginia, together with its affiliate, Catholic Relief Services (CRS), operating from nearby Baltimore, Maryland, also continue a long tradition, dating from 1951 for the first and from 1943 for the second, of organizing foreign humanitarian aid from the Washington area. CRS moved its world headquarters from New York to Baltimore in 1989, judging the location convenient for its proximity to Washington as well as to the Baltimore and Dulles international airports. A Greater Washington location facilitated employees' frequent travels overseas, not to mention coordination with national diplomatic authorities, multilateral bodies, and NGOs.[32]

Naturally, the United States is a fertile base for fundraising on behalf of transnational as well as domestic causes and from international as well as domestic donors. CRS provides a clear illustration. Its public donors include, in addition to the United Nations and the European Union, Washington-based institutions such as the World Bank, the U.S. Departments of Agriculture, Health and Human Services, and Labor, and USAID.[33] In 2012 the U.S. government provided nearly 39 percent of CRS's operating revenue and was by far its largest donor, even though CRS is a transnational NGO with more extensive overseas than domestic operations.[34]

Congressional subcommittees have traditionally heeded religious organizations, due to the moral legitimacy of such groups and their intimate knowledge of local conditions abroad. Relief organizations have often in turn used such knowledge and access to Congress to influence foreign policy thinkers, as Walter Judd and the Committee of One Million did in orienting U.S. China policy firmly toward Taiwan during the 1950s.[35] In the 1970s Catholic and Protestant religious organizations, operating out of Washington, became visible political actors, deepening U.S. interest in Latin American nations such as El Salvador.[36] More recently, during the George W. Bush years, religious organizations successfully pressed for change in aid policy toward HIV-prone countries. Naturally, each cause has typically generated countermovements, as the evolution of Planned Parenthood and other women's rights groups, for example, clearly shows. Such NGO thrusts and counterthrusts have increased the importance of Washington as a principal arena for debate, confrontation, and decision—and hence its role as a global political city.

It is not unnatural for coalitions in the District of Columbia to include seemingly strange bedfellows, from the same physical neighborhood, to serve mutually convenient ends. For example, Planned Parenthood on 16th Street N.W. and the Armenian National Committee's D.C. chapter on N Street—both transnational in their concerns—partner with DC Vote, a newer NGO, also on P Street, created in 1998 to promote the District's right to congressional representation. Geographical propinquity and the sociopolitical networks that close proximity so naturally engenders thus aid the rise of Washington as a political city whose communitarian dimension greatly transcends the U.S. government itself. NGOs interact with one another in patterns that often have little directly to do with the government.

It was World War II and the ensuing Korean War that triggered the meteoric rise of America's formal foreign policy establishment. Not surprisingly, the newly expanding U.S. bureaucracy exhibited a strong political-military cast as a consequence. The growing physical separation of its component parts also intensified the decentralized and accessible character of Washington decisionmaking, with the military and intelligence communities on one side of the Potomac and the diplomats on the other. A major break came in 1943 when the War Department moved physically away from the diplomats at State and established itself on the Virginia side of the Potomac in a sprawling, and self-sufficient, new headquarters (the Pentagon). Decentralization proceeded further in 1947 with the establishment of CIA headquarters at Langley, Virginia.

As Washington came to involve itself more thoroughly in the international scene, just before and after World War II, and became an established presence in world affairs, more and more non–U.S. government institutions found homes in the Washington area. Embassy Row, situated on 16th Street until the mid-1930s, moved to Massachusetts Avenue, as embassies followed the lead of the largest diplomatic establishment, that of imperial Britain. Since then, Embassy Row has expanded, with fifty-six embassies now stretching along Massachusetts Avenue, from Thomas Circle to the Naval Observatory. The influx of newly independent countries' foreign legations after the decolonization of Africa and South Asia in the 1960s forced the District of Columbia to enact, for the first time, zoning laws regarding embassies. Inevitably, when new countries emerged, as after the breakup of the Soviet Union in the 1990s, the foreign presence in Washington expanded still further and, with time, entrenched new international actors in the District's expanding policy community. Foreign business people and lobbyists naturally followed the diplomats.

The rapid recent expansion of America's diplomatic ties with the broader world, keeping pace with globalization, has transformed a traditionally parochial Washington into an increasingly cosmopolitan city. One indicator, presented in figure 1-3, is the steady increase since 1970 in Washington's foreign population. The share of the foreign-born in the U.S. national capital's population nearly tripled between 1970 and 2000, and the absolute number of foreign residents in Washington has continued to rise steadily since then.

Figure 1-3. *Washington's Foreign-Born Population, 1970–2010*

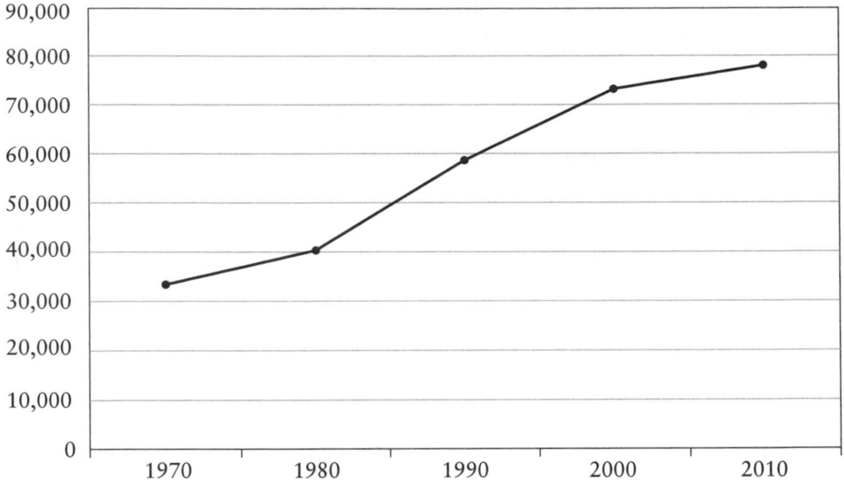

Source: Campbell Gibson and Kay Jung, "Historical Census Statistics on the Foreign-Born Population of the United States: 1850-2000," Working Paper 81 (U.S. Census Bureau, February 2006), table 14 (www.census.gov/population/www/documentation/twps0081/twps0081.html); and U.S. Census Bureau, "Quick Facts" (http://quickfacts.census.gov/qfd/states/11000.html).

Washington's Symbolic Role in Global Agenda Setting

Increasing cosmopolitanism, coupled with political power and diplomatic presence, naturally makes the Greater Washington policy community a center for protests, as well as deal making, regarding the policies of both the United States and foreign nations. Indeed, another particularity of Washington is its *symbolic* nature, an aspect that Roberto Camagni treats as a defining global city characteristic.[37] Associated with Washington are echoes of past political movements—for universal suffrage and civil rights, for example—that hold worldwide implications. These evocative precedents invite the policy-oriented to become part of Washington's microcosm of world affairs, fostering a tradition of political protest and witnessing, thus enhancing Washington's role as a global political city that stands for values that transcend America itself.

The White House and the National Mall, including the Lincoln Memorial, are symbolic locations, but many protests occur in front of embassies as well. Irish Americans in 1920 picketed the British embassy, calling for the end of British involvement in Ireland.[38] In more recent times, protesters have often congregated before the Chinese embassy seeking the PRC's intervention in Darfur, asylum for North Korean refugees, and freedom for Tibet, among other human rights issues. The Uzbek embassy on Massachusetts Avenue sees human rights protests as well.

Many other foreign policy–related activities are more formal. Foreign embassies have spawned such nongovernmental, community-based institutions as the Japan Information and Culture Center (JICC), KORUS House, and the Maison Française. Three Confucius Institutes have been established in the Washington area: at the University of Maryland (2004), George Mason University (2009), and George Washington University (2013); a Confucius Institute U.S. Center now also stands across the street from the Brookings Institution on Massachusetts Avenue, in the heart of the city. The German and the French language schools—the Goethe Institute and Alliance Française, respectively—also have broader sociopolitical ends. These cultural activities are more extensive in Washington than in most capitals and have greater impact precisely because they provide a relaxed and politically neutral venue for the complex information gathering and transnational decisionmaking that far transcend bilateral relations between the United States and individual foreign partners.

These entities attempt to foster understanding and to create ties with Washington residents through culture, although there is often an indirect political referent. The Embassy Adoption Program, organized by the Washington Performing Arts Society, pairs each participating embassy with a local grade school. Since its inception in 1974, more than 35,000 students and 103 embassies have participated.[39]

Embassies work with one another as well, for their mission inevitably involves networking with other nations. Besides formal embassy parties, embassies cooperate to organize cultural events open to the public, such as Euro Night, featuring EU cuisine and music. The Annual Kalorama House and Embassy Tour, for example, sponsored by the Friends of Wilson House, invites the public to visit ambassadorial residences, embassies, and other notable private residences in Washington's Kalorama neighborhood.

The Penumbra of Power: Washington's Emerging Strategic Information Complex

Apart from its well-known formal institutions, which have unquestionable global significance, and its vigorous yet less-recognized NGO culture, Washington's most distinctive and dynamic feature as a global political city—one with economic as well as political significance—is its emerging strategic information complex. This sociopolitical entity has its origins in the formidable information-gathering and information-processing capacities of the U.S. government, leveraged by the technological breakthroughs of the information revolution.[40] The strategic information complex also has an increasingly important private sector dimension, consisting of both government contractors and nongovernment-related research firms, think tanks, and university affiliates.

Washington is a multilayered policy community, where state-to-state relationships are only a minor portion of its sociopolitical interactions. Interpersonal networks involve embassies, think tanks, academic institutions, lobbying firms, politicians, congressional staff, research centers, NGOs, and intelligence agencies. This interaction—heavily oriented toward information gathering and incremental policy modification—is too complex and voluminous to be monitored by top leadership, and much of it lies outside the government. Yet this interaction has important implications for policy, not least due to the analytical capacities it creates outside the government.[41]

Quietly, over the past generation, a new sociopolitical reality has emerged in Washington, fed by the information revolution. It is not purely governmental, yet it also is not purely private. The best analogy is astronomical. It can be compared to the hazy, ambiguous periphery of the moon—the penumbra—where some or all of the reflected light source is obscured by an eclipse. Lawyers also use the term *penumbra* to denote implied rights, by extending the meaning of a rule into its periphery.[42]

I use the term *penumbra of power* here in the legal sense, to denote a netherworld between formal authority and informal action, where private resources monitor, predict, and influence government action and independently set global agendas. The denizens of the penumbra, as suggested in figure 1-4, are individuals seeking to monitor and influence

Figure 1-4. *Washington's Penumbra of Power*

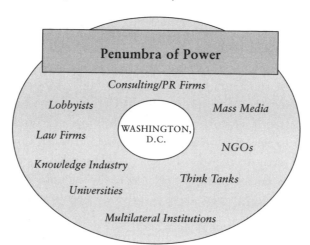

policy. They work for a variety of institutions: law firms, think tanks, consulting companies, multinational firms, universities, and international organizations, with clients throughout the world.

All of these entities converge into a strategic complex for influencing American domestic and foreign governmental activities. Networking and information gathering are the lifeblood of Washington, and these are pursued in diverse forums across the city: embassy parties, think tanks, receptions, presentations, seminars, working groups, and informal meetings. Many of Washington's institutions are a short walk from one another and are highly competitive. Like Silicon Valley and Madison Avenue, Massachusetts Avenue and K Street in Washington are classic "competitive clusters," where rivals generate information and ideas because of close proximity.[43]

Although Washington has an obvious importance in the formal national foreign policy arena, it is an ever more multifaceted policy community as globalization proceeds and as international rules in whose configuration Washington has a central role rapidly proliferate. In this complex and creative arena for transnational interaction, countries can learn both from each other and from lobbyists how to influence congressional policy, World Bank lending, and other globally relevant matters dependent on Washington-determined norms. A fiercer and less hierarchical competition for influence than in the past is thus generated among foreign and local interests operating on Washington's home turf.

Understanding the necessity for proactive lobbying in the fluid, competitive, new environment of contemporary Washington, many rising newcomers have substantially increased their public affairs activities in the 2000s. The Chinese government and Chinese firms, for example, sharply increased their corps of registered lobbyists from one (Jones Day) in 1986 to eleven lobbying and public relations firms in 2010 (not counting ten separate registered agents for Hong Kong entities).[44] In contrast, and perhaps leading to a relative decline of influence compared to the Chinese, the Japanese have historically been significantly more New York oriented.[45] The number of registered foreign agents working for Japan in the United States declined from 120 in 1989 to thirty-five in 2010, with only eight (not including the JICC) based in Washington and one each in Virginia and Maryland.[46]

Under the guidance of PR professionals, national-interest representation practices, to be sure, are changing. Traditionally—indeed, through the 1980s, at least—nations relied heavily, often at considerable cost, on lobbying firms dominated by influential former policymakers.[47] This emphasis has recently moderated, as global trade liberalization proceeds and the power of mass media rises, encouraging a higher premium on lower-budget public education. Embassies coordinate individually with local (and well-known) museums to showcase their art. Some find it easy to maintain close relationships with museums if the latter's central themes are based on a country or a region. The Freer and Sackler galleries, which effectively serve as America's national museums of Asian art, are natural venues for Asian nations to promote their cultures—and, indirectly, their political-economic interests as well.

Embassies reach out to the younger generation, from middle-school students to young professionals. The JICC, among other diplomatically oriented NGOs, sends promotional material to schools throughout the Washington area, welcoming class visits. Embassy officials have also become more accessible to youth by working with nonprofit organizations. The Asia Society, for example, organizes a Diplomatic Dialogue series, featuring face-to-face meetings between young professionals and embassy officials, such as the Indonesian ambassador's "fireside chat" at his embassy and similar informal presentations by China's counselor for political affairs and India's deputy chief of mission. Other Southeast Asian nations, such as Thailand, Singapore, and Pakistan, have been involved as well, sending their representatives to dinner discussions with the Asia Society's young members.

Nations learn from each other's successes and failures in "working the Hill," meaning Capitol Hill, where the U.S. Congress is located. The Koreagate scandal of 1976, for example, was a warning to other nations that contacts with such officials should include legitimate and recognized third-party intermediaries, such as lobbying firms sometimes represented by highly regarded former congressional members and staff, rather than payments or gifts. The Koreans also learned from the acrimonious trade frictions between Japan and the United States, starting in the late 1970s, that early warning systems are necessary to detect potential areas of contention between their home country and the United States. Thus, during the 1980s Korea hired policy-trend analysts and legal experts as a defensive measure to draft policies to inhibit protectionist pressures. Although legal disputes over trade often occurred, Korea was relatively successful in settling most such disputes.[48]

Recognizing the need to systematically analyze the American economic impact on Korea, and to educate the American public about the Korean economy, the Korean government created the Korea Economic Institute in 1982. In doing so, it closely referenced the Japan Economic Institute, sponsored by the Japanese Ministry of Foreign Affairs from 1957 to 2001.[49] Although the JEI is now defunct, the KEI still continues its activities and has, in fact, significantly expanded them over the past decade. As for the Chinese, they have curtailed their past practice of relying on reactive and critical letters to senators and congressional representatives, diversifying and intensifying their methods of lobbying the Hill.

The revolving door between K Street and Congress generates substantial information flows, with lobbying firms' hiring practices reflecting the prevailing balance of political power in Congress. For its part, Congress attempts to gain neutral information by using the Congressional Research Service, which researches solely for Congress and takes pride in its unbiased reports. Nevertheless, Congress cannot help but be influenced by interest group pressure, much of which sparks and sustains foreign policy concerns. Of course, as Congress creates working groups and subcommittees to analyze issues, these bodies also increase both the supply of and the demand for strategic information.

Washington is often considered to have only an American political dimension. Robert Fossaert writes, for example, that its economic activity is mostly due to the creation of domestic and bilateral foreign policy lobbying networks.[50] Yet Washington has also developed important multilateral and transnational functions as a policy community. It has, for example, been the seat of the International Monetary Fund and the World Bank since 1946. The city also hosted the first G-20 financial crisis summit in November 2008. The world clearly recognizes American political-economic power, stimulating determined transnational efforts to influence it, and often to encourage multilateralism.

Both foreign and domestic trade groups also make a point of establishing themselves in Washington in order to assess congressional and executive-branch policies. Naturally, internationally oriented economic institutions, such as the U.S. Export-Import Bank, which provides credit to American firms to facilitate their overseas business, are also attractive to both American and foreign entrepreneurs. Corporate headquarters and offices, as well as trade group offices, have steadily increased in the Washington area. Firms that lack enough funding to have their own offices pool their resources to form trade groups that in turn establish group offices in the District. Although formal national government transactions are, of course, enormously important, strengthening the think tanks, law firms, and lobbying institutions that collectively make up the capital's growing penumbra of power, the professional life of Greater Washington's foreign policy community significantly transcends that formal governmental dimension. This pattern was intensified during and after the 2008 global financial crisis by the shift of significant new financial oversight and regulatory functions to Washington, including the virtual nationalization of major private enterprises such as AIG.[51]

In Conclusion

The international system, as noted earlier, has been classically seen as a world of nation-states. Cities, however, are playing an increasingly important, and highly dynamic, role. Although the importance of cities appeared first, and has been most extensively noted, in the world of international finance they are also increasingly important as sociopolitical communities in configuring international politics as a whole. Yet both the global political role of cities and the forces that enhance that role remain remarkably unexplored.

In this chapter I present and specify the concept of the global political city. By this I mean a metropolitan area with multiple international functions: as a policy hub, as a major political-diplomatic community, and as a strategic political information complex of global import. These functions are related to, yet transcend, the responsibilities of national government, giving global political cities—as transnational, yet geographically linked, policy communities—their importance as objects of independent political analysis. Brussels, Moscow, Beijing, and obviously Washington are examples of major global political cities on the contemporary international scene.

The empirical analysis presented here focuses on Washington—the most important global political city and one that clearly illustrates how such cities can influence the overall profile of international affairs. I situate Washington in comparative context so as to identify distinctive features that merit further explanation. I find that understanding historical origins and their institutional consequences is crucial to appreciating how global political cities function.

In Washington's case, the lack of an extensive imperial past, and the absence of related, entrenched social elites and centralized institutions, makes the U.S. capital unusually decentralized and open to external influence. As America's global power has risen, and as government policy since the 1980s has encouraged privatization, this underlying municipal openness has stimulated the emergence of a distinctive strategic information complex. This dynamic policy community offers unusual opportunities not only for informal foreign influence, much of it located in Washington's expanding suburbs, but also for the consequent flattening of the hierarchical character of American national power relations with the broader world. How this unusual pattern—distinctively amenable to external influence—has evolved, and with what consequences for America's broader role in the world, are the subjects of the next chapter.

2 | Washington's Power Game and Its Transformation

Washington today acts on an international stage and is the capital of arguably the most influential nation on earth. It is the quintessential global political city, whose local dynamics have fateful significance for the broader world. Yet its behavior is by no means a straightforward reflection of American national policy. Indeed, as shown in the preceding chapter, the way Washington operates is heavily shaped by distinctive, historically embedded, institutional features—subtly changing over time—that need to be understood in their own right.

Washington's Parochial Early History

For more than a century after colonial settlers landed at Jamestown and Plymouth Rock, the environs of Washington remained unoccupied Crown Land. For decades thereafter, following distribution to British lords in estates of a thousand acres and over, that territory produced tobacco through slave labor.[1] In 1789, when George Washington was inaugurated president of the United States, the future District of Columbia remained farmland owned by nineteen families, surrounded by a swamp land.[2] Its population varied between 3,000 and 5,000, centered about the sleepy hamlet of Saw Pit Landing and the port of Georgetown, formally established in 1751.[3]

The Constitution drew the contours of the federal city, ten miles on a side, to explicitly include this bucolic realm.[4] Yet Washington as a sociopolitical community was decidedly slow to develop. By the end of the eighteenth century, despite strenuous efforts by George Washington and others to promote its charms, the capital's population was only 8,144, and it remained "a village still nearly wild, with barely passable roads."[5]

U.S. government officials, of course, had little choice but to live in the primitive federal city. But the small community of foreign diplomats accredited to the fledgling America tried their best to avoid it. Only seven nations had relations with the newly established United States in 1800.[6] And of an entire foreign diplomatic corps consisting of fewer than twenty individuals, not a single minister in 1801 inhabited Washington itself.

There were, to be sure, a few exceptions. Llosa Ojeda of Spain did reside in the city for the first six months after its birth. Yet he left soon thereafter, preferring the more cosmopolitan venues of Philadelphia and New York City. The British minister, Robert Liston, likewise arrived in Washington early in 1800, a week before President Adams, but found actually residing there so distasteful that he abruptly departed for the West Indies, to visit his wife's relatives.[7] Ultimately the British gave their officers "hill money," as in India, to enable these afflicted souls to flee in the summertime to the cooler Appalachians.[8]

Due to its total absence of attractions, and the obscure diplomatic profile of the United States itself, Washington hosted no permanent diplomatic establishments for the first sixty-six years of its existence.[9] Of course, the hardy diplomats who did engage with America had few counterparts on the American side either—the State Department employed only ten locally based staffers in 1800, when the department moved to Washington. And it added only thirty-two more—one every two years—in the seven decades to follow.[10] Indeed, it was only after the Civil War, with the Union preserved, the American economy growing powerfully, and the country clearly on its way to global standing, that foreign diplomacy finally began to discover the United States.

Britain appears to have had the longest continuous representation in Washington, although its legation moved several times along Connecticut Avenue between 1791 and the early 1870s.[11] Prussia soon thereafter bought a house for its minister, Friedrich von Alvensleven, only a few blocks away, on 15th Street, with France and others soon following suit. Soon an ad hoc "Embassy Row" emerged—first around 16th Street, fronting the White House, and then (after 1931, when the British moved) on Massachusetts Avenue, where foreign embassies are concentrated today.[12]

Figure 2-1. *Washington's Volatile Population Growth, 1850–2010*

Percent change per decade

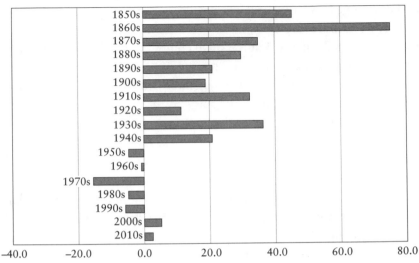

Source: Campbell Gibson and Kay Jung, "Historical Census Statistics on the Foreign-Born Population of the United States: 1850–2000," Working Paper 81 (U.S. Census Bureau, 2006), table 1; and U.S.
Census Bureau, "Quickfacts" (http://quickfacts.census.gov/qfd/states/11000.html).

Domestic Drivers of Early Governmental Expansion

Although the foreign diplomatic presence gradually began to expand in
Washington from the late nineteenth century on, the capital's core, of
course, remained resolutely domestic, responding to a more parochial
logic. The growth of central Washington, quintessentially a city of politics rather than economy, was historically driven by crisis rather than
economic opportunity, as suggested in figure 2-1.[13] And most of the
early crises, such as the Civil War (1861–65) and the Great Depression
(1929–40), were primarily domestic. Although a town of only 75,000
on the eve of South Carolina's secession in 1860, the capital city nearly
doubled in size, to almost 132,000 by 1870, five years after the Civil
War's end. Washington's population nearly doubled once again during
the tumultuous two decades of Depression and war, 1930 to 1950. In
the latter year the District of Columbia—the urban core of Washington
to this day—reached its peak population of 802,178 residents.[14]

It was expansion of federal employment—particularly in times of
crisis—that drove Washington's volatile century of growth after 1860.
The Civil War, as noted above, prompted the first significant municipal

expansion. Federal jobs grew by a factor of six between 1860 and 1880, provoking a doubling of Washington's population.[15] Another spurt came early in the twentieth century, centering on World War I and the rise of new regulatory bodies. Federal employment rose during this period by more than 55,000, or nearly 17 percent, between 1910 and 1920, with population surging by over 30 percent.[16] Apart from the War Department, a number of civilian agencies—the Treasury Department, the Commerce Department, and new entities like the Federal Trade Commission and the Interstate Commerce Commission—also grew rapidly, responding to the political-economic pressures of industrialization and associated human crises.[17]

A further surge of government expansion and local population growth came during the Depression and the New Deal, when federal regulatory agencies expanded still further, and welfare-related agencies began to grow. Yet it was not until later that the U.S. government's foreign affairs bureaucracy began to decisively expand. As with domestic policy institutions in earlier years, it was crisis—this time war and its turbulent aftermath—that until the 1950s drove the transformation to a larger government and a more populous Washington, as we shall later see.

Washington's Classic Power Game

Compared to Napoleon's France and the courts of continental Europe, where the exigencies of monarchy and empire typically shaped the twentieth-century profile of civic expansion in national capitals, the political economy of nineteenth-century Washington had a decided laissez-faire cast. The Progressive Era, mobilization for World War I, and especially the coming of the New Deal, with its ambitious public works projects, moved both civic design and urban life in the nation's capital much closer to the bureaucratically centered pattern, idealized by Max Weber, that was already prevalent elsewhere in the industrialized world.[18] Embedded in the distinctive political context of the 1930s, where government's role appeared basic to national economic viability, this bureaucratic expansion also fostered a breed of Washington politics—static, personalistic, and in many ways predictable—that dominated America's national capital for generations thereafter.

Twentieth-century, "inside the Beltway" Washington politics was parochial and hierarchical, dominated by personalistic and largely nontransparent intragovernmental interactions between executive and legislative leaders.[19] The central actors—the New Deal White House and the legislative leaders on Capitol Hill—were natural allies. Both groups were predominantly Democratic, regulation and compensation oriented, and simultaneously progressive, as well as pragmatic in their relations with the business world. The Congress was dominated by Southern white Democratic leaders—with extraordinary tenure, given the stability of politics in the South and the Democratic majorities in the Congress. And the White House was led for two decades by presidents—Franklin D. Roosevelt and Harry Truman—who shared a populist stance and a taste for regulation.

This coalition naturally spawned a community of formidable downtown brokers personally connected to both ends of Pennsylvania Avenue as well as to the business community.[20] These brokers could mediate the inevitable commercial transactions that a growing and changing America required of the New Deal welfare state. They were frequently retired members of Congress, congressional staffers, and presidential appointees, who maintained networks with their former colleagues that served them in their roles of handling the sensitive tasks of mediation.

The Washington influence brokers came gradually to be concentrated, from the 1930s through the 1950s and beyond, in the major law firms and lobbyist offices of the capital, which increasingly came to be centered on K Street. The classical lobbyists were occupied centrally with domestic regulatory and legislative issues, including finance, transportation, and ultimately trade. After the 1960s, lobbyists gradually moved to other parts of town, and only two of the top twenty lobbying firms remained physically based on K Street itself.

K Street has thus become largely a term of art rather than a physical reality. As Ed Rothschild of the Podesta Group, one of Washington's preeminent lobbying and public relations firms, puts it, "It says you are in the lobbying business."[21] Lobbying itself has merged increasingly with public relations and corporate strategy, giving rise to a new breed of geographically dispersed corporate advisers, many with a strong global orientation, as we shall see later in this chapter.

The decisionmaking system that the Capitol Hill/K Street axis of the transwar period spawned was, as suggested, a stable, predictable, and subterranean one. The Democratic Party held majorities in Congress for fifty-eight of the sixty-two years between 1933 and 1995. Many of the same southern Democratic legislators—people like Lyndon Johnson, Richard Russell, Mendel Rivers, and Wilbur Mills—stayed in office, and in leadership, for thirty years and more. And Democratic presidents occupied the White House for three-quarters of the period, from 1933 to 1969. Precisely because there was so much continuity on Capitol Hill, accompanied by relative stability in the White House, it was easy for a predictable decisionmaking structure to emerge in Washington and for it to be sustained politically by the nation at large.

The classic "inside the Beltway" system, as it began emerging in the 1930s, and as it continued, in most respects, into the 1980s, had seven major characteristics, outlined by a variety of authors.[22] These key traits include broad federal regulatory power over the national political economy, centralized in Washington; the presence of several strong bureaucratic institutions, including preeminently the Department of Defense; chronic fragmentation in the regulatory structure; personalistic power networks linking key institutions; openness to outsiders with the resources to buy access; revolving doors between public and private sectors; and perpetual motion, due to the exigencies of reelection campaigning. The system as a whole was relatively parochial from a global perspective, concentrated geographically within the District of Columbia proper. It was also government-centric and dominated by arcane, subterranean, decisionmaking processes in which mass media and private agenda setters played only a relatively limited role.

Global Interactions with Classic Washington

The foreign side of diplomatic Washington actually began to grow substantially before its American counterpart decisively emerged. On the eve of World War I, there were only thirteen embassies in all of Washington—Argentina, Austria, Brazil, Chile, France, Germany, Italy, Japan, Mexico, Russia, Spain, the United Kingdom, and Sweden.[23] After the war, that number expanded sharply. By 1932 the diplomatic community had reached fifty-three embassies and legations, over four times its scale in 1914, mostly on 16th Street, the first Embassy Row, but with a dozen embassies on Massachusetts Avenue as well.[24]

It was also during World War I and shortly thereafter that the civil society dimension of "international Washington" began to develop. Perhaps the first major U.S. nongovernmental organization to go international from a Washington base was the Red Cross. With the onset of World War I, America's first major conflict since the Civil War, Red Cross membership exploded across the United States, from 17,000 in 1914 to 31 million in 1918.[25] Following the formal establishment of the world-wide Red Cross movement in May 1919—and the American version's affiliation as a central participant—Washington came to have international significance in global humanitarian aid. By 1921 the Red Cross had erected its own permanent national headquarters on 17th Street, next to the Daughters of the American Revolution Hall and just a short walk from the State, War, and Navy Building (today's Old Executive Office Building) as well as the White House. From that strategic location the Red Cross has since influenced the top ranks of the U.S. government on behalf of not only Americans but also of the needy throughout the world.

The next major NGO to go multinational from a Washington base was, ironically, the American Federation of Labor (AFL). The AFL, after all, had been traditionally nativistic, playing a key role in lobbying Congress for renewal of the Chinese Exclusion Act in 1902. Over the following two decades, however, the AFL developed extensive international ties, and in 1921 it established a publicity bureau in Washington to lobby on behalf of the 109 domestic and foreign labor unions associated with the AFL.[26]

The peace movement was another catalyst to increased international consciousness in interwar Washington. The Carnegie Endowment for International Peace, based in the District, spent $500,000 a year publishing the monumental, hundred-volume *Economic and Social History of the World War* as well as the monthly bulletin *International Conciliation*. It also supported smaller peace organizations as well as the Kellogg-Briand Peace Pact. The National Council for the Prevention of War, founded by the Congregational minister Frederick J. Libby, demonstrated against arms manufacturers at the 1921–22 Washington Naval Conference and, with a staff of thirty, then spent $100,000 lobbying in support of peace activists.[27] Women's groups were also prominent: the National Committee on the Cause and Cure of War (NCCCW), a coalition of nine women's organizations that promoted international peace by lobbying for U.S. accession to the International Court of Justice, gathered annually in the city, right up to the eve of World War II in 1941.[28]

Although internationalism and international ties did make modest advances during the 1910s and the 1920s, Washington gradually reverted during the 1930s to its parochial roots. In the course of that decade the population of the city grew to nearly 487,000, as Roosevelt's New Deal increased government influence over the economy through price controls, agricultural subsidies, and extensive public works. This period also brought an expansion of the federal welfare state, giving birth to many relief agencies, as Congress passed a blizzard of legislation in response to the Great Depression.

Many of the institutions created during this period, such as the Civilian Conservation Corps (CCC) and the Works Progress Administration (WPA), were abolished by 1943. Yet holdovers survive, including the Federal Deposit Insurance Corporation (FDIC), the Federal Housing Administration (FHA), the Tennessee Valley Authority (TVA), the Securities and Exchanges Commission (SEC), and the Social Security Administration. Virtually all of these New Deal creations were intensely domestic. Indeed, National Airport, completed in 1941, was virtually the only one with even a modest international linkage.[29]

World War II and its aftermath had a huge impact both on the international role of the United States and on the character of Washington. Not surprisingly, the city's population grew by more than a fifth, from just over 663,000 in 1940 to more than 800,000 by 1950.[30] Federal employment grew by 9 percent, or 83,000 people.[31]

More important for our story, however, Washington began to grow increasingly international and to steadily assume more information-gathering and information-processing functions. At the outbreak of World War II, the nation's capital hosted fifty embassies—twenty-three from Europe, twenty from Latin America, and others from China, Japan, Thailand, Canada, South Africa, Egypt, and Turkey.[32] The diplomatic community expanded substantially thereafter, especially along Embassy Row, with the Icelandic embassy arriving in 1941 and the Saudi Arabian embassy, among others, in 1945.

By 1959 the expansion of foreign embassies in the city had become so pronounced that the D.C. government authorized its board of zoning adjustments to exercise the "city's local prerogatives" in issuing permits for new embassies and legations.[33] Indeed, by 1963 there were 107 missions in Washington.[34] In 1964 Congress approved an amendment, introduced by Senator J. William Fulbright, that barred new chanceries from residential areas and existing chanceries from expanding.[35]

To create appropriate space for new embassies, Congress in 1968 authorized the U.S. government to sell or rent land on the site of the old Bureau of Standards building, near Connecticut Avenue at Van Ness Street, for up to twenty new chanceries and the headquarters of the Organization of American States. Nineteen embassies soon settled there, including several from Asia (China, Singapore, Malaysia, Cambodia, and Brunei). By 2013, counting Embassy Row, the Van Ness area, and other locations, 172 nations were represented in Washington.[36]

Institutional Transformation within the U.S. Government

During wartime America's military began to grow to an unprecedented degree, with nearly 12 million military personnel under arms by mid-1945.[37] This massive expansion naturally had a powerful impact on Washington. In 1943 a huge, five-sided, headquarters for the Department of War was opened just across the Potomac from Washington, in Arlington, Virginia.[38] Appropriately named the Pentagon, the building marked an unprecedented expansion of the city beyond its traditional borders in the District of Columbia. In 1947 this headquarters took on still broader national and international functions, as the U.S. Department of Defense.

America's diplomatic corps also expanded and took on new responsibilities. Until World War II the State Department had been a relative small, genteel, and static part of the federal government. Indeed, in 1940 it had only 1,128 employees and a budget of $2.8 million. By 1945, however, the department had more than tripled in size, to 3,700 employees, and by 1950 it nearly tripled again, to 9,000.

Starting in 1951 the State Department began to create bureaus. In 1951 the Voice of America and an independent U.S. Information Agency—coordinating cultural and public affairs abroad—were formed. In 1952 the Bureau of Consular Affairs was established, followed in 1957 by the Bureau of Intelligence and Research and in 1960 by the Bureau of Cultural Affairs. By 1960, with the third world decolonization process fueling a further expansion, on top of the cold war growth of the early post–World War II years, the State Department had grown to 13,000 career officers.[39] It continued at roughly this level for over half a century thereafter.[40]

Under the National Security Act of 1947, the defense-related bureaucracy expanded in other ways also. The National Security Council was established in the White House. This was complemented by the Central Intelligence Agency, which provided current political-military and political-economic information from around the world. Over the years, the CIA was complemented by the communications-oriented National Security Agency and a host of other new bodies, many of whose names and functions still remain classified.[41]

An Emerging Private Sector Information Complex

Washington's private sector analytical apparatus began expanding also, to meet the new analytical needs of the government. In 1943 the School of Advanced International Studies (SAIS) was founded, literally on Embassy Row, as a policy-oriented graduate school, in a bold initiative by two far-sighted Washingtonians, Paul Nitze and Christian Herter. Nitze, a Wall Street investment banker who arrived in Washington in 1942 to work for the Roosevelt administration at the behest of the White House adviser James Forrestal, was later to serve as State Department director of policy planning and as secretary of the navy.[42] He left his intellectual mark as the author of NSC-68, the blueprint for American postwar containment of the Soviet Union, and also as the father of the strategic U.S. Indian Ocean base at Diego Garcia.[43] Herter went on to become U.S. secretary of state (1959–61), succeeding John Foster Dulles.[44]

Although SAIS was the first major Washington international affairs school, it was by no means the last. George Washington University, located less than a mile from the State Department in Foggy Bottom, expanded its research programs over the 1950s and 1960s, particularly in Soviet and Chinese studies, mirroring the burgeoning national security needs of the federal government. Georgetown University did likewise, with a concentration on Soviet, Eurasian, and Eastern European studies and the addition of its School of Foreign Service.[45] In 1957 the School of International Service at American University was founded in the northern part of the District of Columbia, at the initiative of

President Dwight D. Eisenhower. The school's initial focus was on Latin America. Underlining again the relationship of politics to these academic institutions, Milton Eisenhower, the president's brother, became president of Johns Hopkins University, with which SAIS affiliated in 1950. The University of Maryland, located in suburban College Park, also developed international programs, including its Confucius Institute and its Maryland China Initiative for Asian professionals.[46]

The Rise of Think Tanks

Apart from the government and the universities, but interactive with them, think tanks and specialized analytical consulting firms also began to grow up, creating the glimmerings of a unique Washington-centric research and intelligence complex, which was to grow increasingly important both within the capital and globally in the years to follow. Think tanks, a uniquely American invention, strove to combine the contemplative, long-term analytical orientation of universities with the realism and action orientation of the policy world.[47] Populated by a combination of academics and policy-oriented research professionals, they came to play an increasingly important role in Washington's agenda setting from the 1970s on, exploiting the growing power of mass media, advanced communications, and social networks. Their members testified before Congress, organized study groups nominally presided over by congressional leaders, consulted with government and business leaders worldwide, and spread their personal ideas extensively—in print, on television, and via the Internet.

The first of the recognized think tanks was the Carnegie Endowment for International Peace (1910), followed closely by the Brookings Institution (1916).[48] The first specialized area-studies research body was arguably the Middle East Institute, established in 1946.[49] Although there were less than a dozen think tanks as late as 1950, the number increased rapidly thereafter.[50] Brookings was followed in 1952 by Resources for the Future, in 1954 by the American Enterprise Institute (AEI), in 1962 by the Center for Strategic and International Studies (CSIS), in 1973 by the Heritage Foundation, and in 1977 by the Cato Institute.[51] By the early 1980s Washington was home to more than a hundred think tanks.[52]

Across the 1980s, the 1990s, and beyond, the number of think tanks in Washington proliferated still further, including the Center for Defense

Information (1972), the United States Institute of Peace (1984), and the Center for a New American Security (2007). By the early years of the new century, their number had almost quadrupled from the 1980s, to 393—more than in any other city in the world.[53]

Think tank budgets also increased sharply as their political-economic functions expanded, and began to relate more closely to the operations of other "strategic advisers" in the U.S. capital. During 1998 the five think tanks with the most substantial internationally oriented Washington operations—the Brookings Institution, AEI, CSIS, the Council on Foreign Relations, and the Institute for International Economics—had a combined budget of $79 million.[54] By 2012—only fourteen years later— their combined budget had nearly tripled, to well over $200 million, allowing them to take advantage of new communications and broadcasting technology to further leverage their global role.[55]

This expansion of Washington think tanks was in sharp contrast to somewhat slower growth in Europe and to an actual contraction of think tank activity in some other major parts of the world, such as Japan.[56] In addition to being better funded, Washington think tanks also appear to be freer of government controls and sponsorship and more flexible in forging transnational ties than their counterparts elsewhere.[57] Concentrated in tight geographic proximity, in intense competition with one another, Washington's top think tanks have become a classic competitive cluster, with their rivalries, strategic location, and substantial transnational funding driving them to formidable global prominence. The following list ranks the top five think tanks by their international standing:[58]

1. Brookings Institution, Washington
2. Chatham House, London
3. Carnegie Endowment, Washington
4. Center for Strategic and International Studies, Washington
5. Stockholm International Peace Research Institute, Stockholm

The Transformation of Lobbying

As think tanks steadily increased their size and functions between the end of the 1990s and recent years, given momentum by the information revolution and globalization, parallel trends were unfolding in the for-profit lobbying and consulting sectors. These created new opportunities for synergy within the Washington "idea industry." As indicated

Figure 2-2. *Growing Concentration in the U.S. Lobbying Sector,*
1998–2011

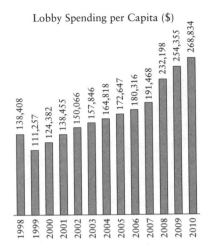

Lobby Spending per Capita ($)

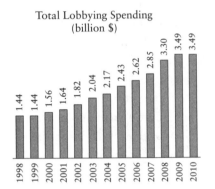

Total Lobbying Spending
(billion $)

Number of Lobbyists

Source: Center for Responsive Politics (www.opensecrets.org/lobby/index.php).

in figure 2-2, expenditures on lobbying in the United States, primarily concentrated in Washington, more than doubled, from $1.44 billion in 1998 to $3.49 billion in 2010. The number of lobbyists followed a more nuanced trend, rising from 10,404 in 1998 to a high of 14,885 in 2007, before falling back by over 10 percent, to 12,982 in 2010. This suggests, however, a steady rise in billings per lobbyist, as also indicated in figure 2-2. This latter pattern reflects a concentration of the lobbying sector into a decreasing number of large, comprehensive service firms, about which more must later be said.

The classical pattern, discussed above, was for law firms, many on K Street, to handle regulatory issues independently of other service firms. Law firm dealings were mainly with the U.S. government and within the regulatory regimes of this special expertise, ranging from finance and telecommunications to transportation. The concerns of the major individual law firms were domestic and largely immutable, involving only a small number of regulators. Specialist attorneys, with a limited range of connections on Capitol Hill and in the relevant administration, were all that was required.

Globalization, the information revolution, and increasing regulatory complexity, both in Washington and in the broader world, however, have created an environment requiring clients to seek a broader range of advisers. In response to this new political-economic circumstance, and to the corporate demand for broader analytical and political skills, new sorts of advisory conglomerates have begun to emerge, to provide comprehensive support known as "strategic advice."[59] One good example is McLarty Associates, chaired by former Clinton White House chief of staff Mack McLarty. This firm specializes in consulting for multinational corporations on regulatory strategies for the varied range of national and local jurisdictions with which such firms must deal. McLarty Associates is not a law firm per se, although many of its partners and associates are attorneys. To provide additional legal expertise, it has forged a strategic partnership with Covington and Burling, one of the most prestigious law firms in Washington, and the old law firm of Truman's secretary of state, Dean Acheson. A similar strategic partnership is that between the Albright Stonebridge Group and Hogan Lovells. The Albright Stonebridge Group is a political-economic consulting firm whose principals include Madeleine Albright, secretary of state in the Clinton administration, and former Clinton National Security Adviser Sandy Berger as principals, on the one hand; and Hogan Lovells, another powerful law firm in which Berger was once a partner, on the other.[60]

Strategic advisory firms and think tanks, of course, have nominally distinct functional roles. The former support particularistic interests, and the latter are dedicated to broader analytical concerns. Some analysts, however, have detected a clear recent evolution from analysis to advocacy at many of the largest think tanks, as their operational needs and functions increasingly converge with those of the advisory firms.[61]

Certainly the two types of institutions overlap geographically in the heart of Washington. And their principals frequently have closely overlapping personal networks as well.

The final key element of the emerging Washington information complex are private service firms, such as Booz Allen Hamilton and SAIC, which gained prominence in the early postwar world, especially after 9/11. Generally specializing in technical support functions that government bureaucrats often do not possess, they have helped handle sudden surges in government procurement, such as wartime buildups in Korea and Vietnam. During the 1980s these firms began to assume even more important functions, as we shall see, with government political-military functions both expanding rapidly and becoming decidedly more technical during the Reagan years, even as policymakers strove to shrink the size of the federal government. Since the World Trade Center and Pentagon attacks of September 2001, their role has expanded even further, as counterterrorism and related communications monitoring have quietly become higher priorities for the U.S. government.

The Geographical Dimension

The emerging private sector information complex grew up in close physical proximity to the U.S. government institutions it was designed to monitor, influence, and support. The information complex also emerged in highly dynamic competitive clusters, as noted in figure 2-3. Powerful think tanks, public relations firms and lobbyists, major embassies, influential multilateral financial institutions, and prominent media are located in close proximity to others of their species, with all of these groups overlapping in synergistic and increasingly intimate geographical and functional connection with one another. This physical proximity is a major factor allowing these private and multilateral institutions to serve so effectively as a penumbra of power (see figure 1-4) to Washington's official policy processes, with the close proximity facilitating networking, recurring social contact, information exchange, and advocacy along many dimensions.

Although the concentration in Washington of competitive clusters with global prominence is distinctive enough, the concentration in certain areas of the city is even more notable, enhancing as it does the synergies of physical proximity. One of the most clear and remarkable

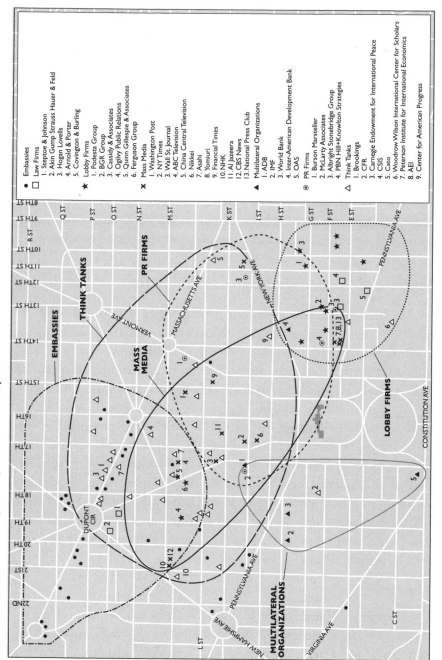

Figure 2-3. *The Washington Information Complex*

illustrations of this phenomenon, and the synergies that are giving it increasing international political-economic momentum, is the Massachusetts Avenue information complex (figure 2-4). Two of the four most influential think tanks in the world, the Brookings Institution and the Carnegie Endowment, are located next to one another on that "policy street," amid embassies, university buildings, and the Confucius Institute US Center, while a third (the Center for Strategic and International Studies), recently moved to Rhode Island Avenue, roughly 500 yards away. Seven of the top twenty think tanks on earth, plus the United Nations Foundation, are located within less than a mile of the 1700 block of Massachusetts Avenue, N.W., and nine are based in Greater Washington.[62] And all of these analytical bodies also lie in close proximity to Washington's increasingly influential strategic advisory firms.

The Rise of Greater Washington, 1945–2010

As America's global role expanded during World War II and its aftermath, America's foreign affairs bureaucracy and its analytical support institutions expanded also, with profound implications for Washington. With the federal government, foreign diplomatic representation, universities, and private analytical support institutions all growing, it became impossible for all these institutions to fit within the established parameters of the District of Columbia, which had been fixed by the Constitution in 1787.[63] It became equally difficult for the expanding number of employees at institutions physically located within the District to find suitable housing close to their employment. Gradually, driven by the dual demands for work space and housing, a Greater Washington, stretching deep into the surrounding countryside, at once more dynamic, more rapidly growing, and more tantalizingly obscure than its traditional urban core, came to be born.

The Profile of Demographic Change

The demographic high point of urban Washington, as suggested earlier, came shortly after World War II. From the 1950s on, surrounding portions of northern Virginia and southern Maryland began to grow much more rapidly, while the District of Columbia's population actually declined. From its high point of over 800,000 in 1950, the District's

Figure 2-4. *The Massachusetts Avenue Information Complex*

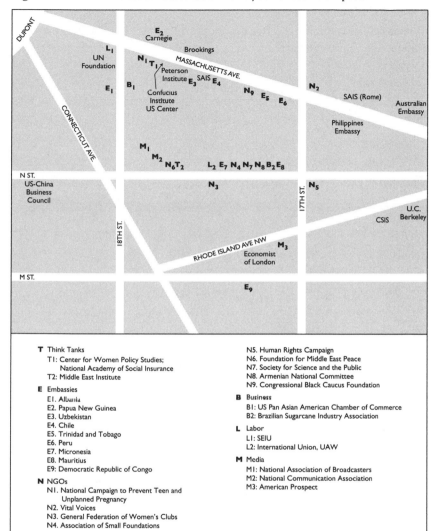

T Think Tanks
  T1: Center for Women Policy Studies;
     National Academy of Social Insurance
  T2: Middle East Institute

E Embassies
  E1. Albania
  E2. Papua New Guinea
  E3. Uzbekistan
  E4. Chile
  E5. Trinidad and Tobago
  E6. Peru
  E7. Micronesia
  E8. Mauritius
  E9: Democratic Republic of Congo

N NGOs
  N1. National Campaign to Prevent Teen and
     Unplanned Pregnancy
  N2. Vital Voices
  N3. General Federation of Women's Clubs
  N4. Association of Small Foundations

N5. Human Rights Campaign
N6. Foundation for Middle East Peace
N7. Society for Science and the Public
N8. Armenian National Committee
N9. Congressional Black Caucus Foundation

B Business
  B1: US Pan Asian American Chamber of Commerce
  B2: Brazilian Sugarcane Industry Association

L Labor
  L1: SEIU
  L2: International Union, UAW

M Media
  M1: National Association of Broadcasters
  M2: National Communication Association
  M3: American Prospect

Figure 2-5. *The Postwar Emergence of Greater Washington,*
1900–2010[a]

Millions of people

Source: U.S. Census Bureau, "American Fact Finder" (http://factfnder2.census.gov).
a. Greater Washington, as defined here, is the area that stretches west to east from Fauquier County, Virginia, to Calvert County, Maryland; and from north to south from Montgomery County, Maryland, to Spotsylvania County, Virginia.

population declined to 601,723 in 2010, although it rose slightly, to 632,323 in 2012.[64] As shown in figure 2-5, the vast majority of Washington metropolitan growth over the past half century has been in those peripheral, yet highly dynamic areas surrounding central Washington.

Thanks in substantial measure to the dynamism of its periphery, Greater Washington as a whole has become one of the most rapidly growing metropolitan areas in the United States, particularly over the past two decades. This expansion is clear from the statistical data, although it is less well appreciated by the general public. As noted in table 2-1, the Baltimore/Washington/northern Virginia metropolitan area (Greater Washington) grew in population by 13.1 percent between 1990 and 2000, even though the District of Columbia expanded very little.[65] Greater Washington's growth during that decade was more

Table 2-1. *Population Change for the Largest American Metropolitan Statistical Areas, 1990–2010*[a]

Units as indicated

Metropolitan statistical area	Population 1990	Population 2000	Population 2010	Population change (%) 1990–2000	Population change (%) 2000–10
Dallas-Fort Worth, TX	4,037,282	5,221,801	6,371,773	29.3	23.4
Washington-Arlington-Alexandria, DC-VA-MD-WV	3,923,574	4,796,183	5,582,170	18.2	16.4
Washington-Baltimore, DC-MD-VA-WV[b]	6,727,050	7,608,070	8,561,799	13.1	12.8
Philadelphia-Wilmington-Atlantic City, PA-NJ-DE-MD	5,892,937	6,188,463	5,965,343	5.0	4.9
Chicago-Gary-Kenosha, IL-IN-WI	8,239,820	9,157,540	9,461,105	11.1	4.0
Boston-Worcester-Lawrence, MA-NH-ME-CT	5,455,403	5,819,100	4,552,402	6.7	3.7
Los Angeles-Riverside-Orange County, CA	14,531,529	16,373,645	12,828,837	12.7	3.7
New York-Northern New Jersey-Long Island, NY-NJ-CT-PA	19,549,649	21,199,865	18,897,109	8.4	3.1

Source: Marc J. Perry and Paul J. Mackun, "Census 2000 Brief, Population Change and Distribution: 1990 to 2000" (U.S. Census Bureau, 2001), table 3; Paul Mackun and Steven Wilson, "2010 Census Briefs, Population Distribution and Change: 2000 to 2010" (U.S. Census Bureau, 2011); "American FactFinder" (U.S. Census Bureau) (http://factfinder2.census.gov/faces/nav/jsf/pages/index.xhtml).

a. The Census Bureau slightly modified the composition of most Metropolitan Statistical Areas between 2000 and 2010. Washington-Baltimore, DC-MD-VA-WV, in 2000, for example, was changed to Washington-Arlington-Alexandria, DC-VA-MD-WV, a decade later. Similarly, Boston-Worcester-Lawrence, MA-NH-ME-CT, became Boston-Cambridge-Quincy, MA-NH, in 2010. Since the major cities in MSAs have remained, however, these changes do not undermine this chapter's argument.

b. "Washington-Baltimore" includes Washington, D.C., Northern Virginia, Baltimore, and Hagerstown, Md.

rapid than that of any other major metropolitan area in the country other than Dallas–Fort Worth and was more than 20 percent faster than the national average for metropolitan areas of over 5 million people.[66] Between 2000 and 2010, Greater Washington continued to be one of the most rapidly expanding urban areas in the nation.[67]

In the governmental sphere, administrative decentralization has become the hallmark of Greater Washington, with the newer, expanding agencies generally being the ones to locate outside of the District. Since 9/11, many of these are intelligence and defense related. Both economic (cost of real estate) and national security imperatives drove this decentralization, which has begun to alter the face of Washington as a whole.

A Changing Spatial Geography

The expansion of Greater Washington was along two main axes: northwest along the Dulles corridor, past Dulles airport, into suburban Virginia; and northeast along the Baltimore-Washington Parkway, toward Baltimore-Washington airport and Baltimore itself (see figure 2-6). Both of these corridors go beyond the I-495 Beltway circumscribing Washington. Yet their location near suburban Washington, and rough proximity to I-495, help justify the term "inside the Beltway," which has come to connote the attitudes, often parochial, at the center of U.S. national decisionmaking.

How and Why Institutions Migrated

The first step in the emergence of the geographically decentralized Greater Washington was the movement during and just after World War II of the State, War, and Navy Departments from a single building next to the White House (now known as the Old Executive Office Building) to Foggy Bottom, in the District, and to Arlington, Virginia. In 1961 the Central Intelligence Agency moved to a bucolic and suitably isolated site at Langley, in Fairfax County, Virginia. The Atomic Energy Commission, founded in 1946, initially established its permanent headquarter in the District, on 19th and Constitution Avenue, N.W. In 1955, however, Congress, fearing the possibility of a nuclear attack on the capital, elected to move the AEC facilities twenty-three miles northward, to Germantown, Maryland.[68]

Meanwhile, in 1957, the federal Bureau of Standards planned facilities for 3,500 federal employees, a substantial number for that small organization, to be located in the vicinity of Gaithersburg, Maryland, by 1980.[69] Two years later, the National Aeronautics and Space Administration (NASA) was set up at the Goddard Flight Center, also in Maryland. The National Security Agency (NSA), together with the Army Military Intelligence Training School, were moved in 1957 to Fort Meade, Maryland.[70] The U.S. Army Military Intelligence and Security Command (INSCOM) was, in the meantime, headquartered at Fort Belvoir, in Fairfax County,

Figure 2-6. *The Geographic Profile of Greater Washington*[a]

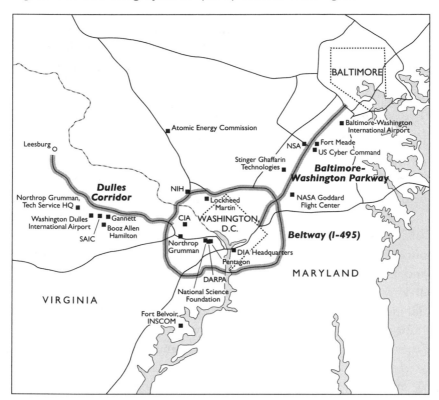

Source: Drawn by William L. Nelson.

a. Abbreviations used: DIA, Defense Intelligence Agency; INSCOM, United States Army Intelligence and Security Command; SAIC, Science Applications International Corporation; DARPA, Defense Advanced Research Projects Agency; NSA, National Security Agency; NIH, National Institutes of Health; NASA, National Aeronautics and Space Administration. Greater Washington, as defined here, is the area that stretches west to east from Fauquier County, Virginia, to Calvert County, Maryland; and from north to south from Montgomery County, Maryland, to Spotsylvania County, Virginia.

Virginia. Meanwhile, the National Institutes of Health and the National Science Foundation, important new postwar federal government affiliates, were located in Bethesda, Maryland, and Arlington, Virginia, respectively.

Washington's Transformation in Microcosm

Since World War II Greater Washington has expanded nearly ten-fold in population—almost exclusively outside the District of

Columbia—sprawling across large parts of suburban Maryland and Northern Virginia. This expansion has been driven, as we have seen, by the emergence of a globally significant strategic information complex that has an important governmental dimension yet extends far beyond that. To understand this transformation, it is useful to view it from several perspectives—micro as well as macro.

The Making of a Greater Washington Strategic Information Complex: An Overview

As the United States grew to become a global power in the wake of World War II, the information needs of its government grew in tandem. The dawn of the nuclear age intensified these requirements, and the coming of the missile age magnified them, in a synergistic way, still further. Amassing and processing stupendous amounts of information—outstripping one's adversaries in that regard—became matters of life and death. Monitoring communications in Kazakhstan or Qinghai, and making sense of developments in such remote locations, became existential matters of national survival, or were so perceived to be.

In the superpower competition between the United States and the Soviet Union, to which the nuclear- and missile-delivery issues were fatefully attached, the ability to monitor minute developments, such as missile preparations and technical command signals deep within the adversary nation, was of critical importance. To improve detection capabilities, as well as command and control systems, the United States spent tremendous amounts on defense research and development as well as on intelligence gathering. These expenditures accelerated with particular intensity during the Reagan administration (1981–89). By 1986, for example, the Defense Department's research budget was double that of 1981, just before the administration's information- and aerospace-oriented buildup began.[71] Of $33.6 billion in such contracts, $19.8 billion, or nearly 60 percent, was paid to non-Pentagon contractors. As a consequence, between 1981 and 1986 these outside contractors more than doubled their revenues.

The information sector was a top priority of defense research and development during the 1980s, due to the rapid technological progress of telecommunications and its deep relationship to aerospace-sector detection, command, and control. Development of the Internet—which had just been invented by Tim Berners Lee of CERN, the European particle physics laboratory, and which subsequently became a major concern of the Defense Advanced Research Projects Agency—was another major priority, due to its enormous national security potential as a battlefield management tool, before its commercialization. To be able to communicate without exposing one's messages to enemy interdiction naturally promised enormous tactical advantages. Many of these defense concerns came together in the Reagan administration's "Star Wars" program and its active efforts—a continuation of Carter administration initiatives— to exploit the revolution in military affairs to America's advantage.

Defense agencies outsourced federal work to the private sector, bringing many contractors and consultants to live and work in close proximity to the Pentagon and other defense-related agencies, consistent with the security imperatives of adequate dispersal. Such firms came to be known as "Beltway bandits," as they were located geographically close to the I-495 Beltway around Washington and because, as one Beltway CEO put it, "they would come in and steal a little subcontracting business away from the big defense companies."[72] Armed with technology developed through defense contracting, the "bandits" also had opportunities to spin off some of their new knowledge to the private sector, especially following the 1984 deregulation of the U.S. telecommunications industry and the sharp pace of commercial innovation that flowed from that.

Opportunities for such information technology–oriented firms, many of which focused on detection and monitoring of Sino-Soviet secrets, were quite dependent on the federal government. It set standards, funded research and development, and supervised start-up projects, especially those concentrated in sensitive national security sectors. Although related contracts plateaued somewhat during the 1990s with the waning of the cold war, they expanded vigorously once again in the wake of 9/11 and the intensification of counterterrorism efforts. And Greater Washington, with its concentration of defense facilities and intelligence organizations, was a natural locus. By 2010 nearly 40 percent of the corporate locations working on top-secret contracts, many of them likely counterterrorism related, were reportedly concentrated in the Greater Washington area.[73]

The information revolution of the 1980s had deeper implications for Greater Washington than for almost any other area of the United

States, because so many defense-related information businesses have traditionally been concentrated there. Many of these later transferred their expertise to civilian applications, making the Beltway a leader in civilian information technology applications as well. These applications in turn triggered transnational interest from around the world.

Greater Washington itself—the very eye of the information revolution hurricane—became so intimately related to the development and operationalizing of the Internet, in both its military and its civilian dimensions, that *Fortune* in 1994 dubbed the whole area the Netplex.[74] By 2012 seven of the top ten contractors for government Internet research nationwide had headquarters in the area: Lockheed Martin, Northrop Grumman, Science Applications International Corporation (SAIC), General Dynamics, Booz Allen Hamilton, Computer Sciences (CSC), and DynCorp.[75] Of these, two were relative newcomers: CSC and SAIC, which relocated their headquarters from California to Greater Washington in 2008 and 2009, respectively. Northrop Grumman also moved its headquarter in 2011 to Falls Church (Northern Virginia) from Los Angeles, where the parent company was founded in 1939.[76]

The emergence of Greater Washington as a strategic information-processing center has resulted in tremendous employment and population increases: between 1990 and 2005, the Washington metropolitan area added nearly 230,000 professional and service jobs, with 96 percent concentrated in the suburbs.[77] Both southern Maryland and the Dulles corridor in Northern Virginia have benefited enormously in financial as well as in employment terms. Not coincidentally, the two richest counties in the entire United States in 2011 were in Greater Washington: Loudon and Fairfax Counties in Virginia.[78] The wealthiest of these counties (Loudon, along the Dulles corridor in Northern Virginia) was also the fifth fastest-growing county in the entire United States in population terms.[79] Five other counties clustered around Washington—in Maryland, Howard and Montgomery counties, and in Virginia, Arlington, Fairfax, and Prince William counties—were also among the most affluent ten. In all, eleven counties in Greater Washington ranked among the twenty-five richest counties in the entire nation.[80]

The information revolution has resulted in the birth of two major technological clusters in the Washington area, as noted previously, where much of the dynamic job growth and rising affluence is concentrated.

The first, as noted above in figure 2-6, is the Dulles corridor. It is situated along Virginia State Route 267 and the Dulles airport access road between Loudoun and Fairfax Counties—the richest in the nation. The Dulles corridor hosts over 2,300 private businesses, with some of the most dynamic firms in America—Accenture, Airbus, AT&T, DynCorp, Electronic Data Systems, ExxonMobil, Lockheed Martin, Orbital Sciences, Nortel Networks, Northrop Grumman, Raytheon, SAIC, and Verizon—conducting major operations there.

Even though AOL and Sprint Nextel have recently moved their corporate headquarters elsewhere, six other Fortune 500 companies maintain national headquarters in the Dulles corridor: Freddie Mac, Capital One, SAIC, NII Holdings, Gannett, and Booz Allen Hamilton.[81] Another three Fortune 500 firms are based nearby in Arlington and Falls Church. Many of these Dulles corridor firms serve the federal government in the defense, telecommunications, information technology, and homeland security sectors.[82] Not coincidentally, perhaps, the corridor is about ten miles from the Central Intelligence Agency and fifteen miles from the Pentagon. The firms in question have a variety of operations, however, facilitating both government contracts and the hiring of former government employees to fill them, including many with little or no direct relationship to national security. Clustered along the corridor and the Baltimore-Washington Parkway are 318 government work locations and 3,716 corporate locations related to counterterrorism, homeland security, and intelligence.[83]

A second technological hub within Greater Washington, on the other side of the Potomac, and also located close to important U.S. government agencies, is the Baltimore-Washington Parkway complex. At the heart of this complex, located about thirteen miles northeast of Washington, lies Fort Meade, the national headquarters of U.S. Army Military Intelligence, with double the number of employees of the Pentagon, and the nearby National Security Agency.[84] In 2010 the U.S. Cyber Command was established at Fort Meade, and in 2011 the Defense Information Services Agency moved onto the base as well. Next door is the high-security National Business Park, with half the footage of the Pentagon.

Just off the Baltimore-Washington Parkway lies the NASA Goddard Space Flight Center, which handles command and control for U.S. deep-space probes. Between Fort Meade and the Beltway also lie the Patuxent

Research Refuge and the Beltsville Agricultural Research Center. Among the major private firms along the parkway is Stinger Ghaffarian Technologies (SGT), founded in 1994 in the early days of the Internet; it ranks among the top federal contractors.[85]

Beyond the rise of dynamic new information technology centers in the District's periphery, the information revolution also profoundly changed the nature of Washington's power game. No longer was it played so quietly and inscrutably in the halls of Congress and K Street, among a small, parochial group of barons. The military and intelligence communities, with their budgets, technology, and security rationales, loomed larger, yet with no stable dominance by any one agency. The power game, after all, was growing increasingly dispersed and complex, making it more and more difficult for a narrow coterie to control it, even on national-security issues. Decentralization also rendered the power game more amenable to knowledgeable outside suasion, from think tanks, mass media, and other information-oriented, private sector operations.

Tysons Corner: A Municipal Perspective

Typical of the communities populating Greater Washington, and generating its dynamism, is Tysons Corner, Virginia. Largely a pasture in the 1950s, it is today what the *Washington Post* describes as "in many ways, the second city of the Washington metropolis."[86] With 25 million square feet of office space, Tysons Corner is host to the corporate headquarters of numerous Fortune 500 companies, such as Capital One, Freddie Mac, and Gannett, as well as one of the most important federal contractors, Booz Allen Hamilton. Its mall, Tysons Corner Center, is the largest mall in Greater Washington and one of the largest malls in the United States, with more than 290 stores and 2.4 million square feet of space.[87] Like Washington itself, Tysons Corner is primarily a working and shopping area. Its daytime population is greater than 70,000, or almost four times its 19,000-plus nighttime inhabitants.[88]

Over the last two decades (1990–2010), Tysons Corner has been one of the fastest-growing cities in the United States. Population growth has been substantial: more than 47 percent over those twenty years, from just over 13,000 to more than 19,300.[89] Yet job growth has been even more rapid—more than 103 percent over the same two decades.[90] Tysons lies in the second-richest county in the country and expects additional job growth of 200,000 workers, together with 100,000 additional nonwork-ing residents, by 2050.[91] Despite some shadows, such as traffic congestion, this suburban community remains a gleaming example of the remarkable political-economic revolution that Greater Washington has wrought.[92]

Booz Allen Hamilton: A Corporate Perspective

To get a concrete sense of the dynamism of Greater Washington over the past several decades and to understand what the birth of Washington's strategic information complex concretely involves, it is useful to chronicle the evolution of knowledge industry firms in the area. Among the most typical and successful is Booz Allen Hamilton, headquartered in McLean, Virginia, which is less than two miles southwest of Washington. Founded in 1914 as an affiliate of one of America's preeminent accounting firms, Booz Allen was originally based in Chicago and made its reputation in World War II designing a strategy to counter German U-boats, a strategy that played a key role in winning the Battle of the Atlantic. The firm has had offices in Washington since 1945, but it moved its entire headquarters and many of its most critical operations to Greater Washington in 1992.

Booz Allen now has more than 24,000 employees worldwide, on six continents, and has expanded its staff more than sixfold over the past three decades. It has been remarkably transformed during that period, from a conventional accounting firm with primarily midwestern U.S. operations into a preeminent global strategy and technology consulting enterprise. It has made this shift primarily through its unique ability to deal, as its website notes, "with complex problems that neither public nor private sectors can address alone" in such areas as health care, transpor-tation, national security, and outsourcing advisory services.[93] Its objec-tive in grappling with such issues is "enhancing the national security, economic well-being, health, and safety of nations around the world."

In 2008 Booz underwent major structural changes that sharpened its strategic focus. It split off its less lucrative commercial consulting arm, under the new name of Booz and Company, and became a pure govern-ment contractor. The new firm is publicly traded and majority owned by the Carlyle Group, a major private equity firm.

Booz Allen Hamilton is typical of many Greater Washington firms in its provision of integrated systems development and systems inte-gration services that cut across the traditional spheres of business and government. In performing such specialized tasks it thus combines strong technical capabilities with proximity to government. Being close to government—mostly by being in Greater Washington—gives Booz an ability to bridge the gap between the U.S. government's expanding global responsibilities and influence and its static personnel capabilities. Private contractors like Booz also reputedly enhance creativity and innovation, provide technical skills as needed, and help government accommodate the volatile swings in government programs and budgets that have become pronounced in recent years. They experience occasional security lapses, as in the Edward Snowden case of mid-2013, although the Snowden case was unusual in its scale and intensity and related to faulty clearance procedures by an outside contractor.[94]

A chronology of Booz Allen's consulting achievements is a history of the federal government's advances in outsourcing critical tasks. The firm has had a particularly long relationship with the U.S. Navy: Secretary of the Navy Frank Knox asked its help in preparing the navy for war in the early 1940s.[95] Throughout World War II, Booz's management engineers focused on cutting through red tape to improve military efficiency. Over time, Booz's client base grew increasingly diverse, while retaining a continuing focus on organizational design.

In 1963 Booz undertook its first consulting project for NASA, predicting the performance of a new satellite. And during the late 1960s it advised both the U.S. government and private firms on automation strategies. In 1967 it helped to structure the newly formed National Football League.

During the 1970s and 1980s, Booz Allen's national-defense business expanded once again, as the government began to outsource more and more security-related activities to the private sector. In 1975 Booz secured a major Trident submarine contract, the largest defense contract ever signed in the United States. Since then, the firm has continued to provide related services, ranging from evaluation and design options for dismantling the Trident in connection with the strategic arms reduction negotiations.[96] No other private management consulting firm has been involved in the Trident program as long as Booz Allen.[97]

Booz has undertaken a remarkable variety of defense and aerospace projects for diverse clients, both domestic and international. In 1978 it planned a naval expansion program for Saudi Arabia. In 1979 it helped

Chrysler design its successful turnaround, which involved a major government liaison. Booz then moved back to aerospace with a major NASA space station contract in 1987.

Booz Allen began its international activities in 1953, with a land-ownership study for the Philippine government.[98] Since the beginning of the 1990s, these international activities have significantly expanded, more than keeping pace with the deepening globalization of Greater Washington in general. In the early 1990s, for example, Booz designed Hong Kong 21, a strategic plan for Hong Kong's international relationships approaching its reversion to China in 1997. In 1992 Booz also began transportation and privatization work in the former Soviet Union and Eastern Europe. In 1996 it secured a massive $620 million U.S. General Services Administration telecommunications contract, and in 1998 it helped design a major transformation of the Internal Revenue Service. In 2000 Tony Blair's administration in Britain commissioned Booz Allen to do a major millennium project on the global digital divide.

Since 2001, in the shadow of the 9/11 attacks, Booz Allen has deepened its homeland security emphasis while continuing to take global developments and global clients into consideration. Major specialties include simulations, cyber security, and consulting. In 2001, for example, the firm simulated a major bioterror attack on the United States, and in 2003 it conducted a major port-security war game. In 2012 Booz markedly expanded operations in the Persian Gulf, establishing a regional headquarters in Abu Dhabi, while also assisting the United Arab Emirates to create its own version of the National Security Agency.[99] In 2013 Booz was also supporting the Saudi government's focus on cybersecurity, in which the Saudis were beginning to actively invest.[100]

In all these activities, the firm has created synergies between government objectives, such as homeland security, and the proprietary organizational and technical expertise that it has accumulated over the years. The technical skills of Booz, and the strong policy-related networks of its top executives, have given the firm the ability both to understand the problems government faces and to lobby for government contracts.[101] Such synergistic interaction between an entrepreneurial, technically competent business, on the one hand, and a government responsible for related policy formation, on the other, lies at the heart of the Greater Washington policy-analytical complex.

Tim Russert's Washington: A Mass Media Perspective

There is a third microperspective that can help us better understand Greater Washington's transformation: that of the journalist. To understand the increasing power of mass media and global information flows, it is instructive to explore what we might call Tim Russert's Washington, after the respected NBC television journalist. Russert, born and raised in Buffalo, New York, served for several years as special assistant to New York's Democratic governor Mario Cuomo. In December 1991 he became the host of NBC television's prime-time Sunday political program *Meet the Press,* the longest-running television series in U.S. broadcast history. He evolved in that role to serve as arguably Washington's most influential journalist for well over a decade, until his untimely death in June 2008.

Russert's Washington, within which mass media and the rapid flow of strategic information loomed large, was profoundly different from the world of the Capitol Hill–K Street axis, described earlier in this chapter, which dominated Washington public life for half a century following the New Deal. Russert's was a much more fluid and public world, in which the mass media, think tanks, spin doctors, and public intellectuals predominated. Quiet understandings among Capitol Hill, the administration, and the private sector, mediated by lobbyists and law firms, held palpably less credibility and durability than they had previously.

The transition from the Capitol Hill–K Street axis to a more fluid and transparent policy world had its roots, ultimately, in broader sociopolitical transitions across America, transitions that undermined the hierarchical power structure of early postwar Washington. First the civil-rights revolution of the 1960s shook the Democratic Party's hold over the previously solid South. Opposition to the Vietnam War mobilized a new generation of Americans, far less respectful of quiet deal making than their seniors, into politics. The Watergate scandal further shook the faith of Americans in the establishment.

In the congressional by-election of 1974 a radically new and more irreverent generation of leaders was elected to Congress, although the Democratic majority continued.[102] The voice of this generation was amplified by crucial structural changes—notably the expanding power of subcommittees, leveraged by the expanding number and influence of congressional staffers.[103] And in 1976 a radically different, and more open, sort of Democrat was elected president of the United States: Jimmy Carter, a peanut farmer who had been elected governor of Georgia and had little federal experience apart from military service.

The conservative Ronald Reagan, who followed Carter in 1981, was naturally of a radically different ideological persuasion, even though he had begun his professional career with the Screen Actors Guild as an active Democrat. Reagan's political emergence intensified both the fluidity and the media orientation of Washington politics, even as Congress was growing more structurally decentralized. Reagan, after all, was a veteran movie actor, for whom media coverage, and symbolic politics, were important. Although his message contained a strong dose of populism, like Carter he lacked both direct Washington experience and deep personal involvement with his party's political machinery, unlike Franklin D. Roosevelt and the previous generation of politicians.

Slowly but surely, the hierarchical, organized, and personalistic compensation politics of the 1930s and 1940s (that involved unions, chambers of commerce, traditional civic groups, and highly institutionalized political parties) began to erode, even as American civil society grew less organized.[104] Mass media, and political reliance on symbolic politics, emerged to fill the gap between politicians and their publics. Yet the media itself also changed, growing more sensational, more short-term oriented, and more preoccupied with crises, while also less inhibited by (and less integrally linked to) the Washington sociopolitical establishment.[105]

This new breed of symbolic, media-oriented politics, prefigured by Carter and Reagan, came to full flowering in the administration of Bill Clinton, just as Tim Russert became host of *Meet the Press*. Clinton, as a relatively obscure southern governor, lacked national organization, but he was young, charismatic, and media savvy. With his eloquent appeals about "building a bridge to the twenty-first century," he upended twelve years of Republican rule in the White House. Two years later, in 1995, the "Contract with America" revolution led by Newt Gingrich ended three generations of essentially Democratic dominance in Congress, contributing further to the fluidity in American politics that the erosion of America's unions and other established civic institutions was producing.

Within Washington itself the dominance of the Capitol Hill–K Street axis was slowly ending. The final coup de grace may have been administered by the Jack Abramoff scandal of 2006, in which revelations of payoffs by the K Street lobbyist Jack Abramoff to the majority leader, Tom DeLay, and other prominent representatives led to a wholesale reshuffling of congressional leadership. Yet the deeper sociopolitical transformation had in reality been many years coming.

The rise of Greater Washington, of course, contributed to the greater fluidity and openness of Washington's power game. From the 1980s on, as we have seen, Washington was becoming more expansive geographically, and more complex in political-economic terms, with a rising number of potential access points for nonestablishment actors. These changes inevitably enhanced both transparency and uncertainty in the system as a whole. Driven by both technological change and globalization, a strategic information complex was unquestionably emerging, and it was ever more difficult for subterranean forces and incestuous personal networks to manage or control it.

Washington in the early twenty-first century was thus, in purely technical terms, growing increasingly knowledgeable about the world. With the coming of the Internet, and with all the think tanks and knowledge businesses around, Tim Russert and his colleagues had virtually instant access to the details of world and domestic developments. Yet whether they had the experience, the personal networks, or the luxury of transcending Washington's parochial past and responding sensitively to developments in the rapidly changing broader world remained troublingly unclear.

In Conclusion

Washington's formal contours were defined by the U.S. Constitution of 1787 as a diamond-shaped federal district ten miles on a side (in 1847 it lost the thirty-one-square-mile area ceded by Virginia). In its early years the national capital, then still a primitive village, was unable to match in reality even the modest expectations of educated Americans, not to mention foreign diplomats. It has evolved remarkably—perhaps even more remarkably than the United States of America itself—over the past two centuries.

Unlike most major cities of the world, Washington has not expanded and grown in tandem with the economy. Rather than prosperity, it has been national crisis that has caused Washington to grow. First there was the Civil War and the years of Reconstruction that followed. Then four tumultuous decades—spanning World War I, the Great Depression, World War II, and the Korean War—transformed a sleepy, parochial Washington into a much more cosmopolitan and affluent city, albeit one with a pronounced domestic orientation.

The heart of early cold war Washington was, symbolically, the line between Capitol Hill and K Street—from the U.S. Congress to the great law firms and lobbyist operations where key policy brokers held court. Policymaking was quiet, conventional, hierarchical, and often subterranean. More than technical expertise, connections were what mattered.

Changing politics, changing technical requirements in government, and a changing world, however, gave birth over the 1970s and 1980s to a different Washington, and a different Washington policy process, which I christened "the world of Tim Russert." The solid South broke down, with the civil-rights revolution, and a new, more volatile, transparent, and in many ways democratic American domestic politics was born. An information revolution began to gather force, with the advent of computers and improved telecommunications, giving leverage to new forms of specialized consulting. Washington physically began to outgrow its boundaries. The suburbs of Greater Washington, a key element of the growing strategic information complex, came to assume a greater role, as did universities, think tanks, consultants, and other private actors, often unbound by national policy constraints. In the new, more plural world of decentralized power and information centers, transparency, complexity, uncertainty, and market orientation inevitably increased.

In this new, more complex Washington, old-style understandings and compromises between Congress and K Street no longer were transcendent. Image, information, public relations, and the specialized, generally more transparent expertise of private actors gained traction. This new Washington was increasingly embedded in the larger world, as the cold war waned, the Berlin Wall fell, and American preeminence grew. The post–cold war world needed Washington. Yet the terms on which Washington would deal with the world, which it understood through a powerful and well-meaning, yet occasionally naive mass-media filter, remained unsettlingly unclear.

3 | *The Washington*
Factor in Asia

Washington is a cosmopolitan city that interacts with its counterparts throughout the world. Many of its international relationships, together with their overall structure, have implications for the global political system because of Washington's standing as the capital of the world's preeminent superpower. It is Washington in both dimensions— as the American national capital and as a global political city—that I consider in this chapter. Its significance in the local political life of America's partner nations clearly varies, both with the nature of their ties to the United States and with the character of their sociopolitical linkages to Washington itself.

The Washington factor looms especially large—with special implications for international relations that I later discuss—among the nations of Asia. Historically the Asian countries as a group have been on the periphery of international affairs, although many of them rank individually among some of the most rapidly growing and most dynamic in the world today.[1] Their explosive recent growth—accompanied by rising military power, in many cases—has given Asian nations substantial latent influence: *power resources,* in the parlance of international relations theory. How and why that latent influence is translated into actual suasion on matters of importance to Asian nations and their partners is of prime importance for global affairs, yet remarkably little empirical work or theorizing has been done on the topic. Indeed, the role of Asian actors in Washington—and their motives for playing their respective parts in the city's political and economic life—are an increasingly

Figure 3-1. *America's Asian Interlocutors*

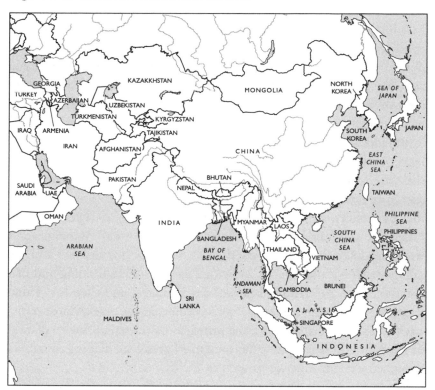

crucial aspect both of the overall Washington equation and of broader international dynamics.

The process of translating power resources into global influence is, of course, a complex interaction between the influencing parties and the influenced. In this chapter I consider the role that the United States—and by extension Washington, as a sociopolitical community transcending the American state—plays in Asia. In doing so, I hope to gauge Washington's power resources on the far side of the Pacific and the impulses within Asia toward transnational influence. In addressing these questions, I focus particularly on the major nations, from India to the east (figure 3-1). (In chapter 4, I examine the converse functional role that Asia plays in Washington, before considering the impact of ethnic politics on Asia's Washington role in chapter 5.)

In assessing first the Washington factor in Asia, I explore the economic, political, and geostrategic meanings that the United States has had for Asia over the two centuries and more since American independence, along with the evolving symbolic role of Washington. In doing this analysis, I note important nuances of difference, both among countries and over time, in the importance that Washington is accorded across Asia. These differences in turn shape the profile of Asian activities in Washington.

Broadly speaking, I find that Washington's importance for Asia has been particularly substantial since World War II, that it rose sharply in the early postwar years, that it stabilized around the 1960s, and that it then rose further during the 1990s, after the cold war. I also find that the functional significance of Washington itself for Asia has recently broadened substantially. Originally just a site for formal communication with the U.S. government, America's capital city has become a prime arena for global intelligence gathering, for personnel training and orientation, for legitimation in intra-Asian conflicts, and even for setting domestic intra-Asian agendas. It also became, in the case of most transpacific bilateral relationships, the principal battleground for mediation of bilateral differences, with Washington's pluralism helping to redress asymmetries with American superpower.

Washington's Early Shadow in Asia

American clipper ships arrived in Canton at the very dawn of the U.S. republic, in 1784.[2] It took close to half a century, however, for the U.S. government to begin establishing diplomatic relations across the Pacific (see appendix A, this volume). America's first formal transpacific diplomatic ties were concluded in 1833, with the kingdom of Siam. Qing China came a decade later, in 1844, and Japan a decade later still.

Opening the Double-Bolted Lands

During the latter half of the nineteenth century, the United States played a key role, as noted above, in opening the two large isolationist nations of Northeast Asia—Tokugawa Japan and Yi Dynasty Korea—to the broader world, initially by force.[3] Commodore Matthew Perry's black ships appeared off Uraga in the fall of 1853 and, after initially being rejected by the shogun's emissaries, sailed south to Okinawa, to conclude a historic bilateral treaty with the kingdom of the Ryukyus. Reappearing in the spring of 1854, Perry's squadron was admitted to Japanese shores, with Perry himself signing the Treaty of Kanagawa, formally opening diplomatic relations between the United States and Japan.

A concrete U.S. presence at the shogun's capital of Edo followed five years later, and Americans played a central role in Japan's historic political-economic transformation and entry into world affairs over the ensuing half century.[4] Guido Fridolin Verbeck, an American missionary in Nagasaki, became a key adviser to the new Meiji government, instrumental in formulating policies for the modernization of Japan.[5] Henry Willard Denison, serving as legal adviser to the Foreign Ministry from 1880 to 1914, drafted nearly all of the important diplomatic documents issued by the Japanese government during that period.[6] William Clark and Horace Capron were central in the development of modern Japanese agriculture, while David Murray was the real architect of Japan's reformed educational system.[7]

The Japanese responded to early American overtures with great ambivalence.[8] Almost universally, they admired American technology and pragmatism and the priority Americans placed on education. Yet the Japanese were not impressed with what passed for American military power at that time. It was ultimately to imperial Germany that Japan turned in that regard.[9]

A little more than a decade after Perry's landing, in the early aftermath of the Civil War, the United States also moved to open Korea, once again initially by force. In 1866 the merchant schooner *General Sherman* sailed up the Taedong River to Pyongyang to test the local stricture that foreign commerce contravened Korean law.[10] A hostile crowd gathered on the shore, and the frightened crew of the *Sherman* discharged their muskets. The local governor ordered the *General Sherman* destroyed; as the tide receded, the vessel was grounded, unable to flee. The Koreans killed the crew and burned the ship. In later years the North Korean government erected a stone monument on the spot where the *General Sherman* burned, which stands to this day, in bitter symbolic commemoration.

Five years later, American forces returned, in a second attempt to open Korea by force. This attempt involved the largest American military action overseas between the Civil and the Spanish-American Wars.[11] After a marine landing on Kanghwa Island and attacks on several strategic forts near Seoul, followed by ultimately fruitless negotiations, the American expedition once again withdrew—and did not come back. In 1882, however, Korea and the United States finally signed a treaty: the Treaty of Peace, Amity, Commerce, and Navigation, which led to the arrival of an American diplomatic envoy in Seoul in May 1883.[12]

The years 1898 to 1902 were, of course, epochal. On May 1, 1898, Commodore George Dewey defeated the Spanish at Manila Bay, and in 1902 a peace was concluded, formalizing the U.S. annexation of the Philippines. The annexation was fatefully important in transforming the United States from a second-rank nation with primarily Western Hemisphere geopolitical concerns into a global power with vested interests in Asia, although the transition itself was tortuous.[13] Even when finally consolidated, the acquisition of the Philippines, which thrust American power into the heart of Southeast Asia, prompted new geopolitical complexities for the United States, particularly in relations with Japan. The new equation compelled Theodore Roosevelt, foremost of the annexationists, to conclude—eight years after he had forcefully put Dewey on the path to confrontation with the Spanish at Manila Bay—that "the Philippines form our Heel of Achilles."[14]

It thus took more than a century after the arrival of American clipper ships at Canton for Washington to establish itself diplomatically in the major Asian capitals, with a major political-military presence in the region to leverage its aspirations. The U.S. entry into Northeast Asia was initially accomplished only by force, although later American contributions to local economic and social development were substantial and met with more regional support.[15] Meanwhile, apart from the Philippines, the bulk of Asia, including India, Indochina, and the East Indies, remained under European colonial rule, with no direct diplomatic links to Washington. Even where that was not true, Europe's presence loomed generally larger than that of the United States.

Japan was a partial early exception to the dominating European presence in Asia, due to the strategic personal roles of a variety of Americans, ranging from Perry himself to William Clark, Guido Verbeck, Charles LeGendre, James C. Hepburn, and Theodore Roosevelt.[16] These remarkable figures were central in introducing Japan to the world, supporting it diplomatically, and transferring key technology and customs, all with long-term implications for Japanese life.[17] Yet even in Tokyo, imperial Britain's commanding strategic and diplomatic influence came gradually to outshine that of Washington, especially following the Anglo-Japanese naval treaty of 1902.

Pursuing Manifest Destiny in the Pacific

The high-water mark of early American influence in the western Pacific was arguably the 1890s and the first decade of the twentieth century. In 1893 expatriate planters, mainly American, deposed the local Hawaiian queen, and soon thereafter they engineered a U.S. annexation of the Hawaiian Islands in 1898.[18] Also in 1898, Dewey defeated the Spanish at the Battle of Manila Bay, and in September 1899 U.S. Secretary of State John Jay enunciated the influential Open Door policy with respect to China.[19] In 1901 the United States consolidated its position in the Philippines with the defeat of Aguinaldo's guerilla insurrection.[20] In 1905 President Theodore Roosevelt mediated a settlement to the Russo-Japanese War, through the Treaty of Portsmouth.[21]

While noting the details of America's emerging Far East policy, it is also important to remember their driving forces and how they began to subtly change early in the twentieth century, under the impact of America's new political-military presence in the Philippines. The United States was originally drawn into Asia, as Griswold notes, by its traders and missionaries. They profoundly, however subtly, influenced the overall profile of U.S. policy.[22]

America's initial orientation was commercial, it should be emphasized, rather than political—an open field for business and proselytizing. This approach did, to be sure, involve more intrusion into local politics and administration—as in support for extraterritoriality and suppression of nativist rebellions like the Boxers—than was typical of U.S. policy elsewhere outside the Americas. Yet the U.S. approach to Asia still remained considerably less intrusive than that of the European colonialists, as epitomized in the notion of the Open Door.[23]

After the occupation of the Philippines, America's Asia policy did, for a time, assume a slightly more geopolitical cast, as America's core national security concerns became more concretely linked to the region. The symbolic high points of early-twentieth-century American involvement with Asia, which bore this geopolitical tinge, were two ceremonial maritime visits of high-ranking U.S. government officials to Asia. One was the so-called imperial cruise to Japan, China, Korea, and the Philippines in the summer of 1905.[24] The other was the voyage of the U.S. Navy's Great White Fleet to Japan, China, and the Philippines in the fall of 1908.[25] The former was principally a diplomatic mission—the largest (numerically) to Asia in U.S. history, while the latter was mainly a show of military force. Both played powerful roles in reinforcing Asian perceptions of the United States as a rising power intent on playing a major role in Pacific affairs, even though two decades later the United States was to fall once again into isolation.

The high-powered American delegation of 1905 included twenty-three U.S. representatives, seven senators, Secretary of War William Howard Taft, and Alice Roosevelt, the comely twenty-one-year-old daughter of President Theodore Roosevelt. It arrived at Yokohama aboard the *USS Manchuria* amid the Russo-Japanese War. Virtually every building in town was decked out in their honor. Perhaps in anticipation of a peace settlement in Japan's favor, on America's home ground at Portsmouth, New Hampshire, the U.S. delegation was greeted with expressions of hospitality, including elaborate fireworks and receptions. The Americans took a special train to Tokyo, where they relaxed overnight at the Shiba Detached Palace. They had lunch the next day with Emperor Meiji, who personally greeted each of the eighty-three-member delegation. Then the Taft group toured the palace gardens, which no westerner and few Japanese outside the imperial household had ever seen.

The Japanese side clearly harbored strategic objectives. The day after the festivities Prime Minister Katsura requested a meeting with Taft. In their ensuing dialogue, fateful understandings emerged: recognizing continued American authority in the Philippines—where Taft had recently served as governor—in return for U.S. recognition of Japanese suzerainty in Korea. What appeared to the Washington group as a triumphal visit was thus used shrewdly by Tokyo to legitimate Japanese colonial rule in continental Northeast Asia—a development that many Koreans resent to this day.

Together with geopolitics, Japan's oligarchic leaders, faced with rising domestic political pressures as their nation urbanized and industrialized, were also concerned about face and legitimacy at home. As they gazed out across the Pacific, rising anti-Japanese sentiment in California, culminating in a 1906 San Francisco school board ruling that children of Japanese descent would be required to attend segregated schools, was an irritant, especially as it stirred public backlash within Japan itself. In 1907 the United States and Japan concluded a so-called gentlemen's agreement: that Japan would restrain further emigration to the United States and that the United States would accordingly refrain from imposing formal immigration restrictions.[26] Yet racial issues continued to cast shadows on U.S.-Japan relations, as they had previously on U.S.-China relations, right down to the Exclusion Act of 1924 and beyond.

In late 1907, calculating that a rising and nationalistic Japan, together with its neighbors, needed to concretely understand the military capabilities of the United States and its determination to play an active role in Pacific affairs, President Theodore Roosevelt dispatched a more martial mission: sixteen U.S. battleships, together with assorted escorts, on a two-year, round-the-world cruise.[27] That cruise, a tangible expression of the Washington factor in Asia, conspicuously included major ports of call across Asia and Australia. Apart from a variety of ranking military officials, the fleet delegation also included journalists, photographers, and painters.[28] It was thus mainly a hybrid exercise in public diplomacy and domestic U.S. politics, although preceded by deft yet separate visits by Secretary of War Taft and others, following the announcement of the cruise itself, that subtly exploited the diplomatic and geopolitical implications.[29]

The high point of the global cruise was no doubt the Great White Fleet's week-long visit to Japan in October 1908. The fleet received a spectacular welcome, just as the imperial cruise of 1905 had done, with the sixteen battleships of the U.S. fleet being escorted into Yokohama harbor on October 18 by sixteen battleships of Japan's own imperial navy, fresh from its historic victory over the Russians. The U.S. fleet was wildly feted in Yokohama and Tokyo and met by crowds of Japanese schoolchildren singing the "Star Spangled Banner" in English.[30] Two days later the Emperor Meiji himself offered an audience and a luncheon in honor of the fleet commander, Sperry, followed by a garden party the next day personally hosted by Admiral Togo Heihachirō, the victor over the Russians at Tsushima.[31]

Upon departure, the Great White Fleet was escorted back to the open sea by Japan's most modern battleships, until the fleet left Japanese waters. It then headed south, dividing into separate squadrons, one of which visited Amoy, China, and the other the Philippines. Then the recombined squadrons headed westward, around the world.[32] The main event, however, had clearly been the eventful visit to Japan, replete with its outpouring of Japanese regard for the United States.

In contrast to the 1905 imperial cruise, Tokyo did not advance specific policy proposals to the U.S. in 1908. Yet the visit of the fleet did impress the Japanese and the Chinese with both the rising political-military capability of the Americans and the rising interest of Washington in Pacific affairs. By reassuring Japan, especially the restive, volatile, and sometimes xenophobic Japanese public, of American friendship, the visit also paved the way for the Root-Takahira agreement of November 1908. That bilateral understanding affirmed not only the U.S. open-door approach to China but also Japanese acquiescence to informal limits on emigration to California. It also implicitly recognized Japan's right to annex Korea and to dominate southern Manchuria.[33]

From the last decade of the nineteenth century, even as the American star was still ascending in the Pacific estimation, the presence of imperial Japan was likewise beginning to loom large across Northeast Asia, constraining potential American influence there and prefiguring the geopolitical tensions of future years. In 1895, following a brief conflict with a weakened China, Japan annexed Taiwan. And in 1905, following the ambiguous dialogue with Washington discussed above, and reflecting Tokyo's wary recognition of Washington's rising regional importance, Japan declared a protectorate over Korea.[34] Five years later it formally annexed that tortured peninsula, thus extinguishing all vestiges of an independent Korea that had successfully preserved its autonomy, as a "shrimp among whales," for over six hundred years.[35]

A Geographically Limited Prewar Role

For the six decades following Perry's visit to Japan, the United States enjoyed strong, interactive ties with both the Japanese government and Japanese society. From World War I until 1945, however, direct American political-economic engagement with Asia was largely limited to the Philippines, an American possession, and China. In the home islands of Japan the United States had substantial investments, especially in the automobile and electronics industries, but little economic involvement with the broader Japanese empire.[36] It likewise had little political-economic intercourse with the extensive British, French, and Dutch colonies.

The substantial U.S. economic and cultural involvement with China, through both business investments and missionary activities, naturally made the United States highly visible to the Chinese and, conversely, China visible to Americans.[37] Not surprisingly, the Japanese invasion of Manchuria in 1931 struck a deep, repulsive chord in both Nanking and Washington. The Chiang Kai-shek regime in Nanking came to rely heavily on the United States both during and after World War II.[38] And American volunteers in the struggle with Japan, such as Claire Chennault's Flying Tigers, created new transpacific bonds, as did the large number of missionaries who remained to work with the Chinese people during the Pacific conflict.

The New Meaning of Washington in the Postwar World

For most of Asia, pre–World War II America was a vaguely attractive nation—a "beautiful imperialist," more idealistic and less predatory than Japan or the major European powers, with economic vitality, dynamic educational institutions, and a clearly rising role in world affairs.[39] For some, such as the Koreans and some Filipinos, the United States also showed a duplicitous streak, subordinating the nationalist aspirations of others to Washington's own reasons of state, through such acts as the Taft-Katsura "understanding" and the suppression of Aguinaldo's nationalist insurgency in the Philippines. Yet with only a limited American military presence in the Pacific during these years, and with the Asian regional economy largely self-contained, transpacific interdependence remained distinctly limited.[40] The United States was useful as a source of technology and as an occasional foil in regional geopolitical struggles, especially with European colonialists, but little more. The Washington factor was thus a distinctly limited one in pre–World War II Asian consciousness, as in Asian political-economic reality.

What Pearl Harbor Wrought

World War II radically transformed this equation. America emerged as the victor in a herculean global contest that exhausted both Japan and

Table 3-1. *Changing Trans-War Patterns of Interdependence
in the Northeast Asian Political Economy*
Percent

Country	Exports		Imports	
	1934–36	1956	1934–36	1956
United States	16	22	25	31
China	18	3	12	3
South Korea/Taiwan	21	6	24	2
Southeast Asia	21	6	24	2

Source: Original data from Ministry of International Trade and Industry, adapted from Jerome B. Cohen, *Japan's Political Economy* (Indiana University Press, 1958), p. 153.

China, not to mention the nations of Europe, leaving the United States as the world's dominant economy and a global superpower. With devastated Asia struggling to regain its economic footing, America loomed as the massive, indispensable market of last resort, generating close to half of total global GDP. And Washington was its capital and decision center, particularly on questions of war and peace.

Early postwar geopolitical realignments intensified capitalist Asia's deepening dependence on the United States by truncating traditional economic ties between maritime Asia and the Asian continent. Most important in this regard were the Chinese revolution of 1949 and the ensuing Korean War. These historic political developments precipitated an American economic embargo of mainland China, which also provoked a sharp reordering of regional trade patterns.[41] Continental Asia had been the primary market and source of imports for prewar Japan (table 3-1). Yet cold war political transformations of the early 1950s sharply constrained this possibility, and by the mid-1950s Japan was instead heavily dependent for both imports and exports on the United States.

Rimming the Asian continent, an asymmetric hub-and-spokes structure of bilateral political-economic relations between a massive American political economy and the noncommunist nations of Asia began to grow. Known as the San Francisco system, after the 1951 San Francisco peace treaty ending World War II in the Pacific, which formalized its structure, this arrangement provided lucrative access to the American market for Asian allies, in return for U.S. bases and other forms of security access with Asia.[42] By radically intensifying transpacific security

Figure 3-2. *Trade Dependence on the U.S. Market: Japan, Taiwan, Korea, Hong Kong, China*

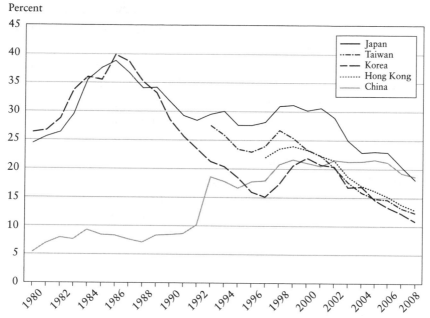

Percent

Source: International Monetary Fund, *Direction of Trade Statistics Yearbook.*

and economic ties in a highly asymmetric fashion, the San Francisco system magnified the importance of Washington in East Asia's political economy and in Asia's internal decisionmaking as well.

The New Washington Factor in Asia's Economic Equation

From the early 1960s through the mid-1970s, the ambit of Asian economic growth began to broaden beyond Japan, to include South Korea, Taiwan, Hong Kong, and Singapore.[43] From 1965 to 1973 the Vietnam War provided substantial stimulus in this regard for Southeast and Northeast Asian allies of the United States, for example. Both directly and indirectly—through exports to the United States as well as through substantial defense procurements in Vietnam and Korea—America provided critical support in the early stages of the rapid and remarkably sustained growth that transpired in these nations. A decade after the war's end, the expansionary policies of Ronald Reagan, coupled with

America's free trade orientation, enhanced economic opportunities in the United States for Asian producers still further. South Korea, Taiwan, and Japan sent between a third and a half of their total exports to the United States throughout this period, a ratio that has declined only slowly in recent years (figure 3-2).

Since the early 1970s, mainland China has also become gradually integrated into the U.S.–centric Pacific political economy, through a series of Washington-driven political-economic decisions. First there was the end of the American economic embargo in mid-1971 and the Nixon-Kissinger overtures to China between 1971 and 1974. In late 1978 Deng Xiaoping initiated the "four modernizations," with Washington fatefully recognizing the PRC a few weeks later, on January 1, 1979.[44] Economic forces responded rapidly to the erosion of political barriers and to the attractiveness of the U.S. market, with Chinese export dependence on the United States rising steadily between the early 1980s and 2002 (figure 3-2).

It is important to note that reliance on the U.S. market varies substantially, from country to country across Asia, in recent years, provoking natural cross-national variations in political-economic sensitivity to Washington. Broadly speaking, as also noted in figure 3-2, trade dependence on the United States has been traditionally high in Japan, Korea, and Taiwan, and although it has gradually declined, it remains substantial. China's dependence was initially low but did rise sharply for two decades, before joining the broader trend toward declining U.S. market reliance in the mid-2000s.[45] Elsewhere in the region, trade dependence on the United States is more limited, and also declining, even in nations favorably inclined toward the United States, such as Singapore (figure 3-3). The one major exception in southern Asia is Vietnam—another communist country where U.S. trade dependency has risen substantially, compared to a generation ago, as in the case of China.

Despite some long-term erosion of trade interdependence, investment dependence on the United States remains quite important in some entrepôt financial centers, such as Singapore and Hong Kong.[46] India and Indonesia are the large nations with the most remote economic ties to the United States. Yet their investment interdependence with the United States has been deepening over the past decade as well, even as relative trade reliance on America has been declining. U.S. foreign direct investment in India during 2010, for example, rose 29.5 percent, to

Figure 3-3. *South and Southeast Asian Trade Dependence on the United States*

Percent

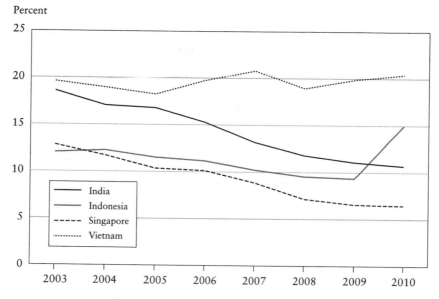

Source: International Monetary Fund, *Direction of Trade Statistics Yearbook,* 2010 and 2011.

$27.1 billion, while Indian foreign direct investment in the United States rose 40.8 percent, to $3.3 billion.[47]

Although the deepening trade and investment relationships between Asia and the United States over the past half century have been driven by market forces, their political-economic dimension—which makes the Washington factor important in Asian calculations—should be noted. It was, after all, political decisions—American foreign aid and then support for Japanese, Korean, and ultimately Chinese accession to GATT, the International Monetary Fund, the OECD, most-favored-nation treatment, and the World Trade Organization, for example—that allowed transpacific economic ties to deepen so rapidly. Had supportive political decisions not been made for many years in Washington, opportunities for Asia in the American market would not have emerged so clearly, as U.S. trading and investment partners in the western Pacific are aware.

As Asian trade surpluses with the United States have risen, and as a capital-surplus Asia has begun investing actively in the United States, the converse fear—of protectionist American political intervention to arrest

Asia's economic rise—has emerged as a central element of the Washington factor in Asia, intensifying Asian incentives to be involved in Washington. The Japanese, who generated the first large bilateral surpluses with the United States, were the first to experience American protectionist pressures in return. This grim reality made them more conscious of and reactive to Washington (in both its executive and congressional dimensions) for nearly two decades, even as their center of economic and cultural activities in the United States remained New York City. South Korea, China, and increasingly India (over outsourcing) have also periodically become the target of protectionist pressures, forcing those countries to keep a careful eye from afar on Capitol Hill, the USTR, and various U.S. economic regulatory agencies as well.

Washington and the Changing Asian Security Equation

While Washington has loomed large on the Asian economic horizon in various ways for over half a century, it has loomed as large or larger in security terms for most Asian nations, although there is substantial intraregional variation. Japan and South Korea formally host American bases and maintain bilateral security treaties with the United States, making them especially close allies (table 3-2). Singapore has deep informal security ties with the United States, including extensive intelligence sharing, while India, the Philippines, and increasingly even Vietnam and Indonesia engage in important informal security cooperation with Washington, as well. Throughout most of the 1980s, amid the cold war, even China had remarkably deep informal security interactions with the United States, including annual briefings by a succession of CIA intelligence directors for top Chinese leaders, coupled with Chinese toleration of highly classified American monitors for Soviet nuclear and missile tests placed strategically along the Xinjiang-Soviet border.[48]

Although the nature of Asian security ties with the United States varies sharply from country to country, most nations of the region follow security policy developments in Washington very closely, for two important reasons. The global superpower status of the United States, of course, is one major factor impelling them to do so. Another very important structural consideration is the absence of a multilateral security framework in Asia analogous to NATO in Europe. For the Asians, in short, there is no analogue to Brussels, where security issues can be reviewed and largely settled on one's own continent. Due to the traditional hub-and-spokes

Table 3-2. *Asian Security Relationships with the United States, 1950–2010*[a]

Country	Treaty	Executive agreements
China	None	None
India	None	1995: Agreed minute of defense relations 2005–15: New U.S.-India defense relationship (NFDR) framework 2006: Maritime security cooperation agreement 2009: End-user monitoring agreement (EUMA)
Indonesia	None	2007: Triborder initiative
Japan	1951: San Francisco peace treaty 1951: Treaty of mutual cooperation and security 1960: Revised treaty of mutual cooperation and security	1960: Status of forces agreement (SOFA) 1991, 1995, 2000, 2006, and 2012: Agreements on host nation support
Philippines	1951: Mutual defense treaty	1947–58: Agreement on military assistance 1993: SOFA 1998: Manila agreement on treatment of U.S. military visitors (amended 2006)
Singapore	2003: Free trade agreement	1990: Memorandum of understanding and its 1998 addendum to allow the U.S. access to military facilities 2005: Strategic framework agreement
South Korea	1953: Mutual defense treaty 2011: KORUS FTA ratified	1960: Nuclear research and training equipment/materials grant 1966: SOFA (amended 2001)
Taiwan	1954–79: Mutual defense treaty 1979: Taiwan Relations Act providing for U.S. arms sales	
Vietnam	None with unified Vietnam	2003: Letter of agreement (LOA) on counternarcotics cooperation 2006: Amendment to LOA previous 2010: Agreement to combat illicit smuggling of radioactive materials

Source: R. Chuck Mason, "Status of Forces Agreement (SOFA): What Is It, and How Has It Been Utilized?" Congressional Research Service, January 5, 2011 (www.fas.org/sgp/crs/natsec/RL34531.pdf); "Background Notes," U.S. Department of State (www.state.gov/r/pa/ei/bgn/); and "Treaties in Force 2007," U.S. Department of State (www.state.gov/s/l/treaty/treaties/2007/section1/index.htm).

a. Items listed are illustrative. This list is by no means exhaustive.

bilateral structure of security ties in the Pacific, all roads inevitably lead back to Washington. The central security role of the United States in the Pacific has powerful implications for how the Washington factor manifests itself in particular Asian nations, as shown in greater detail in chapters 6, 7, and 8. In the divided nations (China and Korea), it impels the competing parties active in Washington (China, Taiwan, and South Korea) to give strong priority to Washington in their overall interaction with the United States. For Japan, a unified nation with strong existing security ties to the United States, the incentives to be proactive in Washington appear weaker than in China or South Korea.

Asian Popular Images of Washington

There is no question that the Washington factor currently looms large—much larger than in the pre–World War II period—for both the economic and security calculations of Asia's elites, especially on both sides of the Taiwan Strait and in Korea. What about the broader public of Asian nations? How important do they feel that Washington is for their countries? And what sort of image does the Asian public have of American policymaking in their respective nations?

The evidence remains fragmentary, but it appears that the general citizenry of most Asian countries, like their leaders, see persuasive reasons both to monitor policy in Washington and to actively try to influence outcomes there. These sentiments are clear from the Pew Global Attitudes survey, which has been carried out annually since 2002 in over thirty countries worldwide.[49] The Pew study suggests that most Asians—a larger share than in most major nations of the world—accept that the United States is both the preeminent global economic power and also one that considers to a substantial degree their own nation's interests.

Asian nations generally appreciate the economic power and leadership capabilities of the United States in world affairs, causing the Washington factor to loom large in their domestic calculations. There are, however, important shades of difference among these countries that are relevant to the analysis here. Accordingly, I present the key findings of the Pew studies along five key dimensions that are central in defining the Washington factor within various national contexts (figures 3-4, 3-5, 3-6, 3-7, 3-8).

Figure 3-4. *"United States as World's Leading Economic Power"*

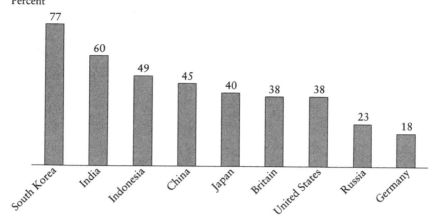

Figure 3-5. *"International Trade Is of Value"*

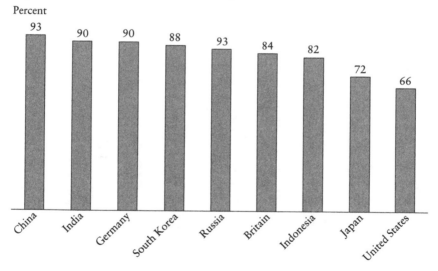

Asians, as suggested above, recognize the United States as the preeminent international economic power more pervasively than do either Europeans or even Americans themselves. The contrast is especially striking with Russians and Germans. Those latter two groups appear to be particularly reluctant to recognize American economic preeminence.

Asians, especially the populous continental giants—China and India—see the value of international trade much more acutely than do

Figure 3-6. *"Is the United States Considerate of Your Country's Interests?"*

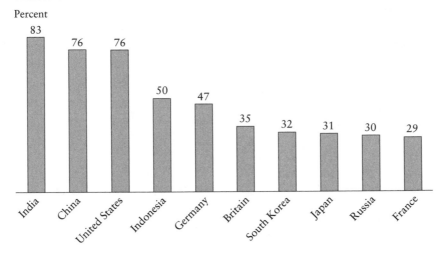

Percent

Figure 3-7. *"Favorable Impression of the United States?"*

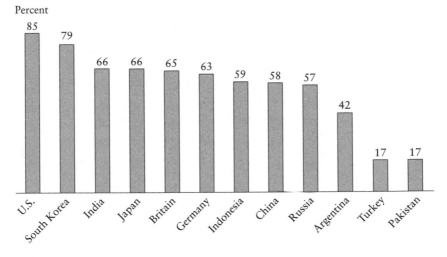

Percent

either Europeans or Americans. The one Asian outlier—less enthusiastic about international trade than any other Asian state—is traditionally insular Japan. Yet even its people appear more prone to recognize the value of trade than do Americans.

The rapidly globalizing Asian giants—India and China—see the United States as more considerate of their interests than Americans

Figure 3-8. *"Confidence in the U.S. President?"*

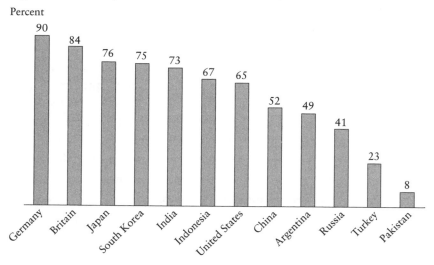

Percent

perceive their own country to be. The Asian developing nations are particularly conscious of American consideration for their interests. The partial outliers are South Korea and Japan, whose skepticism of American intentions is similar to that of the French and Russian publics.

Asians generally tend to have a favorable impression of the United States—much more so than in Latin America or the Islamic world. The publics of some Asian nations—notably South Korea, India, and Japan—appear to think more highly of the United States than Europeans in general do. China and Indonesia, for differing reasons, are more complex cases. In China, geopolitical and ideological differences cloud local impressions of the United States, while in Indonesia—the world's most populous Muslim nation—religious differences appear to be at work.

The Western Europeans and Africans have been generally enamored of U.S. leadership since the 2008 presidential campaign, and that pattern continues. With those exceptions, however, the president seems to be more favorably regarded in Asia than anywhere else in the world— particularly compared to Latin America, Russia, and the Middle Eastern Islamic nations, where latent hostility to American authority figures remains. China, given its contrasting political system and geopolitical differences with the United States, appears to be an intermediate case.

In Conclusion

The U.S. relationship with Asia goes back to the very origins of America as a nation, with the first clipper ship dropping anchor at Canton in 1784, only a year after the Treaty of Paris formally ended the Revolutionary War. The United States did intrude sharply into the consciousness of Japan and Korea during the late nineteenth century as the Western nation that opened both countries—albeit forcibly—to the outside world. Japan saw some value in the United States as a geopolitical partner during the first decade of the twentieth century. America also gained some early appreciation in China for its important educational and humanitarian role, through missionary schools, volunteer activities, and at least nominal opposition to the colonialist designs of the Europeans and the Japanese. Yet the United States and Asia were generally remote from one another, both diplomatically and socially, until World War II.

America's central role in the Pacific war and the early postwar occupation of Japan and South Korea, together with its sudden emergence as the one global superpower with a powerful, prosperous economy, radically transformed the Washington factor in the domestic political-economic equations of Asia. The United States became intimately engaged with many nations of the region in the security sphere, through its military bases and its broader strategic role in deterring aggression, enhanced by its nuclear capabilities. The U.S. also became a primary magnet for Asian exports and a mentor helping Asia liberalize the post–World War II global political economy to its advantage.

Washington, D.C., as capital of the United States, thus began to assume a new, unprecedented importance for Asia in the early postwar years. It was the hub of the hub-and-spokes security system that dominated international affairs in the Pacific. It was also the cold war policy decision center that determined the profile of embargoes against the communist states of the region, notably China, the Soviet Union, North Korea, and later Vietnam. The salience of the United States in Pacific security since World War II seems to have had an especially powerful role in stimulating political activism in Washington on the part of divided nations such as China and Korea.

As economic development in Asia began to accelerate during the 1950s and 1960s, and as Asian nations were admitted to more and more multilateral bodies, Washington also became important to Asia in another sense: as the headquarters of a range of international institutions separate from the U.S. government that supported and helped stabilize the global development process. Relations with the World Bank and the International Monetary Fund became an increasingly important dimension of the Washington factor, as perceived on the western shores of the Pacific. As Asian governments and corporations gained substantial stakes in the smooth and efficient functioning of the global political economy, from the 1980s on, Washington also became increasingly important to them in a third respect: as a venue for intelligence collection and international networking, on issues far transcending transpacific relations themselves. And it likewise began to emerge as a political-economic battleground among them, as Pacific interdependence rose, even as both interests and claims of the major nations—especially Japan, Korea, and China on both sides of the Taiwan Strait—grew increasingly entwined.

4

The Asia Factor in Washington

Washington, as noted in the preceding pages, looms large today in Asia—much larger than before World War II and larger even than a decade or two ago. Given Asia's heavy export dependence on the U.S. market, and the hub-and-spokes structure of security ties, Asian officials feel a strong need to network and coordinate with their Washington-based U.S. government counterparts. And given the presence of the World Bank and the International Monetary Fund in Washington, Asian officials feel an increasing incentive, as the Asian private sector also does, to coordinate in the U.S. capital on multilateral matters as well. Given American commitment to social welfare and democratic values, nongovernmental organizations likewise look to Washington for legitimation. And everyone references the powerful, yet remarkably open, strategic information complex of Washington for insights on global trends.

If Asia focuses on Washington with great intensity, as suggested in chapter 3, then where does Asia's deepening attention fit in the overall Washington scene? How does Asia's obsession with Washington, and its confidence in the capital's capacities on the global stage, influence Washington's own approach to Asia? How much attention does Washington give to the major Asian nations—both their governments and their private sectors? And with what consequences for policy as well as for the transpacific relationship?

In this chapter, I look broadly and comparatively at how Washington as a broad sociopolitical community treats Asia, within the overall context of how it deals with the broader world. In doing so, I explore the aggregate profile that Asia enjoys—compared to other global regions—in U.S. government agencies, in multinational institutions like the World Bank and the IMF, and in NGOs such as the Council on Foreign Relations. I also chart the flow of political, economic, and strategic information from Washington to Asia relative to such flows elsewhere in the world.

In considering Asia's links to Washington from a broader, regional-comparative perspective, there is a much lower level of interaction across the Pacific than prevails with respect to Western Europe or Latin America. It is also clear, however, that Asia's influence on Washington is nevertheless rapidly growing, and that it is quite substantial at certain institutions, particularly think tanks. I likewise note that there is a substantial, asymmetric consciousness gap between the intense Asian awareness of, and interest in, Washington and the lower level of attention that Asia is generally accorded in that city. And finally, I also notice the striking variation in Washington's consciousness of various Asian nations, in ways remarkably unrelated to economic or geographic size.

At the policy level, I find that intensity of interest appears to pay off—that Asian nations collectively appear formidably effective in achieving their principal policy ends, especially defensive objectives, such as forestalling protectionist U.S. congressional legislation that might be damaging to their homelands. At a more theoretical level, the subnational dynamics of lobbying and agenda setting that occur in Washington—including those within the penumbra of power and beyond formal governmental processes—substantially modify the behavioral outcomes that might be expected under classical realist assumptions of unified, rational-actor decisionmaking at the national level. This competitive, subnational process of lobbying and pluralistic agenda setting within Washington itself makes American foreign policy decisionmaking significantly more responsive to foreign pressures—especially those from Asia—than would otherwise be the case.

Asia's Traditional Role in Washington and Its Enduring Challenge

Until World War II, it is fundamental to remember that the transpacific relationship was, with only a few exceptions, of marginal concern for both Asia and the United States. The major European colonial powers were more central in the international system, and they dominated most of Asia. America was a clearly rising economic power, but its political, military, and diplomatic capabilities were unclear. Furthermore, Washington as a sociopolitical community remained a parochial diplomatic backwater.

In the genteel, soporific world of global diplomacy, the major European powers, beginning with Britain and France, loomed large. Asia, as a peripheral, underdeveloped part of the world political economy—most of which remained under colonial rule—loomed small and largely inconsequential. Only Japan, China, and Thailand had any diplomatic presence in Washington.[1] The K Street lobbies and think tanks, which were later to assume such prominence in supporting Asia's rise in Washington, were largely nonexistent.

Like any seat of political power, Washington is a sociopolitical community that allocates valued resources. It includes, in close physical proximity to one another, those who are closely connected to power centers, and able to influence political-economic outcomes, as well as those who are not. Similarly, Washington includes both those with strategic inside information on impending political-economic developments and those without special connections and insights. The heart of Washington's political-economic life is thus *access*—to both strategic information and strategic resources. As political games and relevant political players are continually changing, gaining relevant access is a complex, often deceptive enterprise. As in other global political cities, it takes time, effort, resources, and expertise.

Asia, compared to Europe and even much of Latin America, has been a late developer in the global political economy. It has also been socioculturally distant from the core of the world system as that system has evolved since the mid-nineteenth century. In contrast to these other more integrated regions, Asia has also traditionally lacked the politically active expatriate ethnic ties that have given such relatively small nations as Italy, Poland, Ireland, Armenia, Greece, and Israel disproportionate influence in the American political system.[2]

Asia has thus traditionally lacked systematic access to Washington power centers relative to potential competitors from Europe and Latin America. As long as transpacific interdependence was low, and global competition for influence in Washington remained limited, that lack of political access did not matter too much. Yet as U.S.-Asian interdependence has steadily risen since World War II, in both economic and security dimensions, and as American influence in international affairs has risen with it, systematic entrée into Washington has become an increasingly pressing matter for Asian political-economic actors.

Uncertainty regarding the very parameters of American policy compounds the challenge that Asia confronts in Washington. Such uncertainty is endemic in America's capital to a greater degree than in most Asian or European nations. Intense two-party competition, coupled with the fluid, politically driven processes of staff recruitment for higher level government positions that is typical in the American political system, compounds such uncertainty.[3] Every four to eight years and often much more frequently, the key decisionmakers in virtually all government agencies change. In addition, there is substantial domestic attitudinal volatility, especially within Congress, toward the broader world—and especially toward Asia. Persistent trade imbalances, not to mention differing approaches to democracy, economic regulation, and other potentially contentious matters, ensure that this will be so.

Asia's Postwar Washington Presence in Comparative Regional Perspective

As suggested above, Asia has an unusual problem of access in Washington: for historical and cultural reasons, it is relatively isolated from the U.S. capital's internal decisionmaking, and yet due to intense political-economic interdependence with America it finds access in Washington to be important. As a major and growing part of the global political economy that both needs and supplies development capital, Asia also needs close ties with such globally important institutions as the World Bank and the International Monetary Fund, which are based in Washington.

This section reviews the prominence of Asian nations, relative to other regions of the world, in various aspects of Washington's political-economic life. Clearly there are important cross-national variations within Asia regarding Washington access—among Japan, China, and India, for example (addressed in the following chapters). First, however, it is important to identify general cross-regional patterns and sectoral distinctions that are of consequence for the broader arguments developed in the volume as a whole. Particular attention is devoted to the Asia factor in traditional lobbying and at think tanks, mass media, and multilateral institutions like the World Bank and the IMF. All of these latter institutions are increasingly important dimensions of the Washington scene.

Diplomatic Representation

In terms of sheer scale and opulence of diplomatic representation in Washington, Asia must defer to the Middle East, Africa, Latin America, and Europe. China has a massive, stylish embassy, opened in 2009 on Van Ness Street, and Indonesia boasts the classic Walsh mansion on Embassy Row,[4] but most Asian states are relatively subdued in their formal representation. They generally have modest embassies and do not spend huge amounts of money on entertainment or national day celebrations.

In simple quantitative terms, Asian diplomatic representation in Washington also fails to loom as large as that of several other major regions. There are considerably fewer Asian embassies in Washington than African or even Latin American.[5] And Asian embassies, with the exception of the Chinese and Japanese, have relatively modest staffs, especially in comparison with the large European nations and Canada.[6]

Why formal Asian diplomatic representation in Washington is relatively modest, relative to the substantial and rising political-economic interests of Asian nations, is a legitimate intellectual puzzle. Bureaucratic as opposed to political dominance of many diplomatic corps may be one reason—bureaucrats tend to be bound by universalistic rules and cannot or will not so easily squander scarce national resources on embassy personnel in Washington. A related reason may be that oligarchic sociopolitical interests in home countries have relatively little influence within Asian embassies in Washington, relative to peers from Africa and Latin America. Asian nations are also generally less concerned about ostentatious representation for national prestige reasons than are other parts of the non-Western world, although there are some conspicuous exceptions.

Lobbying

Asian nations do, however, have fundamental economic and security interests at stake in Washington, and these make effective interest articulation imperative. As Asian governments often lack the direct, routine

Table 4-1. *Top Classical Lobbying Nations in the United States,*
1960–2011

Rank[a]	1960	1980	1990	2011
1	France: 50	Japan: 159	Japan: 275	Japan: 34
2	Mexico: 49	Canada: 69	Canada: 151	Korea: 24
3	Cuba: 38	USSR: 58	USSR: 103	Canada: 22
4	Canada: 32	Mexico: 58	France: 54	Taiwan: 16
5	Israel: 30	West Germany: 49	Korea: 51	China: 13
6	USSR: 29	France: 45	Taiwan: 38	Turkey: 13
7	Japan: 28	Korea: 42	Israel 32	UAE: 13
8	Sweden: 25	Taiwan: 30	Italy: 28	Mexico: 13
9	United Kingdom: 24	Israel: 27	Switzerland: 27	Saudi Arabia: 12
10	West Germany: 22	Saudi Arabia: 27	Jamaica: 26	India: 10

Source: U.S. Department of Justice, Foreign Agents Registration Unit (www.fara.gov)
a. Rank is by number of registered lobbyists.

access to the informal side of American policymaking that many of the
NATO members, particularly Britain, enjoy, they tend to employ lobbyists
extensively—as do many private Asian firms. K Street, where lobbyists in
the District traditionally congregate, thus has a large transpacific element.

Asian nations do rank relatively high in their aggregate expenditures
on lobbying and in the number of lobbyists they engage. The Center
for Public Integrity found in 2005, for example, that Japan and China /
Taiwan both ranked among the top ten in terms of lobbying expenditures during the 1998–2005 period.[7] Neither, however, ranked right
at the top—Japan was fourth, after Britain, Germany, and Switzer-
land, while Taiwan was ninth. The PRC, South Korea, and India were
nowhere to be seen at that point.

In the number of lobbyists they engage, Asian nations figure even
more prominently. Half a century ago only Japan, in seventh place,
ranked among the top ten national employers of registered agents. By
2011, however, four of the top five, and five of the top ten lobbying
nations in the United States—with the overwhelming share of their lobbyists in Washington—were Asian nations.

Agenda Setting I: Information Centers

Asian nations devote significant attention and expense to government-
financed information centers in and around Washington—perhaps more

than any other region of the world other than Europe. Japan, China, Korea, and Indonesia, for example, all have fairly elaborate information facilities, detached from yet supportive of their own national embassies. Supplementing the information centers are increasingly elaborate informational websites as well.

Although each Asian nation has a distinctive approach to public diplomacy, all generally focus on deepening local understanding of their country's economic and political circumstances as well as its policy priorities. They generally also teach the national language and sponsor art and film events that deepen American understanding of their national culture. Most also use their national information center as a venue for lectures and addresses by visiting government officials and scholars from their home country.

Language education seems to be common to virtually all information centers in Washington, Asian and otherwise. Asian information centers, however, tend to introduce more political and country-specific cultural content than do such European institutions as the British Council, the Goethe Institute, and la Maison Française. The latter cultivate a more universal cultural focus, with much of their programming lacking a direct relationship to national interests. This may be because very little funding comes from the national governments in question.[8]

La Maison Française, for example, has an advantage over some Asian countries because France is arguably a more familiar country to Americans. As an EU nation and a francophone country, it represents more than itself, thus multiplying its venues.[9] For example, la Maison Française participates in events such as the Kids Euro Festival, organized in part by the French-American Cultural Foundation.[10] The foundation has been active since 2001 in organizing the six-week Francophonie Cultural Festival, which gathers more than forty francophone embassies to showcase their cuisine and art. It also sponsors non-French artists who perform in French.[11] Since la Maison Française hosts la Grande-fete de la Francophonie—the festival's most popular event (1,700 Washingtonians attended in 2011)—French visibility is high at the festival.[12]

Aside from Bastille Day, la Maison Française promotes France through such cultural offerings as a reading of *Genica* by the actress Carole Bouquet and a performance by the chamber rock group Magma. Other events have been a celebration of Beaujolais nouveau and

Valentine's Day soirées, both bows to the conception of France as a romantic and cultured nation. In its use of branding and its sponsorship of diverse activities with a universal human dimension, there is much that Asian nations in Washington can reference in the la Maison Française example.

Agenda Setting II: Idea Generators and Idea Brokers

Crucial to the agenda-setting process in any nation, of course, are the ability to create policy-relevant ideas, to translate arcane concepts from academia into operational policy guidelines, and to offer these ideas and guidelines to those who can realize them in the political arena. All three functions are performed actively in Washington. The city has thus given stimulus to the role of universities as idea generators and to NGOs, especially think tanks, as information merchandisers.

Washington think tanks are not primary generators of original research; that function lies more with universities. The Washington area has several major universities with vigorous research programs on Asia-related topics, including the Nitze School of Advanced International Studies (SAIS, within Johns Hopkins University), Georgetown University, George Washington University, American University, and the University of Maryland. The city also has semiacademic idea generators with substantial propagation functions, such as the Woodrow Wilson Center for Scholars.[13] Much of the input for Washington's idea brokers comes, however, from universities and academic research institutes outside of Greater Washington, especially such northeastern elite universities as Princeton, Harvard, and Yale.

Think tanks are a relatively new type of Washington institution, which has risen sharply in prominence over the past twenty years, aided by the information revolution and globalization. They are the ultimate idea brokers, or intellectual middlemen.[14] Although the Brookings Institution, one of the first think tanks, was founded in 1916, most of its counterparts were born in the 1960s and 1970s and have risen to policy prominence only over the past decade.[15] They are known for their ability to scour the world for attractive ideas, to legitimate them, and to promote them through electronic communications. In the post–cold war world, as decisions made in Washington have become increasingly consequential from a global standpoint, local think tanks have gained an unprecedented opportunity to shape policy agendas and to foster global policy networks.

Washington think tanks have proven useful to policymakers, business people, and academics throughout the world, and actors of all regions interact with them. Think tanks have developed, however, an especially intimate relationship with Asian nations, as their strengths are particularly complementary to the weaknesses and needs of Asian actors in Washington. Representing a dynamically growing region, Asian governments and businesses have financial resources, but they lack, for a variety of cultural, historical, and economic reasons, sufficient access. They also often have difficulty articulating and publicizing their views. Think tanks, which frequently include prominent former government officials on their staffs, can help develop networks and also organize supportive forums within which Asian actors can confidently outline and elaborate their views.

Not surprisingly, think tanks have become a preferred locale for Asians to interact, in their efforts to gain information about developments in Washington. A quarter of a century ago, at the high point of transpacific trade frictions, employing lobbyists was the classic Asian response. Lobbyists remain important articulators of Asian views in Washington, being crucial intermediaries between Asian governments and firms, on the one hand, and American elites, on the other. Yet think tanks have, over the past two decades, emerged as a complement to, and in some cases a substitute for, lobbyists, due to the ability of think tanks to exploit the rapidly growing information search and propagation capacities of electronic communications.

Given their roots and credibility in American society, think tanks can raise and promote issues and positions on which Asian representatives themselves would be less credible, such as particular configurations of exchange rates and asymmetrical patterns of defense spending among allies that raise issues of free riding. Asian nations encourage the role of think tanks as interest articulators and information disseminators for Asia-specific concerns, notably the creation of country-specific endowed positions, such as the Japan, Korea, and Southeast Asia chairs at the Center for Strategic and International Studies and some parallel positions at the Brookings Institution and elsewhere. The incumbents in these positions, together with a small number of academic and other former government officials, play key informal roles in U.S. Asian policy agenda setting.   •

Think tanks are by no means the only information-merchandising NGOs promoting understanding of Asia in Washington. This role is played to some extent by such periodicals as the *Atlantic, National Journal, National Interest,* and *American Prospect.* Another important institution with an explicit regional focus is the Asia Society's Washington Center, which sponsors diverse programming on Asia as a whole, including art exhibits, film screenings, lectures, and periodic orientation events at Asian embassies around Washington.[16] The society is especially important in articulating the concerns of smaller Asian nations, which lack the resources to promote their own countries independently.

Multilateral Institutions

Washington is not just the American national capital—together with New York City and Geneva, it is also a global center of international organizations. The World Bank and the International Monetary Fund are both headquartered in Washington. So are numerous Western Hemisphere multilaterals, including the Inter-American Development Bank and the Organization of American States. Although the Asian Development Bank is based in Manila, it has had a very active office in Washington since 1995, testifying to the city's rising role as a global policy-finance center. Many prominent NGOs with global sweep, such as the World Wildlife Fund, Partners of the Americas, InterAction, Save the Children, and Greenpeace (U.S.), as well as the Pan American Health Organization (the WHO's regional branch for the Americas), are also headquartered in the U.S. capital, pointing to its role as a place where truly global policy networks are created.[17]

The presence of multilateral institutions, of course, is a key element of Washington's role as a global political city and significantly transcends its already substantial nation-state function. The presence of multilaterals like the World Bank allows both public and private actors from countries around the world to transact truly global business in Washington. It also brings them to Washington for reasons other than political representation—training, intelligence gathering, and commerce, to name a few.

For Asia, the presence of such prominent multilaterals as the World Bank and the IMF is a key reason for interest in Washington. As the most

Figure 4-1. *Asia's Large Share of World Bank Loans, 2012*

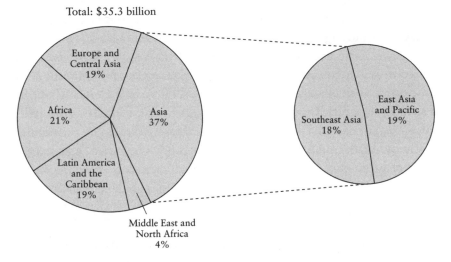

Total: $35.3 billion

Europe and Central Asia 19%

Africa 21%

Asia 37%

Latin America and the Caribbean 19%

Southeast Asia 18%

East Asia and Pacific 19%

Middle East and North Africa 4%

Source: World Bank, *World Bank Annual Report, 2012.*

populous and most rapidly growing part of the developing world—and the pioneer half a century ago in broadening economic development beyond the industrialized West—Asia has been central to the World Bank's operations ever since its foundation. In the 1950s the World Bank built steel mills in Japan, followed by the Tokaido Shinkansen (bullet train) line from Tokyo to Shin-Ōsaka.[18] In more recent years, China, India, and Indonesia have been among its largest borrowers, with 37 percent of total lending going to Asia in 2012 (figure 4-1). Today, in the wake of the World Bank's 2010 voting reform, Japan and China are the largest shareholders in the bank, after the United States, while India ranks seventh.[19]

As Asian nations like Japan and Korea have "graduated" from borrower status—among the first developing nations to do so—such countries have become preeminent sources of capital for further World Bank lending and sponsors of major economic development research projects in their own right.[20] Since 1971, for example, the World Bank has been issuing yen-denominated bonds, in cooperation with the Japanese Ministry of Finance,[21] and in January 2011 it issued its first RMB-denominated bond.[22] China, holding the largest foreign exchange reserves on earth, has also recently been assuming major functions in global development finance, in cooperation with the World Bank.[23] It has, in fact, recently lent more money for global development purposes than the World Bank itself has.[24]

China and the World Bank also signaled their collaborative partnership in a 2007 memorandum of understanding. The initial focus of the memorandum was infrastructure and energy projects in Africa, especially in sustained-growth performers like Ghana, Uganda, and Mozambique.[25] China's transition from borrower to lender has clearly altered its political-economic position within the bank.

The bank has, for example, increasingly recognized China's usefulness in reaching out to third-world countries. President Robert Zoellick (2007–12) frequently underlined the importance of working with China on aid in Africa, despite concerns on the part of some Americans about the strategic implications of Chinese loans to that continent. On his first visit to China as World Bank president in December 2007, Zoellick stressed that the bank's emphasis was "not to reduce cooperation but to expand it, both within China itself and cooperatively with China elsewhere in the world. By being a good partner with China on issues within China itself, it will help us develop a stronger partnership with China in third countries."[26]

As the global role of Asia has risen, the World Bank, and especially its Washington headquarters, have become important to Asian nations. The bank, and particularly the World Bank Institute, have begun to train the personnel of nations like China and Japan for broader functions— economic and even diplomatic—in developing nations. This program leads to smoother working relationships among the nations in question, even among erstwhile adversaries. The bank has also become a source of regional expertise and intelligence on areas far from Asia, such as Africa and Latin America, that would otherwise be difficult for regionally bounded Asian officials to attain.[27] And the bank's headquarters in Washington has become for these officials a social center, a place to nurture the human networks requisite to playing a leading global role.

As Asia's profile at the World Bank has risen, together with its economic role in the world, Asians have come to fill central and critical roles at the bank's Washington headquarters. From 2008 to 2012, Justin Yifu Lin, founding director of the China Center for Economic

Research, served as the World Bank's chief economist and senior vice president,[28] succeeded by the prominent Indian economist and Cornell professor Kaushik Basu. In October 2008 Samjay Pradhand of India became head of the World Bank Institute, where he continues to serve.[29] And since June 2010 Sri Mulyani Indrawati, an Indonesian, has been the World Bank's managing director, the bank's second-ranking position.

Over the years the International Monetary Fund has also been crucially important in Asia's development, helping to provide liquidity for Asia's remarkable growth for more than half a century. It also helped dampen major financial crises that threatened such growth: in Japan in the late 1950s, in India in 1990–91, in Southeast Asia in 1997, and in South Korea in 1997. And the IMF pressed for structural reforms, which were often deeply resented but which have made the region more market oriented and more able to respond to the pressures of globalization than most other parts of the world.

At the Washington global headquarters of the IMF, Asia's role has also steadily been rising, as Asia comes to hold the vast bulk of global foreign exchange reserves. Between 2004 and 2010 Takatoshi Kato of Japan served as deputy managing director of the IMF; he was succeeded by Naoyuki Shinohara in March 2010. Meanwhile, Min Zhu of China served during 2010–11 as special adviser to the managing director, a post traditionally held by a European.[30] In July 2011 he became a second deputy managing director, alongside Shinohara.[31] Given Asia's overwhelming position in global foreign exchange reserve holdings, it seems only a matter of time before Asia assumes additional top spots at the IMF.

Steady accumulation of additional IMF voting shares could well be the mechanism through which this transition—fateful for both Washington and the world—ultimately takes place. In 2011 the Asian nations together held 16.85 percent of total IMF voting shares—slightly more than the United States (16.74) or Germany, France, and the United Kingdom combined (15.57).[32] As Asia's economy grows stronger in global terms, and as further reforms at the IMF take place, increased cohesion among Asian nations will lead to new leadership patterns at the IMF—and thus in the increasingly important multilateral dimension of political-economic life in Washington.[33] The establishment of the G-20 in December 2008 prefigured this change in global political-economic governance: 30 percent of its members are from the Asia-Pacific region.[34]

As at the World Bank and the IMF, Asia is also assuming a larger role in regional financial institutions based in Washington. Japan, South Korea, and China joined the Inter-American Development Bank (IADB)- in 1976, 2005, and 2009, respectively. Japan serves on its fourteen-member board of executive directors, while the other two serve on the forty-eight-member board of governors.

The Beltway Dimension

As we have seen, Asia has often lacked access to traditional Washington institutions and policy processes, such as Capitol Hill, and local social institutions, such as churches, elite private schools, and synagogues. Nor has it been as conspicuously represented on the embassy circuit as some other regions. Yet Asia has nevertheless had substantial—and rising—interests in Washington that need to be addressed; some are bilateral, with the U.S. government, some are multilateral, and some are global. As their global role expands, Asian nations have also had rapidly expanding information requirements. Rather than addressing their diverse needs through classical diplomacy and lobbying—the forms of interest articulation that were dominant when most Asian actors became active on the Washington scene in the 1960s and 1970s—those countries have adopted a less conventional approach, centering on newer, more dynamic institutions and geographic quarters of metropolitan Washington.

One particularly important and interesting part of Greater Washington to consider in this regard is the Beltway—the affluent and rapidly growing suburbs of Washington, which stretch out into Virginia and Maryland. The Beltway is home not only to the major U.S. intelligence organizations, like the Central Intelligence Agency, the National Security Agency, and the U.S. Cyber Command, but also to specialized technical bodies like the National Institutes of Health, and to consulting firms, including SAIC and Booz Allen Hamilton, that cater to both public and private clients.

The private sector portion of the Beltway began to develop during the 1980s, as the Reagan administration privatized a broad range of government functions. It is highly dynamic, growing rapidly, and increasingly globally conscious. Asia, as the most rapidly growing world region and as one with a strong need for access, influence, and intelligence in

Washington, would seem to be a natural partner for the Beltway. That relationship began to develop more than a decade ago, when Booz Allen Hamilton, based in Tyson's Corner, Virginia, did a landmark consulting study for the government of Hong Kong on that territory's international economic future after reversion to China in 1997. It may well only continue to deepen in future years.

In Conclusion

Until World War II Asia had little involvement with Washington, reflecting the limited nature of transpacific political, military, and economic interdependence. This situation changed radically in 1945, as the United States occupied much of East Asia, established military bases across the region, and became Asia's primary market of last resort. As America became a global superpower with deep Asian involvement, Asian nations naturally became active in Washington, and the Asia factor was born.

Asian nations face a distinctive challenge in Washington: obtaining access to the decisionmaking processes and strategic information that, for historical and cultural reasons, has traditionally been beyond their purview. That access has become increasingly important for Asia, as its political-economic dependence on the United States has risen. Fortunately it has had the resources—intellectual and financial—to seek out and obtain the needed access and information.

European, Latin American, and African nations tend to rely on traditional forms of influence in Washington—conventional embassy diplomatic activities and lobbying through established law firms. Europeans, in particular, assiduously cultivate NGOs. Asian governments and corporations, by contrast, rely on the newer, yet formal Washington institutions, such as think tanks, and also on the Beltway—those actors beyond downtown Washington.

Asian actors have had four particular functional objectives in Washington: agenda setting, intelligence gathering, networking, and training for broader global roles. Think tanks, information centers, multilateral institutions, and institutions around the Beltway have been the principal centers through which they have pursued those objectives. By capitalizing on the pluralistic, pragmatic, and relatively open character of metropolitan Washington beyond the government—what might be called the capital city's penumbra of power—Asian countries have been able to offset their initial disadvantages in the U.S. national capital. They have thus been able to create a potent Asian factor in local Washington decisionmaking processes, a factor that moderates the traditionally asymmetrical cast of transpacific relations and that holds major implications for global political-economic governance as well.

Asia across America:
The Changing Calculus

Washington, of course, has a distinctive local dynamic of its own—"inside the Beltway"—as a global political city. Yet it is also deeply linked, both politically and economically, to the rest of the United States, as America's capital. As socioeconomic relationships across the Pacific steadily deepen, as immigration from Asia increases, and as Asian American activities across America intensify, ethnic politics becomes an increasingly important element of "Asia in Washington" as well.

In this chapter, I begin with an overview of Asian American history in the United States, showing how the distinctive features of Asian American political behavior today—and its impact on "Asia in Washington"—flow directly from that ethnic chronicle. In contrast to European, Hispanic, and even African American patterns, Asian Americans have traditionally operated in a distinctive cultural and racial world, which has isolated them from the broad mass of the American population and conditioned them to be wary of a parochial, mass political process, in which they were historically both outnumbered and marginalized. For years, Asian Americans tended toward small-scale, often elite-oriented, political activism and communication, to the extent that they were active in U.S. domestic politics at all. Given the uncertainties of Asian politics and Asian relations with the United States, any possibility of an Asian American role in brokering relations with Asia has been interrupted by war, embargo, and derecognition. As a consequence, Asian Americans until recently found it difficult to exert much influence on matters relating to their homelands, even where they have wanted to do so.

A History of Uncertainty and Marginalization

American economic relations with Asia, as noted in chapter 3, date back to the very early days of the republic. Yet substantial Asian immigration to the United States is a much more recent phenomenon. It really began with the California gold rush, in which 325 Chinese migrants joined the original forty-niners.[1] By 1852 there were over 20,000 Chinese immigrants in California, a near-mythical destination, known in their homeland as Gold Mountain. By the 1860s over 24,000 Chinese immigrants (two-thirds of the Chinese population in the United States) were working in the mines.[2]

Within little more than a decade of the gold rush, the Central Pacific Railway, led by Leland Stanford, aggressively recruited Chinese workers, at $31 a month, to build the tortuous western portion of the transcontinental railway—from the San Francisco Bay across the Sierra Nevada and the deserts of Nevada to Promontory Point, Utah.[3] Driven by a high-pressure, executive-incentive structure that tied corporate bonuses and entitlements for their bosses to speed of completion, the Chinese workers toiled through the dead of winter across Donner Summit and beyond, living in makeshift tunnels beneath the snowdrifts. They completed the project in rapid time, at the cost of numerous deaths and much privation.

Following completion of the transcontinental railway and the waning of viable alternative job opportunities in mining, many Chinese gathered together in San Francisco, which soon featured the largest Asian American population in the United States. In 1860 it numbered 2,719; a decade later that community, almost entirely Chinese, had expanded over fourfold, to 12,022, or one-quarter of California's total Asian population. Outside the Bay area, Chinese helped forge California agriculture—building the Central Valley's elaborate system of canals, for example, and helping the local economy move smoothly from reliance on wheat to the more remunerative fruit cultivation.[4] By 1880, 86 percent of the agricultural labor population of Sacramento County was

Chinese. Immigrants from China also became prominent in small business—by 1890, 69 percent of all the workers in California's laundries were Chinese.

A recurring theme for Chinese immigrants in California, which was repeated all too often across the United States more generally, was discrimination and marginalization. As immigrant numbers rose, a perceived competitive threat to other American workers intensified. When Chinese immigrants began to work in goldfields, a discriminatory tax was imposed on them. When they moved into agriculture, restrictions were clamped on their acquisition of land. In 1882, as their overall numbers began to climb, especially in California, the Chinese exclusion law was enacted; it suspended immigration of laborers from China altogether for a full decade. This domestic restriction was extended in 1892 and made indefinite from 1904.[5]

Early Japanese immigration flowed principally to Hawaii, which from its earliest days of foreign settlement had a different and generally more conciliatory history of ethnic politics and relationships to Asia than did the U.S. mainland. That human flow began with the illegal shipment of 149 Japanese laborers to Hawaii in 1868. It accelerated sharply with passage of the Reciprocity Treaty between the United States and the Kingdom of Hawaii (1876). That document provided, until 1891, for the duty-free importation into the United States of Hawaiian sugar. During the ensuing two decades (1868–91), Japanese contract workers—recruited from Japan in a highly organized way by corporate sponsors and brought to Hawaii in Japanese vessels—flooded into Hawaii to work on the rapidly expanding sugar plantations. Particularly large numbers came from Okinawa, the poorest of Japan's forty-seven prefectures. When Hawaii formally became a U.S. territory in 1900, and contract labor was outlawed, many Japanese workers in Hawaii migrated to the U.S. mainland to work on the railways, in the lumber mills, and on the farms of the West Coast, until President Theodore Roosevelt prohibited the practice of remigration in 1907.[6] Filipinos, who also moved in large numbers to the United States after American annexation of the Philippines in 1898, soon took the place of the Japanese in the cane fields of Hawaii, with some Koreans joining them after 1903.[7]

Two recurring themes in early Asian immigrant politics were the uncertainty of relationships with the immigrants' homelands and their marginal role in any aspect of the American political process—let alone the parochial "inside the Beltway" politics of Washington. Most early Asian immigrants came to America as impoverished, generally uneducated "marginals" from outlying parts of their homelands, ranging from Wakayama to Fujian. They clustered in California and in Hawaii—a continent and more away from the centers of national power in Washington. And the relationships that these immigrants tortuously forged with local inhabitants in the areas where they settled remained delicate—particularly on the mainland. Outside of the self-employed niche occupations, like running restaurants and laundries, Asian immigrants were often perceived to be economically threatening.

The difficulties facing early Asian Americans in influencing transpacific relations directly were compounded—despite the natural cross-cultural sensitivities of these marginals—by the political uncertainties of transpacific relations themselves, through the first half of the twentieth century and beyond. From 1931 to 1945 Japan was at war with China and then with the United States, leaving Japanese Americans in a painful and often unjust cross fire. From 1949 to 1979 the United States lacked diplomatic relations with mainland China, and after 1979 it had no formal ties with Taiwan, creating dilemmas of allegiance for many Chinese Americans as well. And for Koreans in America, a mediating role with the homeland was for many years even more difficult than for the Japanese and Chinese, since Korea was a Japanese colony until 1945 and has been a divided nation ever since that time.

Paralleling and deepening the personal marginalization of Asian American immigrants in the face of a persistently turbulent transpacific relationship were domestic political barriers to Asian immigration. Following the Chinese Exclusion Act of 1882, the San Francisco school board segregated Asian children in 1905. Eight years later, California prohibited "aliens ineligible for citizenship"—every Asian, regardless of national ethnicity—from purchasing land (1913). Meanwhile, American courts were narrowing definitions of immigrants eligible for citizenship.[8] And then a new immigration act denied permanent entry to virtually all Asians in 1924.

The one partial refuge, where Asian Americans were able to both gain local political prominence and gradually come to play a significant mediating role in transpacific relations, was Hawaii.[9] As an independent, non-Anglo-Saxon kingdom during the 1870s and 1880s, with demand for labor on its sugar plantations sharply rising, Hawaii welcomed immigration from Asia, during a period when non-Asian communities in the kingdom still remained small. As a U.S. territory rather than a state from 1900 to 1959—fortuitously removed from the turbulence of mainland U.S. electoral politics—Hawaii remained relatively detached from the broad ethnic controversy in the United States, including the forced relocation of Asian American citizens during World War II.[10] No doubt the distinguished war record of the highly decorated U.S. Army 442nd Regimental Brigade, composed solely of Japanese American soldiers—most from Hawaii but some with families in mainland relocation camps—also helped to legitimate Japanese Americans in Hawaiian and national politics.

Due to their local demographic prominence and national reputation for patriotic service, Asian Americans have been prominent in Hawaii's congressional delegation ever since statehood in 1959. The state's first Representative was Daniel Inoue, who joined the Senate in 1963 and served as chairman of the Senate Appropriations Committee from 2009 until his death in December 2012.[11] Other prominent U.S. senators from Hawaii include Hiram Fong (Chinese American), Spark Matsunaga (Japanese American), and Daniel Akaka (Japanese American)—all of whom have taken an interest in transpacific relations.[12] Hawaii also elected the first Japanese-born senator, Mazie Hirono, who succeeded Akaka in January 2013.

Historic Changes in American Immigration Policies

A development of landmark significance for both American ethnic politics and transpacific relations was the 1965 passage of a new U.S. immigration law. Influenced strongly by the civil rights revolution sweeping America in the early 1960s, it abolished "national origin" as a basis for allocating immigration quotas. Asian countries, which had long faced discrimination in comparison with European nations, inhibiting the migration of Asians to the United States, were at last placed on an equal footing. Through the 1975 Indochina Migration and Refugee Assistance Act, the 1980 Refugee Act, and the 1987 Amerasian Homecoming Act, immigration opportunities for Asian migrants to the United States—particularly those from Southeast Asia—were broadened still further.[13]

Table 5-1. *Asian American Population as Share of U.S. Population,*
1960–2010
Units as indicated

Year	U.S. population (million)	Asian population (million)	Share (percent)
1960	180.0	0.8	0.54
1965[a]	193.5	n.a.	n.a.
1970[b]	203.8	1.5	0.75
1980	221.8	3.5	1.5
1990	248.7	6.9	3.6
2000	281.4	11.9	4.2
2010	308.7	14.7	4.8

Source: U.S. Bureau of the Census, *Statistical Abstract of the United States, 1980,* p. 6; U.S. Bureau of the Census, *Statistical Abstract of the United States, 1990,* p. 1; and U.S. Bureau of the Census, *United States, Race and Hispanic Origin, 1790–1990,* table 1.

a. As the census is conducted only every decade, there is no official ethnic population breakdown for 1965.

b. Data on groups such as Filipinos and Koreans were collected intermittently through the 1970 census. Asian Indians were considered "White," and Vietnamese were included in "Other race." See Jessica S. Barnes and Claudette E. Bennett, "Census 2000 Brief: The Asian Population, 2000" (U.S. Census Bureau, February 2002), p. 2.

Historic Changes in Asian Immigrant Demography

Following these important changes in American legislation, the flow of migrants from Asia to the United States began to expand sharply during the 1970s and 1980s. By 1990 there were nearly 7 million Asian Americans, or 3.6 percent of the U.S. population (table 5-1). By 2000 that figure had risen to nearly 12 million, or 4.2 percent of the population. The 2010 census recorded a total of more than 14.7 million Asian Americans, or nearly 5 percent of all the residents of the United States.[14]

Because of legislative changes in 1965 and thereafter, Asian Americans became the most rapidly growing ethnic minority, on a percentage-increase basis, in the United States. Between 1980 and 1990 the country's Asian American population grew by 96 percent, compared to 4 percent for whites, 12 percent for blacks, and 53 percent for Hispanics (table 5-2). During the following decade (1990–2000), the Asian American growth rate once again outpaced all other major ethnic groups, growing over 63 percent across that decade and rising 43 percent further during the first decade of the twenty-first century.

Table 5-2. *Asian American Population in Comparative Context,*
1980–2010
Percent

	Growth rate by decade		
Racial/ethnic group	*1980–90*	*1990–2000*	*2000–10*
White	4.09	5.08	5.7
Black	11.98	15.26	12.3
Latino/Hispanic	53.02	39.42	43.3
Asian	96.13	63.24	43.0

Source: U.S. Census Bureau, *Statistical Abstract of the United States, 2001*; and U.S. Census Bureau, "2010 Census Data."

This explosive percentage growth almost precisely matched that of Hispanics. America's Hispanic population, of course, remains significantly larger than the number of Asian Americans in absolute numeric terms, but the latter also continues to grow very rapidly by both percentage and absolute measures. It is expected to reach at least 20 million people by 2020 and to approach 40 million by 2050, when Asian Americans will prospectively make up over 9 percent of the entire U.S. population.[15]

Before the immigration act of 1965 the vast bulk of Asian Americans were from one of three countries—China, Japan, and the Philippines. The Chinese community is the oldest, with many of its forebears entering the United States before the Chinese Exclusion Act of 1882. The Japanese community is the second oldest, with much of it leapfrogging the Pacific, given an independent Hawaii from 1871 to 1900, with many Nikkei moving to the mainland shortly after. The Filipinos entered the United States gradually during the half-century that their nation was a dependency of the United States, between 1898 and 1946. All three communities were thus of long standing, although they were relatively isolated from the mainstream political-economic processes of both their homelands and the United States due to their originally humble socioeconomic status and the rapid pace of political-economic change on the western shores of the Pacific.

Following the sharp legislative changes in immigration policy during the civil rights struggle and the Vietnam War era, America's Asian American population grew steadily more diverse. The number of Chinese Americans in the United States continued to grow, on the strength

Table 5-3. *American Asian Population, by Area of Origin and Decade, 1960–2010*[a]

Millions of people

Ethnicity	1960	1970	1980	1990	2000	2010
Total Asians	0.98	1.54	3.5	6.91	11.90	15.50
Chinese	0.24	0.44	0.81	1.65	2.31	3.62
Filipino	0.18	0.34	0.77	1.41	1.85	3.09
Japanese	0.46	0.59	0.70	0.85	0.80	1.30
Asian Indian	n.a.	n.a.	0.36	0.82	1.68	2.73
Korean	n.a.	0.069	0.35	0.80	1.08	1.61
Vietnamese	n.a.	n.a.	0.26	0.61	1.12	1.73
Indonesian	n.a.	n.a.	n.a.	0.03	0.40	0.79
Pakistani	n.a.	n.a.	n.a.	0.081	0.15	0.35
Sri Lankan	n.a.	n.a.	n.a.	0.011	n.a.	n.a.
Taiwanese	n.a.	n.a.	n.a.	n.a.	0.12	n.a.

Source: U.S. Bureau of the Census.

a. Numbers were established by self-identification; n.a. denotes that the ethnic group was not explicitly included in the censuses, highlighting the diversification, growing pluralism, and awareness of diversity among Asians in the United States.

of their homeland's huge population and the country's increasing open-ness under the Four Modernizations (table 5-3). Yet the Chinese American community still did not increase as rapidly, in proportional terms, as did the Asian Indians, the Vietnamese, the Filipinos, and the Koreans. In sharp contrast to other Asian American groups, the number of Japanese Americans actually began to fall.

These contrasting demographic trends have provoked a sharp recon-figuring of the Asian American population (figure 5-1). In 1960 Japanese Americans were by far the largest Asian American community, com-prising over 47 percent of the total Asian American population. Half a century later, however, their share fell to under 7 percent, making them only the sixth largest of the major Asian American communities, even though their absolute numbers began to increase somewhat after 2000.[16]

The new Asian American immigrants who began arriving in America after 1965 were also different in age, educational background, and socio-economic standing from communities that had arrived earlier. Broadly speaking, the newcomers were younger than the prevailing Asian Ameri-can mean, better educated, more affluent, and more professionally accomplished. Many of these new arrivals had broad global experience

Figure 5-1. *Changing Ethnic Composition of the Asian American Community, 1960–2010*[a]

Thousand people

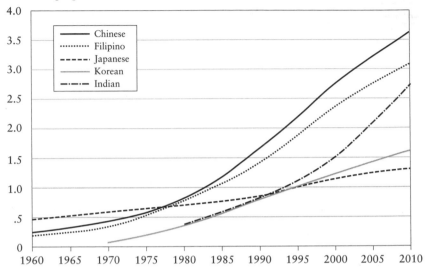

Source: U.S. Bureau of the Census, *Statistical Abstract of the United States,* 1980 and 1990; U.S. Census Bureau, *The Asian Population in the United States,* 2002; and U.S. Census Bureau, *Census Brief 2002,* table C-3.

a. These numbers are tallies of responses, not number of respondents, because of mixed races.

and were also internationally mobile, maintaining close ties with their homelands and traveling frequently back and forth across the Pacific.

Typical were the new Chinese and Indian American transnationals. They arrived from Asia, beginning in the 1980s, to attend undergraduate or graduate school in the sciences, business, or law, especially on the U.S. West Coast.[17] Upon graduation, these young entrepreneurs went to work with multinationals doing transpacific business, linking U.S. design centers with Asian manufacturing or founding their own firms, aided by important legislative changes in U.S. visa regulations.[18]

Asian Americans' Changing Role in the Policy Process

Asian Americans have been classically known as a model minority— law abiding, hardworking, and increasingly well educated.[19] Yet for many years they also tended to be quite detached from both domestic

American and transpacific policy processes. Until India-born Dalip Singh Saund (D-Calif.) was elected to the House of Representatives in 1956, no Asian American had ever served as a member of Congress. And Hiram Fong (R-Hawaii) became the first Asian American senator only in 1959.

Asian Americans, as many of diverse backgrounds would agree, have been subjected to substantial injustice over the years, despite their model minority standing. One case in point is the forced internment of Japanese Americans during World War II.[20] This bitter episode led not only to personal trauma but also to substantial economic losses, as the evacuees were compelled to abruptly abandon homes, businesses, and personal possessions.

The internment, however, led ultimately to one of the early Asian American political successes. After eighteen years of struggle, led by the Japanese American Citizens' League, Congress finally passed, and President Ronald Reagan signed, the Civil Liberties Act of 1988. This provided $20,000 to each internee of Japanese descent, whether they were U.S. citizens or permanent resident aliens. Following a complex struggle over appropriations, President Bill Clinton sent a letter of apology, together with reparation checks of $20,000 each, to all Japanese American internment survivors.[21]

Despite periodic policy successes like the redress legislation, Asian Americans remain significantly underrepresented at various levels of the federal and local governments. There are, for example, only thirteen Asian American members of Congress—2 percent of the congressional total and their highest total ever—even though Asian Americans make up about 6 percent of the U.S. population.[22] In California, Asians have constituted 10 percent or more of the state population for years, but they only recently reached 11 members of the state legislature (9 percent of the total), out of 120.[23] Even though there are many qualified legal scholars nationwide in the Asian American community, only two of over 180 federal circuit court judges nationwide are Asian American. And both were confirmed only in 2013.[24]

One area where some modest recent progress has been made is at the U.S. State Department. In 1985, 5.4 percent of foreign service "professional staff" (including foreign service officers and foreign service specialists) were African American, 3.4 percent were Hispanic, and only

0.7 percent were Asian American. Twenty years later, however, in 2005, the Asian American share had risen to 5.2 percent—the same as the Hispanic share and just behind the 6.5 percent share of African Americans. As the State Department Association for Diplomatic Studies and Training notes, "Despite the small number of Asian Americans reaching senior positions in the State Department, that group is easily the fastest growing minority in the Foreign Service. Within the FSO subcategory, the annual intake of new officers with South Asian backgrounds has been particularly notable."[25]

Despite continuing periodic setbacks, the grassroots political strength of Asian Americans began to rise markedly during the 1990s and has increased still further over the past decade. This trend has been noticeable on local school boards, which articulate, aspiring politicians like Judy Chu, elected to the House of Representatives in 2009 (D-Calif.), often use as their springboard. Chu's first elected position was board member for the Garvey school district in Rosemead, California, in 1985. In 1988 she was elected to the city council of Monterey Park, where she served as mayor for three terms. Elected to the State Assembly in 2001, and then reelected, Chu finally made it to Congress in 2009, becoming chair of the Congressional Asian Pacific American Caucus in 2011.[26] Although Asian Americans are still underrepresented at the national level, they have grown markedly more active nationally in recent years. In the 2012 elections, thirty Asian Americans and Pacific Islanders (AAPIs) ran for national office, up from ten in 2010 and eight in 2008. In 2012 six new AAPIs were elected to the 113th Congress (2013–15), nearly doubling the AAPI contingent on Capitol Hill.

Asian Americans have also won an increasing number of citywide positions in California, Washington, Nevada, and Oregon. Many of these new officials hail from the immigrant groups that began arriving after 1965. In 1992 Tony Lam of Westminster, California, became the first Vietnamese elected official in the United States. In 1998 Chanrithy Oong of Lowell, Massachusetts, became the first Cambodian American elected official in the United States. In the same year Joe Bee Xiong of Eau Claire, Wisconsin, became the first Hmong American elected official in the United States.

The San Francisco Bay area has been particularly fertile ground for local political advances by Asian Americans. Indian American Kamala

Harris, for example, served as elected district attorney in San Francisco from 2003 to 2010 before being elected statewide as California attorney general. Chinese American Jean Quan was elected mayor of Oakland in November 2010.[27]

Most conspicuously, Chinese American Ed Lee was elected mayor of San Francisco in November 2011.[28] The son of immigrants from southern China whose father was a cook and restaurant manager, Lee obtained a law degree from the University of California–Berkeley and then worked with the San Francisco Asian Law Caucus on affordable housing and on immigrant and tenant rights. After twenty-two years at City Hall, working for four mayors, he became interim mayor in January 2011, when Gavin Newsom became lieutenant governor, before Lee ran for election in his own right.

At the statewide level, there have also been noteworthy advances across the United States, half a century after Wing F. Ong became the first Asian American state legislator (Arizona House of Representatives), in 1946. In 1994 Ben Cayetano (D-Hawaii) became the first Filipino American governor. In 1997 Gary Locke, later to become U.S. Secretary of Commerce in the Obama administration and subsequently ambassador to China, was elected as the first Asian American governor outside Hawaii, and the first Chinese American governor (D-Wash., 1997–2005). In 2007, at the age of thirty-six, Bobby Jindal (R-La.) became the first Indian American governor. And in January 2011 Nikki Haley, born Nimrata Nikki Randhawa (R-S.C.), became the first Asian American female governor and the second Indian American governor.[29]

Presidential cabinets have also featured more Asian Americans in recent years than ever before. President Bill Clinton chose the first—former U.S. Representative (D-Calif.) Norman Mineta as secretary of commerce (2000). Mineta became secretary of transportation (2001–06) under President George W. Bush, who also appointed Elaine Chao as secretary of labor (2001–09). Barack Obama also named two Asian Americans to his first cabinet: Nobel Prize winner Steven Chu of the University of California–Berkeley as secretary of energy (2009–13); and Gary Locke, former governor of Washington, as his secretary of commerce (2009–11).

Asian Americans are also moving into senior posts elsewhere in the U.S. government. Julia Chang Bloch became the first Asian American ambassador; she was appointed in 1989 by President George H. W. Bush to serve in Nepal. William H. ("Will") Itoh became the first Asian American career foreign service officer; he served in Thailand in 1996–99. Bill Lann Lee became the U.S. assistant attorney general for civil rights in 1997, while Sichan Siv became the first U.S. ambassador of Southeast Asian origin in 2001, serving as the American representative to the U.N. Economic and Social Council (2001–06).[30] And Gary Locke, after serving as secretary of commerce, was named ambassador to China, his ancestral homeland, in 2011. In late 2011 Korean American Sung Kim was similarly appointed ambassador to Korea.[31]

Why Asian American Influence Is Rising

At least eight factors account for the rising importance of Asian Americans in the American national policy process as a whole. One important factor is a growing and ever more politically strategic geographic base. The first development in this regard was statehood in 1959 for Hawaii, which has the largest proportionate concentration of the Asian American population in the country. Over the years, Hawaii has produced close to half of Asian American congressional representatives. It has also provided an uncommonly stable political base, allowing some—notably Senator Daniel Inoue—to amass sufficient seniority to gain real influence in national legislative politics. During 2011–12 Senator Inoue, reelected in November 2010 to a record eighth term, served as chairman of not only the powerful Senate Appropriations Committee but also its Subcommittee on Defense appropriations, which is responsible for reviewing the entire national defense budget. Together with his wife, Irene Hirano, Inoue played a key role in 2009 in founding the U.S.-Japan Council, a dynamic, agenda-setting NGO articulating Japanese American concerns.[32]

Since the 1960s the Asian American geographical base has broadened greatly on the U.S. mainland, extending far beyond historical communities on the West Coast. By 2008 nearly 14 percent of California's population was Asian American, and there were eight states, spread around the country, with Asian American populations approaching 10 percent of state totals (figure 5-2). Six states with a large Asian American population concentration ranked among the most populous and politically important states in the country.

Figure 5-2. *The Broad-Ranging Asian American Geographical Base*

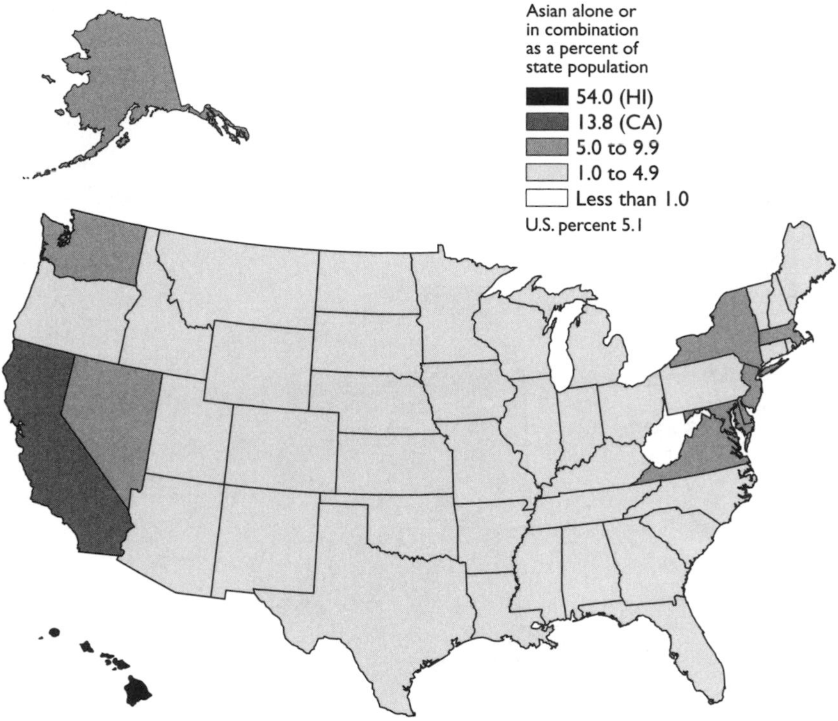

Asian alone or
in combination
as a percent of
state population

- 54.0 (HI)
- 13.8 (CA)
- 5.0 to 9.9
- 1.0 to 4.9
- Less than 1.0

U.S. percent 5.1

Source: U.S. Census Bureau, *The Asian Population in the United States, 2008.*

The speed of Asian American demographic expansion is a second factor enhancing the group's national influence. As suggested in figure 5-3, this trend is especially pronounced recently in the South. In that region, the number of Asian Americans has increased by nearly half over the past decade, albeit from a small base, bringing in many energetic new inhabitants.

A third factor, demographic in character, that enhances Asian American influence is the proliferation—especially in the rapidly expanding new immigrant communities—of young, well-educated, and upwardly mobile professionals who speak excellent English. Indian Americans are a striking case in point. That community is growing extremely rapidly, expanding more than sevenfold between 1980 and 2010, and includes many professionals (see table 5-3). Indeed, there are around 35,000 Indian American doctors in the United States today.[33] And almost 40 percent

Figure 5-3. *Rising Regional Diversity of America's Asian American Population*[a]

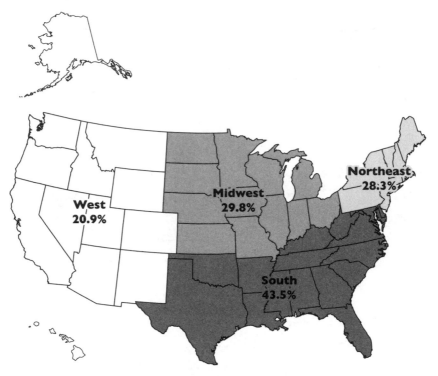

Source: U.S. Census Bureau, *The Asian Population in the United States, 2008.*
a. Percentages represent estimated increase in regional Asian American population, 2000–08.

of Indian American college graduates have master's, doctorates, or other professional degrees—roughly four times the national average.[34]

Given their personal characteristics, including English-language facility, these newcomers tend to mingle easily with—and be recognized by—the broader American population. Bobby Jindal—the Rhodes scholar, governor of Louisiana, and short-listed candidate for vice president of the United States by John McCain—is one iconic second-generation example of this new immigrant prototype. Nikki Haley, the daughter of Sikh immigrants and governor of South Carolina, is another.

A fourth factor behind the rising influence of Asian Americans in U.S. politics, especially at the state and local levels, is the growing strength of homeland-specific ethnic interest groups, which help to leverage politically the rapidly growing numerical strength of Asian Americans. One such group is the National Council of Chinese Americans.[35] Another case in point is the Indian American Leadership Initiative (IALI). Founded in 2000 and currently based on K Street in Washington, this organization seeks to connect with, support, and invest in Indian American Democratic candidates. In 2010 IALI endorsed and supported three Indian American candidates: Manan Trivedi and Ami Bera, who ran (abortively) for Congress in Pennsylvania and California, respectively; and Kamala Harris, who was elected as the first female and first Asian American attorney general of California.[36] The U.S.-Japan Council, designed to bring Japanese Americans more actively into the transpacific dialogue, is another important, ethnically based, agenda-setting group, strongly supported by the core Japanese American community in Hawaii, as discussed above, yet transcending its limited geographical base.[37]

A fifth important new factor aiding aspiring Asian American politicians in the early twenty-first century is the swing constituency character of their community, as its concentration of relatively affluent and educated professionals continues to increase. As Matt Fong, former California state treasurer and 1998 Republican candidate for the Senate from California, perceptively put it, the emerging upscale Asian Americans as a group are a "neutral minority." They can appeal both to mainstream groups, due to their socioeconomic status, and to minority groups, due to their historic experiences with discrimination.[38] This politically pivotal status has become much more pronounced over the past two decades, as the Asian American community's socioeconomic standing has steadily risen, even as its experience with discrimination continues to rankle. It has been magnified by the geographical reality, noted above, that Asian Americans are concentrated in the largest and most politically important states, including swing states like Virginia.

A sixth factor enhancing the political influence of Asian Americans is the emergence of pan-Asian and panethnic organizations and networks. These allow individual Asian groups and politicians to broaden their support coalitions so as to achieve majority standing, avoiding the marginalization that could otherwise occur. With the Asian American community as a whole fragmenting into national blocs (Japanese, Koreans, Chinese, and so on), even as it expands in the aggregate, coalitions among its constituent communities are becoming more important. These communities are also becoming more effective as springboards to national political power.

Probably the most important Pan-Asian political action group is the Asian American Action Fund (AAAF), founded in 1999 to address the political underrepresentation of Asian Americans and Pacific Islanders at every level of government. The AAAF strives to increase the number of Asian American campaign volunteers as well as campaign contributors. It also identifies qualified Democratic candidates for office, providing them with both financial and technical assistance, while nurturing a local network of activists, funders, and supporters. Members of the group include both ethnic Asians and non-Asians who are supportive of AAAF positions on key issues. Candidates endorsed in the past include President Barack Obama, Senator Al Franken of Minnesota (where the Asian American population is only 3.4 percent), and Representative Al Green of Texas (where the Asian American share of the electorate is 9.4 percent). The AAAF has also done fundraising for Japanese-born Mazie Hirano, first during her election to Congress in 2006 (in Hawaii's Second District) and then during her Senate race in 2012. It has likewise added Representative Mike Honda, recently House Democratic senior whip and president of the AAAF honorary board of directors.

The AAAF also works to increase the number of Asian Americans on the federal bench. During 2010–11 it worked for the confirmation of Professor Goodwin Liu of the University of California–Berkeley's Boalt Law School to the Ninth Federal Circuit of Appeals—a cause that attracted considerable national attention. AAAF sponsors include the Democratic National Committee and eight unions, including the AFL-CIO, the American Federation of Teachers, and the International Brotherhood of Boilermakers. The AAAF's honorary board includes Judy Chu, Ted Lieu, Norman Mineta, Neil Abercrombie, Xavier Becerra, Eni Faleomavaega, and Al Green.

The AAAF is by no means the only important Pan-Asian political interest group. Asian Pacific Americans for Progress also works to elect progressive, mainly Democratic, candidates. In 2008 it established a PAC to endorse candidates and train campaign workers. In addition there is the 80-20 Initiative, a national, nonpartisan organization of 700,000 members named for its goal of uniting 80 percent of Asian

American voters to support the presidential candidate that the organization endorses. Under initiative rules, a third of the thirty-three delegates must be Democratic, a third Republican, and a third independent. One of the initiative's signal campaign successes occurred on Super Tuesday 2008, when the Asian American vote produced a 71-25 percentage victory for Hillary Clinton in California, where Asian Americans make up 14 percent of the population. The initiative had endorsed Clinton well before the primary, due to her early responsiveness to their questionnaires on support for Asian American interests.

A seventh factor that leverages Asian American political influence is the emergence of minority networks that transcend the Asian American community. One such network is that of Representative Xavier Becerra (D-Calif.), who represents a diverse constituency in downtown Los Angeles and is promoting an alliance between America's two largest and fastest-growing ethnic groups, Asian Americans and Hispanics. In his efforts to forge such an alliance, Becerra serves both as cochair of the Congressional Hispanic Caucus and as a member of the executive committee of the Congressional Asian Pacific American Caucus. In 2014 Becerra also served as chairman of the House Democratic caucus, while continuing to play a key role in U.S.-Korean parliamentary exchange.

A second key fusion politician with broad catalytic contacts is Representative Michael Honda (D-Calif.), from the San Jose area of Silicon Valley. Japanese American by ethnic background, he has substantial Chinese, Korean, and Hispanic constituencies in his district. A former Peace Corps volunteer, he has traveled widely in Latin America and Africa as well as East Asia and has worked closely with a variety of NGO groups around the world. He sponsored several resolutions in the House of Representatives condemning the Japanese government's failure to admit culpability in relation to the "comfort women" issue, one of which conspicuously passed the House of Representatives in 2007.[39] One reason for his effectiveness in getting this resolution passed was no doubt the breadth of his fusion network on Capitol Hill.

An eighth and final factor leveraging Asian American political influence has been the notable activism of the new generation of Asian Americans, contrasting to the traditional detachment of their elders.

Better educated, more affluent, and more sophisticated than their forebears, the new generation is assuming a larger role in domestic U.S.

politics, especially in garnering cabinet positions. Younger Asian Americans are also more involved in international affairs, including relations with their ancestral homelands. The accelerated immigration of Asian professionals since the early 1990s has created a dynamic, affluent new group of transnationals—heavily Chinese and Indian—that is amplifying the influence of more established, U.S.-born Asian American politicians, and perhaps influencing their agendas as well.[40]

In Conclusion

Although transpacific trade dates back to the very origins of America as a nation, immigration, as a link across the Pacific, is of much more recent provenance. The oldest Asian American community—that of the Chinese—dates from gold rush days, with a heavy influx of Chinese miners, shopkeepers, and laborers following in its wake, between 1850 and the Chinese Exclusion Act of 1882. Two other major communities—those of the Japanese and the Filipinos—also developed before the Exclusion Act of 1924 largely ended Asian immigration to the United States until it resumed on a large scale late in the 1960s.

Major legislative changes of the 1960s and 1970s on immigration policy led to an unprecedented expansion and diversification of the Asian American community in the United States over the last half century. Newer immigrants are, broadly speaking, more educated, more affluent, and more globalized than their forebears. There is also a higher proportion of Southeast and South Asians than in the case of previous immigration waves.

Not surprisingly, given the new demographic mix, and a proliferation of support organizations over the past two decades, Asian Americans are growing more active in domestic American politics, especially at the state and local levels but increasingly in Washington as well. Expanding beyond their original power bases in Hawaii and on the West Coast, Asian Americans are electing governors, congressional representatives, and state legislators across the country, including even in the Deep South. Indeed, two of the eleven states of the once deeply racist Solid South now have Indian American governors.

Even as Asian Americans are growing more influential in domestic politics, their political leaders are also becoming more active in transpacific relations. Asia itself is stabilizing and opening politically to the West. This latter development facilitates deeper contact with the largest Asian powers, China and India, from which many of the new Asian American politicians hail. Improved transportation and communication are making transpacific liaison with Asia much easier than it used to be. And the growing number of Asian Americans living in the United States, coupled with rising Pacific economic interdependence and American public concern for foreign affairs generally, is transforming Asian American identity from a political liability into a political and diplomatic advantage. Barack Obama recognized this new reality by appointing Chinese and Korean Americans to key ambassadorial spots in Beijing and Seoul. Asian America is, in short, becoming a major part of the Asia factor in Washington.

6

Profiles of National Response: Overview and Hypotheses

Asian nations in general, as shown in chapter 5, have an unusual challenge in attaining and sustaining Washington access, for embedded historical and cultural reasons. Since World War II, and especially since the 1960s and 1970s, global growth and rising transpacific interdependence have made resolving that challenge ever more pressing. All the nations of Asia share this common challenge and the deepening urgency of an effective response.

Although all Asian nations do face a common general challenge in Washington, national responses vary in important ways—with implications for both policy and theory. The variations raise questions about the competitive efficacy of these nations' foreign policies in an era where both interdependence and rivalry are deepening. Those national differences in approach naturally provoke issues for American foreign policy as well, since both major allies and significant global competitors of the United States—such as Japan and China, respectively—are involved. These national variations also provide a rare opportunity from the analytical side to employ Aristotle's classic "method of similarity and difference" research design, promising fruitful returns from an analysis for social science theory as well.[1]

Central Problems for Analysis

Among the most important and timeless questions in international affairs is a simple query: What determines power among nations on the global stage? Classical realist theory suggests several elements: military preparedness, industrial capacity, population, geography, and national morale.[2] Washington—capital of the most powerful nation on earth, where Asian nations compete to influence American policy and global affairs more generally—is an excellent place to test such contentions.

Felicitously, from the theoretical standpoint, Washington has a dual character, encompassing both international politics and domestic politics. As a major global diplomatic center and headquarters for important multilateral organizations, it is an appropriate locale for testing propositions about the nature of power in international relations. Yet it is also a uniquely appropriate laboratory, as a national capital, for examining domestic issues and the poorly understood yet critically important interface between domestic and international politics. Although some important conceptual advances have recently been made in this area, as with Robert Putnam's theory of two-level games, the interface of domestic and international political analysis remains a potentially fruitful subject for further political-economic inquiry.[3]

Methodological Approach

For the purposes of this analysis, Greater China (the PRC, Taiwan, and Hong Kong), Japan, Korea, India, Burma, Indonesia, and Singapore have been chosen as subjects of detailed study, for particular analytical reasons.[4] Several actors, including the People's Republic of China, Japan, India, and Indonesia, were selected for their size in terms of the classic criteria of realist international relations theory. Other cases— South Korea, Taiwan, Burma, and Singapore—were selected for converse reasons, being smaller in scale yet active and prominent in Washington. Additional important cases, such as Vietnam and the Philippines, that reflect similar patterns, are treated as relevant and as space allows. Together, the cases represent the most active and geopolitically important instances of Asian governmental presence in Washington, and collectively they provide a composite picture of Asia in Washington today.

As the objective of this research is to understand comprehensively how Asia as a whole represents itself in a changing Washington, the research includes actors from throughout the continent. There are, however, some important subregional differences that deserve examination, and the number of cases considered overall is large in any case. Accordingly, the two chapters to follow, which compare various national approaches to Washington, are divided on the basis of geography, each covering four major cases. The first covers Northeast Asia, with its large economies and generally powerful militaries, where geopolitical rivalries are salient and the stakes of relationships with Washington are uncommonly large. The second comparative chapter covers South and Southeast Asia, where relations with Washington are generally more distant and less invested with geopolitical significance for both sides.

Some might ask why Pakistan or Afghanistan is not in this comparative study. The main reason is that they are special, atypical cases—areas where American troops are engaged in an unusual war against terrorists and Islamic extremists. The wartime environment dominates the relationship of these nations to Washington. This distinctiveness makes it difficult to ascertain the importance of background factors central to the broader analysis of this book as a whole. These factors include national lobbying techniques as well as relationships to think tanks, mass media, and other institutional variables whose configuration appears to significantly affect outcomes.

Since the analysis presented in this section of the book focuses on the comparative profile of national influence in Washington, and the determinants thereof, it begins by presenting the profiles of national prominence and influence in America's capital—ultimately, the dependent variables—along a variety of dimensions. These prominence profiles do not necessarily correspond closely to the classic indicators of national political power, such as population, military capacity, and gross national product. The question then is, What are the determinants of Asian national prominence and influence in Washington?

Visibility and Influence

Of the nineteen Asian political entities with representatives in Washington, eight are especially consequential in political-economic terms. It is these countries on which the research of the following chapters focuses in special detail. Particular attention is given to China, Japan, India, and South Korea, as the largest political economies of the region, and to Taiwan, Indonesia, Singapore, and Burma due to the special dimensions of Asia's overall relationship to Washington that they represent.[5] Other important nations of the region, including several within ASEAN, are also treated as analytically relevant.

There are in the broader world multiple dimensions of political influence, as Robert Dahl and others have long noted.[6] These dimensions do not necessarily covary. Here I consider two central aspects of influence: visibility and positive decisions on matters of importance to the nation in question. Some of these matters of importance, such as invitations to address joint sessions of Congress, are symbolic and relatively easy to quantify. Others, such as free trade agreements and other legislative decisions, are more heterogeneous. As these outcomes are qualitatively distinct, they are considered separately, and the findings are analytically aggregated. I begin with an examination of visibility, the results of which are summarized in table 6-1.

As suggested in table 6-1, it is not necessarily the largest, the most populous, the richest, or the most militarily powerful Asian nation that is the most visible or influential in Washington. Indonesia, for example, is the fourth most populous country in the world, yet it has a remarkably low profile in Washington, rarely being the subject of congressional hearings, for example. Japan is the third-largest economy in the world, America's second-largest transoceanic trading partner, and the most important U.S. ally in Asia, but it has no formal congressional caucus and has remarkably low visibility outside the realm of formal lobbying. Conversely, Burma, Singapore, South Korea, and Taiwan, although relatively small actors, are highly visible, especially considering their geographic and demographic scale. So is Vietnam, on some issues, due to the large number of Vietnam veterans.

Policy Outcomes as Influence Indicators

Asian nations vary widely in their visibility in Washington. That variation, however, does not appear, at first examination, to correlate with national size, GDP, or other variables classically regarded as power resources. If measured by actual policy outcomes, their symbolic and substantive dimensions must be differentiated.

On the symbolic side, one intriguing indicator, broadly comparable cross-nationally, is the number of addresses by visiting leaders of foreign

Table 6-1. *Indicators of Visibility in Washington*

Country	Hearings[a]	Articles[b]	Agents[c]	Caucus[d]	Website	Study group
China/PRC	59	1,387	13	Yes	Forbes[e]	US-PRC Working Group
South Korea	30	448	30	Yes	No	No
Japan	18	631	37	No	No	Congressional Study Group on Japan[f]
Burma	5	90	0	Yes	No	No
China/Taiwan	4	81	20	Yes/H+S[g]	No	No
India	3	560	11	Yes/H+S	Secondary	No
Vietnam	3	241	0	Yes	Secondary and old	No
Philippines	1	75	1	Yes	No	No
Singapore	1	91	11	Yes	No	No
Indonesia	0	109	2	Yes	No	No

a. Hearings are totals of published hearings mentioning the country for calendar year 2011. ProQuest Congressional Publications Database (http://congressional.proquest.com).

b. Articles are 2011 *Washington Post* news articles mentioning the country.

c. Agents denote registered foreign agents or any foreign principal employed during 2011 by the government in question.

d. U.S. Senate caucuses are organized without any official recognition by the Senate itself and are not funded through the appropriation process. The Senate formally recognizes only one caucus—the Senate Caucus on International Narcotics Control—which was established in 1985. See U.S. Senate, "Committees" (www.senate.gov/pagelayout/committees/d_three_sections_with_teasers/committees_home.htm).

e. "Forbes" refers to Representative Randal Forbes's website, where events related to the China caucus are announced.

f. The Congressional Study Group on Japan, while involving current congressional members, is under the auspices of the U.S. Association of Former Members of Congress and the East-West Center. Its activities are supported by the Sasakawa Peace Foundation and the Japan-U.S. Friendship Commission. See U.S. Association of Former Members of Congress webpage (http://usafmc.org/international-programs/congressional-study-groups/congressional-study-group-on-japan/).

g. H+S means the country has caucuses in both the House and the Senate.

nations to joint meetings of Congress.[7] South Korea has been particularly successful, especially since democratization in the late 1980s, in securing these invitations (figure 6-1). Japan, conversely, has incurred much greater difficulty, despite its larger scale, although Prime Ministers Kishi and Ikeda were invited to address subsets of Congress both before and after ratification of the controversial and strategically significant revisions of the U.S.-Japan Mutual Security Treaty in 1960.[8]

Asian nations also engage in Washington with the U.S. government and multilateral agencies on a broad range of substantive security and

Figure 6-1. *Addresses to Joint Meetings of Congress, by Country, up to 2014*

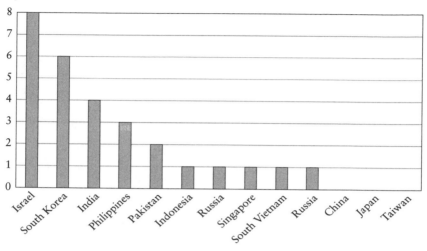

Source: U.S. House of Representatives, "Joint Meeting and Joint Session Addresses before Congress by Foreign Leaders and Dignitaries" (http://history.house.gov/Institution/Foreign-Leaders/).

economic policy questions. Many of the issues that are most important in substantive terms for any given country are sui generis and not readily comparable cross-nationally. Yet there are a few broadly common policy indicators of formal influence in Washington, with some of the most easily quantifiable being presented in table 6-2.

Once again, it is clear that smaller nations can often be more successful than their larger counterparts. Korea and Singapore, for example, have both concluded free trade agreements with the United States. Japan, however, has not.

Understanding Outcomes: Some Hypotheses

Five basic hypotheses concerning Asian national responses to Washington are tested here (figure 6-2):

—The *classical realist hypothesis* that objective, quantifiable "elements of national power" determine influence in international relations (in this case, influence in Washington)

—The notion that *classical diplomacy,* including alliance ties and formal representation, is central

Table 6-2. *Some Comparative Formal Indicators of Substantive Washington Policy Influence, 1979–2012*

Country	Official or working visits	Official development assistance 2010 (US$)	Legislative/political landmarks
Japan	27	n.a.	No FTA Defense technology transfer, 1983 Antiterrorism cooperation, 2001 Futenma Agreement, 2007 (delayed implementation) Host nation support, 2012
South Korea	16	n.a.	Comfort women house resolutions, passed 2007 Visa waivers, 2008 Foreign military sales, 2008 KORUS free trade agreement, 2012
Philippines	10	148.25	World War II veteran benefits, 2009
India	9	108.55	Civil nuclear agreement, 2005
China	6	86.46	World Trade Organization, 1999
Singapore	5	n.a.	Free trade agreement, 2002
Indonesia	3	263.35	Strategic partnership, 2010
Vietnam	3	100.46	World Trade Organization, 2006
Burma	0	31.28	Easing of sanctions, 2012
Taiwan	0	n.a.	Taiwan Relations Act, 1979

Source: "U.S. ODA Disbursements by Recipient," April 2, 2012. Japan, South Korea, Singapore, and Taiwan do not appear in this report.

—The proposition that *classical lobbying* determines outcomes

—The idea that *informal elite networks* shape outcomes

—The proposition that agenda-setting efforts through *public diplomacy* are decisive.

The visibility variable is also assessed and evaluated.

In general, tactical choices among options at the subnational level appear to be decisive. In particular, the most important determining factors are the choices by embassies and home governments of agenda-setting strategies, the personal networks they develop, and the human resources they directly mobilize on the ground in Washington to pursue national ends.

Figure 6-2. *Alternate Hypotheses for Explaining National Response*

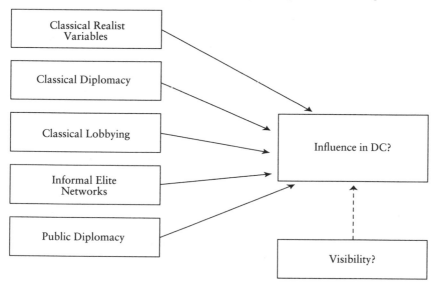

Exploring the Realist Hypothesis: National Profiles of Asian Actors in Washington

To understand how the classical components of national power relate to actual outcomes in Washington, it is first of all instructive to profile the nations of Asia in terms of those components. As noted above, there are nineteen Asian nations represented in Washington, the largest of which, in population terms, are China, India, Indonesia, and Japan. The vital political, economic, and military statistics of the major ones are presented in table 6-3.

In terms of realist criteria, China, Japan, and India should have the most formidable influence in Washington (table 6-3). Indonesia and South Korea also have a significant claim on some parameters. Other ASEAN nations, including Singapore, together with China/Taiwan, are expected to be less influential.

Classical Diplomacy: The Crucial Determinant?

Another important indicator of relative national magnitude, for our purposes, as a proxy for classical diplomatic capacity is the scale of a country's diplomatic presence in Washington. The most succinct and

Table 6-3. *Classical Realist Parameters, Profile of Key Asian Countries*
Unit as indicated

Country	GDP ($ trillion)	Population (number)	Military forces (number)
China	8.25	1,343,239,923	2,285,000
Japan	5.98	127,368,088	247,450
India	1.95	1,205,073,612	1,325,000
South Korea	1.15	48,860,500	655,000
Indonesia	0.895	248,645,008	395,500
China/Taiwan	0.466	23,234,936	290,000
Thailand	0.377	66,091,089	305,850
Malaysia	0.307	29,179,952	109,000
Singapore	0.268	5,353,494	72,500
Philippines	0.241	103,775,002	125,000
Vietnam	0.138	91,519,289	482,000
Myanmar	0.0541	54,584,650	406,000
Brunei	0.0169	408,786	7,000
Cambodia	0.0143	14,952,665	124,300
Laos	0.00927	6,586,266	29,100

Source: International Institute for Strategic Studies, *The Military Balance* (London: 2013).

formal expression of that presence comes from the U.S. State Department, in the form of the diplomatic list. That measure broadly, although not precisely, correlates with gross national product, although not with population (table 6-4). India and Indonesia both have smaller diplomatic missions than their national scale might indicate, while Singapore's mission is larger than might be otherwise expected, particularly relative to its ASEAN partners.

Another classical diplomatic element is alliance relationships. Currently Japan and South Korea have formal mutual security treaties with the United States and host major U.S. bases. Four decades ago, Thailand, the Philippines, South Vietnam, and China/Taiwan also had parallel arrangements. The Philippines and Singapore today have looser formal variants of security cooperation. Paradoxically, Singapore's loosely structured variant appears to convey more access and influence in Washington than more formal and classical diplomatic arrangements, as we shall see, although formal alliance partners enjoy a large number of official or working visits (table 6-2).

Table 6-4. *A Measure of Classical Diplomacy: Scale of Major Asian Diplomatic Missions in Washington*

Country	Number of accredited diplomats
China	194
Japan	106
South Korea	75
India	49
Philippines	35
Indonesia	27
Malaysia	21
Singapore	20
Burma	15
Non-Asian references	
Canada	131
Germany	144
United Kingdom	120
Russia	118
France	55

Source: U.S. Department of State, *Diplomatic List* (Spring 2013).

Classical Lobbying

One element of visibility in Washington deserves special elaboration, as it lies at the delicate borderline between visibility and influence. That is the role of professional lobbyists—registered foreign agents, technically speaking—in the U.S.-Asia relationship (for details, see appendix B, this volume). Lobbyists of foreign countries are required by the U.S. government to register with the Department of Justice under the Foreign Agents Registration Act (FARA) if they receive substantial funds from such sources, so relatively detailed time-series data are available regarding changes in their numbers over time.[9] There was a huge increase in the number of registered foreign agents representing Asian nations between the early 1960s and the early 1990s (figure 6-3). In 1960 France had the largest number of registered lobbyists in the United States (see table 4-1). France was followed by Mexico, Cuba, Canada, Israel, the USSR, and only then Japan, with other Asian nations far behind.[10] Over the following decades, however, the number of lobbyists employed by Asian nations surged to much higher levels than previously.

Figure 6-3. *The Wax and Wane of Classical Asian Lobbying, 1945–2010*

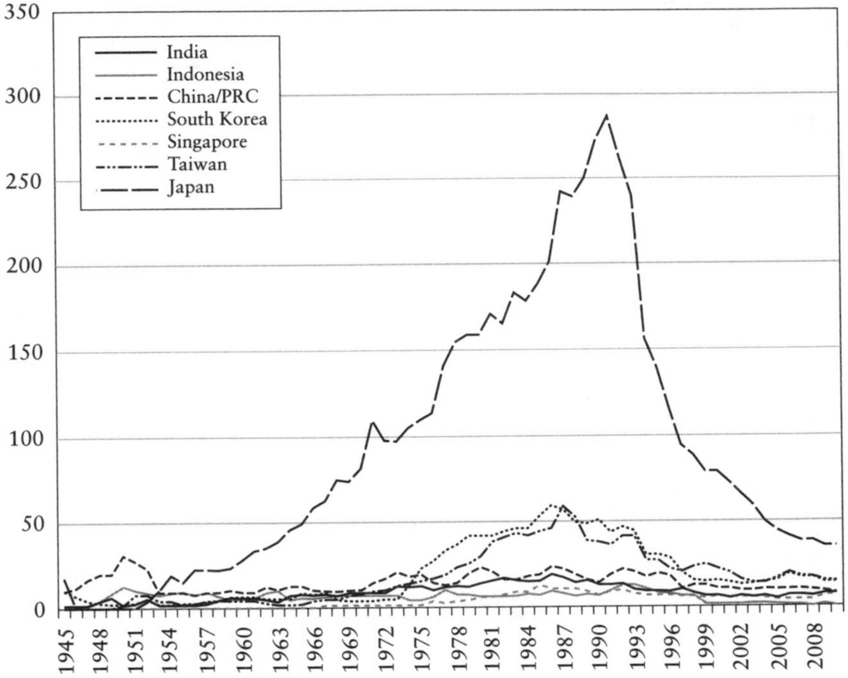

Source: Data provided to the Department of Justice under the Foreign Agents Registration Act (www.fara.gov).

The sharp intensification of Asian lobbying was spearheaded by Japan, which at its high point in 1991 employed 291 registered lobbyists, or over two-thirds of all the registered foreign agents for Asian nations in the United States and 14 percent of the total for all nations.[11] By 1998, however, the number of Japanese lobbyists had fallen by nearly two-thirds, to only 89, and that of Asian agents more generally to just over 160. By 2010 these figures had decreased further still, to 35 Japanese and 53 Asian agents, representing only 6 percent and 9 percent, respectively, of the global totals.[12] So formal lobbying on behalf of Asian interests, while quite intense in the 1970s and 1980s, appears to have been epiphenomenal and to have waned substantially over the past two decades, just as the pace of classical Washington lobbying itself appears to have done.

Apart from Japan, the two most determined lobbyists in Washington appear to have been the divided states of South Korea and China/

Taiwan—both traditionally authoritarian systems with substantial national security concerns, centering on Washington. As figure 6-3 and its statistical correlate in appendix B both indicate, Korea was earlier and slightly more aggressive in the lobbying game, with its contingent of registered agents rising sharply during 1973–74, just after the Paris Peace Accords on Vietnam and the introduction of President Park's anti-democratic Yushin constitution in 1972. Taiwanese lobbying also accelerated sharply after U.S. derecognition of Taiwan at the end of 1978, when the Kuomintang regime was also soft authoritarian. The regimes of South Korea and Taiwan both needed the United States—and both were vulnerable in Washington, both politically and geopolitically. They intensified their formal lobbying when they were most insecure.

Broadly speaking, it thus appears from the data that the function of the registered lobbyists whom Asian nations hire has traditionally been *defensive*: their numbers rise and fall primarily with the self-perceived political vulnerabilities of these countries rather than with realist indicators of national strength, although the financial wherewithal of their employers is also significant. Japan hired large numbers of lobbyists when it faced trade frictions in Congress—and especially when those frictions coincided with Japan's financial bubble of the late 1980s and the early 1990s.[13] Korea and Taiwan similarly hired lobbyists when their authoritarian regimes were under attack and they faced the prospect of retrenchment in U.S. military support following U.S. withdrawal from Vietnam.

Asian regimes also appear to hire lobbyists to defend against one another, since they have conflicting interests over territory, historical issues, and American policy priorities on such matters as nuclear reprocessing, differences that may well be intensifying. After Japan began hiring lobbyists aggressively during the 1960s and 1970s, as figure 6-3 indicates. Korea and Taiwan began to do so also. And after Taiwan hired lobbyists and achieved what mainland China saw as disturbing success on cross-strait issues, the PRC began to do so as well. Asian lobbying, in short, exhibits many of the competitive characteristics that are also found in arms races and electoral campaigns.

Competitive lobbying appears to have escalated in recent years, especially among China, Korea, and Japan, as intra-Northeast Asian tensions have risen. As indicated in figure 6-4, Chinese lobbying expenditures reported to Congress under the FARA more than tripled during 2007–12,

Figure 6-4. *The Shifting Balance of Chinese, Japanese, and Korean FARA Expenditures, 2001–12*[a]

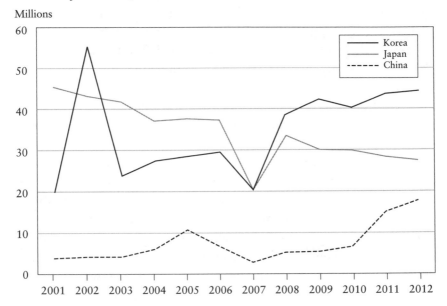

Millions

Source: "FARA Reports to Congress," U.S. Department of Justice, October 29, 2013 (www.fara.gov/annualrpts.html).
a. This figure represents the total receipts and disbursements reported to Congress each calendar year.

while Korean expenditures more than doubled. Japanese spending rose sharply in 2008 but thereafter declined under the DPJ administration, even as spending by highly competitive neighbors continued to rise.

Three significant anomalies in Asian lobbying behavior are the PRC, India, and Singapore. For many years none of these countries hired nearly as many lobbyists as their Northeast Asian counterparts, including even China/Taiwan. In the case of the PRC and India, a relative lack of interdependence with the United States was for many years the likely cause: neither had either a security alliance or deep economic interdependence with the United States during the heyday of lobbying—that is, the 1970s and 1980s. In the paradoxical case of Singapore, alternative means of interest articulation in Washington—more reliance on think tanks and informal personal networks—appear to have been at work. Such methods have become more and more important over the past two decades, so Singapore's approach may have been a future-oriented trend.

Elite Networks and Influence in Washington

Since the 1960s, with the advent of widespread jet transportation and the easing of border restrictions, international travel has grown explosively, particularly among elites. International conferences have proliferated, as has foreign study. Meanwhile, the information revolution has begun to link leaders of nations and their advisers across long distances, in increasingly intimate ways. How do deepening interpersonal networks affect the influence of nations in Washington? My fourth hypothesis suggests that they do so profoundly. As in other dimensions of their local presence, Asian nations vary substantially in the extent and in the strength of their interpersonal networks in the U.S. national capital. This is a complex subject for analysis, in part due to the subjective character of interpersonal networks themselves. A start can be made, however, by comparing the experiential background of ambassadors of various nations accredited to the United States (table 6-5).

What is instructive about this comparison is how little variation there is in the educational and experiential background of Asian ambassadors accredited to Washington. Virtually all have advanced degrees or certificates from elite northeastern U.S. universities. Some of the representatives of the smaller countries, such as Brunei, Papua New Guinea, Mongolia, and Vietnam, have among the most extensive educational credentials in the United States, helping to offset potential disadvantages of their nations' diminutive scale.

Apart from ambassadorial networks, broad sociopolitical networks with local citizens are of course important. Those countries with strong military alliances to the United States, and especially those that host large numbers of U.S. troops, such as South Korea and Japan, often have a relatively large number of citizens with personal ties to senior U.S. military personnel. Those countries that traditionally send large numbers of students to the United States for further education, either at the graduate or undergraduate levels, may also develop interpersonal networks with influential Americans.

Public Diplomacy and Transpacific Relations

The last of the five hypotheses considers the efforts of Asian governments and civil societies to influence policy outcomes in Washington

Table 6-5. *A Measure of Elite Networks: Background of Asian Ambassadors in Washington, 2013*

Country	Ambassador	Foreign study in United States	Previous service in United States	Affiliation with U.S. or international nongovernmental institutions
Brunei	Dato Paduka Haji Yusoff Haji Abdul Hamid	Fletcher School; IV Program, U.S. Information Agency	n.a.	n.a.
Burma	Kyaw Myo Htut	n.a.	Spent several childhood years in Washington, D.C., while his father served as military attaché in the Myanmar embassy	Minister counsel and later ambassador to the permanent mission of the Union of Myanmar to the Office of the United Nations and other international organizations in Geneva
Cambodia	Hem Heng	n.a.	n.a.	Deputy director general, ASEAN directorate
China	Cui Tiankai	School of Advanced International Studies, Johns Hopkins	n.a.	Minister counselor, China's UN mission; interpreter, Department for General Assembly and Conference Management, UN headquarters
India	S. Jaishankar	n.a.	First secretary handling political affairs at the Indian Embassy	Member of the International Institute for Strategic Studies in London
Indonesia	Dino Patti Djalal	McLean High School, Virginia	Washington diplomatic posting; initiator of U.S.-Indonesia security dialogue	Governing board, Institute for Peace and Democracy; executive board of the Indonesian Council on World Affairs; board of trustees, World Resources Institute
Japan	Kenichirō Sasae	Swarthmore	First secretary, embassy of Japan	Research associate, International Institute for Strategic Studies; special adviser to Sadako Ogata, UNHCR, Geneva
South Korea	Ahn Ho-young	Georgetown	First secretary, Korean embassy	Counselor, Korean delegation to the OECD; counselor, Korean mission to World Trade Organization

Laos	Seng Soukhathivong	Asia-Pacific Center for Security Studies	First secretary, Lao embassy; counselor, Lao embassy; deputy chief of mission, Lao embassy	n.a.
Malaysia	Datuk Othman Hashim	n.a.	n.a.	UN resident coordinator and representative, UNDP in Palestine
Mongolia	Bulgaa Altangerel	Columbia University	n.a.	Delegate, UN General Assembly sessions, UN Conference on the Law of the Sea, IPU, and other; board of directors, Trust Fund for Victims, International Criminal Court
Papua New Guinea	Evan J. Paki	Harvard Law School; Kennedy School, Harvard	Multilateral Investment Guarantee Agency	Rotary Club; Harvard Club; Harvard Alumni Association; Fulbright Association; founding chairman, Pacific Islands Ambassadors Group; Sydney office, Baker and McKenzie
Philippines	Jose L. Cuisia Jr.	Wharton School	n.a.	n.a.
Singapore	Ashok Kumar Mirpuri	Harvard Business School	n.a.	Corporate adviser in UK, Asia Pacific region, Shell International
Thailand	Vijavat Isarabhakdi	Fletcher School	First Secretary, Thai embassy	Minister, Permanent Mission of Thailand to the United Nations Office, Geneva
Vietnam	Nguyen Quoc Cuong	Fletcher School; Maxwell School of Public Administration, Syracuse University; Kennedy School, Harvard	n.a.	Deputy director general, Department of Multilateral Economic Cooperation; head of Political and Security Section, APEC Viet Nam Secretariat, when Vietnam was host of APEC in 2006

Non-Asia Reference Case

Israel	Ron Dermer	Wharton School	Minister of Economic Affairs, Israel embassy; worked in D.C. during 1994; born and raised in Miami Beach, Fla.	n.a.

by appealing broadly to public sentiments in the United States. This can involve activities at a wide variety of levels: exchange programs for scholars, study visits for students, events sponsored by think tanks or universities, and major international gatherings in the home country in question, to name a few variants. As in other areas, there is great variation in the activism of Asian nations in this sector

As in multiple other fields, smaller Asian nations have often been the most proactive, politically astute, and successful at their public diplomacy. In the realm of international conferencing, Singapore's Shangri-La Dialogue, cosponsored by the International Institute of Strategic Studies of London, stands out as the premier forum for Track II discussions of Asian security. Korea's Jeju Forum and China's Boao Forum for Asia are also increasingly influential. Singapore, the Philippines, Burma, and China have all recently sponsored major World Economic Forum Asian regional gatherings. The *Nihon Keizai Shimbun* sponsors an influential gathering of ASEAN leaders in Tokyo every summer, but Japan has no real analogue to the large global networking conferences convened by many smaller Asian counterparts.

As is clear from the preceding, many Asian nations engage in active international networking, in support of their broader foreign policy goals. Singapore, South Korea, and China are among the most active. Such effort is often synergistic with the propensity of nations to send students abroad for foreign study, which itself helps to forge transpacific networks. A few nations, such as several of the ASEAN countries, are relatively passive in the area of public diplomacy, engage in unusually specialized or esoteric variants, or have only a limited presence in Washington. In the case studies to follow, I explore further the consequences of policies and practices designed to promote understanding and support for Asian nations among the American public.

In Conclusion

Although there are significant exceptions to the prevailing pattern, the smaller nations of Asia appear to be remarkably effective at achieving their objectives in Washington. They are generally good at attracting attention to themselves—at being visible. They are also remarkably good at achieving legislative and diplomatic outcomes, both symbolic and substantive, that serve their national interests. These findings, of course, run contrary to classical realist contentions and appear not to correlate with either the scale of a nation's diplomatic presence in Washington or the corps of lobbyists in its employ. These findings, clearly in tension with three of the hypotheses regarding influence in Washington, pose a distinct empirical puzzle that requires further explanation. That explanation I seek through more fine-grained empirical case studies of the contrasting Asian national approaches to Washington.

In the following two chapters I consider eight individual country cases one by one, examining how they attempt to shape the Washington political environment that surrounds them. These cases more precisely test the hypotheses regarding influence developed in this chapter, directing special attention to the paradox of small nations with large influence in Washington. I start with Northeast Asia, where the largest nations and those with the most substantial resources in conventional calculations of national power are located, and then move to South and Southeast Asia. The latter encompass more nations that are presumably less influential by realist standards, in the conventional calculus of international influence. As becomes clear, neither national scale nor resources appear to directly determine influence, on either a comparative national or a subregional basis, contrary to what realist theory might suggest. Classical diplomatic scale, and even classical lobbying, are surprisingly ineffective, especially in recent years. Instead, complex, subtle, and ultimately decisive subnational factors, both in the local Washington environment and in the Asian approach to it, appear decisive. Both elite networks and public diplomacy appear particularly important in determining national influence in Washington, as the qualitative national cases, taken collectively, make clear.

Northeast Asia
in Washington

Northeast Asia is a volatile, heavily armed region where many of the great powers of the world come warily into contact. China, Russia, and Japan all surround the divided Korean peninsula, where United Nations forces, with major American involvement, stand along an armistice line between a rapidly growing South Korea and a North Korea that has tested nuclear weapons and is developing long-range missiles. The region is rife with conflict and political ambiguity along many dimensions. Both Korea and China are divided states with the constituent parts competing bitterly for legitimacy. Territorial boundaries between Russia and Japan, China and Japan, Korea and Japan, and China and Korea are all contested. Bitter disputes continue over historical interpretation and even over geographical names.

In this volatile, contentious world of Northeast Asia, relationships with the United States have long mattered greatly. Two key nations—Japan and South Korea—have had strong bilateral alliance relationships with the United States since the early 1950s and are major American trading partners as well. The United States was China's principal ally in World War II and an antagonist in the Korean War, and is its largest export market today.

Washington has become even more important for individual Northeast Asian nations over the past decade, because competition among them for U.S. support has been steadily intensifying, driven by the rise of China and China's increasingly substantial Washington presence. Long-standing territorial and historical issues within Northeast Asia have grown more inflamed politically, and Washington has emerged as a major political battlefield. Competition has also deepened over exchange rates and trade agreements, leading to the robust Northeast Asian activities in Washington that are depicted in coming pages.

This chapter begins by considering the activities of China in Washington, which have expanded substantially in recent years. It then considers the actions of the Chinese on the other side of the Taiwan Strait and why their effectiveness has varied so sharply in recent years. Then it considers Japan and, finally, Korea. As will become clear, classic variables like alliance ties and economic scale can matter, but their efficacy is shaped by Washington-based activism and should by no means be taken for granted.

China

China's relationship with Washington is a study in paradox, and indeed the story of U.S.-China relations is a long one. It goes back to the very foundations of the American republic, with the clipper ships first arriving at Canton in 1784, only a year after the Treaty of Paris confirmed U.S. independence. Chinese Americans have been a major part of the American ethnic mix since the 1840s, and China has had representation in Washington since 1878. Yet China for many years did not exercise influence in the U.S. national capital commensurate with its enormous scale and consequence in the broader world.

China's scale in both Asian and global terms goes almost without saying. China, after all, has for most of recorded history had the largest population in the world, currently over 1.3 billion people. It is also enormous, geographically, being either the largest or the second-largest country on earth since the dawn of recorded history (competing for the past four centuries only with Russia).[1]

China has also consistently held major political-military significance in global terms. Over half a century ago, the People's Liberation Army "volunteers" battled the United States to a bloody three-year stalemate in Korea. Since 1964 China has been a nuclear power. And for more than three decades it has had a sizable and growing economy: since 2010 it has been the second-largest economy after the United States and the largest exporter.

In the early days of the People's Republic, China lacked standing in Washington, despite its scale, due to an absence of diplomatic relations with the United States, coupled with an American economic embargo. That embargo was relaxed—and China was admitted to the United Nations—in 1971, just before Richard Nixon's historic February 1972 visit to China. That trip paved the way for deepening U.S.-China ties, and ultimately bilateral recognition, which was mediated by Zbigniew Brzezinski in 1979. Despite these normalized diplomatic ties, until only a few years ago China's role in Washington continued to be distinctive, contradictory, and limited for a nation of its global consequence. Yet over the past decade China's presence has expanded rapidly in both formal and informal dimensions. Today China maintains the largest embassy in Washington, with nearly 200 accredited diplomats.[2] Its official presence is complemented by wide-ranging mass media and public relations efforts.

China's approach to Washington is distinctive, relative to other national players in Washington, in seven respects:

—It often represents its interests indirectly, through NGOs and American corporations, particularly on Capitol Hill.

—It is more oriented toward Washington than New York.

—Its agenda tends to be highly China-centric, driven by such domestic considerations as relations with Taiwan, prestige opportunities for Chinese leaders, and the marginalization of subversive groups like the Falun Gong.

—Its political strategies have a strong U.S. grassroots orientation, reaching out to local governments and to Chinese American groups across the country.

—Its embassy plays a proactive national role, networking across the country with both embassy staffers and Beijing visitors.

—Its approach has a Beltway dimension, encompassing the think tanks, universities, and corporations of the Washington suburbs.

—Its involvement has a cyclical aspect, alternating between confrontation and conciliation, depending on the American electoral cycle.

Indirect Representation

To a greater degree than most foreign nations, China represents its interests in Washington by working through local American organizations with similar concerns, rather than directly. It supports and encourages such bodies, often by providing them with preferential commercial and personal access in China. In return, these groups, which typically have parallel underlying interests to those of China, typically help promote its objectives, either directly or indirectly.

A good example is the U.S.-China Business Council (USCBC), one of the most effective business promotion bodies in Washington. The USCBC was founded in 1973 and now has nearly 220 corporate members.[3] Unlike parallel international commercial organizations, like the U.S.-Japan Business Council, the USCBC has offices on both sides of the Pacific—a headquarters in Washington, which deals with both U.S. business and government, as well as branches in Shanghai and Beijing.[4] The latter provide active liaison for U.S. member firms with the Chinese government as well as conventional business information and consulting services.

For historical reasons—the need, between Nixon's visit to China in 1972 and U.S.-China normalization in 1979, for a credibly semiofficial entity to coordinate bilateral trade relations—the USCBC is often accorded semigovernmental status within China. Its president, for example, often travels to China and is typically given informal vice-ministerial ranking at bilateral U.S.-China meetings. The USCBC also has, in contrast to its U.S.-Japan counterpart, small but effective local offices in Beijing and Shanghai, which directly support frequent high-level corporate visits from the United States while providing a broad range of other services.

U.S.-China relations also involve a host of other semiofficial support organizations, including the National Committee on U.S.-China Relations (NCUSCR), the China Institute, the U.S.-China Policy Foundation (USCPF), and the Committee on Scholarly Communication with China (CSCC).[5] Many of these semiofficial bodies were also created during the transition years between Nixon's 1972 visit and formal recognition in 1979, with the aim of maintaining forward momentum in the bilateral relationship during those ambiguous times. All of these bodies are endowed with both tacit public support and semigovernmental functions. The NCUSCR mainly supports informal discussions among intellectuals and former officials in the United States and China, building on China's historic role as sponsor of the table tennis friendship matches that preceded the historic Nixon-Kissinger visits of 1971–72.[6]

The USCPF, like the NCUSCR, involves congressional representatives and intellectuals in promoting understanding between the United States and China, this one primarily through educational activities. It sponsors lectures and roundtables in Washington and policy-oriented travel to China.[7] The CSCC, an affiliate of the American Council of Learned Societies, serves as a catalyst for interactions among academics in the two countries. The China Institute, a venerable body with highly contemporary functions, fosters U.S.-China networks and sociocultural understanding through activities ranging from an executive summit and varied elite social events to study-travel programs for teachers and artists and children's after-school workshops and summer camps.[8] Since 2006 it has been assisted in its efforts to enhance American understanding of China by the Chinese government's support of Confucius Institutes, centers for cultural and language study.[9] In November 2013 the activities of these institutes were given greater focus with the opening of the Confucius Institute U.S. Center, across the street from the Brookings Institution, in the heart of Washington's think tank row.[10]

A final private group with a substantial recent role in promoting understanding of China in Washington is the Committee of 100. An invitational body of Chinese Americans initiated by the well-known architect I. M. Pei following the Tiananmen events of June 1989, it does not align with any political party in the United States or government in Asia. It does, however, work to stabilize relations between Greater China and the United States, while also taking China-oriented positions on some important matters of dispute within the region, including territorial questions.[11]

These bodies have collectively helped to stabilize China's role in Washington, including agenda setting, early warning, public education, and informal lobbying. They are gaining legitimacy and access, as nongovernmental Washington's penumbra of power becomes more salient. These NGOs also help to accord U.S.-China ties special legitimacy and priority in the American policy process—despite, or perhaps because of, the mixed conflict-and-cooperation relations between Beijing and Washington. While these mediating NGOs have some analogue in U.S. relations with NATO, and to a lesser degree in American ties with Korea, they have no good parallel in U.S.-Japan relations for a variety of historical reasons, including the protracted transpacific trade conflicts of the 1970s and 1980s.

Most important, these private bodies with public functions help to legitimate the bilateral U.S.-China relationship with both the general American public and Washington policy elites. That has been a formidable task, considering the broad American public hostility toward mainland China during the Korean War, during the McCarthy years, and across the ensuing generation. Yet these China-friendly groups, led by the National Council on U.S.-China Relations, have performed their conciliatory functions effectively, especially considering the tensions induced by massive trade imbalances and the rising sense in America of a geopolitical challenge from Beijing, a point of view that began emerging after 2000.

How far the National Council and its sister organizations have legitimized postrevolutionary Sino-American relations in Washington, compared to the McCarthy era, was manifest in December 2003, when Premier Wen Jiabao visited the United States. The NCUSCR hosted an enormous dinner (600 guests) in his honor at the elegant Ritz Carlton Hotel in Washington. The affair was cosponsored by eight influential local organizations: the U.S.-China Business Council, the America-China Forum, the Asia Society, the Center for Strategic and International Studies, the Committee of 100, the Council on Foreign Relations, the U.S. Chamber of Commerce, and the U.S.-China Policy Foundation.[12] Such massive events held to welcome Chinese leaders and organized by wholly American sponsors are not unusual in U.S.-China relations, as manifest in the elaborate joint event welcoming Vice President Xi Jinping in February 2012, which included a State Department luncheon with prominent Americans from government, business, NGOs, academia, and the arts.[13] In striking contrast, U.S.-Japan events in Washington typically have markedly less extensive local business or NGO involvement.

Washington-Oriented

Foreign countries vary in the geographical locus of their U.S. presence, with Japan and several of the continental European nations, such as France and Germany, having many of their largest and most influential NGOs located in New York City. China, together with Korea, is emphatically Washington-centric: the U.S.-China Business Council is based there, China engages a substantial number of Washington lobbyists, China is active on Capitol Hill, China operates substantial media bureaus, and the Chinese embassy, with the largest diplomatic staff in Washington, looms large. China also places considerable emphasis on cultural events in Washington, even though New York City is America's de facto cultural capital. The Chinese Ministry of Culture, for example, sponsored such major month-long events at the Kennedy Center as the Festival of China and China: The Art of a Nation.[14]

Since 2009 the ministry of foreign affairs in Beijing has placed a priority on public diplomacy, with the generation of soft power in Washington as a principal focus.[15] In October 2009 it established its Office of Public Diplomacy and named Wei Xin, who had just returned from China's embassy in Washington, as its head. Also in 2009 as much as 60 billion renminbi ($8.8 billion) was pumped into the Big Four Beijing media outlets (Xinhua News Agency, CCTV, China Radio International, and *China Daily*) to fund their global expansion.[16]

Chinese governmental and semigovernmental organizations place particular emphasis on public relations and social communications in Washington, recognizing and capitalizing on the growing importance of mass media, in interaction with the idea industry, in informal agenda setting. In late 2011, for example, the government-owned *China Watch*, published in Beijing, began distributing a free supplement in news boxes along Connecticut Avenue, complementing an identical insert provided as an advertising supplement in the *New York Times*. By 2012, using a similar news box strategy, *China Daily* had achieved a U.S. subscription base of over 170,000, much of it in Washington.[17]

In early 2012 China Central Television (CCTV), China's state-run international broadcaster, began broadcasts in English. The broadcast was produced by a staff of more than sixty journalists, most of them Westerners, who were hired from NBC, Bloomberg, Fox News, and other Western news organizations.[18] By mid-2013 that number had expanded to over a hundred. By then, CCTV was operating in English around the clock, through its CNC World Internet channel, and also providing cell phone video. The CCTV network's Washington facility, which began broadcasting from the District in February 2012, is reportedly the hub of CCTV's global news-gathering operation. Jim Laurie,

the former NBC and ABC reporter, who established himself professionally as the only American correspondent to have remained in Saigon
to cover its fall in 1975, serves as CCTV's top adviser for its American
news division.

Why Washington, as opposed to other American cities, has become
uniquely central in China's approach to the United States—even in
media matters, in which New York is traditionally primary—is a question that casts light on the nature of U.S.-China relations more generally. In answer to this question, there are four major reasons.

—First and perhaps foremost, the political struggle with Taiwan is
central to China's diplomacy in the United States, and that is inherently
a Washington-centric struggle. Since Taiwan's derecognition in 1979,
Taipei has placed great priority on cultivating relations with Congress,
and China has naturally worked hard in countering that effort, especially since Congress played a catalytic role, during early 1995, in pressing the Clinton administration to authorize Lee Teng-hui's controversial
visit to Cornell University. Washington—both Congress and the executive branch—has also been central to China's efforts to limit American
arms supplies to Taiwan, which are ultimately proposed by the White
House and authorized by the House of Representatives' Committee on
Foreign Affairs.

—China's trade, finance, and investment concerns are a second
reason for its strong Washington orientation. It has a huge trade sur-
plus with the United States, which has been steadily growing for two
decades, amid persistent congressional calls for renminbi revaluation.[19]
Meanwhile, China has attempted to invest portions of its large surpluses
in U.S.-based direct investment projects, which, as with the attempted
acquisition of Unocal, have at times been controversial. Washington has
necessarily been central in China's defensive fight against American protectionism and in support of favorable regulatory dispensations. Related
to this point, NGOs that have been important intermediaries in Beijing's
delicate relationship with the United States, such as the U.S.-China Business Council, are located in Washington.

—A third reason for Washington's distinctive importance to China in
its relations with the United States has to do with state visits, for which
Washington is, of course, the central arena. Ever since Deng Xiaoping's
triumphal entry into Washington in January 1979, closely following the

U.S. derecognition of Taiwan, Chinese leadership visits to the United States have had high domestic salience, attended by intense semigovernmental publicity.[20] Leaders have typically been accompanied to Washington by large numbers of supportive journalists, with the visits used to enhance leadership prestige and domestic standing.[21]

—A fourth and final reason for China's Washington-centric focus is China's growing global political-economic role and the deepening synergy with the rise of Washington's information industry. Beijing has become an increasingly powerful force at the World Bank and the International Monetary Fund—both Washington-based institutions. Those multilateral bodies have also become crucial arenas for networking and personnel development strategies that are projecting China's influence far beyond East Asia—into Latin America, Africa, the Middle East, and other parts of the world that are more accessible from Washington than from Asia. The penumbra of power in Washington—think tanks, Beltway consulting firms, and so on—is also a useful source of globally oriented intelligence and strategic advice for Beijing as for so many other nations of the world. And the penumbra's rapid yet unstructured growth in turn offers Beijing new opportunities and incentives to engage the influential media-information complex, so as to moderate broader American misgivings about China's rise.

China-centric Agenda Setting

As with most Asian nations, Washington serves as a strategic arena for major Chinese domestic political struggles—obviously including, but nevertheless transcending, Taiwan. Indeed, some of China's official behavior in Washington is not readily comprehensible without considering the domestic political context within the PRC itself. China places great emphasis, for example, on the level of protocol provided at state visits and on the frequency of such occasions, due to the prestige and enhanced leadership legitimacy that such visits confer within China. Indeed, the PRC often appears to make substantive policy concessions in return for such symbolism.[22] The Chinese embassy also carefully tracks the activities in the United States of dissident groups such as the Falun Gong, and responds sharply to their perceived provocations, due to the potential symbolic implications of failing to constrain them. It attacks these dissidents even when, as in the case of "Divine Performing

Arts Spectaculars" at the Kennedy Center, their activities assume what appear to others as only marginally political forms.[23]

Grassroots Orientation

Many nations represented in Washington, including most African and Middle Eastern states, focus their government-related activities almost exclusively on cultivating political-economic elites, particularly within the prevailing national administration. China itself followed this centralized, elite-oriented approach until the 1980s and even beyond, relying on such trusted interlocutors as Henry Kissinger and Zbigniew Brzezinski to convey their strategic objectives to the United States.[24]

Two of Taiwan's spectacular tactical successes, notably the Taiwan Relations Act (1979) and securing permission for Lee Teng-hui to visit the United States (1995), led the PRC to realize that it badly needed to broaden its base of support beyond the White House. It thereafter began a systematic and urgent effort to cultivate grassroots ties, led by President Jiang Zemin himself.[25] Indeed, Jiang made a point of visiting multiple regional cities, including Honolulu, Los Angeles, Boston, New York, Philadelphia, Williamsburg, and Washington, during his 1997 visit to the United States, the first by a Chinese head of state in twelve years. He visited high-tech companies and the Harvard University campus, while also giving speeches in major cities across the country. This practice of extended top-leadership visits to the United States, allowing opportunities to meet with governors, mayors, and prominent local residents while strategically announcing attractive new economic cooperation projects, has become standard for Chinese leaders ever since.

China's recent grassroots efforts, spurred initially by the Taiwan challenge, go far beyond state visits. The Chinese embassy plays a key role. Its staff was substantially strengthened in 1995 and, as noted, is now 50 percent larger than any other foreign mission in Washington. Its physical profile was sharply enhanced in April 2009 with the opening of a new, multibillion-dollar chancery on International Drive, designed by the renowned Chinese American architect I. M. Pei.

The embassy actively courts local leaders and congressional members in both Washington and their home districts. It routinely hosts receptions in honor of the U.S. National Governors Conference, for example. Senior embassy officials also have a busy travel schedule, visiting local centers ranging from Springfield, Illinois, and Lincoln, Nebraska, to Los Angeles and Sacramento, California. They also meet actively, at the embassy and elsewhere, with third country representatives, and multilateral bodies such as the World Bank, pursuing an increasingly global Chinese diplomacy not only in Beijing, but also out of the Chinese Embassy in Washington, D.C.[26]

A key part of this new grassroots strategy is deepening relations with the large Chinese American ethnic community in the United States, which is now around 4 million strong. To this end the Chinese embassy has established the Compatriots Department. This department sponsors a variety of events to deepen understanding between the embassy and Chinese Americans; these include sumptuous receptions commemorating the Chinese Spring Festival and National Day.[27] In cultivating ties with Chinese Americans, local U.S. politicians, and other groups, the embassy takes advantage of the spacious auditorium and the reception rooms in its large new chancery.

Beltway Ties

Many nations focus their D.C. lobbying narrowly on downtown Washington's formal institutions, particularly the U.S. State Department. China adopts a much broader approach, one that extends beyond both downtown Washington and America's grassroots to encompass the strategic "penumbra of power," not only in the downtown information industry, but in Washington's growing suburbs as well. Interacting with the suburbs seemingly allows better information flow, with lesser visibility, than would be possible in the heart of Washington itself. Significantly, two of the three Confucius Institutes in the Washington metropolitan area are located in suburban Washington: the University of Maryland and George Mason University in Virginia.

Cyclical Patterns

Among the most distinctive features of Chinese activities in Washington is the pattern of response to the American electoral cycle. Typically, American administrations start with decidedly delicate relations with Beijing, marked by rhetorical statements in support of human rights, veiled sympathy for Taiwan, and sometimes outright conflict with China. Around the first midterm election, however, the incumbent president's relations with Beijing markedly improve.

This cyclical pattern in China's relations with Washington has persisted with remarkable consistency from the Nixon years (1969–75) through the Bush administration and beyond. Richard Nixon had no relations to speak of with China until the "ping-pong diplomacy" of 1970. Relations deepened after the 1970 midterm elections, with the removal of trade sanctions and Kissinger's secret visit to China. As elite networks began to deepen during the latter part of Nixon's tenure and throughout the Ford administration, which included numerous Nixon-era officials such as Henry Kissinger, relations with China became much better.

Jimmy Carter, like Richard Nixon, began his career markedly critical of China, in part due to his strong human rights emphasis. Although Carter entered office resolved to normalize relations with China, he and his secretary of state, Cyrus Vance, also desired to preserve ties with Taiwan.[28] Vance made a frustrating August 1977 trip to Beijing, futilely attempting to secure China's assent to a normalization that preserved American consular rights in Taiwan. Following the 1978 midterm election, however, through the mediation of National Security Adviser Zbigniew Brzezinski, Carter recognized China, withdrew recognition from Taiwan, and enjoyed positive relations with Beijing thereafter.

Ronald Reagan began his presidential tenure as a strong Taiwan sympathizer, from his days as California governor, and had very delicate personal relations with Beijing. Yet those ties warmed markedly after Reagan agreed to limit arms sales to Taipei, following the 1982 midterm elections, and he enjoyed an amicable visit to Beijing shortly thereafter. Reagan's successor, George H. W. Bush, a former envoy to China, experienced the Tiananmen massacre early in his term, which naturally chilled relations with Beijing. Yet following the Houston summit of 1991 he promoted a gradual revival of bilateral ties.

Patterns of the Clinton and George W. Bush administrations in U.S.-China relations were similar to those under Nixon, Carter, and Reagan. Clinton, like Reagan, entered office as an established Taiwan sympathizer, who had been a guest of honor at Taiwan's National Day, on October 10, 1985, and visited the island at least four times as governor of Arkansas.[29] During 1993–94 Clinton persistently stressed human rights issues and an annual review of most-favored-nation treatment for China to provide leverage with that country. During Clinton's second term, however—after the 1994 midterm election, the 1995 Lee visit to Cornell, and the 1996 Taiwan missile crisis—the Clinton administration established markedly positive relations with Beijing, including an amicable exchange of state visits between Jiang Zemin and Bill Clinton.[30]

George W. Bush, like Nixon, Reagan, and Clinton, started his presidency markedly pro-Taiwan. During his first few months in office, he also experienced a major crisis with China, as an American EP-3 surveillance plane was forced down in Hainan. Yet following the 9/11 attacks on the United States, and American intervention in Afghanistan, relations significantly improved, with the United States also quietly acquiescing in harsh Chinese steps against Uyghur separatists. In 2003, following the 2002 midterm elections, George W. Bush began enjoying relatively good relations with the new Chinese president, Hu Jintao. In 2006 and 2008 they exchanged major reciprocal visits, with Hu visiting Washington in April 2006 and Bush attending the Beijing Olympics with his wife, father, and mother in August 2008. Bush's first overseas trip as a former president was also to China, to speak at the Boao Forum for Asia, in April 2009.[31]

The pattern of the Barack Obama years has been broadly similar to that of Obama's seven predecessors, although it has also been shaped by the rising geopolitical shadow of China on the world stage. During the 2008 presidential campaign, Obama, like his competitor, John McCain, was relatively critical of the PRC, noting human rights violations and an allegedly undervalued renminbi.[32] His wariness continued during the first two years of his presidential term. Following the 2010 midterm elections, however, in January 2011 Obama hosted Hu Jintao in Washington at a relatively amicable summit. Tensions rose thereafter over the South China Sea and the administration's "Asia pivot" in the political-military sphere.[33] However, in February 2012 the White House hosted Hu's heir apparent, Xi Jinping, at another conciliatory summit.[34]

Relations grew more delicate during the 2012 presidential campaign, with Obama keeping a low profile in the face of Mitt Romney's criticism of China.[35] Yet following his reelection, Obama became even more solicitous, inviting Xi to an unprecedented "G-2" individualized summit meeting in Palm Springs, California, in June 2013.[36] Cyclical oscillation in the dynamics of the Sino-American relationship thus continues to prevail, with campaigns a recurrent time of tension, followed repeatedly by reconciliation.

The seven distinctive features of China's approach to Washington all have their origins in three critical junctures: the June 1950 American interposition in the Taiwan Strait to save Chiang Kai-shek; the ambiguous 1972–79 informal U.S. recognition of China; and the fateful 1995 visit of Taiwanese President Lee Teng-hui to Cornell. The first of these separated Taiwan decisively from China, despite the Red Army's triumph on the mainland, while the second entrenched informal institutions like the U.S.-China Business Council in quasi-formal roles. And last, Lee's 1995 visit to the United States triggered a dramatic shift in China's approach to the United States—away from a focus on White House elites to a much broader concern with grassroots diplomacy, and the cultivation of Chinese American support for Beijing.

Summary

China is a massive nation—the largest in the world in population and second-largest in both geographic and economic scale. Yet for many years it paradoxically lacked the political-economic clout in Washington even remotely commensurate with its formidable dimensions. Division across the Taiwan Strait and a bitter history of cold war estrangement from the United States limited Beijing's influence for many years following the Chinese revolution and the onset of the Korean conflict.

It was ironically defensive responses to the action of outsiders, rather than the direct assertiveness of a rising China itself, that first set the country on the path to real influence in Washington. Henry Kissinger's and Richard Nixon's visits, followed by Jimmy Carter's gestures toward normalization, regularized U.S. relations with Beijing. And Lee Teng-hui's Cornell visit shocked Beijing into a more proactive and realistic approach to inside-the-Beltway politics.

Beijing has steadily gained standing in Washington of late, even if its current influence still does not match its global scale. The country has enhanced its position through indirect representation, a Washington orientation, China-centric agenda setting, grassroots sensitivity, a central role for the Chinese embassy, its Beltway dimension, and its cyclical involvement in Washington.

The distinctive profile of China's Washington involvement, which has involved several abrupt shifts in orientation, is attributable to critical junctures that encouraged major shifts in China's approach. We have identified three: the June 1950 American interposition in the Taiwan Strait; the eight-year period of informal entente between Washington and Beijing (1971–79); and the 1995 U.S. decision to admit Taiwanese President Lee Teng-hui to the United States, and its aftermath. Collectively, these events bred a dynamic, grassroots-oriented Chinese approach to Washington that has been increasingly successful at influencing the American policy process—more because the "trees in the forest" tactical approach is intrinsically effective, rather than due to the PRC's imposing geographic, demographic, or economic scale, as realist theory might suggest.

Taiwan

Taiwan would appear, on the face of matters, to be one of the weakest Asian political entities in Washington.[37] For well over three decades (since 1979) it has not even been recognized by the U.S. government as a nation-state, and the number of other nations supporting it diplomatically is small and steadily declining.[38] Taiwan is only 0.3 percent the geographical size of mainland China, less than a hundred miles to the west, which claims it as an integral part of the People's Republic. And Taiwan's population is only 3 percent of the PRC total. To make matters even more delicate, the PRC, a nuclear power, reportedly has well over 1,600 short-range missiles, including the high-precision Dong-Feng 12, targeted on Taiwan.[39] Further, the United States needs the cooperation of mainland China—the world's most rapidly growing major power—on a broad range of global issues, not least the funding of its massive and growing national debt.[40]

Taiwan's position in Washington, and its evolution over the past several decades, is a complex and often contradictory one. It has not evolved in a straight line. Yet despite Taiwan's small physical size relative to mainland China, not to mention its vulnerability in both the geopolitical and the diplomatic spheres, the island has nevertheless exerted remarkable influence in Washington, its formal diplomatic handicaps notwithstanding. Diminutive Taiwan's persistent visibility and capability to shape the course of American Asia policy present a genuine empirical puzzle that shows once again the shortcomings of classical realist notions of power, which all too uncritically privilege economic, geographic, and political-military scale in international affairs.

Considering the importance of both policy and theory to Taiwan's substantial role in Washington politics, and the vigorous interest in the subject among Chinese on both sides of the Taiwan Strait, there is remarkably little recent English-language literature on Taiwan's role in Washington. Douglas Mendel offers the most authoritative work on this topic, using primary sources, in his 1970 classic, *The Politics of Formosan Nationalism*.[41] Yet it was nearly forty years before his research was updated, based on interviews with influential Taiwanese and American figures.[42] As Thomas Robinson, the long-time course chairperson for China at the U.S. Foreign Service Institute, observes: "In a very large literature on American-Taiwanese relations, almost no work deals with this subject. Indeed, most deal with American policy and Taiwan's changing diplomatic status."[43]

Taiwan's Embedded Historical Advantages

"Lobbying efforts on behalf of Taiwan are noteworthy for their sophistication, strong message, and long history," a veteran observer of cross-strait relations puts it.[44] Today's Taiwan lobby has its origins in the China lobby of the 1940s, born of the World War II struggle against Japanese aggression and the sympathetic American response. Madame Chiang Kai-shek's eloquent 1943 address to the U.S. Congress, the only one ever given by a leading figure of the Chinese state, elicited a powerful emotional response from the American public and helped to consolidate the U.S. alliance with Chiang's Republic of China for years into the future. It also gave legitimacy to the Kuomintang's determined efforts to preserve control over mainland China during the ensuing civil war, which garnered substantial U.S. support.

The China lobby remained one of Washington's most powerful interest groups for over two decades. It secured a continuous flow of aid to Chiang Kai-shek, first on the mainland and later on Taiwan. Simultaneously, it also forestalled virtually all bilateral contact between the

U.S. government and the Chinese communists until the dramatic Nixon-Kissinger overtures of the early 1970s.[45]

After the Nixon "shocks" of late 1971, the China lobby, in cooperation with the KMT government on Taiwan, fought a sustained, and remarkably effective, rearguard action to prevent the U.S. government from establishing diplomatic relations with China. This effort ultimately proved futile. Yet the China lobby's efforts were successful in preventing both President Nixon and President Ford from establishing diplomatic relations with Beijing, as they often assured the Chinese that they planned to do.[46]

Much of the classical China lobby's influence lay in a conservative support base that carried over to the Taiwan lobby of ensuing decades. Religious opposition to the advance of "godless forces" on the mainland—first Japanese imperialism and then the Chinese communists—lay at its base. Former missionaries in China, such as longtime House member Walter Judd (R-Minn.), served as catalysts, supported also by conservative media, such as *Newsweek* magazine and the *Time-Life* communications empire, and by various business interests.[47]

The China lobby blocked U.S. consideration of recognizing the newly established People's Republic of China in late 1949 and early 1950, before the Korean War.[48] It also blocked the Kennedy administration's serious consideration of recognizing Mongolia in 1961, and sustained national political support for Taipei's UN Security Council role until the early 1970s.[49] The lobby's extraordinary domestic political influence was enhanced beyond its core constituency by the reality that several of its key members, such as Henry Luce and Walter Judd, both knew China well from their childhoods, were highly opinionated, and had the powerful media connections to shape public opinion on matters in which the bulk of the American people had little background.[50]

For many years Taiwan also benefited from U.S. anticommunist geopolitical fears—that any lack of resolve in the cross-strait conflict, or at least in containing mainland China, would undermine America's global security. These fears were magnified by China's steady economic rise and growing military budgets, from the early 1980s on. And there was also a growing population of Taiwanese—rising from 6,000 in 1970 to 200,000 a decade later and roughly 600,000 by 2010—that passionately opposed any concessions to mainland China regarding their vulnerable island home.[51]

Jimmy Carter noted the continuing power of pro-Taiwan sentiment in the late 1970s, terming it "very strong . . . particularly in Congress."[52] "In the absence of consistent presidential leadership," Carter observed, in recounting his 1979 decision to transfer recognition to Beijing, "Taiwanese lobbyists seemed able to prevail in shaping United States policy on this fundamental issue in the Far East." He also remarked that "we realized that we would have a firestorm on our hands as soon as this announcement was made," referring to the transfer of recognition from Taiwan to mainland China.[53] National Security Adviser Zbigniew Brzezinski apparently shared this wariness of the Taiwan lobby, while stressing the Carter administration's success in finessing its influence during the late 1970s.[54] White House apprehensions regarding the lobby's power in Congress delayed U.S.-China normalization talks until after the Panama Canal treaties were passed.[55] These apprehensions also led President Carter to insist on utmost secrecy and on negotiations being conducted by only a small number of White House officials, led by National Security Adviser Zbigniew Brzezinski, rather than by the State Department.[56]

Crisis-Driven Birth of a New Taiwan Lobby

Carter transferred U.S. recognition from Taipei to Beijing on January 1, 1979, thus signaling Taiwan's most traumatic defeat ever in Washington. That bitter setback intensified pressures on the autocratic KMT regime in Taipei to make changes that would enhance its Washington legitimacy, leading ultimately to the birth of an authentic democracy in "Island China."[57] Derecognition also, however, catalyzed the emergence of a new support coalition for Taiwan in Washington, which was proactively nurtured by Taipei. This new and potent coalition led to a surprising yet pronounced revival of Taiwanese influence in the nation's capital over the course of the 1980s and the early 1990s, in sharp contradiction of realist foreign policy paradigms, stressing the correlation of size and power in international relations.

Following the derecognition of Taiwan by America's executive branch in 1979, the last refuge in Washington for the Taiwan lobby was naturally Capitol Hill. To provide a modicum of continuity in U.S.-Taiwan relations, the Carter State Department proposed bland legislation supporting limited, informal economic and administrative ties between Taiwan and the United States but leaving critical political-military issues such as arms sales untouched. Congress, upset at what it considered cavalier treatment of Taiwan, and lack of consultation in the normalization process, sharply bolstered the tepid legislative draft, advancing its own far bolder ideas.[58] Thus was born the Taiwan Relations Act of April 1980, which authorized de facto American diplomatic relations with Taiwan, defensive arms sales, and assurances that the United States would consider any attempt to determine the future of Taiwan by other than peaceful means as a threat to the peace and security of the western Pacific.[59] None of these assurances had been clearly included in the original State Department legislative draft.

Across the early 1980s proactive congressional support for Taiwan was undermined by mainland China's geopolitical shift toward the West under Deng Xiaoping.[60] Support was further muted by three additional considerations: U.S. recognition of the PRC in 1979, which resolved the issue of de jure sovereignty across the Taiwan Strait; the presence of the Reagan administration in the White House, which conservatives assumed would care for Taiwan's fundamental interests; and the political oppressiveness of the KMT regime, which disenchanted congressional liberals and undermined their backing for Taiwan.[61] The House of Representatives' Subcommittee on Asian and Pacific Affairs, chaired by human rights advocate Stephen Solarz (D-N.Y.), held numerous hearings on the KMT government's treatment of political dissidents.[62] Solarz, together with Representative Jim Leach (R-Iowa), as well as Senators Ted Kennedy (D-Mass.) and Claiborne Pell (D-R.I. and Senate Foreign Relations Committee chairman), also organized the Committee for Democracy on Taiwan, to sponsor legislation calling for political liberalization.

In the face of derecognition and the escalation of criticism regarding its human rights practices, Taiwan embraced one classical defensive Washington remedy—it hired more lobbyists. The number of registered agents working for Taiwan more than doubled, from 26 in 1979 to 59 at the high point in 1987 (figure 7-1). Ultimately, however, the KMT under Chiang Ching-kuo and Lee Teng-hui also strategically decided to liberalize Taiwan's local political system. In doing so, the KMT

Figure 7-1. *The Rise and Decline of Formal Taiwanese Lobbying,
Compared with the PRC, 1972–2011*[a]

Number of lobbyists

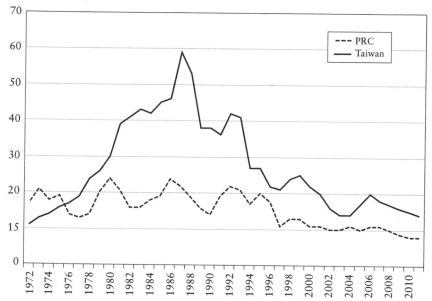

Source: U.S. Department of Justice, FARA Quick Search.

a. Lobbyists who worked for more than one organization, representing either China or Taiwan, are counted as a single unit.

leveraged its precarious backing from lobbyists, helping to further stabilize Washington's support for the beleaguered island.[63] Throughout this period, the formal Taiwanese lobbying contingent was also far more numerous than that for mainland China (see figure 7-1).

Across the 1980s Taiwan thus radically transformed—and strengthened—its political support base in Washington, laying the groundwork for some spectacular political successes in the United States during the 1990s. In place of the direct, explicit White House and Pentagon backing that had been so important in earlier days, Taiwan proactively developed a lower profile yet a much broader base of support, anchored in Congress, think tanks, universities, and statehouses across the country. In many ways its new and remarkably successful efforts prefigured a broader decentralizing trend in Washington policymaking toward Asia, and in fact it accelerated that tendency.

Informal-Formal Representation

One major force in Taiwan's new post-1979 Washington presence was its de facto embassy—initially known as the Coordination Council of North America (CCNA) and later as the Taipei Economic and Cultural Representative Office (TECRO). Despite derecognition, Taiwan, through CCNA/TECRO, continued to maintain an elaborate presence at 4201 Wisconsin Avenue, in Georgetown. Various annexes contained virtually all the functions of a conventional embassy while also servicing twelve regional offices across the United States.[64] Taiwan also retained a palatial residence, Twin Oaks, the largest privately owned estate in Washington. Twin Oaks had been the home of Alexander Graham Bell's father-in-law and the first president of the National Geographic Society, Gardiner Green Hubbard, before serving as the official home of eight Nationalist Chinese ambassadors to the United States between 1937 and 1979.[65]

Since 1979 Taiwan's unofficial representatives have continued to use the twenty-six-room Twin Oaks mansion, located within sight of Washington's stately National Cathedral in one of the capital's best residential districts, for a variety of CCNA/TECRO functions directed toward strengthening Taiwan's sociopolitical network in Washington. On one occasion, outdoor Taiwanese film screenings were held on the south lawn. On another, Ambassador Jason Yuan hosted a dinner in honor of the board of directors and the executive staff of the American Conservative Union. Earlier, Yuan hosted a luncheon in honor of the ambassadors of Taiwan's diplomatic allies to the United States and the Organization of American States.[66]

In October 2011 Jason Yuan moved to broaden his intellectual network by hosting the Harvard Club of Washington at Twin Oaks. Also in October 2011 Twin Oaks was the scene of a special celebration commemorating the centennial anniversary of the Republic of China, attended by three thousand Taiwanese expatriates and fifteen members of the U.S. Congress. This was the first "double-ten" commemoration at Twin Oaks in thirty-two years.[67] On July 18, 2011, Yuan also hosted a Mongolian barbecue for the U.S. Senate Chiefs of Staff Association, which was attended by twenty-one Senate chiefs of staff. In January 2011 Ambassador Yuan hosted a dinner at Twin Oaks in honor of the newly elected chairman of the Republican National Committee, Reince Priebus, and his wife, together with seventy members of the RNC.[68]

Tools for Expanding Influence

Although conventional Taiwanese representational functions at the non–executive branch level have been continuing through TECRO—to a remarkably normal degree, considering the formal derecognition of 1979—the broader structure of Taiwan's activities in the United States changed significantly during the 1980s. There were four major innovations: creation of a grassroots ethnic lobby, deeper ties with state political leaders, deeper ties with Congress, and increased financial support in the intellectual area (universities, think tanks, and individual researchers). These changes, together with the revitalized, quasi-diplomatic operation described above, stabilized and actually enlarged Taiwan's influence in Washington over the decade following derecognition. They led ultimately to such stunning successes, from Taipei's vantage point, as the Lee Teng-hui visit to Cornell in 1995, when Taiwan's president was allowed to pay a full-scale alumni reunion visit to his U.S. alma mater.

Grassroots Ethnic Politics

The Taiwanese population of the United States, as noted above, began to grow significantly during the 1970s—from around 6,000 in 1970 to 200,000 in 1980, and then to 500,000 by 2000, and roughly 600,000 by 2010. Their numbers were thus approaching those of the Japanese American community, one of the five largest in the country. Taiwanese immigrants were concentrated in California, the most populous state in the United States and, fortuitously, in the congressional districts of some increasingly powerful members of Congress, such as Nancy Pelosi and Tom Lantos.[69] There are also prominent Taiwan-born U.S. political figures, such as Elaine Chao, secretary of labor during the George W. Bush Administration (2001–09), who have enhanced Taiwanese American national influence.[70]

Taiwanese have long had an ethnic consciousness in the United States distinct from that of mainland Chinese, due to the traumatic political and psychological effect on Taiwanese people of the bloody February

28, 1947, massacre of local Taiwanese by the KMT. This unique Taiwanese consciousness has been reinforced in the United States by the fact that many Taiwanese Americans are Christian, especially members of the internationally linked Taiwanese Presbyterian Church, which traditionally supported Taiwanese dissidents against the KMT.[71] Thus following derecognition in 1979, it is not surprising that beleaguered Taiwanese Americans should band together both in support of their home island and in opposition to the KMT.

The product of these new grassroots political yearnings among ethnic Taiwanese in the United States was the Formosan Association for Public Affairs (FAPA), which had an anti-KMT, Taiwan-independence, and mildly left-of-center cast at its inception. FAPA was founded in 1982 by Peng Ming-min, a political science professor at the University of Michigan, who had long been a leader of the Taiwan independence movement as founder of World United Formosans for Independence. A victim of the 1945 Nagasaki nuclear bombing, Peng later studied at both Kyoto and Tokyo Universities and was arrested for anti-KMT activity in Taiwan, before escaping from house arrest and fleeing overseas—eventually, in 1970, to the United States.[72]

FAPA, with only around ten paid staffers together with a few unpaid interns, was registered as a nonprofit educational body rather than as a formal lobbying organization.[73] It declared its objectives to be fivefold: promoting international support for the rights of the people of Taiwan to establish an independent and democratic country and join the international community, deepening relations and cooperation between Taiwan and the United States, protecting the right of self-determination for the people of Taiwan, promoting peace and security for Taiwan, and advancing the rights and interests of Taiwanese communities throughout the world.[74]

Many of FAPA's early members were young Taiwanese American professionals who had migrated to the United States as students during the 1960s. They were concentrated in Los Angeles, San Francisco, and New York. They became an important source of political contributions for some members of Congress, notably Stephen Solarz. That passionate human rights advocate fortuitously headed the House of Representatives' Subcommittee on Asia-Pacific Affairs for twelve years (1981–93) and was thus able to give FAPA affiliates a highly visible platform to promote agendas in support of Taiwan.[75] During the 1980s, FAPA lob-bied against repressive KMT human rights policies and increasingly also, as democracy steadily emerged across the 1990s, for broader Tai-wanese security interests.

Liaison with Local, State, and Congressional Politics

With relationships to U.S. national leaders in the executive branch disrupted by de-recognition, Taiwan focused its attention on rising U.S. governors and state-level political leaders, whom it expected to play significant national roles in later years. U.S. presidents in the late 1970s and the 1980s were coming uniformly from the ranks of governors, such as Jimmy Carter and Ronald Reagan. They were a group on which Taiwan resolved to focus due to their inherent future potential influ-ence, and fortuitous distance from the complexities of international diplomacy. One emerging object of Taiwan's far-sighted attention in the 1980s was Governor Bill Clinton of Arkansas. Clinton made four gubernatorial visits to Taiwan—the first less than a year after diplomatic relations with the United States were severed in 1979—and developed a rapport with the Taiwanese that went far beyond the export of soy-beans. On October 10, 1985, the two main guests of honor at Taiwan's National Day parade and rally were Clinton, representing Arkansas, and the well-connected governor of Virginia, Charles Robb.[76]

Deepened Congressional Ties

With executive branch ties disrupted, Taiwan intensified its efforts to deepen relations with Congress, where it already had many allies, as had been manifest in passage of the Taiwan Relations Act. Taipei expanded and intensified its cultivation of congressional members and their staffers in a variety of ways, ranging from receptions and dinners at TECRO's elegant Twin Oaks estate to all-expense-paid study tours to Taiwan. FAPA was also periodically involved. Among the issues recently considered in Taiwan-congressional dialogues are the merits of a U.S.-Taiwan FTA, the implications of the ECFA cross-strait agreement, and the rationale for increased U.S. arms sales to Taiwan.[77]

Taiwan's relations with Capitol Hill were helped greatly by the com-ing of democracy to "Island China" during the mid-1990s, which had been supported strongly by the high-powered Committee for Democracy on Taiwan. Taiwan was also strengthened politically in Congress by the presence of key supporters in positions of real influence: Claiborne Pell, who had spent time in Taiwan during the late 1940s and was chair of the Senate Foreign Relations Committee from 1987 to 1995; Steve Solarz, who was chair of the House of Representatives' Asia and Pacific Affairs Subcommittee from 1981 to 1993; Tom Lantos and Jim Leach, who were both ranking House International Relations Committee members; and Tom DeLay, who was Republican House majority leader from 2003 to 2005, to name just a few.[78] Taiwan developed this powerful congressional network partly due to fate and partly due to far-sighted Taiwanese strategy, which had been cultivating members of Congress with strong future personal prospects for years.

Cultivation of Universities, Think Tanks, and Research

The KMT government of the 1970s generally regarded American intellectuals as antagonists and largely avoided them. After derecognition, and particularly as Taiwanese democratization moved forward during the 1980s, this inclination significantly changed. Taiwan became much more engaged with the U.S. academic world, reducing parochialism on both sides, while measurably improving Taiwan's image in Washington and across America as a whole.

American think tanks, including the Center for Strategic and International Studies, the American Enterprise Institute, the Heritage Foundation, and the Brookings Institution, were expanding rapidly in this period. Taiwan took advantage of their new entrepreneurial spirit and their expanding global interests to establish ties with all of them. With their strong policy networks of high-level former government officials, their inside information on recent policy developments, their informal, nongovernmental status, and their need for soft-money support, the think tanks held a naturally symbiotic relationship with governments in Taiwan's ambiguous diplomatic position. They rapidly became a key part of Taiwan's new political-economic network in Washington.

Universities and individual researchers also were, for different reasons, natural candidates for membership in Taiwan's new Washington support coalition, particularly following democratization. Island China was eager to be favorably understood, to be considered progressive and altruistic, and to play a significant informal role in the U.S. foreign policy agenda-setting process. Relationships with universities and researchers served all those ends. Conversely, researchers were perennially in need of research funds, and newly democratic and increasingly affluent Taiwan was a tempting and ever more legitimate source of potential support.

Particularly attractive new opportunities arose for Taiwan to show-case its democratic transition before U.S. intellectuals following the Tiananmen massacre of June 1989 in mainland China. Numerous mem-bers of the democracy movement, such as Fang Lizhi, Wei Jingsheng, Wang Dan, Wuer Kaixi, and Chai Ling, fled from the Chinese main-land, and many Americans became interested in researching Chinese political development from a critical perspective. Conversely, prominent comparativists like Harvard University's Samuel Huntington became increasingly interested in the sociopolitical context of Taiwan's emerg-ing democracy.[79] Avenues of research that were intellectually appealing and also congenial to Taiwanese political ends were suddenly expanding.

It was at this juncture, in 1989, that the Chiang Ching-kuo Foun-dation for International Scholarly Exchange was established. Funded initially by the Taiwanese Ministry of Education through a one-time $53 million grant, it rapidly became a major funding source worldwide in China studies.[80] The foundation's activities deepened relationships between Taiwan and U.S. intellectuals as well as political leaders across American society.

Conspicuous Successes of the 1990s

The high-water mark of Taiwan's influence in Washington, building on the important structural changes of the 1980s, was almost certainly the 1989–97 period. That era began with the Tiananmen massacre in Bei-jing, just as Taiwan's own democracy was beginning to flourish, sharp-ening the cross-strait contrast in Taiwan's favor within the minds of most Americans. Taiwan's democratic tenor and its respect for human rights no doubt lay in the background of important policy steps in its favor that Washington took in succeeding years. The waning of the cold war, which reduced the geopolitical importance of the "China card," reinforced a growing tendency to treat Beijing lightly, even as respect for Taiwan continued to grow in step with its democratization.

Two striking policy successes for Taiwan in the first half of the 1990s stand out. Both may seem paradoxical in light of Carter's abrupt 1979 derecognition, yet they are thoroughly understandable given the marked improvements over the ensuing decade in Taiwan's Washington standing. First, in the fall of 1992, the Bush administration agreed to sell 150 F-16 A/B combat aircraft (defensive models) to Taiwan, substantially augmenting Taiwanese air defense capabilities in the face of Russian delivery of advanced SU-27 fighters to mainland China.[81] Second, in May 1995 the Clinton White House approved the application of Taiwanese President Lee Teng-hui to visit Ithaca, New York, in order to speak at his alma mater, Cornell University, overruling recommendations against the visit by the State Department.[82] The controversial visit went ahead, even in the face of furious opposition from mainland China, leading ultimately to the Taiwan Strait missile crisis of early 1996.

Taiwan adopted somewhat different lobbying strategies in the 1992 and 1995 cases, although both were stunningly successful. In 1992 Taiwan's campaign concentrated on the Pentagon, with only a few members of Congress getting involved—late in the process and due to economic concerns. In July 1992 General Dynamics indicated that it would fire 5,800 workers from its Fort Worth factory that produced the F-16s. Subsequently, the Texas congressional delegation, including Senator Lloyd Bentsen, who had run for vice president on the Democratic ticket in 1988, started pressuring President George H. W. Bush to sell the jets to the Taiwanese.[83] There was thus high-level, bipartisan support for the F-16 sale to Taiwan, in the midst of a presidential campaign, making it particularly easy to justify.

In 1995 Taiwan concentrated mainly on Congress and state legislatures, although it preceded its explicit lobbying on the Lee visit with broad-based spadework, cultivating newspaper editorial boards, Democratic campaign contributors, and several governors.[84] FAPA mobilized thirty state legislatures to pass support resolutions on the Lee visit issue, so as to pressure Capitol Hill.[85] Then the 104th Congress near-unanimously passed Congressional Resolution 53, supporting the Lee visit, by a vote of 396-0 in the House and 97-1 in the Senate. House Speaker Newt Gingrich, then at the height of his political powers, also strongly endorsed the idea.[86] Confronted with these multiple pressures, and lacking clear signals of resistance from the Clinton White House, the State Department had little choice but to recant its earlier promise to China and allow Lee to visit Ithaca.

Figure 7-2. *U.S. Exports to Taiwan and the People's Republic of China, 1985–2011*[a]

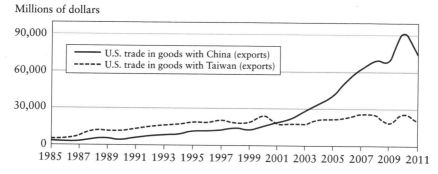

Millions of dollars

Source: U.S. Census Bureau, "Trade in Goods with China" (www.census.gov/foreign-trade/balance/c5700.html).

a. Figures are for combined exports and imports, based on U.S. trade data.

How Taiwan's Influence Has Recently Waned, and Why

Lee's historic visit to Cornell was arguably the high-water mark of Taiwanese post-derecognition influence in Washington. In 1997 the House did pass a supportive missile defense bill, the U.S.-Taiwan ABM Defense Cooperation Act.[87] And in 1999 Taiwan did get permission to buy over-the-horizon early-warning radar systems with sophisticated missile detection capabilities from the United States.[88] Yet legislative defeats, such as congressional failure to pass Senator Jesse Helms's 1999 Taiwan Security Enhancement Act (TSEA), became increasingly common. The U.S. business community, which had played little role in the 1995 Lee case, was becoming nervous at the prospect of offending China, as the PRC's expanding economy grew more important for U.S. firms, especially with China's pending entry into the World Trade Organization. The Helms TSEA legislation was ultimately pigeonholed; it died on the Senate legislative calendar, without being called up for a vote, at the end of the 1999–2000 congressional session.[89]

Despite its relatively small population—less than 1/75 that of mainland China—Taiwan for many years had loomed remarkably large, relative to the PRC, as a U.S. trading partner. Until 2001 Taiwan was actually a larger U.S. export market than mainland China (figure 7-2). This situation was beginning to change during 1999–2000, however.

After the PRC joined the World Trade Organization in 2001, the relative economic importance of Taiwan and mainland China to the United States began to shift rapidly, giving American business deepening stakes in conciliating the much larger and more rapidly growing trading partner on the far side of the Taiwan Strait.

Equally damaging to Taiwan's Washington influence, in political terms, were deepening divisions within Taiwanese ranks. These ironically reflected democratization and the declining resultant legitimacy of TECRO, caught between competing partisan interests, in its role as representative of Taiwan as a whole. In 1994, for example, Lee's KMT government set up a new organization in Washington, the Taiwan Research Institute.[90] The institute signed a three-year, $4.5 million, contract with Cassidy and Associates, Taiwan's principal lobbyist.[91] A year later, in early 1995, the opposition Democratic Progressive Party (DPP) opened an office of its own in the National Press Building.[92] In 2004 the KMT/PFP (People-First Party) opposition coalition also set up a representative office in Washington.[93]

The fragmentation of Taiwan's representation in Washington, in short, has intensified, reflecting the increasing pluralism and diversity of opinion within Taiwan itself. Groups with independent representation in Washington—apart from TECRO, the formal governmental representative—now include the Taiwanese Chamber of Commerce of North America, World United Formosans for Independence, the Formosan Association for Political Activity, and both of Taiwan's major political parties—the KMT and the DPP. There is no unified Taiwan lobby outside the Taiwanese government, and TECRO's own position is often weakened by divisions within the Taiwanese political environment as well as a proliferation of messengers from Taipei. These conflicting inputs make it difficult for Taiwan as a whole to communicate a unified message. As Taiwan's political-economic challenges in asserting a distinct identity in Northeast Asia continue to deepen, its problems of coherent representation in Washington do so as well.

Summary

Taiwan in Washington presents a distinct empirical paradox. Taiwan itself is a small political entity in terms of geography, population, and even economic scale, that is not recognized by the United States—or any other major world power—as a nation. Yet for many years it continued to prosper, maintain visibility, and retain significant influence in Washington even after derecognition and despite its small size and distinct political vulnerabilities. Its apparent success presented a clear challenge to realist theory.

The preceding pages outline this paradox and try to explain what influence in Washington Taiwan has been able to retain since derecognition—and how it has done so. Taiwan started with some embedded advantages—chiefly the historical respect it was accorded during World War II and the cold war as "free China" and the established ties with religious groups, news media, and members of Congress that it built up over more than half a century of common struggle, from the 1930s into the 1990s. Taiwan's authorities also had, in their elegant Twin Oaks ambassadorial residence in Cleveland Park, one of the finest entertainment locations anywhere in Washington—an excellent place for building networks.

Despite these structural advantages in the nation's capital, Taiwan lost its favored formal role as a cold war protégé of the United States when the Carter administration recognized mainland China—and simultaneously derecognized Taiwan—in 1979. In deconstructing the crisis of derecognition, however, another paradox emerged: that Taiwan actually grew more influential over the 1980s and early 1990s—as an ambiguous, unrecognized nonstate—than it had been as a recognized nation. Washington's 1992 decision to sell 150 F-16s to Taiwan and its decision only three years later to allow Taiwanese President Lee Teng-hui to lecture at Cornell in the face of fierce Chinese objections show the formidable influence that Taiwan retained more than two decades after the United States recognized Beijing.

Despite its formidable informal standing of the 1980s and early 1990s, especially on Capitol Hill, Taiwan has not been able to sustain its influence in Washington at the levels of the 1990s. Mainland China's economic power and political influence, to which U.S. business is particularly sensitive, is a contributing factor in Taiwan's decline. But it is by no means the most important one. More damaging is the fragmentation of the Taiwan lobby, a fragmentation that ironically flows from the deepening democratic pluralism within Taiwan itself. As Taiwanese politics grows more contentious at home, and as homeland conflicts are transposed to Washington almost instantaneously through the power of twenty-first-century communications, differences are exacerbated by the establishment of conflicting party representation in Washington. Taiwanese appeals to the United States become fragmented, and the activists making them grow increasingly mistrustful of one another. The challenge of offsetting small size and lack of formal diplomatic representation through superior tactics is growing more difficult for Taipei, even as its geopolitical need for influence in Washington is deepening. How Taiwan can address the multiple obstacles that it faces in Washington politics is increasingly unclear, its formidable and venerable association with the local "penumbra of power" notwithstanding.

Japan

Japan is the most economically and technologically advanced nation in Asia, the third-largest economy in the world, and a long-standing ally of the United States. It is also America's second-largest overseas trading partner, the second-largest supplier of direct foreign investment to the United States, and the second-largest holder in the world of U.S. Treasury securities. Tokyo's stakes in a stable U.S.-Japan relationship, and in American policies supportive of Tokyo's economic interests worldwide, are enormous. Yet over much of the past two decades, both the Japanese government and the country's private sector had a remarkably low profile in Washington, even as their competition has grown more active.

Japan in Washington

Japan's relative inactivity in Washington is clear from a comparative perspective, as the data presented earlier in this chapter suggest. Japan has long lacked a congressional caucus, although the Chinese, Koreans, Taiwanese, Indians, and even Indonesians established parallel organizations years ago. Japan has no dedicated website in Washington, and there is no formal U.S.-Japan study group established by present congressional members, in contrast to China, India, and even Taiwan.[94] Neither the Japan Foundation nor the Japanese Federation of Economic Organizations (Keidanren) have auxiliary offices in Washington, unlike their Korean counterparts. Nor do any of the Japanese political parties have offices in Washington, in contrast to the Germans, and even the Taiwanese.

Comparative Benchmarks

Top-level Japanese officials based in Washington, to be sure, have been personally active in local community affairs in recent years, as have local representatives of individual Japanese corporations. Yet the home offices of Japanese institutions have responded rather slowly to the rising activism in Washington of nearby Asian nations, with absolute levels of formal Japanese involvement in Washington actually declining along many dimensions. That trend has persisted for at least two decades and helps account for the growing gap between Japanese involvement in Washington sociopolitical life and that of many other Asian nations.

Cross-National: Japan versus Korea

The contrasts with nearby Korea, in particular, are striking, with Koreans playing an increasingly proactive role in Washington sociopolitical life even as Japan's role is receding. The Japan Foundation, for example, closed its Washington office in 1996, while the Korea Foundation opened an analogous facility in 2008. Nomura Research Institute closed in 1997, while Samsung Research Institute opened in 2008. The Japan Economic Institute closed in March 2001 just as the Korea Economic Institute, with similar functions and a similar diplomatic affiliation, began markedly expanding its functions in 2001. And the Keizai Kōhō Center, public relations arm of Keidanren, closed in March 2009.

Subnational: Washington versus New York City

The decline in Japanese Washington involvement is also striking in comparison with trends of Japanese activity in New York City. For more than a century, New York, after all, has been the central base for Japanese economic and cultural activities in the United States. Japan, in contrast to divided countries like Korea and China, is emphatically New York-centric rather than Washington-centric. This orientation is epitomized by the fact that Washington is a sister city to Beijing and Seoul but not to Tokyo—despite the long tradition in Washington of the Cherry Blossom Festival. Tokyo's sister city in the United States has always been, and continues to be, New York.[95]

The Japan External Trade Organization, similarly, has its U.S. head-quarters in New York, as does the U.S.-Japan Foundation. The Japan Society, also based in New York, is by far the largest Japan-related NGO in the United States, with a membership of around 1,400, or roughly six times the membership of the Japan America Society of Washington. The New York–based Japan Society, with stronger corporate support, is also growing more vigorously than its Washington counterpart. And several of the Japan-related organizations that moved out of Washington over the past two decades and that did not withdraw to Tokyo, such as the Japan Foundation's U.S. headquarters, have moved, not surprisingly, to New York City.

Embedded history has much to do with the relative weakness of Washington in representing Japan within the United States.[96] Since at least 1907, when the Japan Society was founded there, New York City has been the traditional center of Japanese activities in the United States.[97] The society's early leaders include financier Jacob Schiff of Kuhn Loeb, who played a key role in arranging war loans for Japan during the Russo-Japanese conflict; Henry W. Taft, a brother of President William Howard Taft; and Arai Rioichirō, president of the Nippon Club.[98]

The Japan Society gained even greater influence, from the early 1950s on, when John D. Rockefeller III served as its president (1951–78) and John Foster Dulles (1951–53) as its chair, following his central role in organizing the San Francisco Peace Treaty conference.[99] During Dulles's subsequent tenure as secretary of state (1953–59), the Japan Society became the standard forum for policy pronouncements on Japan by both Japanese and American leaders, despite its distance from the nation's capital.

New York also gained importance in U.S.-Japan relations as the base of the influential early post–World War II American Council on Japan (ACJ), with which Japanese business groups had strong ties. The ACJ, like the Japan Society, also drew strength and credibility from relations with the national media, especially from the strong support of *Newsweek* magazine, based in New York. The ACJ undertook, from its New York base, important occupation-era lobbying, managing to blunt MacArthur's reforms and thus to preserve the core of the prewar

Zaibatsu during the turbulent, uncertain early days of the U.S. occupation of Japan.[100]

Historical: The Origins of Japan in Washington

There was a fleeting period during which Washington did loom particularly large in the context of Japan's overall presence in the United States, and also relative to other major Asian nations in the nation's capital. That period was over 140 years ago—both Japan and the United States, as well as their bilateral relationship, have changed profoundly since. Yet the contrasts to the present situation yield some clues as to the underlying sociopolitical dynamics of contemporary Japan in Washington.

The first emissaries of the Japanese government arrived in Washington during 1860, led by Shinmi Buzen-no-kami, to ratify the initial U.S.-Japan Treaty of Friendship.[101] A permanent mission was formally established in 1870, with Japan's first resident envoy arriving at Washington in late February 1871, after an extended transcontinental journey of close to two weeks from San Francisco. That first representative was a twenty-three-year-old samurai from Kagoshima, with three years of study in Britain and the United States: Mori Arinori. He soon established himself and his mission at the corner of 24th and M Streets, in a building that served both as a chancery and as a residence for himself and his two Japanese secretaries.[102] Mori was also assisted by an American staff—secretary, butler, cook, chambermaid, and gardener. Consulates were maintained in New York and San Francisco under the honorary consulship of American citizens.

Japan's representation in the United States, in short, was small, its staff was young, and it had numerous start-up challenges.[103] It was not upgraded to formal embassy status until 1906. Yet the legation bore heavy responsibilities, not least hosting the Iwakura Mission of top Japanese leaders and arranging its appointments only a year after Mori's arrival. The small outpost nevertheless did a remarkable job of establishing itself and engaging with politicians, scholars, military leaders, and diplomats across the United States at a critical point in Japan's own national development.

The core of Mori's personal accomplishments as minister was his successful hosting of the Iwakura Mission, for which he served as chief interpreter. The mission included Ōkubo Toshimichi and Itō

Hirobumi—both future prime ministers—and sixty students, many of whom would become intellectual and political leaders.[104] Mori arranged a highly successful White House reception, numerous substantive meetings, and a historic final dinner in Boston, which included Henry Longfellow, Ralph Waldo Emerson, and Oliver Wendell Holmes.

Apart from his work on the Iwakura Mission, Mori recorded several signal accomplishments during his short two-year tenure (1871–73): the first postal convention between Japan and the United States; abolition of discriminatory tonnage fees on Japanese ships; admission of Japanese cadets to the U.S. Naval Academy at Annapolis (although not to West Point); and establishment of a cultural dialogue with the Smithsonian Institution, involving exchange of natural history and ethnology-related specimens.[105] During his tenure Mori also published three English-language books.[106]

Mori was a pronounced activist in his dealings with American society, immersing himself in the life of the capital. He developed a close personal relationship with Secretary of State Hamilton Fish, a sixty-three-year-old lawyer turned statesman, who seems to have had an avuncular affection for the young Mori.[107] Mori personally briefed the Foreign Affairs and Appropriations Committees of both Houses of Congress regarding the Meiji Restoration, helped American orientalists to import Japanese books, sponsored translations of Japanese poetry, and wrote frequent op-ed pieces for the *Washington Evening Star,* while also giving numerous public addresses.[108] In his dealings with Tokyo, Mori was an inveterate internationalist. He insistently presented candid views of developments in the United States in dispatches typically written in English. He also encouraged the use of English within the Japanese mission.

Over time, the vigorous precedents that Mori established—active engagement with Washington society, far beyond the diplomatic world; concrete steps to deepen bilateral cultural, military, and economic exchange; and determined efforts to deepen understanding of the United States back in Japan—were compromised by more parochial instincts within Japanese society. The mission became more ingrown, even as it expanded in scale, moved to the prestigious Embassy Row, and gained embassy status, from 1906.[109] New parochial forces—preeminently, the military—began intruding into the diplomatic process, as the embassy grew. Transpacific relations inevitably deteriorated, thus complicating bilateral diplomatic communication, isolating the Japanese embassy itself, and leading down the tragic road to Pearl Harbor.[110]

Although the Japanese mission in Washington, following the dynamic Mori years, failed to maintain its intense pace of interaction with American society, it did serve as a training ground for some key Japanese leaders of the future. One such figure was Yamamoto Isoroku, a young military attaché and former Harvard special student, charged with analyzing the energy production capacity of the United States. Yamamoto two decades later was to serve as commander of the Combined Fleet *(rengo kantai)*, charged with the December 1941 surprise attack on Pearl Harbor.[111]

The first two decades of the twentieth century were the high point of U.S.-Japan relations between the Mori years and the end of World War II. Although the locus of interaction was primarily New York City, the one symbolic highlight in the nation's capital was the arc of cherry trees surrounding the Tidal Basin in Washington, and blooming every spring. Donated by the Tokyo mayor, Ōzaki Yukio, and the Nippon Club president, Takamine Jōkichi, to fulfill a plan conceived by First Lady Helen Taft, the first trees were planted on March 27, 1912, inspiring a Cherry Blossom Festival that has continued for a full century and more.[112]

Formal representation of Japanese interests in the nation's capital did revive somewhat following the end of the American occupation of Japan in April 1952, when the Japanese embassy was reopened at its prewar Massachusetts Avenue location. In April 1957 the U.S.-Japan Trade Council, funded by the Japanese Foreign Ministry to supply research on Japan's economy and on legislation affecting U.S.-Japan relations, was founded in Washington.[113] In the same year, the Japan America Society of Washington, a private initiative between State Department officials and friends at the Japanese embassy, was also founded, to give a "human face" to U.S.-Japan relations that complemented the official relationship between the two countries.[114] Despite the personal enthusiasm of its members, however, the JASW lacked the powerful financial base and historical tradition that its influential counterpart in New York, presided over by John D. Rockefeller III, and supported by the U.S. corporate headquarters of numerous powerful American and Japanese firms, so clearly enjoyed.[115]

Deepening U.S.-Japan trade frictions, between the early 1970s and the mid-1990s, did finally spur the Japanese government and Japanese businesses to pay more attention to Washington. The number of registered foreign agents employed by Japan, mainly in Washington, rose sharply—from none in 1950, to 28 in 1960, 82 in 1970, 159 in 1980, and 295 in 1990—more than five times the number employed by any other Asian country.[116] Japanese corporations were supportive of academic and think tank initiatives in Washington, including the Japan Chair at the Center for Strategic and International Studies, established in 1981, and the Reischauer Center for East Asian Studies at SAIS/Johns Hopkins University, established in 1984.[117] In 1987 the Japan America Society initiated its annual public affairs dinner to deepen interaction between prominent Washingtonians and the Japan America community.[118] In 1988 the Japanese Commerce Association of Washington, composed of local Japanese corporate representatives, was founded.[119] These efforts were leveraged from Tokyo by the establishment, also in 1988, of the Council for Better Investment in the United States, led by SONY's long-time chair, Akio Morita.[120]

Anatomy of Transformation

From its high point around 1990, Japanese involvement with and visibility in Washington has been declining in terms of several other statistical indicators, in addition to the Washington presence of major Japanese institutions, as discussed above. The number of registered foreign agents hired by the Japanese government and Japanese firms, for example, peaked at 275 in 1990. By 2010 it had fallen to 35.[121] As recently as 2005–06 there were 598 hearings in the U.S. Congress (Senate and House combined) that mentioned Japan; by 2009–10 that number had fallen to 133.[122] During the decade of the 1980s more than 52,000 *New York Times* articles mentioned Japan; two decades later (between 2000 and 2010) that number had fallen by more than half, to just over 25,000.[123]

Japan's involvement with Washington has declined in at least four other respects over the past two decades, with a particular acceleration of this downturn since around 2000:

—*Congressional exchanges.* In the late 1990s an average of fifty congressional members, and at times as many as ninety staffers, would annually visit Japan, on either publicly or privately sponsored travel.[124] Between 2007 and 2009, however, only an average of fourteen congressional members—less than one third as many—visited. In 2011 the visit of six members, including Senator Jim Webb, to Japan to attend the New Shimoda Conference was one of the largest in recent years,[125] although several key members, including Senate Foreign Relations Committee chair Robert Menendez, did visit in August 2013, just before Caroline Kennedy's ambassadorial confirmation hearings.[126] Visits by congressional staffers declined even more precipitously, with the 2009 figure less than a quarter that of 1997 and roughly a quarter of those visiting China.[127] The number of Diet members visiting Washington has also been declining, although not as sharply as that of U.S. congressional members to Japan.[128]

—*Think tank activities.* The role of think tanks in Washington's policy agenda setting has risen substantially since the 1980s, as we have seen, with think tank budgets also rising sharply.[129] Yet the number of think tanks with major U.S.-Japan activities conversely fell for many recent years, from twenty in 1998 to only ten in 2009, although it has since rebounded slightly.[130] In September 2012, for example, Brookings established the Philip Knight chair in Japan Studies: Mireya Solís is the first to hold this position.[131]

—*Washington-based Japan specialists.* Paralleling the decline in Japan-related think tank activity in Washington, the supply of Japan specialists in Washington has also stagnated, with numbers being surpassed by specialists on other Northeast Asian nations. In 2009, for example, there were only four Japan specialists at Washington think tanks, compared to seven Korea specialists and forty-two who focused on China. And only one of those Japan specialists was of Japanese origin.[132] There were only three senior Japanese politics specialists at major area universities, although several able adjunct professors were also active.

—*Japanese students and researchers.* The number of Japanese students in the United States generally has been steadily falling for a decade, and this trend is clearly observable in Washington. At SAIS/Johns Hopkins University, where Japanese students a decade ago were the largest foreign contingent, only one new Japanese master's degree candidate matriculated in 2013. Although a U.S.-Japan Research Institute (USJI) program, initially involving five of Japan's preeminent universities, did interject additional vitality from 2009, as has the Woodrow Wilson Center for Scholars, the USJI has not yet reversed the long-term decline in the number of Japanese scholars resident in D.C.[133]

Institutional Profiles

To understand comparative national patterns and the long-term implications of historical trends regarding Japanese involvement in Washington, it is important to understand the institutional base of that involvement and the activities that emerged from that structure. There are three physical venues of formal government activity: the embassy chancery, constructed in 1931; the ambassador's residence, completed in 1977; and the Japan Information and Culture Center (JICC), which moved to its current location at 18th and M Streets, NW, in 2012.[134] There are also several Japanese community organizations and Japan-related NGOs with their own private venues, such as the Japan Commerce Association of Washington and the Japan America Society of Washington, although they are not nearly as large or as active as their New York counterparts. According to Japanese consular data, there are fewer than a thousand Japanese registered residents in the Washington area, compared to almost 55,000 in New York.[135]

The Japanese embassy itself is one of Japan's largest anywhere in the world, with over 200 employees—well over ten times its scale in Mori Arinori's day. It is divided into eleven sections, including a powerful political section, which deals intimately with the State Department, the Pentagon, the White House, and various intelligence agencies.[136] The embassy also features an influential trade and economic policy contingent, which deals actively with the office of the U.S. Trade Representative, the U.S. Department of Commerce, and the U.S. Department of State. It is divided institutionally with staff from Japan's Ministry of Foreign Affairs (MOFA); Ministry of Economy, Trade, and Industry (METI); Environment Ministry; Agriculture, Fisheries, and Forestry Ministry; and other agencies. Finance is likewise influential but is relatively self-contained. The embassy also engages in congressional research and liaison—but less extensively than a decade or two ago.

Japan's broader government representation in the United States, like that within the embassy itself, is of course much more elaborate than in Mori Arinori's day. The number of consulates general in the United States has expanded from two to sixteen.[137] In addition, both MOF and METI have largely autonomous representation in the United States, through the Japan Center for International Finance and the JETRO New York office, respectively.

In its U.S. public diplomacy, through both the embassy and JICC, the Japanese government targets essentially two audiences: one, an advocacy community consisting of political groups, individual politicians, think tank and media analysts, and academics; and two, the general American population, including Japanese residents in the United States. The Foreign Ministry assigns distinct roles to its Washington embassy and to JICC, with each allocated an audience and each promoting Japanese interests through different means. JICC concentrates on introducing Japanese culture to the general American public as well as to subgroups with special cultural interests. Meanwhile the Japanese embassy concentrates on enhancing the U.S.-Japan relationship among Americans with more specific policy interests, expertise, and involvement. JICC maintains its credibility as an independent cultural institution through physical separation, while coordinating closely with the embassy through the embassy's press and information section.

Of the fifty-three JICCs worldwide, four are in the United States—in Washington, New York, Chicago, and Los Angeles. The Washington office is relatively small—three diplomats and five local staff—but quite active for its size, and leveraged by its 130-seat auditorium, where it holds biweekly Japanese film screenings, a weekly anime program, and a broad range of lectures. It publishes the *Japan Now* newsletter, distributed to 6,000 people, which focuses on three types of activities: art and cultural exchange, intellectual exchange, and grassroots exchange.

One of JICC's key priorities is to reach out to the black community in Washington, especially its young people, and thus build a positive view of Japan to offset negative images periodically created by the offhand statements of Japanese politicians. JICC has developed a special relationship with Howard University, and in 2008 it brought the Tateshina High School Jazz Band from Japan to perform with the Howard

University Jazz Ensemble at the Kennedy Center.[138] JICC also actively participates in the D.C. school board's Embassy Adoption program.

In 2009, for example, JICC adopted a class of forty-two in a Southeast Washington school, with JICC personnel visiting the school ten times to introduce them to premodern Japanese history and to hold workshops on *sumie* and *obon*.[139] Numerous visitors, including judo heavyweight gold medalist Yamashita Yasuhiro, were also dispatched to the adopted school. In 2007 Abe Akie, wife of the then prime minister, watched the school's class presentation on Japan when the couple visited the United States.[140] Following up on these precedents, Ambassador and Mrs. Fujisaki Ichirō visited adopted schools multiple times, with students at Thomson Elementary School, for example, learning about traditional Japanese court music (*gagaku*) in February 2012 from Japanese specialists, with the ambassadorial couple in attendance.[141]

In recent years anime has been a central element in what many see as an increasingly prominent form of Japanese global soft power—and a way to transcend cultural barriers.[142] Originally approached by the D.C. Anime Club, a small local NGO consisting mainly of African Americans, JICC offered a venue for special monthly showings of anime films. It has also been providing technical assistance to the Anime Club in developing that group's own presentations on anime. Such activities appear to be having substantial local resonance, especially with African Americans, because the greater Washington area is one of the major centers of anime activity in the United States. Indeed, the biggest Otakon conference in the nation has been held annually in Baltimore's Inner Harbor since 2005, and another large Katsukon conference has been held in the Washington area since 1998.[143]

Transpacific Challenge

In Mori Arinori's day, as noted earlier in this chapter, the Japanese embassy was small and its staff inexperienced, but it has played a remarkably dynamic role in Washington—and in U.S.-Japan relations more generally. Both the embassy's staff and Japan's representation in the United States are much larger now. Yet bilateral relations have grown much more complex and more difficult to manage. Operational pressures on the embassy to network closely with Tokyo-based politicians and officials have also risen, especially during periods of protracted political fluidity in Tokyo, such as prevailed for most of the past decade. The difficult challenge has been for working-level officials to respond both to their Tokyo and Washington constituencies at the same time.[144]

Agawa Naoyuki, a Keio University professor who served as minister for public affairs at the Japanese embassy from 2002 to 2005, notes that the embassy, particularly the political section, gathers large amounts of information regarding Washington and the United States as a whole, which could provide it with a think-tank function in relation to the broader Japanese society. Yet he contends that this information is closely held, and insufficiently shared, despite its broader prospective utility.[145] Governmental cultural affairs programs, he asserts, focus heavily on relatively exotic and expensive activities, such as Kabuki and Noh drama.[146] To the extent that they concentrate on Americans, informational activities also allegedly tend to focus on what some see as exotic concerns, such as anime and manga. Meanwhile, budgets for more prosaic yet mainstream educational outreach activities, such as Japanese-language education; the Japan Bowl competition for American high school students; and Japanese-language advanced placement programs for U.S. high schools, have encountered difficulty in being funded.[147] So have the JET program, supporting foreign English teachers in Japanese schools, and publications such as *Japan Echo,* an English-language periodical providing translations of major Japanese policy-related journal articles, which enjoyed substantial following in the U.S. academic and media communities until it was cancelled due to budget-cutting pressures from the *shiwake* (budget-downsizing examiners) in 2010.[148]

Communication problems go beyond inadequate budgets and parochialism in Tokyo regarding financial priorities with respect to U.S.-Japan cultural communications. Tokyo all too often appears to misread political trends in the United States, and the embassy finds it difficult to adjust to American realities. In the very recent past, the embassy also appears to have been slower than several European nations, and than Korea, in embracing the potential of social media, such as Twitter and Facebook, for burnishing Japan's public image in Washington, although the JICC has to some extent filled the gap in Japanese official visibility in this respect.

A vivid illustration of the embassy's difficulties in reconciling volatile, delicate Washington realities with parochial pressures from Tokyo was the painful "comfort women" controversy of 2007. In that instance, the embassy spent substantial political capital trying to head off a congressional resolution of censure against comments in Tokyo that offended both major human rights and Asian American constituencies in the U.S. Congress and the Democratic Party. Yet the struggle ended with a motion of censure, opposed by the embassy, passing the U.S. House of Representatives, albeit only on a pro forma voice vote.

The embassy does appear to place very high priority on hosting prominent visitors from Japan, who have become much more numerous over the past two or three decades, as transpacific travel has become more commonplace. In the case of Japanese government ministers, the ambassador typically meets visitors at Dulles airport and briefs them on current developments in the United States, while also organizing receptions and other official meals.[149] The deputy chief of mission, and sometimes lower-ranking officials, are also heavily involved in such travel-related activity. The hospitality naturally deepens relations between the embassy and Tokyo, but it also focuses embassy concerns away from Washington and back toward Tokyo.

Noncareer staff help balance the focus of embassy activities between Washington and Tokyo, enhance outreach within Washington, and relieve career officials of a preoccupation with travel-related appointments. Agawa Naoyuki's 2002–05 appointment as minister for public affairs, for example, had this effect. During his tenure, Agawa testified before Congress, initiated policy-oriented seminars at JICC, lectured broadly across the United States, and published articles for a Japanese weekly magazine while resident in D.C.[150] His noncareer appointment was not continued when he returned to Japan in 2005, although Agawa was succeeded by other able career officials.

If the foregoing critiques are correct, they raise an important question: Why does the Japanese embassy exhibit such a strong Tokyo-oriented bias, paradoxically passive in relation to much of Washington, despite the rising complexity of U.S.-Japan relations, the pressures of globalization, and the increasing activism of many other Asian nations in Washington? The paradox is deepened by the sharp contrasts to the embassy's early history. Even though the embassy is much larger and more seasoned now, it seems to be less interactive with Washington in sociopolitical terms than was once true.

Understanding the recent relative isolation and passivity of the Japanese embassy is, of course, difficult from the outside, but several factors appear to be at work. Lack of resources and rapid rotation of embassy staff, including, in many cases, ambassadors, are two reasons often suggested by Japanese observers.[151] No doubt the heavy stream of visitors itself takes a toll and makes a sharply focused Washington orientation difficult. Japan has had generally excellent ambassadors to the United States, but an additional factor may be the selection process for ambassadors itself, which has intensified a strong Tokyo orientation.

Professionally, most Japanese ambassadors to Washington in recent years have been former vice ministers of foreign affairs—career officials who have spent their entire careers in the Foreign Ministry.[152] Personally, most have also grown up in diplomatic families that have often for generations been key members of Japan's ruling elite.[153] It is also common for Japanese ambassadors to Washington to be married to the daughters of former diplomats or other bureaucrats.[154] As individuals, these ambassadors are typically gifted and unusually sensitive in human relations, but they naturally have personal networks that are powerfully oriented to official Tokyo. And they serve at the center of a large, complex bureaucratic organization that has strong Tokyo ties of its own, in a society that greatly values established human relations in cultural terms, and exerts great effort in maintaining them.

The Broader Japanese Washington Community

Apart from the Japanese embassy and the JICC, the JASW has traditionally been the most active institution in Washington that is devoted explicitly to promoting understanding of Japan. Its annual Public Affairs Dinner is a major local social event, normally featuring a high-profile political or diplomatic speaker. Past speakers have included Senator John D. Rockefeller IV (1987), Representative Dick Gephardt (1989), House of Representatives Speaker and ambassador to Japan Thomas Foley (1990, 1997, and 2001), chair of the Federal Reserve Board Paul Volcker (1992), Vice President Walter Mondale (who also served as ambassador to Japan in 2007), and Kurt Campbell, assistant secretary of state for East Asian and Pacific Affairs (2012).[155] The JASW also sponsors the annual Japan Bowl, a College Bowl–type quiz program on Japan for high school students; teaches the Japanese language to adults (which the JICC is forbidden from doing); and coordinates a variety of other cultural events. Most conspicuously, it supports the renowned Cherry Blossom Festival and organizes its popular street festival.

The Japanese Commerce Association of Washington, D.C. (JCAW), founded in 1988 and led by Washington representatives of major Japanese firms, is growing increasingly active, both in community welfare activities and also as an educational body promoting deeper understanding of American society and global issues on the part of its members.[156] It supports Japanese-language programs in the Fairfax County Schools, at the Washington Japanese Language School, and at Georgetown University, while also organizing the annual traditional Japanese New Year celebration at the Washington Plaza Hotel.[157] JCAW also helps fund the National Japan Bowl, together with the JASW, and plays a key role in supporting the annual Cherry Blossom Festival.[158] During 2011–12 it sponsored a creative, future-oriented review of U.S.-Japan relations, led by young American scholars and professionals; this was unveiled in the spring of 2012 on the centennial of Tokyo Mayor Ōzaki's historic cherry tree gift.

The JCAW has also been playing an increasingly important community role in Washington. It has been giving aid beyond the Japanese American community to the hearing impaired, as well as financial and educational assistance to low-income families and to infants with incurable diseases. Following 9/11, JCAW naturally encouraged member donations to the Pentagon Memorial fund.[159]

The Sasakawa Peace Foundation USA (SPF-USA), established in 1990, has also recently grown active in Washington. Headed by Japanese executives, it has also involved Daniel Bob, a former senior legislative aide in both the Senate and the House of Representatives, with two decades of experience on Capitol Hill. The new program has cosponsored seminars with a wide variety of D.C. think tanks and universities, on subjects ranging from security issues to the Trans-Pacific Partnership (TPP).[160] In June 2013 SPF-USA also created a U.S.-Japan Commission on the Future of the Alliance to generate recommendations for cooperative responses to twenty-first-century problems.

For many years the Japanese community in Washington—both official and corporate—had a surprisingly distant relationship to Japanese Americans across the United States. The painful history of U.S.-Japan relations as a whole over the wartime years contributed to this complexity, as we saw in chapter 5. During the past decade, however, the two sides have come measurably closer, with the Japanese embassy and business community becoming markedly more supportive, even as Japanese Americans have begun to embrace their ancestral homeland in new ways. The JCAW began contributing actively to local Japanese American activities through the Japanese American Care Fund, founded in October 1999 to provide everyday assistance, optionally in Japanese, to those in need, especially the elderly.[161]

The mutual rapprochement began to gain momentum in 2000, when the Japanese embassy, in collaboration with the CGP, inaugurated an annual Visit Japan program for Japanese Americans, whereby MOFA and the CGP periodically invite groups of ten to fifteen Japanese American leaders to Tokyo, to meet with prominent Diet, Foreign Ministry, U.S. embassy, and business leaders.[162] In 2005, after speaking at Nippon Keidanren, the group, for example, met with Prime Minister Koizumi Junichirō. In 2010 delegation members met with Foreign Minister Okada Katsuya, U.S. Ambassador John Roos, and leaders from Nippon Keidanren, Kankeiren, Keizai Dōyukai, and Forum 21.[163] In 2012 the delegation visited Sendai to show support for the region devastated by the Great East Japan Earthquake and met Prime Minister Noda Yoshihiko, Foreign Minister Gemba Kōichirō, and other Japanese leaders.[164] In 2013 the Japanese American Leadership Delegation visited Fukushima Prefecture and Tokyo, meeting Prime Minister Abe Shinzō, Foreign Minister Kishida Fumio, and holding a major symposium.[165]

In 2003 Japan's Ministry of Foreign Affairs also began working to help deepen ties among Japan-related groups within the United States. In that year it began to help organize annual conferences among Japanese American leaders, Japanese executives in the United States, and Japanese consuls general from across the nation. Since early 2009, when the U.S.-Japan Council (USJC)—a group of Japanese American leaders devoted to maintaining effective working relations among American, Japanese, and Nikkei communities—was founded, relations between the embassy and the Japanese American community have grown even closer.[166] In November 2009, for example, Ambassador Fujisaki Ichirō held a major, and unprecedented, networking reception at his residence in honor of a range of Japanese American groups, including both USJC and the Japanese American Citizens' League (JACL).[167] In September 2010 the USJC took further initiative in nationwide networking activities, inaugurating an annual conference series on the future of U.S.-Japan relations, with Vice President Joe Biden as the keynote speaker.[168] Subsequent keynotes included, in 2012, Acting U.S. Secretary of Commerce Rebecca Blank and, in 2013, Yamanaka Shinya, the Nobel Prize Laureate in Medicine.[169]

Like other Asian government organizations, the Japanese Ministry of Foreign Affairs sponsors broader, nonethnic institutionalized study travel activities, such as the Japan-U.S. Leadership Network Program and the Kakehashi youth exchange project, to encourage interest in Japan-related topics among emerging leaders and to deepen transpacific personal networks.[170] These activities have become more vigorous in recent years as broad understanding of U.S.-Japan relations appears to have waned on both sides of the Pacific. Yet the embassy, and the broader Japanese community in Washington, relies also on periodic festivals and other informal events to deepen consciousness and understanding of Japan in the general American public.

The Kennedy Center and other cultural institutions periodically stage Japan-related events. The most important consciousness-raising event for Japan in Washington, however, is the annual National Cherry Blossom Festival, commemorating Tokyo's gift in 1912 of 2,000 Japanese cherry trees, now lining the Tidal Basin surrounding the Jefferson Memorial.[171] The festival itself dates from 1927, when the first reenactment of the original planting, undertaken by a group of American school children, was held. By 2010 more than a million tourists annually were visiting Washington to attend festival events during late March and early April, heralding the beginning of spring in the nation's capital.[172]

The centennial in 2012 of this original gift provided a historic opportunity for Japanese and American groups, both public and private, to work together to revive a consciousness of Japan in Washington that has receded dangerously in recent years. The centennial celebrations involved, among other events, proposals on the future of U.S.-Japan relations by the Mansfield U.S.-Japan Young Leaders Program. Two full weeks of additional festivities took place, accompanied by historic exhibitions of Japanese artistic masterpieces at the National Gallery and the Sackler Gallery.[173]

The tragic March 2011 earthquake and tsunami in Japan also provided a catalyst for new initiatives that held promise of reinvigorating

Japan-related activities in Washington. Building on the spirit of cooperation and friendship flowing out of the vigorous American response
to the tragedy, the U.S. government and the U.S.-Japan Council—based
in Washington—launched the Tomodachi Initiative, a tax-exempt, nonprofit organization supported by the Japanese government as well as
by private groups in both countries. In 2012 alone, the initiative implemented twelve educational, seven cultural, and six skills-development
programs, involving nearly a thousand young people, mainly residents
of Japan's stricken Tohoku region.[174]

U.S.-Japan cultural exchange also intensified in 2013 with the activities of the Tomodachi Initiative: the American Council for International
Education and the U.S.-Japan Council announced the launch of the
Tomodachi U.S.-Japan Youth Exchange Program; and Goldman Sachs,
Morgan Stanley Japan, and United Airlines, among others, announced
sponsorship of the initiative, which held a two-week seminar on engaging American and Japanese students in D.C. during February 2014.[175]

Summary

Despite the immense scale and sophistication of its economy, its substantial population, advanced technological level, and massive foreign
exchange reserves, Japan has maintained a remarkably low profile in
Washington. There has been no Japan congressional caucus, there are
relatively few congressional hearings on Japan, and Japan is not prominently featured in the Washington media, except in case of disasters like
the tragic March 11, 2011, tsunami. Yet competition with Asian neighbors is deepening, along many dimensions. In bilateral skirmishes within
Washington against East Asian neighbors over territorial and historical
issues, for example, the neighbors typically come out ahead, although
Japan achieves its policy goals bilaterally with the United States on most
important security questions.

To understand the paradox of Japan's distinctive Washington profile, it is instructive to look to history. Japan was largely absent from
the modern Washington diplomatic scene as America became a global
power in the 1940s and early 1950s, during an interlude when Japan's
Washington presence was disrupted by war and occupation. As a preeminently economic power, postwar Japan focused primarily on New
York rather than on Washington. The vicissitudes of twentieth-century

history thus left the Japanese diplomatic corps, as well as local Japanese Americans, in an awkward, ambivalent relationship with one another and with Washington until recently. The trade war heritage of the 1980s also convinced many Japanese that the prudent approach to Washington was a near invisible silent diplomacy.

Globalization and the deepening intra-Asian competition for influence within Washington itself have made visibility and a proactive role in agenda setting increasingly important for all foreign nations active in Washington. Japanese authorities in Tokyo have been relatively slow to see this emerging imperative. Since 2005 they have been reassessing the situation, as locally based officials reach out more actively, but political uncertainties and declining policy research capacity in Japan itself have made a decisive response in Washington difficult.

Korea

Compared to China, Japan, India, and Indonesia, South Korea is a relatively small nation, especially in the Asian context.[176] The 108th-largest nation in the world geographically, it is only slightly larger than Indiana. Korea's population of 50 million is only a fraction of that of China, and only 40 percent that of neighboring Japan. Even Korea's substantial GDP is dwarfed by that of its giant neighbors: it is less than a third the economic size of either China or Japan.[177]

Despite its relatively small scale within Northeast Asia, Korea enjoys both considerable visibility in Washington and also remarkable success in pursuing its national policy goals. Korea-related issues are reported frequently in the major national news media, and Congress holds frequent hearings on Korea, as well. As indicated in table 6-1, there were more congressional hearings on Korea over the past decade than on any other Asian country except China. Korean presidents have spoken to more joint meetings of Congress than representatives of any other Asian nation. And Korea is effective at influencing the U.S. government—both the executive and the legislative branches—even in head-to-head competition with other major powers and on global and historical issues that do not relate directly to U.S. government actions at all.

The recent record of Korean competitive success in Washington is a lengthy one, with some of the landmark achievements being the following:

—In 2007 the U.S. House of Representatives passed a resolution of censure against Japan for its mistreatment of Korean "comfort women" during World War II.

—In 2008 Korea succeeded in joining the U.S. visa waiver program, allowing Koreans to travel to the United States for purposes of business or tourism for up to ninety days without obtaining visas—a benefit that the Korean Ministry of Foreign Affairs and Trade described as being worth at least 100 billion won (roughly U.S. $100 million) to Korean citizens annually.

—In 2008 the U.S. Congress also upgraded Korea's foreign military sales status to that of the countries of NATO, Australia, New Zealand, and Japan—the highest level provided to U.S. allies. Korea buys close to $4 billion annually in U.S. military equipment—over 90 percent from U.S. firms.[178] As a result of the upgrade, Korea became able to purchase U.S. arms in quantities under $25 million without approval from Congress, and items over $25 million are subject only to a nominal, fifteen-day review process.

—During the summer of 2008 Korea beat back an adverse bureaucratic decision by the U.S. Bureau of Geographic Names: to change the subject heading for what Korea claims as its Dokdo islets from Tok Island (Korean) to the more neutral Liancourt Rocks and to file the new appellation under Islands of the Sea of Japan.

—In late 2008 Korea was invited to join the new G-20 global leadership group, designed to supplant the G-8 as the principal vehicle of international economic and financial coordination, with the strong support of the United States.

—In 2009 Korea was invited to chair the G-20, with the 2010 G-20 summit—the first in Asia—actually convened in Seoul.

— In 2012 Seoul hosted the second nuclear summit, following Washington, with strong U.S. support. Fifty-three heads of state and government participated.

—Most significantly, from a bilateral U.S.-Korea perspective, in October 2011 Seoul finally secured the ratification by the U.S. Congress of the Korea-U.S. (KORUS) free trade agreement—the largest bilateral free trade agreement in U.S. history—after more than five years of negotiation.[179] The following month ratification by the Korean National Assembly finalized the agreement.[180] Korea was only the second Asian country to conclude and ratify a free trade agreement with the United States, after Singapore in 2003.[181]

Recent Success in Historical Perspective

Korea has a long history of representation in Washington, although for many years it was not nearly as successful in achieving national strategic ends as it has become over the past decade. The first Korean legation office in Washington opened at 1513 O Street in 1888. Roughly a year later the legation moved to a mansion at 1500 Thirteenth Street (now 15 Logan Circle, N.W.), which it purchased in 1891—Korea's first diplomatic property in the West.[182] Until the legation was turned over to the Japanese for a nominal payment of $5, two months before Korean annexation in 1910, the building served as an active base for the promotion of Korean culture through receptions and displays of artifacts (such as Korean costumes and men's horsehair hats).

Korea lacked formal representation in Washington for four decades thereafter, although the Korean Commission to America and Europe, representing Korean nationalists overseas, did have an active office at 4700 16th Street until 1922. Upon Korea's annexation by Japan, the locus of émigré activity shifted temporarily to Hawaii, where the bulk of the 5,000 Koreans in the United States resided at the time.[183] Syngman Rhee, first president of the Korean Provisional Government (KPG), lived there for several years before moving to Washington in the early 1940s to spearhead a wartime initiative by the KPG to gain formal diplomatic recognition. It was due in substantial part to Rhee's wartime Washington activities that he developed an influential U.S. policy network and gained legitimacy from the Korean community as its representative.[184]

Few countries under colonial rule have both organized a coherent government in exile and used it as a focal point for implementing independence activities for as long as Korea did (1905 to 1945).[185] This distinctive pattern, under which nationalist exiles live for many years in the local Korean American ethnic community, representing their occupied nation and its people, had an important consequence for Korea in Washington. It brought the prospective politicians and diplomats of postindependence Korea, including future ambassadors to the United States such as Chang Lee Wook, into much more intimate and egalitarian contact with their local ethnic compatriots than was common in other Asian countries, such as Japan.[186]

The typically wide status divide between penniless, blue-collar immigrants and elite, generally wealthy political émigrés undermined the effectiveness of many other captive nations in their Washington activities. Yet such caste distinctions did not emerge in the Korean case. Among Koreans in the United States, the immigrants and the exiled nationalist conspirators were for many years part of a single community, unified in their struggle for Korean independence, with Koreans actually living in Washington ultimately playing a central role.

Korea reestablished its formal diplomatic presence in Washington in 1949 but was initially handicapped by a chronic lack of staff. At its reopening, the embassy had only two diplomats—Ambassador Chang Myun and a purchasing agent, together with clerical help.[187] It expanded only slowly until 1990, when a new embassy chancery was purchased.[188] Over the past two decades, however, the Korean embassy's expansion has been markedly more rapid.

Until the early 1970s the relationship between the United States and South Korea was chronically one-sided, with Korea dependent on the United States for both security assistance and economic aid. Despite this dominance/dependence relationship, bilateral conflicts naturally occurred from time to time. Yet Korea made little effort to influence Washington by circumventing formal diplomatic channels.[189] The American ambassador to Korea was Seoul's primary point of contact with Washington, and the Korean embassy in Washington—usually understaffed—remained quiet and politically inactive. The direct link between the four-star general commanding U.S. forces in Korea and the Pentagon further undermined the leverage of Korea's D.C. embassy in bilateral relations.

Circumstances began to change dramatically in the mid-1970s. Under the Nixon Doctrine, the United States began gradually to withdraw American ground forces from Korea, despite strong Korean protests, as it was also doing from Vietnam. To make matters more difficult for Korea, Congress delayed approval of the $1.5 billion American military aid package that was to compensate for troop withdrawal, in protest against President Park Chung-hee's authoritarian Yushin constitution of 1972. Seoul realized that conventional diplomacy alone could not prevent the troop withdrawal, ensure congressional approval of military aid, or secure support for Park's authoritarian rule. The U.S. embassy in Seoul was no longer an adequate contact point, given the delicate and largely Washington-centric issues involved. Aggressive, direct lobbying in America's capital clearly appeared necessary for the Korean government.

Seoul's response, beginning around 1970, was to engage Tongsun Park, a socialite of Korean origin, sometimes called the Asian Great Gatsby.[190] Park charmed members of Congress with his Washington dinner parties and cash payments, in an attempt to reverse President Richard Nixon's decision to withdraw American troops from South Korea.[191] The Korean Central Intelligence Agency (KCIA) allegedly funneled bribes and assorted favors through Park, in an attempt to further Korean objectives. Some 115 members of Congress were supposedly involved, together, by many accounts, with Unification Church founder Sun Myung Moon, former KCIA director Kim Hyung Wook, and former South Korean prime minister Chung Il Kwon.

Tongsun Park and U.S. House Representative Richard Hanna (D-Calif.) were the two protagonists in what became known as the Koreagate scandal. Park represented the Korean side of the secret agreement, while Hanna was responsible for the American side. According to their understanding, both parties would share the commissions from American rice sales to Korea and use the proceeds to obtain favorable decisions for Korea's military regime in the U.S. Congress. Park was also responsible for providing extra financial incentives to Hanna and other members of Congress—a task made easier by the large rice sale commissions that he received. The financial "incentives" that Park provided reportedly ranged from $100,000 to $200,000 at a time, per individual.[192]

Once rumors of Park's activities began to spread around Washington, there was a strong political, and ultimately legal, backlash. In 1976 Park was charged with bribing members of Congress in an effort to convince the U.S. government to keep troops in Korea. In 1977 he was indicted by a U.S. district court on thirty-six counts, including bribery, illegal campaign contributions, mail fraud, racketeering, and failure to register as an agent of the Korean Central Intelligence Agency. He avoided federal trial by testifying to the court in exchange for immunity. Representative Hanna, however, was convicted and sentenced to from six to thirty months in prison.

The Shift to Knowledge and Expertise

The fallout from the Koreagate scandal badly damaged U.S.-Korea relations for years, especially during the Carter administration (1977–81).[193] In its wake, the Korean government, in cooperation with Korea's private sector, began to adopt a very different approach to Washington—one placing a premium on knowledge and expertise as instruments of influence rather than direct financial incentives.[194] This new approach proved to be better adapted to the increasingly open, fluid, and media-sensitive Washington that was emerging in those years.

As American trade policies became more restrictive over the 1980s, and as legal disputes proliferated, the Korean government, firms, and manufacturers' associations also began to hire lawyers. Under pressure from deepening protectionist sentiments on Capitol Hill, Korea's Washington strategy became increasingly defensive and preventive. To secure their newly modest, largely defensive goals, Koreans cultivated technical consultants, such as Harold B. Malmgren Associates, the International Business and Economic Group, and Manchester Associates. With these consultants, the Koreans focused on spotting regulatory trends and technical loopholes in the American policy process while also devising realistic countervailing strategies and tactics for Korean clients.

Korea during the 1980s did not by any means ignore conventional lobbying, however wary it may have become in the wake of the Koreagate scandal. Korean diplomats had some trouble in the Washington of those years, due to the poor human rights record of the military regimes that dominated their country at the time. They did, however, succeed in recruiting several prominent former officials with extensive contacts for Korea, such as William Rogers (U.S. secretary of state from 1969 to 1973), Thomas Kuchel (former Republican senator from California), Michael Deaver (former deputy chief of staff to Ronald Reagan), and Alexander Haig (Nixon's White House chief of staff and Reagan's first secretary of state).

Mass-media relationships and grassroots connections also became increasingly central in Korea's approach to Washington during the 1980s and 1990s. This more open approach was facilitated, of course, by Korea's own democratization after 1986, which made Washington's liberal community, in particular, increasingly receptive to Korean entreaties for support. Shared existential memories of the Korean War had made American conservatives receptive to Korean concerns from even earlier days. Korea from the mid-1990s on thus enjoyed an unusually broad, bipartisan fund of support in Washington that aided its efforts to articulate national interests.

The number of Koreans and Korean Americans manifesting strong familiarity with Washington, and with the United States generally, was also rapidly growing. In 1980 there were only 350,000 Korean residents in the country. That number rose to 800,000 by 1990 and doubled again, to over 1.6 million, by 2010. One of the largest communities nationwide is in northern Virginia. The number of Korean students in the United States rose by more than a third over the last decade; it is now greater, relative to population, than in any other major Asian nation.[195] Ethnic and old-school ties naturally become the bases of interpersonal networks—a deepening foundation for Korea's remarkable recent Washington success.

As the battle for influence in Washington broadened from K Street and Capitol Hill toward mass-media outlets, think tanks, and universities, Korea broadened its Washington institutional presence as well as its interpersonal networks. The Korean embassy first established a cultural service within the embassy itself. In 2004 it also set up KORUS House, converting it into an official Korean Cultural Center in 2010.

The center, housed in an elegant old mansion on upper Massachusetts Avenue, close to both think tanks and the diplomatic community, offers a broad range of activities: a speaker series on current events, official briefings, art exhibits, NGO receptions, displays on the history of the U.S.-Korea alliance, and a variety of other cultural offerings.[196] It also coordinates a multimedia program to disseminate information about Korea and U.S.-Korea cooperation across the United States. In addition, the Cultural Center sponsors Korean-language study as well as academic programs through its King Sejong Institute.[197]

On the economic side, the Korean embassy has an impressive array of affiliate bodies in Washington, both public and private, which it coordinates to gather intelligence, to help network, and to persuade. The earliest was the Korea Trade Investment Promotion Agency's Washington office, established in 1962. The Korean Chamber of Commerce and Industry was founded in June 1992, representing the private sector, supplemented by the Federation of Korean Industries and the Korea International Trade Association.[198]

In 1982, taking a tactic directly out of Japan's economic playbook, the Korea Institute for International Economic Policy, a semigovernmental organization based in Seoul, set up the Korea Economic Institute (KEI) in Washington.[199] Although lacking the capacity to do much in-house research, KEI has served for three decades as an important convener, agenda setter, and supporter of work on modern Korea, especially that by younger scholars. The institute organizes annual collaborative conferences with major academic institutions; publishes and supports scholarly research on Korea; and hosts seminars and policy addresses by a variety of scholars, think tank experts, and Korean policymakers.[200]

Recent topics of special interest to KEI include U.S.-Korea trade relations, green growth, Korean family reunification, and energy security. With an office on the tenth floor of 1800 K Street, formerly occupied by Kissinger Associates, KEI provides a convenient, informal, speaking venue for visiting Korean officials and for outreach programs involving Capitol Hill.[201] KEI also helps organize the ambassador's dialogue program, which has frequently taken the two ambassadors—the Korean ambassador to the United States and the U.S. ambassador to Korea—across the United States for paired presentations on such politically salient topics as the KORUS free trade agreement.

In the new information age, Korea employs an articulate corps of mainly U.S.-educated representatives to interface with the mass media, think tanks, and universities in Washington. Ambassadors Lee Tae-sik and Han Duk-soo spoke frequently during the 2007–11 period at think tanks like the Heritage Foundation and KEI in support of the KORUS agreement.[202] In late 2013 Ambassador Ahn Ho-young similarly celebrated the sixtieth anniversary of the U.S.-Korea alliance through mammoth invitational gatherings at the Kennedy Center and on Capitol Hill.[203] Korean business, with government support, endowed a Korea chair at CSIS, with the first incumbent being Victor Cha of Georgetown University, previously director for Asian affairs at the National Security Council in the George W. Bush administration. Korea also cultivated major universities in the Washington area, making substantial contributions to the U.S.-Korea Institute at SAIS, while also endowing Korea-related positions at Georgetown, George Washington, and American Universities.

The Korean embassy is simultaneously doing more and more out-reach across America. Recent ambassadors have made frequent and extensive speaking tours across the country. Both Lee Tae-sik and Han Duk-soo, for example, spoke extensively about the importance of ratifying the KORUS FTA. In September 2009, Ambassador Han, along with Kathleen Stevens, the U.S. ambassador to Korea, visited Detroit and Chicago in support of the KORUS agreement. In October 2009 Ambassador Han also went to Dallas and Houston to meet local leaders and businessmen with a similar appeal. Final ratification of the agreement in the U.S. Congress and the Korean National Assembly was reached in the fall of 2011.[204] Ambassadors Han and Stephens made the prospective benefits of ratification a central theme of their annual ambassadors' dialogue discussions across the United States during late November and early December 2011.[205] In 2012 Ambassadors Y. J. Choi (Korea) and Sung Kim (United States) continued the bilateral tradition, jointly visiting Houston, Los Angeles, San Diego, and Honolulu.[206]

In addition to direct embassy efforts, Korea-related NGOs are also expanding, reflecting an expansion in the Korean American community.[207] These NGOs are amplifying support for Korean interests as they grow and gain political experience. Among the most active is the Korean American Voters' Council (KAVC), which mobilizes Korean voters throughout the country in support of priority causes.[208] KAVC is particularly strong at on-line mobilization, through its vaunted 121 network.[209] Also active is the Network of Korean-American Leaders (NKAL). These are second-generation Korean Americans in their thirties and forties who work in fields ranging from business to entertainment to government. KEI has periodically offered its facilities in midtown Washington to NKAL for weekend organization and strategy sessions.

Anatomy of Success

Five recent cases, contrasting sharply to the spectacular failures of the Tongsun Park era, illustrate the changing nature of Korean political activity in Washington and the reason that the new, civil-society-oriented recipe is proving so successful. Those cases include the comfort women struggle (2007), the Tokdo (Takeshima) question, foreign military sales (2008), the visa waiver program, and ratification of the KORUS free trade agreement. In the first two, the Korean side was essentially defensive, while in the latter three it was attempting new policy advances. In each of the five cases, the Korean embassy was a central, but far from the only significant, actor. Characteristic of all five cases was a complex yet cooperative interaction between the embassy and supportive Korean NGOs. This collaboration provided early warning to the embassy of possible policy or real-world developments adverse to Korean interests. It also helped mobilize grassroots support to implement solutions or policy changes that the embassy and colleagues in Seoul were able to negotiate with the United States.

The Comfort Women Case

On July 31, 2007, the U.S. House of Representatives unanimously approved H.R. 121, regarding the comfort women case. The resolution was cosponsored by 168 congressional members. A month earlier, on June 26, the resolution had passed the House International Relations Committee by a huge majority of 35-2. Predecessors of this remarkably outspoken resolution had failed to get out of committee in several previous Congresses.[210] H.R. 121 provided that the Japanese government should formally acknowledge, officially apologize, and publically take historical responsibility for coercing Asian women into sexual slavery during the World War II period while educating current and future generations about the tragedy.[211]

The overwhelming passage of H.R. 121 in mid-2007 was a particular puzzle in two respects: one, that it should gain so much backing, after having failed several times in previous Congresses; and two, that Korean Americans should back it so strongly, even though they had nothing tangible to gain through its passage. The course of the struggle is best explained by two factors: the tactical missteps on the Japanese conservative side and the shrewd tactics of the Korean opposition. Both factors were necessary, yet not individually sufficient, conditions in producing the ultimate outcome.

The comfort women resolution was first proposed to the 2007–08 Congress in January 2007 by Representatives Mike Honda (D-Calif.) and Frank Wolf (R-Va.).[212] At that point, it had only six cosponsors. Two provocative developments in Japan, however, gave it critical momentum. The first was a casual statement by Prime Minister Abe Shinzō on March 1 that the comfort women had not been coerced by the Japanese government, which consequently bore no responsibility for the "private actions" involved. Abe's Washington visit in late April did reduce tensions to some degree, as did a conciliatory Japanese tea event two weeks later on Capitol Hill, conducted by the distinguished Japanese tea master Sen Genshitsu and hosted by House of Representatives International Relations Committee chairman Tom Lantos.[213]

Then on June 14 a full-page *Washington Post* ad—sponsored by Japanese conservatives and making a similar, and equally provocative, point as that of Abe's original pronouncement—reignited the controversy. The various Japanese declarations incensed the growing Korean American community, much of it recently arrived from Korea, and imparted critical momentum to the Korean NGOs. Korean American anger could not have been translated into a congressional resolution, however, without thoughtful advocacy and politically shrewd tactics. Three elements of the advocacy were decisive. It was couched in universalistic terms (human rights, women's rights, and peace). It was a request from U.S. citizens (Korean American) rather than a foreign government (Japan). And it was bipartisan.

In terms of tactics, four factors were crucial. The movement had a strong strategic headquarters (KAVC). Activists collaborated closely with existing community institutions like the churches, which have strong social standing in the Korean American community. The movement had experienced leaders.[214] And the movement cooperated closely with non-Korean NGOs, including both Asian American ethnic groups and Amnesty International.[215]

The Tokdo (Takeshima) Question

Korea and Japan had had a running diplomatic dispute since 1952 over ownership of small islets east of Korea and west of Japan, known as Tokdo in Korean and Takeshima in Japanese. The long-standing territorial conflict exploded in July 2008, when the U.S. Bureau of Geographic Names quietly proposed to reclassify the islets in a manner offensive to the Koreans.[216] A Korean studies librarian at the University of Toronto, Hana Kim, alerted the Korean embassy in Washington to this development, suggesting that it was the result of quiet Japanese lobbying.[217]After a short, sharp defensive struggle, in which the embassy, driven by fierce Korean media pressure and a political backlash in Seoul, pressed top officials of both the State Department and the White House—up to and including President George W. Bush—the adverse change was withdrawn.

Foreign Military Sales

In October 2008 Korea secured congressional support (H.R. 7177) to provide an important upgrade to its foreign military sales status, allowing it to purchase more advanced weaponry, in larger amounts, and through simplified procedures. This policy coup was achieved through a two-level process: first, threats at the international level to develop and procure new military aircraft (the KMX project) from a third party (Sweden) that were traditionally secured in the United States; and second, astute domestic lobbying within the United States involving traditional lobbyists (the Loeffler Group) as well as a transnational coalition of American supporters in Korea (United States Forces Korea and Amcham) and related firms (especially Boeing) in the United States. All these groups combined to put strong pressure on Congress, which in turn authorized more favorable foreign military sales for Korea.

The Visa Waiver Program

The U.S. VWP allows citizens of participating nations to enter the United States for business or tourism for periods up to ninety days without visas. Korea was admitted to the program in 2008, after three years of effort, due to the intensive work of a young Korean American lobbyist, Thomas Kim, who was sponsored by the Korean embassy in Washington. Kim, the president of Scribe Strategies and Advisors, succeeded in convincing two members of Congress (Jim Moran and Dan Burton) to intervene with their colleagues and the White House on this issue, complementing active, and ultimately successful, Korean diplomatic efforts.

The KORUS Agreement.

On June 30, 2007, trade representatives of the U.S. and Korea signed the KORUS FTA. The U.S. Congress, however, was slow in ratification. A renegotiated agreement, providing expanded opportunities in Korea for the U.S. auto industry and American agriculture, was signed in December 2010, after tense bilateral negotiations the month before at the G-20 summit in Seoul had fallen through.[218] The Korean embassy in Washington played a key role in the long struggle for ultimate ratification in three ways. It hired lobbying firms (Parven Pomper Strategies), it aired relevant issues extensively at Washington think tanks, and it popularized the importance of KORUS around the country through Korean embassy outreach.

A key additional catalyst was the North Korean shelling of Yeonpyeong Island, just off Korea's west coast, in November 2010. That provocative act convinced the publics and legislatures of both the United States and South Korea that reinforcement of their relationship in all its dimensions, including the economic, was imperative on national security grounds.

Summary

Korea, relative to its giant neighbors, is a small nation—in geographic, demographic, and even economic terms. It does not loom large in the realist power calculus. Yet Seoul has, particularly in very recent years, wielded considerable influence in Washington, attaining substantial visibility. It has done so through an eclectic and distinctive combination of traditional tactics and grassroots and media-oriented innovations that suggest the way that transnational politics in Washington is evolving more generally.

On the traditional side, Korea engages lobbyists, both large and small. It also independently mobilizes long-standing allies in the American defense-industrial complex who value their role as major suppliers to the Korean military. Political-military developments on the Korean peninsula—North Korea's nuclear tests, the March 2010 *Cheonan* sinking, and the November 2010 shelling of Yeonpyeong Island—have given Seoul additional leverage in its efforts to influence U.S. government policy.

On the innovative side, Korea's government perceives knowledge and expertise as an increasingly important dimension of influence in an ever-more-global Washington and aligns its strategies accordingly. It has established and sustained the Korea Economic Institute, run by American analysts and former policymakers, while also reaching out actively to local think tanks and universities.

Meanwhile, the Korean embassy in Washington plays an unusually proactive role for a foreign actor in swaying American opinion. It capitalizes on several factors: its historical cooperative relationships with the growing Korean American community, its grassroots intelligence, and its political support. Both the embassy and Korean American NGOs are creative in employing social websites to promote a deeper understanding of Korea as well as to support specific policies that the NGOs and the Embassy mutually espouse. And Koreans at all levels mobilize such social networks as school ties and ethnic bonds and defense-industrial relationships to further their nation's interests in Washington.

8

South and Southeast Asia in Washington

South and Southeast Asia have forged longer and in many ways deeper historical ties with Washington than have their neighbors in Northeast Asia (see chapter 7). Thailand was the first nation in Asia with which the United States established diplomatic ties (in 1832), while the Philippines was the only Asian nation to have been under U.S. sovereignty (1898 to 1946). As we shall see, India and the Philippines, as early democracies, arguably had the strongest early post–World War II Asian presence in Washington, and Vietnam was a central preoccupation of American foreign policy (as a whole) until the mid-1970s.

Following a hiatus after the fall of Saigon in 1975, South and Southeast Asia became major objects of U.S. attention again over the past two decades. India's 1999 nuclear tests and the intensification of the "war on terror" beginning in 2001 were catalytic factors. The dramatic rebirth of democracy in Burma has increased the region's visibility as well.

Although South and Southeast Asia have periodically inspired American policy attention, and often achieved public visibility in Washington both in the media and on Capitol Hill, the nature of their involvement in D.C. has been very different from that of the Northeast Asians. These countries are smaller economically, further from America, and not—with the partial exception of Singapore—as directly engaged with core American political, economic, and strategic concerns. Their rivalries with one another are also less pointed. The result is a less intense and less insistent interaction with Washington, marked—as we shall see—by

bureaus. The Nepal/India desk was also divided to facilitate a more concentrated focus on India. And in July 2009, the Obama administration assigned a senior director at the National Security Council to focus specifically on India.[14] Attention to India within the U.S. government was also subsequently amplified by creation of the U.S.-India Interparliamentary Exchange Program, under legislation proposed in May 2009 by Representative Jim McDermott (D-Wash.), cochair of the Congressional Caucus on India and Indian Americans.[15]

Paralleling institutional changes in U.S. legislative and executive branch relations with India has also been a symbolic deepening, especially over the past decade, in Washington's cultural and intellectual relations with India. In 2003, for example, the first Diwali celebration was held at the White House—ironically in the White House Indian Treaty Room, where North American Indian issues were traditionally considered, with White House political adviser Karl Rove, rather than President George W. Bush, in attendance.[16] In 2009 the Obama White House celebrated Diwali in the East Room, with President Obama personally lighting the single lamp traditionally symbolizing the advent of the festivity. Also attending were the Indian commerce minister, Anand Sharma, and Ambassador Meera Shankar.[17] In the early spring of 2011, the Kennedy Center for the Performing Arts also held a major three-week India festival.[18]

Washington think tank and research centers have also sharply increased their attention to India in recent years. One important platform is the East-West Center's Washington office. The Asia Society has also inaugurated two major seminar series in Washington: the Global India Series, showcasing films, books, and speakers on India, often in coordination with the Indian embassy; and INDOvations—a series that showcases India-inspired innovations and their impact on the global knowledge economy. The innovations range from concepts in affordable and environmentally sustainable business to social and cultural innovation. The series promotes collaborative partnerships between Indian innovators and potential American supporters of their entrepreneurial ventures.

At a more systematic Track II level, the Aspen Institute in 2002 inaugurated a U.S.-India Strategic Dialogue, in cooperation with the Confederation of Indian Industry based in New Delhi. This bilateral dialogue is convened twice annually, once in the United States and once in India, and also involves biannual reciprocal governmental visits and joint roundtables in both national capitals. Fifteen to twenty delegates from each country take part in each session.

India's Lengthening Shadow

Clearly India, since the economic reforms of 1991 and the waning of the cold war soon thereafter, has taken greater interest than previously in rapprochement with the United States at the national level. This concern has been intensified since 9/11 by a desire to combat terrorism jointly with the United States and to influence American policies toward Afghanistan and Pakistan. Yet there have also been major domestic changes within the United States that make Americans increasingly receptive to expanded engagement with India in Washington.

Most strikingly, the Indian community in the United States has been rapidly expanding. It more than doubled between 1990 and 2012 (from roughly 1.1 million to over 3 million), becoming the second-largest Asian population after the Chinese, which was 3.7 million in 2012, and surpassing the Filipino community, with its 2.7 million.[19] By 2010 direct first-generation immigrants from India totaled around 1.6 million, making them the largest such immigrant group in the country, after Mexicans and Filipinos.[20] In 2007–08, the number of new Indian immigrants—more than 43 percent of whom had arrived since 2000—surpassed the number of Chinese immigrants in the United States for the first time since 1960.[21]

Indian immigrants to the United States tend to have a powerful impact on domestic American politics for three reasons. First of all, they are numerous and becoming more so. Just as important, however, Indian immigrants are largely proficient in English, unlike many Chinese, Korean, and Mexican immigrants. The Indians also tend to be well educated, with nearly three-quarters of Indian-born immigrants having at least a bachelor's degree. Many are educated in the United States; indeed, in the 2011/12 academic year, India was the second leading country of origin for foreign students in the United States, following only a more populous and affluent China.[22]

Indian Americans thus tend to have relatively high incomes and to be concentrated in high-status fields. Despite constituting less than 1 percent of the U.S. population, Indian Americans comprise 3 percent of the nation's engineers, 7 percent of its IT professionals, and 8 percent of its physicians and surgeons.[23] Nearly a quarter of Indian immigrants work in the IT area, with the rest split among management, science/engineering, health care, and sales.[24] Almost 40 percent of Silicon Valley start-ups founded by immigrants in the 1990s had at least one founder of Indian origin.[25] There are more than 20,000 Indian millionaires in the United States, many of them engineers living in the San Francisco Bay area.[26] Indian Americans also tend to have strong extended-family ties, which give them a sense of group cohesion and facilitate their rapid assimilation into new social settings. Indeed, in 2012 half of Indian immigrants were admitted to the United States on a family basis.[27]

The impact of Indian Americans on American domestic politics over the past decade has been dramatic and more substantial than at any point since the 1940s and 1950s. In 2007 the Rhodes Scholar Bobby Jindal became governor of Louisiana, at age thirty-six. In 2011 Nikki Haley (born Nimrata Nikki Randhawa) was inaugurated as governor of South Carolina, at age thirty-nine. Also in 2011 Kamala Harris became attorney general of California. Meanwhile, President Barack Obama approved more than two dozen Indian Americans to serve in his administration—more than any previous president.[28] Many others are prominently involved with influential NGOs, such as USINPAC and the American India Foundation.

Deepening business interest—both American business interest in India and Indian business interest in America—also helps leverage India's rising role in Washington. Foreign investment, both to and from India, has been rising sharply since India's economic growth began to accelerate in the early 1990s.[29] So too, though to a lesser extent, has bilateral trade, especially in service sectors like outsourcing.[30] In 2010 U.S.-India bilateral trade in goods and services combined jumped more than 30 percent, exceeding $60 billion.

Roughly a third of that total represents outsourcing, mainly in the rapidly growing computer services area. The vitality of the industry has given rise to a powerful industry association, the National Association of Software and Service Companies (NASSCOM), in India.[31] Since 2010 NASSCOM has been lobbying actively in Washington for an outsourcing-friendly immigration policy and against the outsourcing restrictions imposed by American state and local governments.[32]

Support from other influential interest groups is also leveraging India's role in Washington. Most conspicuously, since the tragic 9/11 attacks the Indian community has forged close ties with the Jewish lobby, including powerful groups like AIPAC and the American Jewish Committee (AJC). As Sanjay Puri, chairman of USINPAC puts it: "In some ways the Indian community is like the Jewish, because it is a community that cares about strong relationships, not just because it's good for India but because it's good for the U.S. too."[33] For its part, the AJC includes USINPAC among its "advancing inter-ethnic and inter-religious partnerships."[34] At the working level, the AJC has also held periodic training sessions for Indian Americans around the country, showing them the ropes of grassroots lobbying.[35]

A final important multiplier for India's rising influence in Washington is its proactive embassy in the nation's capital. Although relatively small in comparative terms, with less than a third the accredited diplomats of China and less than half of Japan's contingent, the Indian embassy has a strategic location, at the heart of Embassy Row, and many experienced diplomats. It also has a distinctive emphasis on the sciences and community affairs.[36]

As in the case of other effective nations in Washington, India's embassy fills a broad and expanding range of functions, both defensive and offensive. Defensively, the work of Ambassador Naresh Chandra (1996–2001), a mathematics graduate with a strong understanding of technology and over thirty-five years of experience in dealing with the United States, was especially noteworthy in allaying strong backlash on Capitol Hill to India's May 1998 nuclear test.[37] On the offensive side, the embassy under Ambassadors Ronen Sen (2004–09), Meera Shankar (2009–11), Nirupama Rao (2011–13), and S. Jaishankar (2013–) has been moving actively beyond conventional diplomacy and lobbying, toward a heavier emphasis on public diplomacy. The ambassador has been speaking frequently at universities and think tanks while also hosting a variety of cultural events and participating in multilateral forums.[38]

Varied Cases of Lobbying Success and Failure

Judging the efficacy of any nation's attempts to enhance its influence abroad is inevitably a subjective enterprise. Understanding can be increased, however, by looking at specific cases. The way that India has handled nuclear issues—including adverse American reaction to its 1998 nuclear tests and negotiations over the civilian nuclear agreement a decade later—reveals the effectiveness of India's lobbying techniques. Economic cases such as outsourcing illustrate, however, some of the political constraints that continue to confront India in Washington.

Neutralizing the Backlash to the 1998 Nuclear Tests

Following India's surprise nuclear tests in May 1998, New Delhi was thrust sharply onto the defensive in Washington. Almost immediately after the first tests, President Bill Clinton condemned the Indian government for its actions, contending that "they were unjustified" and that "they clearly create a dangerous new instability in their region."[39] In a display of Washington's commitment to the international nuclear non-proliferation regime, the United States imposed tough economic sanctions on India. All pending applications with the U.S. Ex-Im Bank for export projects to India, all applications for insurance with the Overseas Private Investment Corporation, and all direct aid to India, as well as export of goods subject to licensing, were suspended. The United States also expressed a determination to oppose loans to India through international financial institutions, including the World Bank.[40]

As indicated earlier, Ambassador Naresh Chandra and his staff played an important role during the nuclear crisis as a defensive "shock absorber" between India and the United States. Immediately after the Indian nuclear tests, there were strong suspicions in Washington that the U.S. government—whose vaunted intelligence community apparently did not foresee the tests—was deceived by false Indian government assurances offered to forestall untoward pressure.[41] Soon after the tests, Ambassador Chandra went to work, meeting with senior members of Congress to allay suspicions of Indian veracity, emphasizing India's continuing commitment to ultimate global nuclear disarmament, and reaffirming India's offer to join Geneva discussions on the Fissile Material Cut-off Treaty in a constructive manner.[42] He also worked intensively with the media—TV, radio, and press—while participating in every discussion between high-level delegations from India that were visiting Washington and U.S. counterparts led by Deputy Secretary of State Strobe Talbott.[43]

The Indian embassy also helped to mobilize Indian Americans with a tangible stake in U.S.-Indian relations to support a stabilization of India's relationship with the United States. Ambassador Chandra saw the role of these ethnic allies as highly strategic: giving a "greater breadth and richness of engagement" between Indians and Americans, and dispelling the "old image of Indians as poor and poverty stricken, without appearing to be Maharajahs."[44] He systematically worked to maximize contacts between successful Indian American business people and government officials in the United States, on the one hand, and, on the other, Indian government ministers and opinion makers in India. The ambassador also encouraged the Indian government in New Delhi to appoint Indian Americans to its advisory committees in information technology and telecommunications, as well as other areas. For their part, Indian Americans, with embassy support, funded and established university chairs in Indian studies in Berkeley, Santa Cruz, New York, and Chicago.

Empathetic nonethnic members of Congress—encouraged not surprisingly by the Indian American community—also worked to stabilize India's position in Washington amid the nuclear crisis. Among the most important backers was Representative Frank Pallone of rural Long Branch, New Jersey (D-N.J.), cofounder of the Congressional Caucus on India and Indian Americans.[45] Pallone subsequently received India's third-highest civilian award, the Padma Bhushan, for his critical contribution to the caucus and to U.S.-India relations.[46] Senator Sam Brownback (R-Kan.), responding to wheat growers in his home state and intense Indian American lobbying, also played a key role in moderating sanctions against India, as chairman of the Senate Subcommittee on Near Eastern and South Asian Affairs. In that capacity, he also sponsored the Brownback amendment, mitigating preexisting nuclear sanctions legislation.[47]

American business groups also stepped in to help stabilize U.S.-Indian relations in the wake of the nuclear tests. Especially active was the India Interest Group, founded by Michael Gadbaw, long-time vice president and senior counsel for General Electric's International Law and Policy program.[48] Ambassador Chandra coordinated with representatives of U.S. multinationals like GE who were active in India, as he also did with Congress, the Clinton administration, and Indian American representatives.[49]

The confluence of Indian embassy, Indian American, multinational business, and congressional efforts catalyzed a dramatic rollback of the early nuclear sanctions, introduced in the wake of the May 1998 Indian nuclear tests. In July, two months after the tests, Congress exempted food products from the trade sanctions for humanitarian reasons. In September the so-called Burton amendment, which sought limitation of U.S. assistance to India due to alleged Indian infringement of Kashmiri and Khalistani human rights, was routed 342-82 in the House of Representatives, with the adamant support of the nearly hundred-strong India Caucus, despite the nuclear tensions.[50] On October 20 Congress passed an omnibus spending bill for fiscal 1999 that included the Brownback amendment, empowering President Bill Clinton to dilute sanctions.

On November 7 the president in fact waived most of those punitive measures. Finally, during late 1999 he dispensed with the remainder as well. These steps, and conciliatory reciprocal Indian gestures, paved the way for a series of mutual high-level visits that sealed the Indo-American reconciliation—India's new status as a nuclear power notwithstanding.[51]

Implementing the 2005 Civilian Nuclear Deal

India's successful efforts to neutralize backlash in Washington to its 1998 nuclear tests was followed seven years later by a landmark U.S.-Indian civil-nuclear energy deal. In July 2005 President George W. Bush and Indian Prime Minister Manmohan Singh announced that "the President would . . . seek agreement from Congress to U.S. laws and policies, and the United States would work with friends and allies to adjust international regimes to enable full civil nuclear energy cooperation and trade with India, including but not limited to expeditious consideration of fuel supplies for safeguarded nuclear reactors."[52] Formalizing the initial heads-of-government agreement required approval from the U.S. Congress and also a waiver from the Nuclear Suppliers Group allowing the export of nuclear fuel to India.

From the very outset, several influential members of Congress fervently opposed the nuclear deal. Allowing the sale of nuclear fuel and technology to India—a nation that had refused to sign the Non-Proliferation Treaty (NPT) and that had tested nuclear devices in the face of fierce international opposition—was seen by many as violating the very concept of nuclear nonproliferation. It also suggested gross American inconsistency. At the same time that Washington was pressuring North Korea and Iran to end their nuclear programs, it was also proposing to negotiate a deal with India, according that clear violator of NPT norms unique privileges.

In the House of Representatives, Massachusetts Democrat Ed Markey forcefully stressed Bush administration inconsistency and the perverse prospective consequences of that inconsistency for negotiations with Venezuela, Pakistan, and North Korea.[53] In the Senate, Daniel Akaka (D-Hawaii) underlined the moral hazard created by making special rules for India: "India will gain all the rights of a nuclear state and bear none of the responsibilities."[54] He also warned that India could potentially aid Iranian nuclear weapons development.

Despite such objections, the nuclear deal was approved overwhelmingly in October 2008: 86-13 in the Senate and 298-117 in the House. In the Senate, twelve of those voting against the bill were Democrats, with independent Bernard Sanders of Vermont as the thirteenth vote. The House opposition consisted of 10 Republicans and 107 Democrats. The multilateral Nuclear Suppliers Group also approved the waiver, however, thus bringing India into the civilian nuclear mainstream despite its military nuclear tests.[55]

The U.S.-India civil nuclear agreement did, to be sure, face domestic obstacles in India as well as in the United States.[56] Yet regardless of the complications in New Delhi, the agreement itself represented a clear success for India's lobbying efforts in Washington. What were the forces making this success possible, and what does the case suggest about the state of India's recent Washington presence?

There was, of course, an underlying geopolitical logic to the civil nuclear deal. As leaders in both countries stressed, it had potential to consolidate their bilateral ties as a central international relationship of the twenty-first century.[57] The agreement was, however, problematic in political terms for the United States, since it contradicted long-standing NPT norms and attached burdensome amendments to domestic legislation, only a decade after India had defied those very global norms with its 1998 nuclear tests. Indian concessions to Washington on the terms of the agreement were also politically difficult in New Delhi. The arrangement itself represented, after all, an unprecedented deepening, for a traditionally nonaligned nation, of a controversial tacit entente with a global superpower.

In Washington three catalytic actors were critically important to the legislative success of this complex agreement. First, of course, there was the Indian government, in the local incarnation of the Indian embassy in Washington. Second, there were business interests—both federations and individual firms—with a stake both in the deal itself and in the broader stability of Indo-American political-economic relations. Finally, there were NGOs—both Indian American and those with broader concerns—that favored the agreement.

Within the Indian government, Ambassador to Washington Ronen Sen took the lead, playing a critical role both in negotiations leading to an agreement and in mediating its complex, three-year voyage through the U.S. Congress. Sen was especially appropriate as a spokesperson, as he had previously served as secretary to the prime minister of India, responsible for foreign affairs, defense, and technology in the delicate 1986–91 period during which India prepared for its nuclear tests. He also served as secretary to the Indian Atomic Energy Commission. Highly knowledgeable on the technical side of nuclear issues, Sen engaged actively with the American media, and at think tanks and universities across the country, during the three-year period of debate in Washington preceding final congressional passage of the nuclear legislation in the fall of 2008.[58]

The Indian embassy also hired a D.C.-based law firm, Barbour, Griffith, and Rogers (BGR), to lobby for the bill's passage in Congress.[59] BGR's efforts on the nuclear deal were led by Robert Blackwill, who had served in the Bush administration as ambassador to India.[60] Ambassador Ronen Sen personally signed a second contract with another Washington law firm, Venable, whose work on the project was led by former Senator Birch Bayh (D-Ind.).[61] The Indian embassy thus engaged two major law firms, each with powerful connections in one or the other of the country's political parties.

The nuclear agreement also had diverse, powerful business backing. The U.S.-India Business Council (USIBC), first of all, supported the deal strongly, stressing its financial benefits for American firms.[62] The USIBC claimed that India would spend $175 billion on nuclear infrastructure and fuel by 2030, and that passage of the deal would allow U.S. firms to compete strongly for those contracts.[63] To enhance the effectiveness of its rhetorical support, the USIBC hired one of Washington's best-connected law firms, Patton Boggs, to lobby Congress; indeed, Patton Boggs was to claim that it "led the legislative drive to pass the Act on behalf of the U.S.-India Business Council."[64] Its strategy was to extol not only the immediate nuclear-related contracts made possible by the deal, but also the "halo effect" of increased trade in related sectors: producing opportunities in retail, banking, insurance, pension, military procurement, and infrastructure, while generating potential increases in contracts to U.S. firms of more than $200 billion. Apart from its work with USIBC, Patton Boggs was also hired in August 2008, shortly before the final vote on the nuclear deal in Congress, to aid the Indian embassy in its Washington lobbying.[65]

The U.S. Chamber of Commerce, which shares operational resources with the USIBC, also conducted its own campaign in support of the nuclear agreement. It appealed for "stronger ties between the two great democracies" and "$100 billion worth of new opportunities in India in the energy sector alone," while stressing the agreement's potential to reduce Indian reliance on coal-generated electricity as a way to reduce global greenhouse gas emissions.[66] The chamber's Indian counterpart, the Confederation of Indian Industry (CII), also conducted its own lengthy campaign in support of the legislation, beginning in 2000.[67] In 2005 CII also hired BGR, separately engaged by the Indian embassy, to lobby on the deal.[68]

Individual companies likewise lobbied on behalf of the nuclear deal. Among these enterprises, surprisingly, was AIG, which paid its lobbying firms $2 million during the summer and fall of 2008, even as the global financial crisis was building, to see if the agreement might have a business dimension beneficial to AIG.[69] Other American companies that directly lobbied Congress on behalf of the agreement included Ford, Dow Chemical, Lockheed Martin, Boeing, General Electric, and JP Morgan.[70]

Nongovernmental organizations based in Washington also joined the struggle to pass the U.S.-India nuclear deal. Chief among them, of course, was USINPAC. It hosted public briefings with State Department and congressional leaders discussing the arrangement; set up meetings with key congressional leaders, such as Speaker Dennis Hastert and Representative Charles Rangel; and organized a high-profile fact-finding mission to India to meet with leaders of the Indian parliament to report their viewpoints on the bill.[71] USINPAC also engaged in some unique, twenty-first-century transnational lobbying: it released a press statement encouraging residents of Indian origin in Nuclear Suppliers Group member countries throughout the world to encourage their governments to support the granting of a nuclear waiver for India.[72]

The U.S.-India nuclear deal also mobilized some cross-issue political allies with little direct stake in the legislation itself. The American Jewish Committee, for example, sent a letter strongly supporting the nuclear deal to key members of Congress, including Senators Joseph Biden and Richard Lugar, as well as Representatives Henry Hyde and Tom Lantos. The letter emphasized the strategic benefits of the legislation, such as its potential to strengthen the "natural alliance between India and the United States."[73]

Ratifying the U.S.-India civil nuclear deal was thus a protracted struggle, highly contested on nuclear proliferation grounds. It lay at the center of India's activities in Washington for more than three years, from mid-2005 to late 2008. The struggle to pass the legislation was ultimately successful, however, due to the powerful coalition of business and NGOs, catalyzed by the Indian embassy, lobbyists, and congressional supporters that stood behind it. Powerful networks were fundamental to the legislation's success.

Occasional Failure and Frustration

India's efforts in Washington have often met with striking and sometimes paradoxical success. Yet they have on occasion met with frustration as well. India has had mixed success, for example, in its battle to forestall protectionist American steps with regard to outsourcing. It has also had trouble inhibiting U.S. measures to restrict the hiring of foreign skilled workers by U.S. corporations.

The Outsourcing Controversy

For years American companies such as General Electric and American Express have been outsourcing significant and growing portions of their operations to India to take advantage of lower wages, providing major stimulus to what now is a substantial industry in India.[74] As the Council on Foreign Relations cautions, it is difficult to authoritatively say how many jobs have been lost to outsourcing, but careful studies have been carried out. Since 1983, 2 million manufacturing jobs are estimated to have moved offshore from the United States.[75]

Outsourcing began emerging as an issue in American politics shortly after the election of 2000. In 2002 New Jersey State Senator Shirley Turner proposed a bill to prevent outsourcing of New Jersey Department of Human Services contracts to Mumbai. Provoked by this initiative, several other states, including Connecticut, Maryland, Missouri, Wisconsin, and Michigan, considered following suit. By 2003 the Indian media had already picked up American domestic political discontent with outsourcing to India. In 2002 Forrester Research estimated in one detailed study that 400,000 service jobs had been lost to offshoring since 2000 alone, with jobs leaving at a rate of 12,000 to 15,000 a month. It further projected that by 2015, 3.3 million U.S. service jobs would have moved offshore, including 1.7 million "back office" jobs, such as payroll processing and accounting, as well as 473,000 IT jobs. Seventy percent of those outsourced jobs were projected to go to India, with a resulting wage loss to American workers of $136 billion.[76]

In June 2003 Indian Trade Minister Arun Jaitley visited Washington to assess the issue. Shortly thereafter, the U.S. House and Senate passed restrictive bills regarding outsourcing, as well as H-1B and L-1 visas. The House Small Business Committee held two related hearings (June 18 and October 20, 2003) while, at Congress's request, the Government Accountability Office prepared a report on outsourcing's impact on the U.S. economy—which, though critical, did not provide extensive supporting data.[77]

The Senate passed an omnibus appropriations bill in January 2004, restricting U.S. government contractors to the Department of Transportation and the Treasury from outsourcing offshore. By 2004 a hundred bills were pending in thirty-eight states to limit the use of offshore contractors by state and local governments. Five states had actually passed such legislation by 2004.[78]

Outsourcing also became a contentious political issue during the 2004 presidential campaign, with public interest provoked by the congressional, state, and local attempts to limit it. The outsourcing issue was raised, in particular, by Democratic presidential candidate John Kerry. Yet it gained little traction in the campaign and resulted in no significant policy shifts during the second George W. Bush administration.[79] As U.S. unemployment began to rise sharply during the 2008–09 financial crisis, however, Congress, the media, and ultimately the White House grew more critical, especially with the advent of a Democratic administration in January 2009. President Barack Obama, for example, criticized laws allowing corporations to "pay lower taxes if (they) create a job in Bangalore, India, than if (they) create one in Buffalo, New York."[80]

Skilled Foreign Worker Visas

Despite the economic utility of Indian outsourcing firms such as Tata Consultancy Services, Wipro, and Infosys, from a corporate and consumer perspective, these companies became the target of restrictive legislation in Congress, presenting a new challenge to the Indian lobby in Washington. The lobby successfully resisted sweeping anti-outsourcing measures, such as a 2010 bill that would have placed a ban on U.S. government contractors using the money of American taxpayers to shift American jobs offshore.[81] Yet outsourcing did become the target of two successful pieces of legislation that illustrate India's continuing political vulnerabilities in Washington. In August 2010 President Obama signed a border security bill that increased the guard force along the Mexican border by 1,500 officers, at a cost of $600 million. To pay for this increase, the bill targeted foreign corporations if at least 50 percent of their U.S.-based employees were H-1B visa holders. The fees paid by these corporations to sponsor worker visas would rise by $2,000 for a period of four years.[82] This legislation passed both houses of Congress easily, aided by the fact that the visa fees were attached to a border security measure that they in fact funded.

The second bill extended these fees an additional seven years, until 2021. This second bill was also part of a larger piece of legislation, in this case providing health care for first responders to the September 11, 2001, terrorist attacks. These health care benefits were to be partially funded by the extension of the visa fee hikes.[83] The cosponsors, Senators Kirsten Gillibrand (D-N.Y.) and Charles Schumer (D-N.Y.), candidly stipulated the bill's target: "This (bill) affects outsourcing companies such as Wipro, Tata, Infosys, Satyam—but does not affect American companies such as Microsoft, Oracle, Intel, and Apple."[84]

Both USINPAC and the Indian government did respond negatively to this new wave of anti-outsourcing legislation. USINPAC argued that ultimately costs for the American consumer would rise and that protectionist action could trigger a trade war.[85] The Indian commerce minister submitted a statement protesting the legislation, arguing that the surcharges ran contrary to mutual sentiments in favor of free trade expressed by both President Obama and Prime Minister Singh at their New Delhi summit of November 2010.[86] In September 2010 the Senate blocked the Creating American Jobs and End Offshoring Act, an act designed to end tax breaks for U.S. companies that move jobs and manufacturing plants overseas.[87] However, on January 2, 2011, President Obama signed into law H.R. 847, parallel legislation originating in the House of Representatives.[88]

India responded fiercely. Yet the intended American recipient of the protest, a senior U.S. trade official, did not even bother to reply. And Indian officials in Washington did not subsequently press for redress, either with the Obama administration or with Congress.[89]

Summary

India is of course a large and highly consequential nation in global terms. Yet like many large Asian nations, for many years its visibility and influence in Washington lagged far behind its global prominence. To add to its other handicaps, India lacked alliance relations with the United States, a particular drawback during the cold war. For many years its determined nonalignment caused New Delhi serious political complications in Washington, especially during Republican administrations, such as those of Dwight D. Eisenhower, Richard Nixon, and Ronald Reagan.

Democratic administrations, like those of Harry Truman and John F. Kennedy, were more congenial for India in Washington. Indeed, it was Harry Truman himself who gave India one of its historic legislative victories, by backing the 1946 Luce-Celler bill. That landmark legislation gave Indians, as well as Filipinos, immigration and naturalization rights not available to other Asians, in recognition of their fledgling democratic traditions and their support of America's World War II war effort. The Kennedy administration, through its active foreign aid program and support for India's military following China's attack in the 1962 border war, also gained Indian appreciation.

India's prominence in Washington began to rise systematically with the end of the cold war, a rapid increase in the Indian American population, and the emergence of a coherent India Caucus in Congress during the mid-1990s. New Delhi's representatives demonstrated their political finesse in Washington by fielding two difficult political challenges: the American backlash against India's May 1998 nuclear tests; and the ratification a decade later, in 2008, of the U.S.-India civilian nuclear legislation. In both cases Indian officials succeeded in forging complex coalitions involving both business and NGO supporters as well as sympathetic members of Congress. There is little question that India's influence in Washington has risen sharply over the past decade, but the limits to that influence have also been clearly shown in controversies related to outsourcing since the global financial crisis of 2008.

Burma

Burma has one of the smallest economies of any Asian nation represented in Washington—less than $50 billion in 2012.[90] Only Brunei, Cambodia, and Laos—with either minuscule populations or highly underdeveloped economies—are smaller. Burma's economy remains only one-seventh as large as that of Thailand, next door, and the country trades very little with the United States.[91]

For many years Burma, also known as Myanmar, was virtually invisible in Washington.[92] For over two decades following the violent suppression of peaceful demonstrations in the fall of 1990, no U.S. ambassadors were posted in Rangoon.[93] The USAID program was suspended, and Burmese leaders were denied entry into the United States. Burma lay under pervasive U.S. and multilateral sanctions, bringing already minimal bilateral trade with the United States to a virtual standstill.[94]

Even when diplomatic relations between Burma and the United States were finally restored at the ambassadorial level in 2012, Burma's formal presence in Washington remained small. The fledgling Burmese embassy consisted initially of only thirteen diplomats.[95] The Burmese simply did not have the local Washington network of more established Southeast Asian counterparts like the Philippines and Singapore.

Yet Burma since the late 1980s has become one of the most visible nations in Washington—not only among Asian countries, but worldwide.[96] Its prominence in Washington decisionmaking has become especially pronounced in the Obama years, since early 2009. Secretary of State Hillary Clinton made a historic trip to Yangon in December 2011—the first by a principal U.S. diplomat since the 1950s. This was followed by President Barack Obama's late November 2012 visit (accompanied by Clinton)—the first ever by a sitting U.S. president. Burmese President Thein Sein visited the United States twice during 2012–13 as well, the first time simultaneously with Nobel Laureate Aung San Suu Kyi. Numerous congressional hearings have been held on Burma—far more than on larger nations such as Japan. And pronouncements by Burmese leaders, including President Thein Sein and opposition leader Aung San Suu Kyi, appear frequently in local Washington media.[97]

How Burma Gained Prominence in Washington

As suggested above, Burma's prominence in Washington politics, and in American foreign policy, presents something of a paradox, given the country's geographic remoteness, small economic scale, and its limited trade and other contact with the United States. As in the case of so many empirical paradoxes, however, this incongruity reveals important dynamics of broader analytical importance. In this case, Burma's new prominence demonstrates the rising influence in recent years of Washington's penumbra of transnational power, discussed in chapter 1—particularly NGOs, think tanks, and mass media that are inside the Washington Beltway yet outside the government. Such groups, as noted, are gaining unprecedented ability to set U.S. foreign policy agendas. Burma's rise among Washington's priorities also shows the increasing salience in American foreign policy of idealist agendas such as human rights.

During the 1950s Burma attracted substantial attention among U.S. diplomats and strategists, despite its distance from Washington, as a neutral power on the borders of both Communist China and the turbulent and contested Indochinese peninsula. As David Steinberg notes, "If we were sitting in a hotel bar in 1956 asking ourselves which countries in Asia would develop most quickly and compared Burma, Thailand and South Korea—each with a similar per capita income and population at the time—Burma would have been the obvious choice." His reasoning was that Burma "was the world's largest rice exporter," that it "exported oil to India," and that it had "timber, gems, minerals and good supplies of many other natural resources. It was also under-populated," he notes, "with a well-educated workforce and had a parliamentary system."[98] Reflecting Washington's priorities of the time,

Vice President Richard Nixon made a two-day visit to Burma in 1953. Secretary of State John Foster Dulles visited Rangoon in February 1955, shortly after the defeat of the French in Indochina appeared to make Burma more strategically vital than ever in the cold war.[99]

Dulles, however, was the last secretary of state to set foot in Burma for over half a century. Following the neutralization of Laos at the 1962 Geneva conference, and Burma's self-imposed isolation from the mid-1960s on, U.S. strategic and economic interest waned substantially. America's one remaining policy concern was drug eradication, as Burma rose by 1987 to become the largest producer of illicit opium poppies in the world.[100] That sobering reality led the United States to support the termination of World Bank loans to the country that year, although no other significant diplomatic or public policy action was taken.[101] Inside the Beltway, within Greater Washington itself, Burma remained effectively nonexistent.

It was the fitful stirrings of democracy—paralleling developments of the same period in the Philippines, South Korea, and ultimately China—that began to make Burma visible in Washington. The catalyst for American interest, as with respect to the other countries, was popular demonstrations, followed by dramatic suppression. On "8/8/88" (August 8, 1988), more than a thousand protesters were killed in a brutal Burmese government crackdown, followed by a military coup and the ascension of the State Law and Order Restoration Council (SLORC) to power.[102] SLORC's ascent provoked additional unrest that led to the deaths of 3,000 more protesters. Vehement backlash from Congress then led to the cessation of all U.S. nonmilitary aid and, in April 1989, to the suspension of Burma's GSP trade status in the United States.[103]

The Burmese military responded to international pressure with intensified repression. In July 1989 Aung San Suu Kyi, leader of the opposition, was placed under house arrest, beginning a serial incarceration that ultimately led to her imprisonment for fifteen of the following twenty-one years. It was only in November 2010 that she was to be conclusively released.

Washington's consciousness of Burma rose further in September 1989 through congressional hearings, led by House of Representatives Asia-Pacific Subcommittee chairman Stephen Solarz, concerning what was termed the crackdown in Burma.[104] Initially the United States took no further policy action, but further human rights infringements were to come. In 1990 the National League for Democracy, led symbolically by Aung San Suu Kyi from confinement, won national elections, with 82 percent of the vote. The elections were voided by the military, however, followed by a wave of arrests.

A protest government in exile, the National Coalition Government of the Union of Burma (NCGUB), was established soon thereafter in Thailand, with Sein Win, a first cousin of Aung San Suu Kyi, as prime minister. A few months later, however, the NCGUB moved to the Washington area, clearly manifesting the importance of America's capital in Asian dissident politics. For several years the NCGUB was based in Rockville, Maryland, a Washington suburb of around 61,000, its headquarters supported by a $75,000-a-month rent subsidy from George Soros's Open Society Foundation.[105]

Ultimately the NCGUB moved to downtown Washington, before dissolving itself, in deference to Burma's ongoing domestic reforms, on September 14, 2012.[106] Over the years Prime Minister Win and his colleagues played a key role in the politics of Asia in Washington, testifying at congressional hearings on Burma, and consulting with the State Department. They also participated in countless discussions on human rights and democracy in Burma, sponsored by NGOs and think tanks in Washington, giving visibility to their cause, and thus intensifying pressure on the U.S. government to support reform in their native land.

After the NGCUB government in exile moved to the Washington area, consciousness of Burma's tortured politics naturally began to rise further in the broader world. In December 1991 Aung San Suu Kyi was awarded the Nobel Peace Prize. In April 1994 Congress declared Burma to be an "outlaw state." In July 1995 Senator Mitch McConnell, later to become Republican Senate minority leader, introduced the Free Burma Act, which proposed sweeping prohibitions on trade with and investment in Burma.[107]

McConnell's proposal was followed in June 1996 by the even more severe Massachusetts Burma Law, an unusual state-level attempt to force more decisive action against the Burmese military by prohibiting state contracts with companies doing business in Burma. The law had immediate repercussions—at least thirteen major firms, including Apple Computer, Eastman Kodak, Philips Electronics, and Hewlett Packard, pulled out of Burma. Between 1995 and 1998, the Free Burma Coalition, the principal lobbyist for the Massachusetts law, also convinced twenty-four cities, including San Francisco, Los Angeles, and New York, to adopt similar legislation.

The Massachusetts legislation and its broad national impact inspired a quiet bipartisan attempt, begun a month after its ratification by Senators William Cohen and Dianne Feinstein and supported by the Clinton White House, to legislate clear national sanctions against the Burmese military, while heading off more radical action against Burma that might erode the White House's negotiating authority. This they proposed to achieve through indirection, in the form of an amendment to the Foreign Operations, Export Financing, and Related Programs Appropriation Act of 1997 (HR3540). This compromise legislation, approved in the Senate by a 54-45 vote, preempted the Free Burma Act. It also led ultimately to investment sanctions, through executive order, that were introduced on May 20, 1997, seven months after the Cohen-Feinstein amendment was passed.

Conservative Groups Join the Action

Liberal NGOs, such as the Free Burma Coalition, the New England Burma Roundtable, Amnesty International, and Human Rights Watch, together with the Burmese expatriates, were the first to raise consciousness of Burma in Washington. They were followed in smaller numbers by conservative libertarians and pragmatists like Senator Mitch McConnell, as noted. Conservatives grew most active, however, when embedded U.S. business investment interests—mainly in the oil industry—came under threat due to sweeping sanctions proposals, such as the Massachusetts Burma Law and the Free Burma Act, together with their proliferation at various levels of government. The United States was, after all, the second-largest investor in Burma during the late 1980s and early 1990s, with $125 million at stake, mainly in the oil industry.[108] Firms such as Unocal, Amoco, Arco, Exxon, and Texaco all had stakes in the country, mainly investing in offshore reserves within Burma's economic resource zone.

In 1997, responding to the proliferation of sanctions measures, the National Foreign Trade Council (NFTC), a nonprofit corporation representing U.S. companies engaged in foreign commerce, unveiled a multifaceted strategy for fighting sanctions. On the one hand, it mobilized powerful law firms such as Hogan and Hartson, one of the oldest and largest law firms in Washington, on its behalf. At the same time, it also inspired establishment of its own affiliated NGO, USA Engage, led by Anne Wexler, director of the Office of Public Liaison during the Carter administration. In 1998 the NFTC moved from New York to Washington, paralleling actions of the Burmese dissidents two years earlier. The escalating battle within the United States over Burma's future thus increasingly centered on Washington.

The business counteroffensive against sanctions had many dimensions. Individual firms such as Unocal, with large interests in the Shwe offshore gas fields, both supported the NFTC initiatives and hired their own lobbyists, such as Tom Korologos of Timmons and Company.[109] They also contributed to tax-exempt NGOs such as the Asia-Pacific Exchange Foundation and the International Center's Burma-Myanmar Forum, which sponsored fact-finding missions to Burma by prominent members of Congress and senior former government officials, including Morton Abramowitz and Richard Armitage.[110] Frances Zwenig, former chief of staff for John Kerry, also organized several trips to Burma for members of Congress and congressional staff while heading the Burma-Myanmar Forum.

The conservative counterattack also included a legal dimension. In April 1998 the NFTC challenged the Massachusetts Burma Law in U.S. District Court. The litigation wound its way ultimately up to the Supreme Court, which in June 2000 declared the Massachusetts law unconstitutional; it was a unanimous decision. While this judgment gave U.S. business somewhat more flexibility in its dealings with the Burmese military, it conversely also weakened the hand of the U.S. government in pressing the SLORC for concessions.

Escalating Pressure on Burma Driven by Congress

Over the years, under both Democratic and Republican presidents, the White House has been consistently conservative on Burma policy, with Congress being the driving force for policy change, often in response to dramatic and flagrant human rights abuses. So it was in May 2003, when seventy NLD supporters of Aung San Suu Kyi were murdered in what many saw as an attempt to assassinate Suu Kyi herself. The so-called Depayin massacre triggered even tighter U.S. sanctions—the Burmese Freedom and Democracy Act, which remains the basis of punitive measures against the Burmese military to this day.

In 2007 suppression of the so-called Saffron Revolution by Buddhist monks in Burma led to the Block Burmese JADE (Junta's Anti-Democratic Efforts) Act, sponsored in the House of Representatives by the eloquent human rights advocate Tom Lantos. That legislation forbade the import into the United States of both Burmese jade and Burmese rubies. At the time, Burma accounted for around 90 percent of world production of both gemstones. This tightening of sanctions, initiated by Congress, was also strongly supported by the White House, partly due to First Lady Laura Bush's personal contact with Christian NGO groups protesting human rights abuses against Karens and other Christian groups in Burma. By 2008 a broad and powerful bipartisan coalition against the Burmese military had clearly emerged, while business interest in Burmese investments had declined. The coalition's indignation against the Burmese authorities was intensified still further following Cyclone Nargis in May 2008, when the ruling State Peace and Development Council, successor to the SLORC, initially banned virtually all foreign disaster relief specialists from entering the country to minister to the injured.

Transformation of Burma Policy under Obama/Clinton

Although Cyclone Nargis was a great human tragedy, leading to the deaths of an estimated 138,000 people, it proved ultimately to be a political-economic blessing in disguise, by accelerating Burma's interdependence with the broader world.[111] Burma's military regime reached out to ASEAN and, after two weeks of hesitation, also allowed U.S. C-130 military transports to fly relief supplies into Rangoon. Ultimately, the United States provided over $75 million in humanitarian relief. China, a close ally of the regime, was unable or disinclined to provide equivalent assistance, with Szechuan being struck by a major earthquake little more than a week after Cyclone Nargis hit the Irrawaddy Delta.

More important than the diplomatic response was that of international NGOs. The disaster both forced the Burmese government to accept more NGO involvement and also drew in international NGOs (INGOs) with primarily humanitarian (as opposed to human rights) concerns, further allaying local political complexities within Burma. For a variety of reasons, the number of INGOs involved in Burma thus grew sharply, from around forty before Cyclone Nargis to more than a hundred shortly thereafter, including many INGOs with global operations, such as CARE, World Vision, and the International Rescue Committee.[112]

Since the Nargis disaster of 2008, INGOs, their transnational activities, and their linkages to Washington have become increasingly important factors in the deepening of the U.S.-Burma relationship, with the newly supportive role of INGOs contrasting sharply to the inhibiting role they had played previously in U.S.-Burma relations. Two principal reasons for this change, of course, have been the changing attitude toward democracy on the part of the Burmese regime and the positive response to these changes from Washington. The political changes within Burma may have been modest and incremental, and the modification in the structure of American sanctions correspondingly modest also. Nevertheless, those changes have led to a major expansion in the latitude afforded to NGOs and multilateral organizations based in Washington, such as the IMF and the World Bank, to engage in confidence-building exercises, agenda setting, and concrete support to both the Burmese economy and its civil society. Interaction with the penumbra of power in Washington has thus been a critical factor in Burma's evolution and in the evolution of the Burma-U.S. relationship. Conventional diplomacy and classical lobbying have conversely played lesser roles than traditional analysis would suggest.

The Obama administration's own approach to Burma policy has been a key reason for the extraordinary NGO and multilateral influence apparent in this case. When Assistant Secretary of State for East Asian and Pacific Affairs Kurt Campbell unveiled the results of the administration's seven-month policy review in September 2009, he stressed an incremental, "pragmatic engagement," approach. That involved a "targeted easing" of sanctions, which left broad implicit latitude for NGOs and multilaterals to serve as intermediaries, interpreters, and informal agenda setters.[113] Actors within the penumbra of power outside the U.S. government, most based in Washington or with strong links to it, rapidly began to fill the void.

The administration has chosen to accord nongovernmental actors, as well as multilateral institutions, an unusually large role in the evolution of Burma policy, because the key interlocutors that it seeks to legitimize and support are outside the Burmese government. Aung San Suu Kyi, Nobel Peace Prize laureate and leader of the Burmese democratic opposition in a country dominated by the military, looms largest among them. The United States naturally cannot ignore the government in its dealings with Burma, but it wants to enhance Suu Kyi and her democratic movement, rather than the military. Empowering NGO intermediaries naturally helps to serve that end.

In contrast to earlier periods in U.S.-Burma relations, many of the NGOs most active since 2009 support a revival and intensification of U.S.-Burma ties, rather than their diminution. Rights-oriented groups like Human Rights Watch, Amnesty International, and the U.S.-Burma Council have injected periodic cautionary notes, but they have also generally backed some degree of engagement and have not in any case dominated the central line of policy. Instead, think tanks and diversified public affairs organizations have been especially influential.

In the fall of 2009, soon after the Obama "pragmatic engagement" report, the Asia Society organized a heavyweight Track II task force on Burma policy, co-chaired by former NATO commander Wesley Clark and former USAID administrator Henrietta Fore. The group also included an influential group of policy intellectuals, combining generalists and specialists—Amartya Sen, Thomas Pickering, George Soros, Donald Emmerson, Frances Zwenig, and Maureen Aung-Thwin among them. In March 2010 this group issued a detailed report with nuanced suggestions on how to concretely pursue "pragmatic engagement" that later had significant influence on policy.[114]

The Asia Society, well connected with the policy process in part through Democratic Party stalwart Richard Holbrooke, who had been president of the society until entering the Obama administration early in 2009, continued to influence Burma policy through its task force and its network of veteran policymakers.[115] In January 2012 the society began a Track II dialogue on policy reforms with the newly created Myanmar Development Research Institute, Burma's first think tank. Aung San Suu Kyi also gave a major address at the Asia Society during her September 2012 visit to Washington, where she shared the podium with U.S. Secretary of State Hillary Clinton.[116] The Asia Society served both as a forum for informal engagement between U.S. and Burmese leaders and also as a source of ideas for strengthening a delicate relationship in transition, where government policymakers prefer to be tentative and discreet.

Other major Washington think tanks played parallel roles, helping to define and informally advance rapprochement between Burma and the United States during the Obama years. The U.S. Institute of Peace, located directly adjacent to the State Department in Foggy Bottom, was one major forum in which Hillary Clinton and Kurt Campbell explicated new developments in Burma policy. Another venue, and contributor to policy, was the Center for Strategic and International Studies (CSIS), which undertook a major study mission to Burma in August 2012, followed by a major international conference in Washington.[117] CSIS has had particular credibility regarding Burma policy, as both of the key working-level State Department architects of the Obama administration's Burma policy—Assistant Secretary for East Asian and Pacific Affairs Kurt Campbell and Ambassador to Burma Derek Mitchell—are CSIS alumni and had been close professional colleagues during their years there.[118]

Universities have also played a role in the rapprochement. Johns Hopkins University, for example, reestablished a presence at the University of Yangon, where President Barack Obama spoke, that it held originally in the mid-1950s. Burmese President Thein Sein in turn used the Paul Nitze School of International Studies (SAIS), a Johns Hopkins University affiliate in Washington, as the location for his major Washington policy address in May 2013; in addition, he has met in Burma with senior Johns Hopkins faculty, including President Ronald Daniels and Southeast Asian Studies Director Karl Jackson.

Washington's penumbra of power, including think tanks, universities, INGOS, and multilateral institutions, has had a particular impact on the evolution of U.S.-Burma relations in functional, relatively noncontroversial sectors such as health and education. This has been leveraged by the resumption of official development assistance from the United States, Japan, and other industrialized nations. The United States formally resumed assistance in April 2011, with an initial $55 million in development assistance directed mainly at local NGOs.[119] And Japan, together with Korea, has complemented this with even larger support.[120]

Multifaceted U.S. policies, with substantial NGO input, have produced a dramatic deepening of U.S.-Burma relations. Breakthroughs include top-level visits in both directions, the naming of ambassadors in both directions, the freeing of large numbers of political prisoners in Burma, the cancellation of the environmentally destructive Myitsone Chinese hydroelectric project, and the loosening of multilateral Western sanctions on foreign investment in Burma. Washington in all its dimensions has, in a short five years, become deeply engaged with Burma, with potentially substantial consequences for the future, spanning both economics and geopolitics.

Summary

Burma is a relatively small economy, located far from the United States, and Washington's interest in that country, and concern for its future, has waxed and waned over the years. During the 1950s it attracted attention from U.S. policymakers as a neutral nation in the cold war, strategically located next to both China and India. Over the succeeding two decades, it also gradually became infamous as a narcostate, with the largest opium poppy production on earth.

Burma really began to attract anguished attention in Washington, however, in the late 1980s, when its military brutally suppressed democratic protesters in the infamous "8/8/88" massacre. Two years later, in 1990, its military also voided a democratic election that would likely have made Aung San Suu Kyi, daughter of the country's martyred founder, Burma's prime minister. It compounded that illegitimate political intervention with brutal suppression of the widespread demonstrations that naturally followed, leading to ostracism of Burma from international society for the ensuing two decades.

The political process of ostracizing Burma from the world was not a strategic diplomatic decision but rather a spontaneous response by Congress and NGOs based in Washington to the human rights transgressions by Burma's military rulers. Civil society actors like Human Rights Watch, the Open Society Foundation, Amnesty International, and the Massachusetts Burma Coalition played key roles. More conservative NGOs from the business world were also active, particularly in moderating economic sanctions, in coalition with more conservative senators such as William Cohen (R-Maine) and Dianne Feinstein (D-Calif.).

Following Cyclone Nargis, which killed over 138,000 Burmese in May 2008, Burma faced new economic imperatives for rapprochement with the outside world. Relationships with Western NGOs began to multiply. The Obama administration, entering office in early 2009, immediately embarked on a Burma policy reassessment, leading ultimately to a new "pragmatic engagement" approach, first articulated in September, which offered substantial scope to informal Washington in defining the new parameters of interaction and in articulating options for further mutual contact. Private groups such as the Asia Society, the U.S. Institute of Peace, Johns Hopkins University, and CSIS came to play important new roles, capitalizing on their extensive Washington networks, in brokering a deepening bilateral relationship. By mid-2012 that new relationship had produced mutual exchange of ambassadors, historic leadership visits in both directions, and deepening policy cooperation, especially in functional areas such as education and health. Burma, despite its diminutive economic scale and lack of established contacts, had become a dynamic new part of Asia in Washington.

Indonesia

Indonesia is the world's fourth-most-populous country, after China, India, and the United States. It is also the third-largest democracy, with the largest Muslim population on earth: Muslims in Indonesia are nearly as numerous as the combined Muslim populations of all the Arab nations. The country is also strategically situated, near important sea routes like the Strait of Malacca. Yet Indonesia could well, as Colin Powell once observed, be "the most misunderstood country in the world."[121] And as *Asia Times* aptly notes, "It is also the most important country that Americans know virtually nothing about."[122]

The comparative sections of this volume confirm Indonesia's puzzling, and remarkably low, visibility in Washington. The *New York Times,* for example, published only one-seventh as many articles about Indonesia as about China, during the first decade of the twenty-first century, and less than one-fifth as many as about Japan, less than one-quarter as many as about India, and less than one-third as many as about Korea.[123] And in 2009–10 there were only thirty-one congressional hearings (House and Senate) that even mentioned Indonesia— only one-eighth the number about China, or one-fifth the number about Korea. This relative lack of congressional attention persisted, despite the rapid deepening of U.S.-Indonesian ties during that period, spurred by the personal interest of President Barack Obama, who had lived in Java as a boy.[124]

Indonesia's lack of visibility in Washington presents a genuine empirical puzzle. How could such a large, important country—particularly an Islamic one, in the post-9/11 era—remain so invisible? In its generally unrecognized state, how does it promote its interests in Washington? In promoting itself, what are its assets and disadvantages? Just where has it failed and, occasionally, succeeded? How have patterns in all these areas evolved over time?

This section addresses these questions in an effort to understand the largest "silent power" of Asia and to portray it more accurately in the context of Washington. Indonesia in Washington, despite its counterintuitive low profile, should tell us much about the political, economic, and social dynamics that generate visibility and influence in Washington.

Sources of Indonesia's Counterintuitive Low Profile in Washington

Our comparative research suggests six potential determinants of political-economic visibility in Washington: historical origins, presence of U.S. bases and alliance commitments, trade relationships, ethnic ties, political leadership, and bilateral political-military crises. In this section I outline how these factors relate to the case of Indonesia in Washington. My hypothesis is that low readings, in terms of these variables, generate low visibility in Washington.

Historical Origins

The U.S.-Indonesia relationship has been, historically, a distant one, in both ideological and interpersonal terms, from its very beginnings. As Andre Roadnight points out, "Washington thought communism posed a threat to Asian nationalism, while the Indonesians viewed Cold War competition as a danger to their independence."[125] Washington policymakers were determined to identify communist subversion in virtually every aspect of Indonesian political life, preventing them from understanding the nature of Indonesian nationalism, and taking actions that intensified its anti-American dimension. Washington saw many of Indonesia's early actions, especially under Sukarno, as flagrantly subversive and as actually abetting communists in the Manichaean world of the cold war. Foremost among these "provocative" steps was the Bandung Conference of 1955.[126] The conference was attended by Chou En-lai and other American antagonists, confirming to Washington its subversive and anti-American character.

Apart from deep-seated cold war anticommunism, bureaucratic and strategic factors were also at work: the European Bureau of the State Department had more influence within the department than the East Asia and Pacific Bureau; the stability of Europe's economy, which many U.S. officials thought might be threatened by decolonization, held primacy in U.S. government priorities over Indonesian nationalist designs.[127] This balance of considerations prevailed both during Indonesia's independence struggle (1945–49) and during the subsequent *Konfrontasi* between the Netherlands and Indonesia over the fate of West Irian (1949–63).[128]

Washington's lack of Indonesia expertise helped give rise to a neutralist Indonesian government that rejected alliance ties with the United States; to a CIA-sponsored rebellion in Sumatra in 1957–58; and to near-total estrangement between the Sukarno administration and the United States until the Suharto military countercoup of 1965. Following the Untung left-wing power grab, Suharto's initiative ousted the Sukarno regime itself from power. It was thus only after 1965 that enduring interpersonal networks between Americans and Indonesians began evolving on a major scale.

Presence of U.S. Bases and Alliance Commitments

The second determinant, the presence of U.S. bases and alliance commitments, has not been operative in Indonesia due to its nonaligned orientation. It rejected U.S. bases and any discussion of alliance. This removed the U.S. military and its close supporters as a consistent prospective advocate for Indonesian interests in Washington, in contrast to the Korean pattern, where national security concerns consistently enhanced Seoul's Washington prominence.

Trade Relationships

As for trade relationships, in contrast to China, Japan, Korea, and Taiwan, Indonesia is not a major U.S. trading partner. It ranks only thirty-seventh as a market for American exported goods and twenty-eighth as a supplier of goods imported into the United States.[129] There is also only limited cross-investment, especially from the Indonesian side. Indonesia thus lacks the business support in Washington enjoyed by China, European nations, and even Japan. This problem of limited business support is compounded by Jakarta's failure to employ many lobbyists, especially those registering as foreign agents—there are typically only one or two annually.[130]

Ethnic Ties

In contrast to China, Korea, Vietnam, and many non-Asian nations such as Italy, Poland, and Israel, ethnic ties to America do not affect Indonesia. The country has no substantial expatriate community in the United States. There are few immigrants from Indonesia living in the United States and only a few resident Indonesian students, although alumni of U.S. universities, such as UC Berkeley, have powerful technocratic influence in Jakarta. This paucity of ethnic ties has impeded the expansion of all-important interpersonal networks.

Political Leadership

Regarding political leadership, few American leaders have stressed the importance of U.S.-Indonesia relations or called public attention to them except for some devoted former ambassadors, such as Ed Masters, and a few supportive members of Congress, like Dan Burton (R-Ind.) and Robert Wexler (D-Fla.).

This situation, of course, changed with the election of Barack Obama as president in late 2008, because Obama lived in Indonesia for four years, from age six to age ten. During 2009–10, however, he twice postponed scheduled visits to the country.[131] The importance of the leadership variable in affecting the visibility of a nation in Washington is clear from the case of Indonesia. Jakarta's visibility has clearly waxed and waned with the perceived precedence accorded to it by President Barack Obama.

Bilateral Political-Military Crises

The final determinant of visibility, bilateral political-military crises, is also largely absent in U.S.-Indonesian relations. Unlike American relations with the two Koreas or with China and Taiwan, U.S. relations with Indonesia have been relatively stable and predictable, though distant. This has been especially true since the advent of the Suharto administration in 1965, controversies over military conduct in East Timor excepted. Previously, there was a pattern of anti-American bombast, together with a CIA-supported rebellion in Sumatra and dramatic confrontations with Malaysia and the Dutch that attracted media attention and U.S. governmental concern. Those stimulants to Washington visibility, however, disappeared by the mid-1960s, superseded by Washington's long Southeast Asia obsession, due to the Vietnam War. Only human rights issues relating to East Timor, especially from 1999 until that area's independence in 2002, made Indonesia a topic of even moderate general discussion in Washington.[132]

Where Indonesia Matters in Washington, and Why

Clearly there are a few notable exceptions to the general pattern presented here, in which Indonesia attained major visibility in Washington and significantly influenced U.S. policy outcomes. This research identifies at least four such cases of enhanced visibility in recent years:

—The formation of the U.S.-Indonesia Society (USINDO) (1994)
—The founding of the Congressional Indonesia Caucus (2004)
—The revival of U.S. military aid to Indonesia (2005)
—The establishment of the U.S.-Indonesia Comprehensive Partnership (November 2010).

In each case, a combination of crisis consciousness and strong personal initiative by a credible American leader was essential to the policy innovation in Washington that broke the general pattern of low-profile drift in U.S.-Indonesian relations. Due to the low overall consciousness of Indonesia in Washington, even strong personal initiatives by single individuals culminated in dramatic policy and institutional shifts.

The establishment of USINDO in early 1994 demonstrates this pattern. This was clearly a counterintuitive development. USINDO is one of the few single-country organizations in Washington, and it was founded to deepen American relations with a nation that had not previously attracted much attention in Washington.

The impending APEC Bogor summit of November 1994, which involved a presidential visit to Indonesia supported by corporate sponsors with special stakes in Indonesia, including Freeport Moran,

ExxonMobil, and General Electric, was an action-forcing event for the executive branch. Former ambassadors to Jakarta Ed Masters and Paul Wolfowitz provided leadership in promoting policy innovation.[133]

Action-forcing, crisis-inducing events were also important in the establishment of the congressional Indonesia Caucus in 2004. Among these action-forcing events were the Bali terrorist bombings (2002), East Timor independence (2002), the advent of Indonesia's first democratically elected president (2004), and a devastating earthquake and tsunami in Sumatra (2004). Collectively, these catalytic developments created a sense of urgency and crisis that provoked key congressional figures interested in Indonesia and the problem of terrorism—Representatives Dan Burton (R-Ind.) and Robert Wexler (D-Fla.)—to visit Indonesia, after which they decided that a formal friendship caucus should be established.

Establishment of this caucus was clearly event-driven and issue-driven, rather than grassroots politics driven. Representative Wexler's district—Florida's nineteenth—has no Indonesian communities to speak of, and Asians in general make up less than 3 percent of his constituency.[134] Representative Burton's district is less than 2 percent Asian American.[135] However, there are major issues pending in the bilateral U.S.-Indonesian relationship that concern both members, including funding for Indonesian military assistance and training, cooperation in relation to emergencies like tsunamis and bird flu, and business issues.

On the other side of the equation was Senator Patrick Leahy (D-Vt.), chairman of the Senate Judiciary Committee. Senator Leahy, a major force in the rarefied world of Indonesia in Washington due to his personal interest and ethical concerns, spoke out about and introduced legislation on a broad range of Indonesia-related issues, including East Timor atrocities (2001–02), restriction on military assistance to Indonesia (2002), human trafficking (2005), the untimely death of Indonesia human rights defenders such as Munir Said Thalib (2006), and protection for Indonesian rain forests and ecosystems.[136] Senator Leahy played a particularly important role in the suspension of U.S. military assistance to Indonesia in 1999, following atrocities by the Indonesian military in East Timor and a strong backlash on Capitol Hill against Indonesian human rights abuses in the same region.[137]

Pressure from political realists for a resumption of military aid gradually began to rise in the ensuing years, leading to establishment of the

Indonesia Caucus in 2004. This pressure for reinstatement intensified in 2005, following China's offer to provide large-scale military assistance to Indonesia. Faced with this direct geopolitical challenge, the Bush administration, with the consent of a Republican Congress, finally dropped its prohibition of military aid to Indonesia on November 22, 2006, despite Senator Leahy's misgivings.[138]

The final major recent policy innovation in U.S.-Indonesian relations, the Comprehensive Partnership of November 2010, was similarly leadership driven. The crucial catalyst, of course, was the election of Barack Obama as president of the United States. Obama had lived for four years in Indonesia as a boy, while his mother was conducting anthropological research in a small Javan village. Yet there were also supportive steps by other key actors that gave policy direction to the political momentum generated by Obama's election. Indonesian President Susilo Bambang Yudhoyono ("SBY") made a landmark visit to Washington to attend the first G-20 summit, convened less than two weeks after Obama's victory, and delivered a policy speech appealing for the deepening of the U.S.-Indonesian partnership.[139]

Six months later, in May 2009, USINDO organized a three-day dialogue in Washington between U.S. and Indonesian officials, on issues ranging from democracy to maritime security. This conclave was intended both to reaffirm Indonesia's importance and to make concrete policy recommendations to the U.S. and Indonesian governments. Presidents Obama and Yudhoyono officially launched the Comprehensive Partnership during Barack Obama's November 2010 visit to Jakarta.[140] It proposed long-term bilateral cooperation on a wide range of issues, including education, finance, environment, health, energy, and food. Among the concrete projects undertaken under the partnership were a "mobile money" microcredit initiative intended to reach 10 percent of Indonesia's unbanked population, and a five-year program to increase agricultural production in West Irian.[141]

Creative leadership at the embassy level has also occasionally broken this low-profile pattern. Dino Djalal, President Yudhoyono's forty-six-year-old spokesman, who served as Indonesian ambassador to the United States from September 2010 until December 2013, showed graphically the importance of effective use of media instruments in early twenty-first-century Washington.[142] Soon after arrival Djalal announced that he would become Indonesia's first "Twitter ambassador." Within a year Djalal, who has written five books and frequently appears on television, had 60,000 Twitter followers and 4,300 Facebook friends.

In July 2011 the Indonesian embassy, in cooperation with the Asia Society and various Indonesian groups, organized an Indonesia festival that drew over 5,000 people to the National Mall.[143] Organized around a theme of multiculturalism, which resonates well in Washington, it included an interfaith celebration involving Muslim, Christian, and Jewish groups.[144] The event featured subnational booths promoting such organizations as USINDO and BKPM (the Indonesian Investment Coordinating Board) as well as unique aspects of Indonesian culture, such as batik. The tour de force was a successful effort to set a Guinness world record, with 5,182 people simultaneously playing "We Are the World" on the *angklung*—a traditional Indonesian bamboo musical instrument. Ambassador Djalal, demonstrating his new-media savvy, played a key role in organizing and publicizing the event, doing a major interview for the *Washington Post,* published the day before the event, and starring in an appeal on the embassy website, encouraging people to attend.[145]

Yet despite such periodically successful events, the structural obstacles in the United States to an intensified U.S.-Indonesian relationship remain, illustrating the powerful impediments to sustained attention toward Indonesia. President Barack Obama's promised visit back to his boyhood home, Java, accompanied by his family, was twice postponed. Indeed, it did not finally occur until November 2010, more than two years after his election.[146] Obama visited again in November 2011, to attend the Sixth East Asia Summit, convened in Bali.

Domestic electoral pressures and policy commitments in Washington kept diverting White House attention away from a much-needed strengthening of bilateral relations, offending the prospective hosts as well. On October 3, 2013, Obama canceled his third trip to Indonesia to attend the APEC economic meeting, as well as meetings with Indonesian President Yudhoyono and leaders of TPP negotiating countries, due to a government shutdown.[147] The innovative Ambassador Djalal himself resigned his post at the end of December 2013 to return to Jakarta and run for president.[148]

Despite these symbolic setbacks, quiet yet substantial progress was nevertheless made during the first post-9/11 decade on deepening

U.S.-Indonesian relations, through the efforts of a remarkably small number of people in the NGO community, of corporations interested in Indonesia, and of interested members of Congress.

The Indonesia Policy Process: Comparative Perspectives

Indonesia, as suggested above, has traditionally attracted remarkably little attention from senior American policymakers, despite its enormous size, large population, strategic location, and political importance within the Islamic world, as a populous yet moderate Muslim nation. Yet Washington has nevertheless responded in a remarkably sensitive manner to the difficult technical problem of making policy on Indonesia, despite frequent top-level neglect. How has that been possible?

An important role has been played by area specialists, particularly in the State Department and academia, such as former Ambassador Edward Masters. As Japan specialists once did half a century ago in the Reischauer era, Indonesia specialists have actually benefited politically from the limited attention that senior generalist policymakers in Washington have accorded Indonesia.[149] In this power vacuum, specialists have often been able to dominate policymaking and to formulate policies sensitive to the local realities of Indonesia, with only minimal interference from the less-knowledgeable generalists. They have also been able to entertain more input from transpacific interests than is common in politically entwined Asia policymaking elsewhere, which tends to mobilize more parochial American domestic political interests. Thus despite the huge discrepancy in U.S. and Indonesian global political-economic influence, the lack of an Indonesia consciousness in Washington helps create a relatively well-aligned U.S.-Indonesian policy process more cognizant of local realities in Indonesia than is common in American Asia policymaking as a whole.

Enduring Achievements: The Key Role of USINDO

Despite the general lack of attention to Indonesia in Washington, some important institutional innovations have been achieved in the bilateral relationship, as noted above, due to a felicitous crisis-driven process in which area specialists tend to hold an unusually powerful role. Chief among these innovations is USINDO, a unique "umbrella provider" of information and contacts on Indonesia. USINDO, founded in 1994, is one of the few single-country organizations in Washington that rejects many of the traditional tools of influence in the nation's capital. To understand why U.S.-Indonesia interactions in Washington have been surprisingly fruitful over the past two decades, despite limited public awareness of Indonesia, it is useful to recognize both how issue politics operate in the low-profile transpacific relationship just described and also how distinctive organizations like USINDO—well adapted to operating in low-information, low-profile environments—actually function.

USINDO, it is important to note, is not a lobbying organization. It does receive corporate support—primarily from firms like Freeport-McMoran, Exxon, BP, and Chevron, which have business in Indonesia. Yet USINDO explicitly stresses that it cannot represent the corporate interests of these firms in any proprietary way, due to restrictive U.S. national lobbying statutes that would undermine USINDO's legal standing as a nonprofit, public interest corporation. USINDO also stresses that it is not funded by the Indonesian embassy, although the two bodies do in fact work closely together.

Rather than serving as a lobbyist, USINDO serves as a platform—an information provider, a gathering place, a speaker's forum, and a provider of educational and career opportunities for Indonesian students and for Americans interested in learning more about Indonesia. It provides detailed information on issues of interest to the business community, including labor law, environment, politics, and Indonesian education. In its various activities, USINDO cooperates closely with the Indonesian embassy. Indeed, it holds many of its receptions and miniconferences in that classic old mansion on upper Massachusetts Avenue.[150] This conjunction implicitly nurtures the corporate perception that associating with USINDO will be favorable to their relationship with the Indonesian government.

USINDO has also been the venue for several major policy pronouncements by top Indonesian leaders, including President Yudhoyono. It has likewise served as the site for major agenda-setting conferences, such as a historic three-day session in May 2009 called Comprehensive Partnership. To strengthen its image as the authoritative interlocutor between Indonesia and the United States, USINDO also works hard to co-opt all Indonesia-related organizations, so that they operate under its umbrella.

USINDO has programs in both Indonesia and Washington. Its central linkage programs are educational. It supports Indonesian university students who wish to travel to the United States for further study, so that they may improve conditions in Indonesia upon their return. USINDO has also set up language and cultural-immersion programs in Indonesia for American students, as well as a university consortium for reshaping teachers' education. In addition it sponsors a presidential scholars' program and fellowships enabling students to do fieldwork in both the United States and Indonesia.

In many respects—particularly in its information provision, agenda setting, and networking, as well as its rejection of explicit lobbying—USINDO operates like a single-country, niche think tank. It has paradoxically prospered for nearly two decades in its niche, without providing proprietary services, precisely because Washington has paid so little attention overall to Indonesia. USINDO thus provides services not available elsewhere. Whether it would prosper in a more integrated Pacific community, where information and understanding of Indonesia is more broadly diffused and where vested interests regarding Indonesia are in clearer competition, is open to question.

Summary

Indonesia in Washington is an empirical paradox: a nation of first-rank global consequence in many dimensions, especially in the post-9/11 era, with a remarkably low profile in the nation's capital. It is the world's fourth-most-populous nation, with more Muslims than all the Arab states combined. It extends for three thousand miles, across some of the most strategic sea-lanes on earth. Yet it is remarkably unknown in Washington. The management of U.S.-Indonesian relations presents a second paradox. Although public understanding of the bilateral relationship is low in Washington, that relationship seems to be well managed. The United States and Indonesia seem to get along fairly well and to respond efficiently to the problems that arise between them.

From time to time, Indonesia explodes into Washington's consciousness, as it did following the East Timor atrocities (1999), the Bali bombings (2002), and the Sumatran earthquake (2004). It also at times suddenly attracts positive local attention, as through the July 2011 Indonesia Festival on the Mall. And major policy innovations occasionally occur in U.S.-Indonesian relations. Normally, it is determined leadership, and often crisis, that drives such transformations in the general pattern of limited Washington consciousness of Indonesia.

Barack Obama, S. B. Yudhoyono, Ed Masters, Paul Wolfowitz, and Dan Burton, to name a few, have had a measurable impact on the bilateral relationship. So has the distinctive single-country think tank USINDO, which often plays a more active role in Washington than the Indonesian embassy itself, although the two are by no means in conflict. Due to the low profile of U.S.-Indonesia relations in Washington, area specialists, both governmental and private sector, with more sophisticated expertise on Indonesia than most U.S. Asia policymakers, have also been able to hold inordinate sway.

A low national profile in Washington has thus, in the case of U.S.-Indonesia relations, not necessarily led to a perverse set of ties across the Pacific. Broad mutual understanding between the second- and third-largest democracies in the world has seemingly not been imperative. Whether this pattern of Washington's benign neglect can be functional in the long run, however—particularly should Indonesia's interests vis-à-vis the United States come in conflict with those of neighboring Asian nations—is in greater question.

Singapore

In contrast to the giants of Asia, Singapore is a tiny city-state, with a population of only 5.4 million people, or roughly that of Minnesota. Its area is less than 700 square kilometers, or just 3.5 times the size of Washington, D.C.[151] In global terms, Singapore ranks no higher than 191st internationally among the world's nation-states in land area, and 117th in population. Even on the GDP calculus, affluent Singapore ranks only forty-first. And in contrast to the armies of registered lobbyists mobilized by some nations, Singapore relies on only seven, whose activities center largely on noncontroversial fields such as business promotion and tourism.[152]

Singapore's, in short, is a remarkably small-scale operation, run by a remarkably diminutive city-nation. Yet that virtual state manages somehow to cast a remarkably long shadow in Washington.[153] It was the first Asian nation to negotiate and then, in May 2003, to conclude a free trade agreement with the United States. It was a founding member, in 2008, of the Trans-Pacific Strategic Economic Partnership (TPP) talks, championed by Washington. Singapore is also consistently ranked inside the Beltway as one of America's most trustworthy military and intelligence partners, even though it has no formal mutual security treaty with Washington and hosts only 200 American troops on its soil.

This chapter outlines—and attempts to unravel—the empirical puzzle that Singapore in Washington presents. It suggests that Singapore's unlikely influence in Washington has three important origins:

—Singapore's willingness to present its underlying interests as transcendent global and regional concerns and to work cooperatively and concretely with others to realize those broader systemic goals

—Its acceptance of declared American national security priorities and its active operational support for them

—The formidable personal networks and astute tactical sense of Singapore's Washington embassy staff, which capitalizes on the open, fluid political-economic environment of a global political city remarkably well.

These underlying sources of Singaporean strength in Washington have grown progressively more formidable over the past decade, making Singapore one of the most effective Asian actors in the nation's capital today, despite its modest size and its sparing use of conventional lobbyists.

Why Singapore Is Influential in Washington

Among the most powerful underlying reasons for Singapore's remarkably high standing in Washington is its discreet yet clear and consistent support for U.S. national-security concerns, and for the underlying concept of bilateral security cooperation. Singapore's air force F-16 crews routinely train at Luke Air Force Base in Arizona and participate in joint exercises with their U.S. counterparts.[154] Both Singapore's navy and its air force routinely carry out combined exercises with a U.S. Navy task group, under the Cooperation and Readiness Training Program. Also, the Singapore army has, since 1980, routinely conducted exercises with U.S. Army Pacific units.

Singapore gained particular credibility with the U.S. military and key members of the executive branch with its offer in the early 1990s—well before the United States entered basing negotiations with the Philippines—to conclude an access agreement that would help disperse the

U.S. presence across the Southeast Asian region, thereby diffusing the political responsibility of hosting the often-controversial U.S. strategic presence. Ultimately, at the end of 1991, following a volcanic eruption that destroyed Clark Field—and followed by the Philippine Senate's rejection of the draft U.S.-Philippines base agreement—the U.S. military left the Philippines, which had hosted some of the Pentagon's largest overseas facilities for nearly a century.[155] The far-sighted 1990 U.S.-Singapore memorandum of understanding has thus been instrumental in sustaining the American military presence in Southeast Asia, despite political turbulence elsewhere in the region.

Although few U.S. personnel are permanently assigned to Singapore, a functionally important naval logistics unit—Commander, Logistics Group Western Pacific—was relocated there from Subic Bay at the time of the U.S. military withdrawal from the Philippines. That group assists critically in fleet support and continues to coordinate bilateral naval exercises involving U.S. forces throughout Southeast Asia. Meanwhile, Singapore quietly provides other low-profile support functions to the U.S. military:

—The only large-scale dry dock between Yokosuka, Japan, and the Persian Gulf capable of repairing and reconditioning U.S. aircraft carriers

—Back-office accounting functions that issue most of the U.S. government checks in the Western Pacific

—Transit facilities at Paya Lebar Airport and Sembawang port, which moved huge amounts of strategic transit cargo to the Persian Gulf and Diego Garcia during the Desert Storm conflict of 1991.

More than a hundred U.S. Navy ships annually continue to call at Singapore, and U.S. fighter aircraft also regularly deploy there, on their long yet strategic movements between the Pacific and the Middle East.

Singapore also cooperates closely with the United States in the intelligence area, especially with respect to terrorism. Singapore has arrested at least thirty-five Islamic militants on its soil, including at least thirteen who were members of Jemaah Islamiah (JI), the group reportedly responsible for the 2002 Bali bombings. Joint cooperation between the United States and Singapore also led to the arrest of a key JI cell leader in Indonesia as well as a senior member in Thailand.[156]

A second reason for Singapore's surprising influence in Washington, related to its defense commitments in also reflecting proactive support for U.S. global policy objectives, is the economic dimension: Singapore promotes free trade and enthusiastically backs the rule of law and liberal investment opportunities for foreign corporations. Singapore has actively participated in all of the major recent global trade liberalization rounds, including those initiated at Tokyo and Doha. Further, it welcomes American corporations, many of which maintain regional headquarters and research centers there. Singapore's supportive policies toward U.S. companies like IBM, of course, enhance its influence in Washington, where it generally enjoys the tacit backing of multinational firms and their local lobbyists.

Singapore policies on security, trade, and investment illustrate some broader reasons why Singapore is highly regarded in Washington. In the words of one veteran U.S. Asia hand, "Singapore gives, as well as takes." It provides intelligence, base support, and diplomatic backing in an area of the world with considerable, and rising, importance to U.S. interests. Americans find this two-way policy interaction attractive and tend to respond in kind.

The value to Washington of Singapore's policy contribution is leveraged by that city's active efforts to define its interests in terms of an inclusive regionalism—a geographical conception that includes both the ASEAN nations and the United States, connected through policy vehicles such as APEC, TPP, and the U.S.-ASEAN policy dialogue. Given Singapore's small geographic scale and its Chinese-majority population, defining interests in narrow national terms could stir a serious backlash among the neighbors. In giving precedence to the broader interests of ASEAN, the Singaporeans may thus only be making a virtue of necessity. Yet there is little doubt that this regional approach also enhances Washington's appreciation of Singapore. It allows American diplomacy to use Singapore, with which it has intimate ties, as an entry point to relationships with other strategically important neighboring nations, such as Indonesia, Thailand, and even Vietnam, with whom America's bilateral relationships are not nearly so well developed.

Singapore has also been aided politically in Washington—both within the White House and on Capitol Hill—by a perception that it is a coherent, unified state, capable of delivering effectively on the commitments that it makes. This predictability makes the U.S. government's internal planning easier and improves the credibility within the American internal policy process of the officials that deal with Singapore. The impression of a reliable, proactive ally is enhanced by the unequivocal positions that Singapore officials typically hold and by their often formidable personal eloquence and intelligence, as epitomized by veteran diplomat-scholar Tommy Koh.[157]

A final reason for Singapore's effectiveness in Washington is the high quality of that nation's embassy staff. It is remarkably small—only nineteen officers, including the ambassador.[158] Singapore has no affiliated cultural center in Washington, unlike most major embassies in the U.S. capital, and the Singapore embassy itself is relatively new, in operation only since 1966.

The ambassador personally is one principal reason that Singapore's embassy in Washington is so effective. Ambassador Chan Heng Chee, who served in Washington from 1996 to 2012, and who recently returned to Singapore as a global ambassador-at-large, is a case in point. With a master's degree from Cornell and a Ph.D. from the National University of Singapore in political science, Chan has a strong academic background and considerable personal experience in policy research.[159] She has served both as director of the Institute of Southeast Asian Studies and as founding director of the Institute of Policy Studies in Singapore. Chan has also received two major book awards and remains a professor of political science on secondment at the University of Singapore.[160] After joining Singapore's elite diplomatic corps, Chan served as permanent representative to the United Nations (1989–91) before being accredited to Washington. She served in the United States for fifteen years (1996–2012), and was, on her departure, the second-longest-serving foreign ambassador in the U.S. national capital.[161]

Ambassador Chan's seniority was an important enhancement to Singapore's effectiveness in Washington, as it enabled her to gradually develop a formidable local network. This network was augmented both by the embassy's social events for local dignitaries and also by the ambassador's participation in activities outside her embassy. Ambassador Chan often attended small-group seminars and special functions at Washington think tanks, the Library of Congress, and other analytical centers, even when other ambassadors were presenting. She also served on several prestigious advisory boards, further expanding her international network. Among these were the International Advisory Board of the Council on Foreign Relations, the Council of the International Institute for Strategic Studies, and the International Council of the Asia Society. She also worked closely with the Asia Foundation. Ambassador Chan's broad global range of first-rank think tank and NGO affiliations parallels that of Tommy Koh, her academic colleague and predecessor as ambassador both to the United States and to the United Nations. Her successor, Ambassador Ashok Kumar Mirpuri, an Advanced Management Program graduate of the Harvard Business School, is also rapidly developing a diversified personal network in Washington.[162]

Embassy Activities

The Singapore embassy is eclectic in its programming, which often subtly combines culture and entertainment with an analytical, political, altruistic, and ultimately diplomatic dimension. Ambassador Chan called the embassy a "do-it-yourself" institution.[163] In 2009, for example, Singapore hosted the APEC summit, providing a rationale to convene an unusually broad range of events in Washington. Over the course of 2009, the embassy hosted nine major functions, concentrated in the spring and fall.

In the cultural area, the Singapore embassy began the year in April, hosting a cast supper of the Washington National Opera's *Turandot,* featuring classical recitals by students from the Peabody Conservatory of Johns Hopkins University. The Peabody Conservatory has a partnership agreement with the Yong Siew Toh Conservatory of Music at the National University of Singapore. In mid-November, the embassy, in partnership with the D.C.-based musical organization, the Embassy Series, hosted a concert by Singapore violinist Lee-Chin Siow, accompanied by pianist Enrique Graf. The concert at the embassy was aptly titled "Tribute to America: A Thanksgiving Celebration" and was attended by over 130 guests.

The embassy balanced its cultural events with a range of analytical offerings. It began the year by hosting a distinguished panel of economic forecasters, including David Rubenstein, managing director of the Carlyle Group; Steven Preston, former secretary of the Department of Housing and Urban Development; and Ambassador Chan Heng Chee. In late April it organized a panel discussion on Singapore's educational system, focusing on Singapore math. The following day it convened a dinner honoring the Stimson Center's twentieth anniversary, including a tribute to Ambassador Thomas Pickering, one of America's most distinguished former diplomats. Complementing this social function was a panel discussion the same evening of twenty-first-century multilateralism, with Anne-Marie Slaughter, director of State Department policy planning, and Ambassador Vanu Gopala Menon, Singapore's permanent representative to the United Nations, as central participants.

In the diplomatic area, the Singapore embassy's main event of the year was classic: celebration on July 30 of Singapore's National Day and Armed Forces Day. The guest of honor for the evening, Assistant Secretary of State for East Asian and Pacific Affairs Kurt Campbell, remarked on the strength and closeness of U.S.-Singaporean bilateral relations, reflecting his frequent personal comments to that effect in a variety of contexts, for more than a decade. Over 430 guests attended, including two former cabinet secretaries, representatives of the Obama administration, congressional staffers, and members of the business community, the diplomatic corps, and the Washington media. Later in the year, on September 23, the embassy hosted an Asian ambassadors' dinner organized by the Asia Foundation and featuring as keynote speaker Representative Howard Berman, chairman at the time of the House of Representatives Committee on Foreign Affairs.

Many Singapore embassy functions are altruistic. It was the venue, for example, for the May 2010 spring cocktail party of St. John's Community Services. The reception was a benefit, organized to support St. John's mission of providing education, housing, and personal services to needy children.[164]

Apart from locally scheduled functions, the embassy also capitalizes on Singaporean leaders' visits to Washington, using them as a form of entrée into the U.S. administration. When the U.S.-ASEAN Business Council presented Lee Kuan Yew with a Lifetime Achievement Award in 2009, for example, many members of Congress attended, giving embassy staffers a golden opportunity to deepen personal relationships with Capitol Hill. They thereby gained an additional chance to voice their interests and concerns directly to the U.S. government, thus helping once again to set Washington's policy agenda.

Lobbying Singapore Style

As noted, Singapore hires very few lobbyists, having only a fifth as many registered agents as Japan. To be sure, the embassy or branches of the Singapore home government, such as the Singapore Economic Development Board, have on occasion hired counsel for defensive reasons. These have happened in connection with the following: criticism of Temasek, the country's sovereign wealth fund, the emergence of legislative proposals in the international tax area threatening to undermine Singapore's attractiveness as a business destination, CFIUS reviews of Singapore-related investment ventures; and lawsuits against defamation of the Singapore judiciary.[165] Singapore also stages international events in Singapore itself, to influence Washington and U.S. policy indirectly. One example is Singapore International Water Week, inaugurated in 2008.[166]

Among Singapore's classic cases of success in Washington—one that illustrates that tiny but nimble nation's distinctive "do-it-yourself" lobbying techniques—is the U.S.-Singapore Free Trade Agreement (USSFTA), signed by Prime Minister Goh Chok Tong and President George W. Bush in Washington on May 6, 2003.[167] The USSFTA Implementation Act was the first American free trade agreement ever signed with an Asian nation and the second bilateral USSFTA worldwide, following only America's path-breaking agreement with Israel. Despite traditional congressional aversion to free trade agreements, the USSFTA Implementation Act was smoothly ratified in less than three months by both the House of Representatives and the Senate.[168]

Singapore employed a distinctly unorthodox strategy to achieve its landmark diplomatic victory, as noted above. The process began with a USSFTA lobbying strategy paper, completed in January 2002, that laid out the details.[169] Instead of hiring large, prominent lobbying firms, Singapore engaged only a small boutique operation, Fontheim Associates, which helped interpret arcane trade legislation and introduce trade-friendly Blue Dog Democrats.[170]

Most of the networking and coalition building was done personally by the ambassador and her staff.[171] The embassy engaged in a degree of preemption, speaking early in the negotiation with labor unions traditionally antipathetic to FTAs, so as to defuse their opposition. Yet rather than concentrating on dialogue with existing groups, Singapore focused primarily on creating new support groups, thus transforming the political context within which the USSFTA was to be forged.

The embassy's early lobbying strategy paper presciently recommended creating two major support groups: the Singapore Congressional Caucus, and the USSFTA Business Coalition. These two bodies were identified as the "main pillars of the lobby plan."[172] Although Ambassador Chan noted that "the Caucus as conceived was not trade-specific, and was expected to last beyond the USSFTA," the caucus was doubtless important in rallying congressional support.[173] From the beginning, Singapore strategists worked hard to ensure that the caucus would be bipartisan, and they in fact succeeded in this objective when Representative Curt Weldon (R-Pa.) and Solomon Ortiz (D-Tex.) agreed to serve as cochairs. The fact that the Singapore caucus is explicitly bipartisan—indeed, formally named the Bi-Partisan Singapore Congressional Caucus—is likely a significant enhancement to its influence on Capitol Hill.

Weldon and Ortiz then waged an aggressive campaign to get their Capitol Hill colleagues to join, noting both the strong security ties linking the United States and Singapore as well as the powerful economic bonds that underlie their bilateral relationship. "For a country with no more than 4 million people, Singapore ranks as a more important trade partner for us than countries such as China, France, Italy, and Brazil," they wrote.[174] Ultimately more than fifty members from both major parties joined the Singapore caucus in the House of Representatives alone, making it one of the largest such groups in Congress. Deputy USTR Jon Huntsman, former U.S. ambassador to Singapore under George H. W. Bush and subsequently ambassador to China in the Obama administration, was among the many prominent participants at the inaugural reception for the caucus, held in the Rayburn House Office Building on October 9, 2002.[175]

The second pillar of Singapore's FTA strategy was the creation of a U.S.-Singapore FTA Business Coalition, composed of seven key U.S. trade associations. First the Singapore embassy invited a few leading American corporations with a presence in Singapore and related business interests in Southeast Asia to a brainstorming session on the formation of such a coalition.[176] Many major U.S. firms responded positively, with Boeing, ExxonMobil, and UPS—among the most supportive—chosen as cochairs. In the first year of the coalition, more than 50 multinational firms, as well as some smaller companies, signed on. By the time the FTA was concluded in 2003, the coalition had grown to 114 companies, industry associations, and other organizations.[177]

Even after the formal USSFTA was signed by President George W. Bush and Singaporean Prime Minister Goh Chok Tong, it still needed to be vetted by the International Trade Commission (ITC). The Trade Promotion Authority stipulated, after all, that the commission release its report concerning the impact of the FTA on the U.S. economy within ninety days of its signing. The coalition was important at this stage, as the ITC's impact statement was based heavily on input from the American business community. The coalition's work on the ITC report was thus synergistic with the efforts of the congressional caucus, as the Singapore strategists had supposed. The caucus had, in the final analysis, spearheaded the ratification of the agreement by Congress, and the coalition ensured that it passed regulatory muster thereafter.

Summary

Singapore is one of the smallest nations in Asia, in both population and geographical area. Even in absolute economic terms it does not loom large, compared with giants like China, Japan, and Indonesia. It also employs many fewer professional lobbyists than the larger nations.

Yet despite its do-it-yourself approach, Singapore has been able to amass and sustain remarkably formidable influence in Washington since establishing formal relations with the United States in 1966. The smooth, three-month ratification of the 2003 U.S.-Singapore free trade agreement—the first bilateral FTA ever concluded by the United States in Asia, and the second one worldwide, following only a politically and strategically distinctive FTA with Israel—clearly demonstrates the island nation's political skills.

Singapore has generated its formidable influence with the United States—and positive visibility in Washington—through an unorthodox strategy that combines shrewd cultivation of U.S. business and national security interests with the development of broad interpersonal networks. A Washington embassy that prioritizes sending intellectually gifted and politically astute personnel to Washington, and also keeping them in strategic positions for long periods of time, appears to have played a central catalytic role in such counterintuitive successes.

Global Implications

Washington, as we have seen, is a complex, fluid, political community—one whose boundaries far transcend the formal institutions of the American nation-state. It includes, conspicuously, a penumbra of power surrounding the U.S. government that performs important global functions in its own right. Both the informal and formal sides of Washington are continually evolving. Indeed, political Washington has changed dramatically over the three decades and more since Ronald Reagan served as president. It has changed even more profoundly since Franklin D. Roosevelt and his associates began forging the modern presidency eight decades ago.

Within America's national capital, the countries of Asia occupy a pivotal yet precarious place. They represent collectively the most dynamic and rapidly growing actors in the international system. Yet those nations and their leaders are also traditional outsiders—peripheral, until recently, to the core global governance structures of international affairs. How a rising Asia interacts with all of Washington—including, critically, those parts beyond the U.S. government—is thus a central determinant of stability and change in international affairs and a seminal issue for both policy and theory.

This chapter explores how the day-to-day functioning of Washington, in its varied interactions with Asia, is quietly reshaping the world as we know it. The chapter summarizes, first of all, the distinctive sociopolitical features of America's national capital in comparison with other major global political cities. Such a comparative perspective helps clarify why Washington as a policy community is generally more congenial to Asian interlocutors than are such European and Asian alternatives as London, Paris, Moscow, and Beijing. The chapter then summarizes Washington's concrete significance for Asia as a whole and how varied foreign national approaches to the U.S. capital differ within Asia itself.

Based on this summary of earlier findings in the book, this chapter considers how Washington's unique local character has affected the functioning of the international political economy as a whole, especially over the past twenty years. The distinctive nature of the Asia factor within Washington conceived as a transgovernmental and transnational political community, I argue, constrains American hegemonic power, while also rendering both Washington and the international system as a whole less hierarchical, more open, and more stable than they would otherwise be.

Washington as a Global Political City: Comparative Perspectives

As discussed in chapters 1 and 2, Washington today has three major structural characteristics rendering it distinct from other major global political centers. These traits in turn profoundly influence Washington's functioning as a political-economic community, distinct from the American nation-state itself. First, Washington has an unusually *parochial yet egalitarian heritage* for a major national capital, having never served historically as the seat of a major formal empire. Second, and related to the foregoing, Washington is remarkably *pluralistic and open,* allowing nonresidents and informal local actors a multitude of access routes to influence. This openness has become accentuated since the 1980s by the widespread privatization of governmental functions, by an increase in the number of former officials working in local research institutions, and by the broad geographical sweep of local political-economic activity, with the rise of the Beltway and of the Dulles and Baltimore-Washington corridors. Third, Washington has an expanding *multilateral* dimension, due to the local clustering of increasingly important global institutions, such as the World Bank and the IMF.

Most of the other major national capitals—London, Paris, Rome, Moscow, and Beijing among them—served for much of their history as the seat of substantial, and generally cosmopolitan, empires. The

European capitals, in particular, had well-established aristocratic courts, powerful bureaucracies, and a clearly defined hereditary elite, making them both exclusivist and sophisticated in their response to outside forces. Not so Washington.

At its foundation more than two centuries ago—and indeed for a century and more thereafter—Washington was a remarkably parochial town, as we saw in chapter 1, with distinctly limited governmental organization and international exposure. It hosted, for example, no resident foreign embassies at all until after the Civil War. The domestic side of official Washington, to be sure, grew steadily during the 1930s. Yet it was not until after World War II that the foreign diplomatic and cultural presence in the U.S. national capital began to grow substantially—within a sociopolitical context dominated by parochial, long-standing, domestically oriented institutions, both public and private.[1]

Despite its parochialism, early Washington was also remarkably open to outside contact and suggestion, especially compared to major European and Asian capitals. For half a century after the U.S. capital's founding, it was not unknown for ordinary citizens, including backwoodsmen, to casually drop by the White House to visit.[2] The federal government traditionally had multiple access points, and lobbying institutions that provided ready governmental access to outsiders were well institutionalized.[3] The egalitarian, democratic American political tradition also legitimated transparency and the rule of law, facilitating external access to the internal functioning of government.[4]

As the United States suddenly rose to global superpower standing in the wake of World War II, the outside world naturally began to take a special interest in steering the "great unwieldy barge" of American policymaking.[5] Fortuitously, it was this sort of an open, cumbersome, episodically naïve Washington policy process that foreigners, including local representatives of Asian powers, often confronted. Since the 1980s the transparency and accessibility of American policymaking have been enhanced further by the geographical spread of both public and private research entities across the Washington metropolitan area, far beyond Foggy Bottom, and also by the privatization of many government functions, as noted in chapter 2. Such developments have made technically oriented Beltway consulting firms like SAIC and Booz Allen Hamilton, manned extensively by seasoned former government officials, important potential access points, supplementary among the initiated to traditional K Street lobbies.

A third key structural feature of modern Washington, seen from a comparative perspective, is the proliferation since World War II of multilateral institutions with important local operations. Not only are the International Monetary Fund, the World Bank, the Organization of American States, and the Inter-American Development Bank based in the U.S. capital but also multilateral NGOs like the Aspen Institute, the Bretton Woods Committee, the Center for Global Development, Freedom House, the G-7 Group, Human Rights Watch, the World Wildlife Fund, and the United Nations Foundation. To be sure, European counterparts, such as London, Paris, and Rome, as well as less explicitly political metropolitan centers like New York and Geneva, also host some multilateral institutions. Yet the concentration in Washington of large and globally consequential multilateral actors is unusually high.

As a result of these three distinctive structural features—a parochial, domestic heritage; an open, egalitarian community structure; and a large multilateral dimension—-the U.S. national capital has an expansive, unusually well-developed, nongovernmental penumbra of power. Its importance is magnified by the global pressures on Washington stemming from America's preeminent global role. This unofficial sociopolitical community often rivals institutions of the American state itself in ability to set global agendas and influence global outcomes.

Given America's preeminent international standing, and the myriad ways in which U.S. power projects beyond national shores, vested interests from throughout the world naturally compete to influence Washington in both its formal and its informal incarnations.[6] Asia, it should be noted, drawing on our findings from chapters 3 and 4, is unusually energetic in trying to shape Washington's perceptions and actions. Asia's major powers have only limited formal political-military influence in world affairs, especially outside their own region, so operating in a congenial informal milieu with linkages to a global superpower is particularly attractive for them.

The nations of Asia naturally have increasingly global political-economic interests after all—ranging from the security of energy sea-lanes to the security of direct investments far from Asia itself. Those interests need sympathetic consideration from a global hegemon. In an era when formal empire has grown passé, in which Asia lacks the global political-military sway to secure its more distant concerns, the Washington economic community—both government and nongovernmental—has a key role, in Asia's eyes. Asian nations are also, in general, heavily dependent on the U.S. market, reliant on dollar-based finance, and hold their massive and rising foreign exchange reserves largely in dollars.

Asia as a whole is thus uniquely intertwined with Washington along a broad range of political-military and political-economic dimensions. These connections intensify Asia's interest in a U.S. national capital where Asian nations have traditionally had much more limited access to the formal levers of power within America's sociopolitical establishment than many of its transatlantic acquaintances. In order both to influence outcomes and to gain information, Asia tends to be intensely interested in the informal penumbra of power surrounding formal U.S. government institutions. The importance of one-on-one personal relationships in Asia's own politics reinforces this interest in informal personal access to Washington.

Governance in a Global Age

For analytical purposes, it is useful to distinguish between official Washington, consisting of U.S. government institutions and foreign transactions with them, on the one hand, and Greater Washington, which includes both official Washington and also the penumbra of power. That penumbra—the informal side of Washington—is the focus of this volume, especially chapters 1 through 4. The penumbra is being critically expanded, and its functional role in world affairs enhanced, by changes in the international system since 1970. These include the erosion of the Bretton Woods trade and financial regime, the end of the cold war, and the rise of globalization. Such historic developments, taken together, have greatly increased the uncertainty of international political-economic parameters and the importance of Greater Washington, including its "penumbra of power," in shaping global outcomes.

The basic political-economic dimensions of globalization, concentrated in the fateful decades of the 1970s, 1980s, and 1990s, are clear.[7] International finance, which had been dormant in the early post–World War II years, began to recover, and rising liquidity outside the United

States put severe pressure on the prevailing Bretton Woods, dollar-based, fixed exchange-rate system.[8] During the wrenching global financial crises of 1971–73, the system collapsed, and the world moved precariously forward to floating exchange rates.

Over the ensuing two decades, global liquidity sharply increased, due to rising international affluence, coupled with rising deficit spending in the major industrial economies led by the United States. Federal debt quadrupled in the United States between 1981 and 1993, for example, from under $1 trillion to over $4 trillion in only twelve years. Meanwhile, new public debt averaged 3–4 percent of GDP in the largest industrialized countries, 5 percent in Canada, the Netherlands, and Spain, and 11 percent in Greece and Italy.

Reflecting both enhanced global affluence and rising OECD debt, and fed by enhanced cross-border liquidity brought about by rising financial liberalization, global financial markets began to rapidly expand. In 1973 the pool of capital available in offshore international markets totaled around $160 billion, with some $35 billion being lent annually. By the early 1980s international capital markets were roughly ten times larger, at $1.5 trillion, than only a decade before, while lending had also risen ninefold, to $300 billion a year. As the global financial system continued to expand, by the early 1990s it held over $5 trillion in net assets and liabilities and was meanwhile lending out more than $1 trillion annually.

By the dawn of the twenty-first century, after further expansion, a huge pool of global capital, totaling over $150 trillion, was available to finance an infinite variety of transactions.[9] Yet capital was accompanied by the simultaneous emergence of immense, potentially volatile, cross-border capital flows, which by the year 2000 totaled well over $1 trillion daily.[10] Such flows were easily capable of destabilizing exchange rates, local financial markets, and entire economies in all but the largest and most robust industrial nations.

The new globalized world of trade and finance that began emerging in the 1970s created a host of new challenges for global governance and international collective action.[11] Most dramatic, of course, were the intermittent financial crises: Argentina (1982), Mexico (1995), Southeast Asia and Korea (1997), and Russia (1998), to name a few. There were also the worldwide trauma of 2008 and the global uncertainties of 2013 and beyond.

Outside the sphere of finance, there were issues of trade liberalization—the Tokyo, Uruguay, and Doha Rounds, as well as the Trans-Pacific Partnership (TPP). There was also the specter of trade protectionism in myriad forms, ranging from orderly marketing agreements, import quotas, and export embargoes to nontariff barriers. And there were burning questions of how the world should cope with negative externalities like global warming while simultaneously generating global public goods such as defense against pandemics and global terrorism. Beyond these political, economic, and military questions, there were also issues for the global community of human security and human rights.

As global issues proliferated, in the late-twentieth-century world of deepening interdependence, nation-states as a category became increasingly incapable of solving them—at least, solving them alone. The problems themselves were growing more complex and more transnational. And as public debt among the advanced nations steadily rose, with welfare demands commanding larger shares of national product as "graying" proceeded, nation-states themselves had diminishing resources to harness to the task of resolution.

Functional Imperatives for a Global Age

The evolution of the global political economy since the 1970s, as briefly described above, has created at least five new functional imperatives for global system management: a stabilization imperative, a development imperative, an agenda-setting imperative, and feedback and legitimation imperatives. These functional imperatives are necessary to prevent international chaos and to ensure optimal global economic development.

The first, and most pressing, is the *stabilization imperative,* with its locus in the financial sector. Enormous global liquidity and huge amounts of capital flowing freely across national borders call for an international mechanism to inhibit financial crises, ensure economically efficient macroeconomic adjustment, and inspire long-term structural change.

Second, the *development imperative* addresses the problems of some of the areas just entering the global political economy, including South Asia and Africa. Although most of these regions have bright long-term prospects, markets may be hesitant over the short term to provide capital, especially in the form of microcredit to promising small enterprises, and especially when local political conditions are turbulent.

Third, the *agenda-setting imperative* would be a mechanism for vetting issues and finding best solutions. It would need to act rapidly and realistically, given the dynamism of global capital markets discussed above.

Fourth and fifth, the *feedback and legitimation imperatives* would provide a mechanism for assessing the value and effectiveness of policy initiatives on problems of common import. They need to determine as expeditiously as possible whether the remedies being implemented are efficacious or not—both for individual actors and for the system as a whole. They also need to provide confidence that such remedies reflect the values of the international community.

These functional imperatives clearly need to be addressed at some level of government—national, supranational, or subnational. Structurally, a historic transition has been occurring in the global political economy, from the centrality of the nation-state, which began with the Peace of Westphalia (1648), to the current, more decentralized age. In this new era, multinational corporations have become important integrators in international affairs.[12] In many countries, local governments have also been growing increasingly dynamic and efficacious.[13] Transnational networks are also more important.[14] And there is both room for and a need for multilateral organization.

The Global Importance of Washington's Penumbra of Power

As shown in the preceding pages, the world in this global age needs financial stabilization and development capital as well as globally sensitive agenda-setting and feedback mechanisms. National governments, including even that of the United States, are increasingly unable to fill these functions alone. And subnational entities, due to their parochialism and limited resources, are clearly unable to do so either.

Washington's multifaceted, non–U.S. government policy community is of tremendous and increasing importance for all four functional imperatives. In the all-important area of financial stabilization, the International Monetary Fund is of central significance. With a staff of nearly 3,000, many of them first-rate technical economists, the IMF prides itself on being cohesive, consistent, and tightly disciplined.[15] Its decisions are made on the basis of weighted shares, so that economically powerful G-7 nations, beginning with the United States, are preeminent, in contrast to the UN pattern. Within the IMF, a European traditionally serves as managing director, with an American as first deputy managing director; Japanese and Chinese technocrats were added recently, as deputy managing directors.[16]

The IMF thus has both the contacts and the expertise to monitor the global financial system—and especially the domestic finances of the developing nations, which are its weakest link. It also has the political heft, with close relationships to both the commercial banks and the governments of the major industrialized powers, to ensure respect for its mandates. If there is a serious weakness in the current structure, it is the alleged insensitivity to the human dimension of global finance, coupled with pronounced solicitousness toward the large money-center banks.[17] This bias is counterbalanced, however, by the World Bank, with its stronger egalitarianism. Both are within a five-minute walk of the White House or the State Department and a five-minute cab ride to the U.S. Federal Reserve.

With respect to the second global imperative—development finance—Washington's penumbra of power is also strategic, with the World Bank and most of its 10,000 employees oriented to address that challenge. The White House nominates the bank's president, who is traditionally a figure of considerable weight with the prevailing administration.[18] Yet the United States by no means calls all the shots, either at the World Bank or at the IMF, and lending patterns do not necessarily reflect U.S. priorities.[19] In cases where the United States has no particular interests at stake, or where U.S. preferences are neither clear nor obvious, other nations play an influential role. And where no large shareholder has particular stakes, the staff and management become very influential, especially in the case of the World Bank. So interpersonal interaction across the penumbra of power—within Washington but outside the U.S. government—plays a central role in shaping many outcomes.

The physical reality that the IMF and the World Bank are literally next to one another in Washington—just across from each other on 19th Street, and also connected by an underground tunnel—is also important to their credibility in serving both stability and development objectives in a coherent fashion. Their respective goals, of course, can easily come into conflict, as they apparently did during the 1997 Asian financial crisis.[20] Yet over the past decade World Bank objectives have begun to converge with those of the IMF. The IMF has been moving toward longer-term, more structural lending, with the World Bank increasingly focusing on policy-based lending, and also helping indebted countries to achieve the structural transformations necessary to sustain economically desirable exchange rates.[21] Due to their physical and functional proximity, these institutions have numerous mechanisms for coordination, ranging from semiannual meetings, to collaboration in staff and management reviews, to appointment of former officials of one organization to positions in the other, to informal meetings at neighborhood coffee shops by staffers of both institutions.[22]

The presence of both the World Bank and the International Monetary Fund in Washington—not to mention other parallel or complementary bodies, such as the Federal Reserve Bank, the Multilateral Investment Guarantee Agency, and the Inter-American Development Bank—leads to a consolidation of impressive economic and intellectual resources in a remarkably compact geographical area.[23] Economists, research, data, personnel, and lendable funds are all readily accessible. That concentration, plus a degree of constructive competition among the people concerned, provides the classic circumstances suggested by Michael Porter as a precondition for a "competitive cluster."[24]

Clearly, Greater Washington has created—in interaction among the multilateral financial institutions, local specialists, and the U.S. government—a potent competitive cluster in the realm of international finance. That cluster contributes more to stabilizing the volatile and increasingly complex global financial system and to securing public finance for global development than any other analogous community on earth, apart from possibly Wall Street itself. It is not unrelated to U.S. governmental influence. Yet the cluster far transcends it.

Washington's penumbra of power has also become increasingly important in filling the three other key global governance functions that emerged in the wake of globalization: agenda setting, feedback monitoring, and legitimation Thanks to high-speed global communications and to deepening transnational interpersonal networks, those processes are all technically capable of being centralized. Because of the presence of the U.S. government, the city of Washington, D.C., is a natural setting for flexible, dynamic agenda-setting and feedback-monitoring processes. America's considerable soft power gives Washington a role in global legitimation as well.

Institutionally, the think tanks, semigovernmental research centers, and universities of the Washington area are uniquely suited to serve as arenas for agenda-setting debates and background research. Heavily staffed with veteran government officials, technically skilled academics, and a horde of interns who undertake basic research, these research institutions have the personnel to handle the intellectual dimension of this work. They can also mobilize transnational networks, including a heavy flow of specialists from other parts of the world who pass through Washington in increasing numbers. And the growing prominence of major think tanks in the media, coupled with policy credibility, attracts increasing amounts of financial support.

One particular dimension of global agenda and policy evaluation where Washington plays a potent, if sometimes neglected, role, is human rights. Since America's foundation more than two centuries ago, human rights and democracy have been foundational to the American people and their Congress. Even though the national government has waffled on this issue, American geopolitical influence, together with the broad sympathies of the American people and the power of communication, have made Washington a powerful arena for furthering human rights and countering human tragedies, ranging from the interests of Soviet Jews to genocides in Bosnia and Darfur.

The Washington penumbra of power is thus admirably suited to agenda setting, and its members have the personal expertise, information sources, and interpersonal networks to fill monitoring functions as well. The potential problem resides in the natural tension between financial support (most of the think tanks, in particular, are heavily dependent on soft money) and the monitoring function. Institutional and ideological competition, however, is still vibrant in Washington, reflecting the deepening political cleavages in the American political economy. That competition helps to improve prospects for competitive monitoring, despite the inherent difficulties involved. The rising importance of mass media in Washington, and the city's growing diversity with the coming of the Internet, further enhances this competitive monitoring process.

Implications for Asia of a Greater Washington

Greater Washington, in the sense of a heterogeneous D.C.-based policy community with a penumbra of power extending far beyond the U.S. government, has quietly assumed a highly influential, strategic, and much-needed role in global governance, a role that has yet to be broadly appreciated by specialists in international political economy. Washington helps to fill five increasingly important functions in the globalized international system now emerging: stabilization, economic development, agenda setting, feedback monitoring, and legitimation. All of these functions are uniquely important for Asia, with its special need for the sort of informal access to authoritative global decisionmaking processes that Washington's penumbra of power provides.

In the areas of stabilization and economic development, Washington beyond the U.S. government is crucially important to Asia due to that continent's distinctive pattern of rapid, capital-intensive, and often highly leveraged economic growth. Asian nations are typically reliable, efficient borrowers, but many have unusually large populations and developmental needs, as well as high aspirations and a pronounced sense of urgency. They need the multilateral institutions based in Washington. India, for example, is currently the World Bank's largest borrower, just as Japan and China once were; Indonesia also stands high on the World Bank's list of clients. All of these nations, and others in the region as well, have been through financial crises, with many continuing to fear a recurrence. So the conditions for stabilization are a continuing concern, with respect to which Asia needs and wants to interact with the multilaterals and other development specialists—often including but not restricted to the U.S. government.

It is in the area of agenda setting where Asia wants the greatest help from the panoply of actors concentrated here, and where mediation by the nongovernmental penumbra of power can most emphatically be of global consequence. Crucially, the think tanks, universities, and research centers of Washington can alert the U.S. government specifically, and the Washington policy community more generally, to issues of consequence to Asia that tend to be neglected in the American policy process, such as energy efficiency and energy security, or to issues on which Asia has a distinctive view.

Through intensive efforts at influencing the Washington agenda-setting process, Asian nations can also help counter the substantial asymmetries with the United States in military and economic power that have traditionally prevailed across the Pacific. Their efforts can thus help to make transpacific relations less unequal than they appear on the surface. Attention to "Asia in Washington" in agenda setting can be especially important for smaller nations, as they strive to enhance their global influence beyond Washington itself.

Informal, international, agenda-setting efforts can likewise be very important for unrecognized political actors who cannot easily use formal diplomatic channels. Their access is through the region's informal network of media, universities, and think tanks—the knowledge-industry network. Taiwan, with its 17 million people and a GDP of over $800 billion (the twentieth-largest in the world) is an example of this sort of formally unrecognized yet highly dynamic actor.[25]

The importance of Washington as an arena for legitimation cannot be neglected. Even as American political-economic power begins to wane in relative terms, interpersonal networks and soft power remain. Many Asian political systems are also structurally inclined to be reactive, particularly to pressures from the seat of the American superpower.[26]

Washington in its largest sense is also important for Asian countries in some particular respects that relate more to their own specific inexperience than to unofficial Washington's powerful new functions in the globalized world. Specifically, as Asian nations assume a global role transcending their traditional regional relationships, Washington institutions help them orient toward parts of the world, such as Africa, the Middle East, and Latin America, which they do not know well. Multilateral entities like the World Bank are especially suited to performing this global intelligence, monitoring, and training function. Yet universities and think tanks, especially those with strong regional studies programs, also play a key role.

In Conclusion

Washington is distinctive among major world capitals for not only its parochial past but also its relatively open, egalitarian present. Washington's openness, flowing from an absence of entrenched bureaucratic or imperial institutions, has been enhanced by local transformations of the recent past, including the privatizations of the 1980s and the geographical spread of many policy-related enterprises across the Beltway area. The local presence of important multilateral institutions, including the IMF and the World Bank, has also fostered a globally influential non-U.S. governmental policy community in Washington—a transnational penumbra of power. That diffuse community interacts dynamically with the government of the world's sole remaining superpower to create a more potent, accessible unofficial Washington than local lobbies, universities, and think tanks alone could provide.

The Washington policy community today thus confronts a world starkly different from the parochial community that began globalizing in the 1970s. The emerging international political economy of the early twenty-first century, in contrast to its predecessor a century ago, has a massive, highly integrated, and remarkably open global financial system, which provides a versatile, sophisticated, and flexible pool of capital for international development. At the same time, however, the emerging financial system is potentially highly volatile and has been wracked over the past four decades by numerous highly destructive financial crises—national, regional, and global.

Recent globalization has also been accompanied by remarkable political-economic change, the consequences of which continue to challenge the stability of international affairs and to leverage the importance of global Washington, with its diverse, cosmopolitan capabilities. Economic development has spread far beyond the G-7 nations to embrace Russia, China, India, Brazil, and many smaller powers. Meanwhile, political change swept the communist world in the early 1990s, bringing an end to the cold war, and has been transforming the Islamic world more recently as well.

Greater Washington is uniquely equipped to address the deepening global imperatives of stabilization and economic development, due to its unmatched concentration of globally oriented financial institutions, beginning with the World Bank, the IMF, and the U.S. Federal Reserve. Washington is also well equipped to provide global governance functions in the areas of agenda setting, feedback monitoring, and legitimation, due to that city's concentrated presence of think tanks, universities, and semigovernmental research institutes. All of these special functions of Greater Washington are especially attractive to Asia—and supportive of Asia's rising role in the world—due to Asia's rapid rate of economic growth and its traditionally peripheral role in world affairs, a circumstance that can be substantially offset through interaction with the unusually open, permeable, and globally regarded institutions of Greater Washington. These penumbra structures contrast with the greater rigidity, opaqueness, and parochialism of national government institutions, even those of the United States itself.

10 | Policy Implications

As has become clear over the past nine chapters, paradox abounds in the transnational politics of Washington. Emerging historically from a distinctly parochial heritage, the District of Columbia has grown to become one of the most global of cities. In conventional realist terms, however, many of the largest and most powerful nations in the world have less visibility and influence within its confines than some of the smallest and seemingly most insignificant.

Many of the greatest sociopolitical paradoxes in America's national capital relate to the subject of this volume: Asia in Washington. Asia lies on the other side of the globe from Washington, but appears to be intensely and unusually concerned about local developments in America's national capital. Asia's myriad cultures are all markedly distinct from that of the United States, yet Asian representatives strive insistently to enter the Washington mainstream. Washington, for its part, appears in its internal functioning to have a reciprocal interest in a part of the world to which it has remarkably limited historic ties.

In this concluding chapter, I recount the central problem for analysis: understanding Washington as a global political city, encompassing much more than the U.S. government, in a complex relationship with the nations of Asia. This problem, as I noted at the outset, is significant from a global standpoint. Several countries of Asia, including China, India, Japan, and Korea, are rising actors in the international system, and their interaction with the unofficial penumbra of power in Washington critically shapes the pace and contours of their ascent. Growing economic and military power alone does not guarantee them entrée.

Asian interactions with Washington are both intense and globally significant for three special reasons. First, the United States is a global superpower, with a highly permeable and relatively transparent domestic political process that is unusually accessible to outside interests. Second, Washington is an unusually convenient venue for bilateral, multilateral, and private sector political-economic transactions, including those engaging multilateral actors like the World Bank and the International Monetary Fund. And finally, Washington is a useful site for global NGO agenda setting, due to the presence of U.S. policymaking, the presence of powerful multilateral institutions, and the presence of globally influential mass media, universities, think tanks, and NGOs, which help confer legitimacy on and conformity to worldwide standards.

Mode of Analysis

The analytical objective of this volume, as outlined in the introduction, is to understand how various Asian nations have responded to the challenge of representing their interests in the changing sociopolitical environment of Washington in the post–cold war world. The first half of the book outlines how Washington itself has evolved, as an increasingly globalized sociopolitical community, over the past thirty years. The latter half of the book considers comparatively how Asian nations, both large and small, respond to this transformation and the relative efficacy of the tools they employ in that effort.

As Robert Dahl and others note, there are multiple dimensions of political influence in the world, and those dimensions do not necessarily covary. In this research I focus on two central aspects: one, visibility; and two, the positive decisions by the U.S. government on matters of importance to the nations in question. I chronicle examples of visibility from a comparative perspective: congressional hearings, media coverage, and leadership addresses at joint sessions of Congress. I also examine concrete cases of decisions demonstrating Asian influence, such as free trade agreements and mutual security treaties.

Chapter 6 lists five hypotheses regarding the origins of Asian influence in Washington. These hypotheses are examined in eight country cases in chapters 7 and 8. These putative explanations for national influence in Washington policy outcomes include the following:

—Realist criteria, such as GNP, population, and military spending
—Diplomatic capabilities, as measured by embassy size and alliance relationships
—Classical lobbying efforts, as indicated by number of registered agents and related spending
—Personal networks in Washington
—Agenda-setting influence

Indicators suggesting the magnitude of effort in each category are given.

Findings

Through the analytical process outlined above, two main intellectual targets are addressed: theory, primarily in international political economy, and comparative public policy, both in the United States and among America's diplomatic partners, especially those of Asia. This contribution to an understanding of Washington's transition is expressed in terms of the concepts presented, accompanied by a review of their heuristic significance, as follows:

—*Global political city*. For more than 350 years, nation-states have been considered the principal unit of organization in the international system. Yet rival units, both supranational and subnational, have been gaining strength, even as the capacity of nation-states has been declining, eroded by conflict, globalization, and a declining resource base. Global political cities, of which Washington is a prime example, have been quietly assuming many traditional nation-state functions.

—*Penumbra of power*. In global political cities such as Washington the multilateral and nongovernmental dimension has been steadily rising in importance. Like the penumbra, or dark shadow that encircles the bright moon, this shadow around the central core of American superpower can be highly consequential for the way the unit as a whole functions. Global public financial institutions like the World Bank and the IMF, together with the law firms of K Street and the think tanks of Massachusetts Avenue, as well as the NGOs and universities stretching from Dupont Circle to Foggy Bottom and from Georgetown to Capitol Hill, are all consequential elements of this penumbra of power.

—*Strategic information complex.* The influence of Washington rests on a much broader base than proximity to American governmental power. Proximity to strategically and economically relevant information, provided by dynamic clusters of researchers at universities, think tanks, multilateral institutions, and individual firms, is another key dimension, and it is rising rapidly in importance in the Internet age.

—*Competitive clusters.* Competitiveness arises and is deepened through a combination of rivalry and knowledge diffusion among nearby actors, a concept elucidated by Michael Porter in a business-strategy context.[1] The concept is useful in understanding how political Washington operates and why it is growing globally preeminent in the supply and analysis of geostrategic and political-economic information. Rival think tanks, research centers, and policy-oriented university programs are numerous and located in close proximity to one another in downtown Washington, especially around Massachusetts Avenue, Capitol Hill, and K Street, as well as outside Washington, along the I-495 Capital Beltway. The growing, globally oriented, analytical capabilities of these knowledge clusters are increasingly synergistic with the rise of Asia, which desperately needs more transregional intelligence and expertise as its economic concerns and geopolitical stakes increasingly transcend Asia itself.

New concepts are proposed and empirically tested in the early chapters, while analytical conclusions of broader relevance, particularly to the classic question of what determines political influence, flow from the comparative analysis in the second half of the book.[2] The study's findings include the following:

—*Common values as a catalyst for influence.* National credibility in Washington and the ability to achieve desired policy outcomes appear to relate closely to a nation's perceived trustworthiness, especially on security matters. The case of India shows this clearly. Indians and Filipinos obtained early rights to immigration and naturalization, relative to other Asians, due to their military cooperation with the United States during World War II, combined with their democratic evolution approaching independence, leading to the Luce-Celler Act of 1946. Conversely, India suffered a sharp loss of credibility in Washington from the mid-1950s until the late 1990s. Its neutralism during the cold war and socialist economic management created the perception among many in Washington that it did not share the concepts of national security and of a market economy with the United States. Similarly, the Philippines lost credibility when it rejected a renewal agreement for U.S. bases in 1992, although it has since gradually recovered.

—*Relationship between national scale and national influence.* Realist theory has classically suggested that a nation's scale—geographic, economic, and demographic—determines its power resources and, hence, its influence in international affairs. The research presented here strongly challenges this generalization. If anything, there appears to be an inverse relationship between national scale and national influence among Asian nations in Washington. The smaller actors—Singapore, South Korea, and Taiwan, in particular—are often the most dynamic, while some of the larger nations—Japan, Indonesia, and, for many periods, both China and India—have been slower to respond effectively to Washington's distinctive, rapidly changing political environment.

—*Declining relative importance of classical diplomatic and lobbying efforts.* Asian nations have gone to considerable lengths to present their views formally in Washington, employing large numbers of diplomatic personnel and expending large amounts of money on conventional representation. During some periods, such as the 1970s and 1980s, they have been the dominant lobbying presence in Washington. That formal presence, and the vigor of Asian representation efforts, has been highly visible. Yet the substantive impact of such efforts on U.S. policy and global governance has been less clear, and the efficacy of individual Asian nations in achieving their objectives in Washington has varied substantially. The successes of Taiwan in the 1980s and early 1990s—when it had no formal diplomatic representation at all in the U.S. capital—and Singapore over the past two decades, with a small embassy and limited conventional lobbying, contrast with the difficulties occasionally experienced by Japan, despite its strong bilateral alliance with the United States and substantial conventional diplomatic resources. When Asian societies have been divided internally, however—as has Taiwan since around 2000, for example—they have lost credibility and influence.

—*The rising importance of interpersonal networks and public diplomacy.* These variables appear to have become of increasing importance in Washington over the past two decades. The information revolution, changing patterns of global finance, and increasing global elite mobility have led to the critical importance of rapid, proactive representation based on flexible, on-the-spot evaluations of rapidly changing local conditions. Interpersonal networks based on trust are important, as they facilitate rapid, candid evaluation. And effective public diplomacy—focused on issues of current policy relevance as well as cultural "grace notes"—requires an active, relatively autonomous local presence so as to respond proactively to rapidly moving Washington issue cycles. Asian nations can no longer afford to regard Washington only as a source of information; they need to consider it as a crucial arena for proactive agenda-setting efforts, as well.

Considering Implications

Over the past decade a vigorous international debate has raged over whether Washington, in the post–cold war world, has become the center of a "new American empire" and, if so, how that ostensibly powerful yet amorphous unit is configured. This debate follows an earlier and to some extent parallel discussion, provoked by the steady rise of Japan in the 1980s and of China since 2000, as to whether Asia is replacing the United States as the global center of political-economic gravity. A close examination of Asia's growing role in Washington adds new insight to these overly generalized debates and suggests why the truth probably lies somewhere in between the classic standpoints.

Washington, with its parochial, egalitarian heritage, has from its origins had a broader range of local access points for outside influence than most other global political cities. The broader world has been sharply increasing its ability and propensity to interact with Washington over the past two decades, due to the rise of a dynamic penumbra of power surrounding formal governmental institutions, which includes law firms, NGOs, think tanks, and policy-oriented universities and other research institutions. This deepening transnational interaction has been a major reason for unofficial Washington's rising global influence—clearly apart from the capabilities of the U.S. government. Just as the city of London has a transcendent influence in international finance, apart from the British treasury and the Bank of England, so Washington's penumbra, too, is gaining global political-economic legitimacy.

The emergence of this penumbra has several implications for international affairs generally, that are highly relevant to the global role of Asia specifically, as follows:

—It diffuses geostrategic information much more broadly across the world than heretofore, thereby stabilizing the mutual expectations of major nations and, thus, contributing to broader geopolitical stability.

—It helps broaden the political-economic networks of participant actors around the world.

—It socializes outside actors in the norms and modus operandi of the international system, while also providing them with technical knowledge.

—It provides a platform for the viewpoints of nonlocal actors, giving them an enhanced role in global agenda setting.

—It enhances foreign access to the U.S. government, including both the executive branch and Congress.

Issues for Future Research

In an increasingly interdependent twenty-first-century world, where transnational relationships are proliferating, the realist, nation-centric model of international relations is becoming increasingly obsolete. Sophisticated alternatives, of course, have been proposed. Yet few of these have come to terms with the important new reality that cities—as significantly as supranational bodies, multinational firms, and NGOs— are becoming major actors and arenas in their own right for decision-making in international politics.

Some interesting work already exists, of course, on city-state political actors such as Singapore.[3] The international role of major municipalities such as New York City has also been considered, especially with respect to export promotion and service-trade regulation.[4] Yet the important transnational role of nongovernmental actors within cities (law firms, think tanks, NGOs, and multilateral organizations among them), and the way that a community of such nongovernmental actors can reshape international affairs, have rarely been considered.

This research shows that the institutional history, sociopolitical structure, and internal competitive dynamics of a city can significantly affect its international role—and indeed, can crucially define that role. Local dynamics thus have implications for the world as a whole. This insight, based on the consideration here of Washington as a global political city, could productively be tested elsewhere in the world. Brussels, Paris, Beijing, New York, and Shanghai are all global political cities in their own right and would make excellent subjects for the sort of comparatively grounded, city-level, and subcity level analysis—sensitive to implications for the global political economy as a whole—that has been undertaken here.[5] Similarities to and differences from prevailing patterns in Washington could then provide the basis for more refined research on the systemic role of particular global political cities as well.

This book also, of course, involves a second axis of comparison: cross-national consideration of the varying approaches by different national and subnational actors to Washington, D.C. The objective in this latter instance has been comparative in nature, directed at clarifying national lobbying and public relations strategies, while evaluating the effectiveness of those efforts. Special attention has been given to the differences among Asian political economies in their approaches to Washington. Only eight cases—China, Taiwan, Japan, India, South Korea, Indonesia, Burma, and Singapore—are considered in detail; clearly, others could be added. Vietnam and the Philippines, in particular, would be prime candidates, given their historically intimate relations with the United States. Pakistan and Afghanistan could also usefully be included, if the geographical ambit of consideration were expanded further west, and if the peculiarities of conflict situations with broad political-military significance could be held constant.

Implications for Policy

Asia's interactions with Washington reshape both Asia and Washington, as well as the broader world. Within Asia they have implications both for individual countries and for Asia collectively. These nuances need to be clearly distinguished in any coherent policy analysis.

For an emergent, yet all too often marginalized, Asia, Washington—and especially its non-U.S. governmental penumbra of power—is vitally important, for both its equalizing and its stabilizing effects on the broader international system within which Asia must operate. Asia's relations with the West, as we saw in chapters 3, 4, and 9, have on the whole historically been hierarchical. Virtually all of Asia's major nations were once colonized or otherwise occupied by a Western power, in an age when the Atlantic nations, led by the United States, were globally preeminent. Informal Washington provides many vehicles for redressing the underlying inequities—in information, network contacts, and other power resources—that Asia persistently confronts in its relations with Europe and the United States.

Washington also fills an important stabilizing function for Asia in trade, financial, and security dimensions, both through specific actions and through general support for cosmopolitan regimes that Asian nations typically find congenial. With respect to trade, Washington plays a key role, through the U.S. government's powerful influence, coupled with lobbyist encouragement, in sustaining an open global trading regime. In finance, U.S. authorities—in concert with the IMF and the World Bank—play a key role in stabilizing foreign exchange rates, and in promoting long-term capital flows to developing nations, while also supporting an open foreign investment regime. Meanwhile, American security guarantees have a key function in stabilizing international political-military affairs. The U.S. role in assuring freedom of navigation in the energy sea-lanes from the Persian Gulf to Northeast Asia, while also ensuring the stability of the Middle East, is a case in point.

All these existing functions of Washington as a political community—comprising the U.S. government plus the surrounding penumbra of power—are highly desirable for Asian nations. The policy implication of this research for them, generally, is thus to support the open, prevailing structure of political Washington and to do everything possible to sustain it. The evidence suggests, however, that maintaining that cosmopolitan structure is not an easy task.

Congressional relations are especially demanding, since the overriding concern of congressional members, especially in the House of Representatives, must be domestic—so as to secure their own reelection. The evidence suggests that nations maintaining continuing ties with Capitol Hill—on a broad range of matters, including many in which the nation in question is asking for little—elicit a more sympathetic response on matters of importance to them than those that engage with Capitol Hill only sporadically. Conversely, the countries that engage only when they have a specific policy agenda to press do more poorly than their more consistently engaging counterparts.

Another increasingly important challenge for Asian nations is consolidating relationships with ethnic compatriots in the United States itself. Since 1965, and especially since 2000, the number of Asian Americans has grown sharply, even as the political activism of individual Asian Americans has also increased. The recent NGO activities of Indian Americans and of the Japanese American–led U.S.-Japan Council illustrate this rising activism—as also does the near doubling of the Asian American congressional delegation in the 2012 elections. Asian Americans can provide increasingly powerful support to both presidential and congressional candidates, while also playing a rising role in directly shaping national policy agendas. More Asian governments need to make cultivating such support a major policy priority of their Washington operations, as nations like India and China already have clearly done.

In enhancing their relations with Congress, ethnic Americans, and local governments, Asian nations inevitably find their embassies in Washington increasingly important. Some, such as Singapore, recognized the potential of their Washington embassies long ago and benefited from that realization. In general, Asian countries need to devote even more resources to expanding the staffs of their Washington embassies, broadening their local activities, and increasing their level of professionalism. Asian nations can also usefully expand information centers, trade promotion offices, political party offices, and other forms of local presence in Greater Washington, as many European nations have already done.

Cultural activities, both under local embassy auspices and more indirectly, can be a crucial tool in meeting the challenge to the transpacific relations enumerated above. Cultural events are one of the most effective tools for simultaneously broadening transpacific networks, deepening mutual understanding, and inspiring trust. They can also, as in the case of U.S.-China relations, help to neutralize geopolitical tensions that could otherwise so easily emerge between rising and status-quo powers of sharply divergent cultural backgrounds. Again, European nations like Britain, France, and Germany are potential models.

Leadership visits are a second tool, in addition to embassies, that Asian nations can and should use to enhance their presence in Washington. Such visits give Asian officials occasion to network with top American leaders and their senior staffs, to set agendas, and to force action on pending issues of special importance. Ongoing, institutionalized, high-level policy dialogues—such as the Track I U.S.-China Strategic Economic Dialogue (SED) and the U.S.-India Track II Strategic Dialogue, can also be functionally important for similar reasons. Both Asian and U.S. policymakers, of course, can use Washington leadership visits to political advantage, but the access that they provide is especially important on the Asian side, due to the underlying asymmetry of attention that is typical in most transpacific bilateral relationships.

Business diplomacy can also be an important tool of influence in Washington and should be a priority of Asian nations. This tool is mostly effective, from the Asian standpoint, when it brings American firms actively to the support of partners across the Pacific, through reciprocal backing in the Asian home country, for example. The U.S.-China Business Council (USCBC) and USINDO are important examples of this pattern in operation. Asian nations can increase the prospects of U.S. business support by providing face time with their leaders, as well as regulatory dispensations and commercially useful information on the ground in Asia, mediated through U.S. business organizations that in turn play a supportive Washington role for these Asian nations.

There is no one strategic approach that optimally suits all Asian nations. For some, such as Indonesia, which are relatively far from Washington and have limited agendas, a low-profile approach that does not attempt to direct public attention to the country works well. For countries with a more urgent need to spur Washington to action, however, silent diplomacy can be counterproductive. There is substantial variation cross-nationally in the effectiveness of any given tool at promoting specific national ends. This book accordingly generates specific policy recommendations for specific nations, especially the larger ones that have not been as effective as they could have been.

For Japan, the most important recommendation of the research is to recognize the growing importance of informal Washington—outside the traditional lobbies and pressure groups. Tokyo has a more classic view of Washington than many of its Asian counterparts, and it has been relatively slow to see how radically the locus of power and influence in agenda setting has been shifting to the think tanks, university research centers, and mass media. Japanese public and private sector actors need to be more conscious of this shift and of the need to engage Washington broadly, rather than through a narrow range of parochial personal contacts. They also need to be conscious that Washington itself is growing in political-economic and intellectual stature, relative to New York City, and to reallocate their resources more toward Washington so as to accommodate the new American political-economic realities.

In reorienting itself toward the emerging Greater Washington, Japan—and for that matter other nations—should take note of the success of their peers, especially the smaller nations like Singapore. These smaller countries have developed several practices worth referencing:

—Managing the Washington environment rather than placating visitors from back home. Several of the larger nations, Japan included, spend a substantial part of their effort in Washington at the latter task, making them markedly less responsive to what is happening in the United States itself.

—Adopting a coherent long-term strategy, giving the local embassy a central role within it.

—Cultivating individual legislators on Capitol Hill, so as to build give-and-take relationships with them.

This book also has significant implications for American policy toward Asia, many of them mirroring the implications for Asian policy toward the United States. The research suggests that many of the most critical transactions in transpacific relations occur literally on the U.S. government's doorstep—within the penumbra of power but not directly involving the government itself. U.S. authorities, in short, need to pay more attention to that informal penumbra of power: how it operates, whom it benefits, and how it can be used more effectively for public purposes.

To be concrete, the U.S. government needs to intensify its international diplomatic efforts within Washington itself, to complement existing efforts abroad. One critical target needs to be the foreign media in Washington. The U.S. government should give priority attention to the foreign press and increase opportunities for informal discussions with foreign visitors. It could also work more vigorously with local universities and think tanks (such as the Woodrow Wilson Center for Scholars) to esure that foreign visitors engage with the full intellectual resources of the U.S. national capital.

The research suggests that the U.S. government should also be highly conscious of the Washington policy calendar and use it to advantage in relations with Asia. Many Asian domestic policy processes are bureaucratized and operate on predictable schedules. Supplementing intuitively plausible dates on the calendar, like the beginning of a fiscal year, state visits to Washington can also serve as especially useful decision-forcing events from a U.S. policy perspective, because matters of "face" for top leaders, closely related to the details of such visits, tend to be important in Asian domestic politics.

The research also suggests, finally, that the U.S. government should be keenly aware of the intense intraregional competition within Asia and subtly use such differences to encourage countervailing cooperation with the United States. This does not, however, imply the desirability of an offshore balancing strategy. The United States does, after all, have formal alliances with nations like Japan and South Korea, whose credibility is important, in turn, to regional stability. Those alliances need the reinforcement of forward-deployed U.S. military forces and would be seriously undermined by offshore balancing. In addition, trade and financial interdependence across the Pacific is so great that a lack of the institutionalized political-military ties that alliances and bases provide could be regionally destabilizing in many dimensions.

Most scholarship in international relations has heretofore focused on nation-states and their behavior, seeing states as the principal and most dynamic actors in international affairs. This book has given an alternate view, privileging global political cities. Clearly they are only a part of the international political-economic equation, but also clearly an important yet heretofore neglected dimension, a gap that this book has striven to redress. This effort to define and elucidate the role of global political cities like Washington, although vigorously pursued, has generated a host of new questions for scholarly research. They in turn open new fields of inquiry, which should occupy a next generation of scholars for many years to come.

Appendix A. Important Events, America and Asia, 1784–2013

February 22, 1784   The *Empress of China* departs from Canton to open U.S.-China trade on George Washington's fifty-second birthday.

March 1833   The United States establishes diplomatic relations with the Kingdom of Siam, America's first formal transpacific connection.

July 1844   The United States establishes diplomatic relations with Qing China.

July 8, 1853   Commodore Matthew Perry and his squadron of black ships attempts to land in Japan at Uraga, but are rebuffed.

March 31, 1854   Matthew Perry concludes the Treaty of Shuri with the Ryūkyū Kingdom.

June 1854   Matthew Perry returns to Japan and concludes the Treaty of Kanagawa, establishing diplomatic relations.

February 9, 1860   Japan's Tokugawa Bakufu sends the first diplomatic mission to the United States, aboard the *Kanrin Maru*.

August 1866   The U.S. merchant schooner *General Sherman* sails up the Taedong River to Pyongyang, contrary to Korea's isolationist strictures. The schooner runs aground, and the Koreans kill all the crew, burning the ship.

June 1871	U.S. Marines land on Kanghwa Island in Korea, undertaking the largest U.S. foreign military action between the Civil War and the Spanish-American War.
January 15, 1872	The Iwakura mission arrives in the United States from Japan.
June 21–September 3, 1879	Former U.S. President Ulysses S. Grant visits Japan and meets Meiji emperor.
May 22, 1882	The United States and Korea sign the Treaty of Peace, Amity, Commerce, and Navigation.
May 1883	An American envoy arrives in Seoul, Korea.
May 1, 1898	Admiral George Dewey defeats the Spanish at Manila Bay.
September 1898	Secretary of State John Jay enunciates the Open Door policy with respect to China.
July 4, 1902	Peace is concluded that formalizes the U.S. annexation of the Philippines.
September 1903	The United States opens Clark Air Base in the Philippines.
August 1905	President Theodore Roosevelt mediates the Treaty of Portsmouth, ending the Russo-Japanese War.
July 8, 1905	The United States undertakes a U.S. imperial cruise to Japan, China, and the Philippines.
1907	The United States and Japan agree to informally constrain Japanese immigration to the United States.
Fall 1908	The U.S. Navy's Great White Fleet visits Japan, China, and the Philippines.
November 30, 1908	The Takahira-Root agreement between the United States and Japan is signed.
June 1924	The Immigration Act of 1924 (Johnson-Reed Act), based on a national-origin formula, formally ends new Asian immigration to the United States.
December 1941	The Japanese military attacks Pearl Harbor, the Philippines, the Dutch East Indies, and

	British possessions throughout the western Pacific.
May 1942	Corregidor falls, consolidating Japanese occupation of the Philippines.
June 1942	The Battle of Midway decisively shifts the balance of Pacific naval power.
October 1944	At the Battle of Leyte Gulf, General Douglas MacArthur returns to the Philippines.
February 1945	The fall of Manila effectively ends Japanese dominance in the Philippines.
August 6 and 9, 1945	The United States drops atom bombs on the cities of Hiroshima and Nagasaki, Japan.
August 15, 1945	Japan surrenders.
September 2, 1945	The formal surrender ceremony is held aboard the *USS Missouri* in Tokyo Bay.
July 4, 1946	The Philippines gains independence from U.S. rule.
August 15, 1948	U.S. occupation of South Korea ends.
October 1, 1949	Mao Tse-Tung announces the formation of the People's Republic of China.
June 25, 1950	The Korean War begins with the North Korean invasion across the thirty-eighth parallel.
October 1950	Chinese "people's volunteers" intervene in the Korean War.
September 8, 1951	The World War II peace treaty with Japan is signed at the San Francisco Opera House. The U.S.-Japan Mutual Security Treaty is signed at the Golden Gate Club, Presidio, San Francisco.
April 29, 1952	U.S. occupation of Japan ends.
July 27, 1953	The Korean War armistice is signed.
January 19, 1960	The revised U.S.-Japan Mutual Cooperation and Security Treaty is signed in Washington.
June 1960	Massive demonstrations in Tokyo against the U.S.-Japan Mutual Cooperation and Security Treaty in Tokyo force the

	cancellation of President Dwight Eisenhower's Japan visit.
March 8, 1965	The United States begins full-scale military intervention in South Vietnam.
July 9–11, 1971	Henry Kissinger makes a secret diplomatic visit to Beijing.
August 15, 1971	The United States suspends convertibility of the dollar into gold and imposes a surcharge on Japanese exports to the United States.
December 18, 1971	The Smithsonian Agreement realigns global exchange rates.
February 21–28, 1972	President Richard Nixon visits the People's Republic of China and concludes the Shanghai Communiqué.
May 15, 1972	Okinawa reverts to Japan.
January 27, 1973	The Paris Peace Accords formally end the Vietnam War.
February 1973	A floating exchange rate system is introduced for the U.S. dollar.
April 30, 1975	Saigon falls to North Vietnamese forces.
November 17, 1976	Gerald Ford becomes the first U.S. president to visit Japan.
January 1, 1979	The United States recognizes the People's Republic of China.
January 28, 1979	Deng Xiaoping visits Washington.
December 1980	Revision of Japan's foreign exchange law inaugurates an era in that country of massive capital outflows, principally to the United States.
September 22, 1985	The Plaza Accord realigns the world's exchange rates.
January 1991	Japan provides $13 billion of support for U.S. and allied forces in the Gulf War.
November 24, 1992	The United States withdraws the last of its military forces from the Philippines, after nine decades of occupation.

October 21, 1994	The KEDO agreement attempts to cap the North Korean military nuclear program.
June 1995	The U.S. government approves Lee Teng-hui's Cornell visit.
July 11, 1995	The United States establishes diplomatic relations with Vietnam.
March 1996	A missile crisis occurs in the Taiwan Strait.
December 2, 1996	The United States concludes an agreement with Japan to move the Futenma U.S. Marine Corps air station to Henoko, in northern Okinawa.
September 23, 1997	The U.S.-Japan guidelines agreement operationalizes transpacific military cooperation.
September 11, 2001	Terrorists attack the World Trade Center and the Pentagon.
October 29, 2001	Japan passes an antiterrorism law, facilitating dispatch of Japanese forces to the Arabian Sea and, ultimately, to Iraq.
May 6, 2003	The U.S.-Singapore Free Trade Agreement is signed; it is ratified two months later.
September 20, 2006	A U.S.-China strategic economic dialogue is initiated.
June 30, 2007	A U.S.–Republic of Korea free trade agreement is signed. It is ratified four years later.
March 2008	The United States joins negotiations for a transpacific trade partnership.
April 2009	A U.S.-China strategic and economic dialogue is established.
November 9–10, 2010	President Barack Obama, the first "Pacific president," returns to Indonesia, where he lived as child for four years.
March-April 2011	The U.S. military helps Japan recover and rebuild, following a disastrous earthquake and tsunami.
February 13–18, 2012	Vice President Xi Jinping visits Washington.
May 8, 2013	President Park Geun-hye addresses a joint meeting of Congress.

June 2013	President Xi Jinping and President Obama meet in Sunnylands, California.
October 6–12, 2013	President Obama's 2013 Asia trip is cancelled because of the government shutdown.
October 16, 2013	Caroline Kennedy is confirmed as U.S. ambassador to Japan.

Appendix B. Registered Foreign Agents in Washington, Key Asian Governments, 1945–2010

Year	India	Indonesia	China/ PRC	Korea	Singapore	China/ Taiwan	Japan
1945	2	0	9	11	0	0	18
1946	3	0	12	7	0	0	0
1947	1	3	17	4	0	0	0
1948	4	5	20	3	0	0	0
1949	6	9	20	3	0	0	0
1950	2	13	31	2	0	1	0
1951	3	11	27	3	0	8	1
1952	6	9	23	5	0	7	4
1953	2	8	9	3	0	4	11
1954	3	9	9	2	0	4	19
1955	2	10	9	3	0	2	15
1956	2	8	8	3	0	3	23
1957	3	9	9	4	0	4	23
1958	4	7	9	4	0	4	22
1959	5	5	11	7	0	4	24
1960	6	6	9	6	0	4	28
1961	6	6	9	6	0	4	34
1962	4	9	13	5	0	3	35
1963	4	10	11	5	0	2	39
1964	8	5	13	5	0	2	46
1965	8	6	13	9	0	2	49
1966	8	5	11	8	0	4	59
1967	7	7	10	9	1	5	63
1968	7	9	10	4	1	5	75
1969	8	6	11	4	1	7	74
1970	8	7	11	4	1	8	82
1971	10	7	15	4	1	10	110

Year	India	Indonesia	China/ PRC	Korea	Singapore	China/ Taiwan	Japan
1972	9	7	17	5	1	11	98
1973	13	7	21	4	2	13	97
1974	12	5	18	14	2	14	106
1975	13	5	19	24	2	16	110
1976	10	6	14	27	4	17	114
1977	12	10	13	34	3	19	143
1978	13	8	14	37	4	24	155
1979	12	8	20	42	5	26	159
1980	14	6	24	42	6	30	159
1981	16	6	21	42	6	39	172
1982	17	6	16	45	8	41	165
1983	16	6	16	46	9	43	184
1984	15	8	18	46	9	42	178
1985	16	7	19	54	13	45	190
1986	19	9	24	59	11	46	202
1987	17	8	22	57	11	59	243
1988	14	6	19	50	11	53	239
1989	16	8	16	48	9	38	251
1990	13	7	14	51	7	38	275
1991	13	9	19	43	9	36	288
1992	14	13	22	47	10	42	260
1993	9	13	21	45	8	41	239
1994	8	11	17	30	7	27	156
1995	9	8	20	31	7	27	138
1996	9	8	18	29	7	22	115
1997	11	6	11	19	6	21	93
1998	8	6	13	16	6	24	89
1999	6	1	13	15	5	25	79
2000	6	2	11	16	6	22	79
2001	5	1	11	14	6	20	73
2002	6	2	10	13	5	16	65
2003	5	2	10	14	6	14	60
2004	6	2	11	15	5	14	50
2005	5	2	10	16	5	17	45
2006	7	1	11	19	4	20	41
2007	6	1	11	17	4	18	39
2008	6	0	10	17	4	17	39
2009	8	1	9	14	6	16	35
2010	8	0	8	15	7	15	35

Source: Foreign Agents Registration Act data.

Bibliography

Agawa, Naoyuki. *Massachusetts Dōri 2520 Banchi* [2520 Massachusetts Avenue]. Tokyo: Kōdansha, 2006.

Allison, Graham. *Essence of Decision: Explaining the Cuban Missile Crisis.* Boston: Little, Brown, 1971.

Asahi Shimbun. *The Pacific Rivals: A Japanese View of Japanese-American Relations.* New York: John Weatherhill, 1972.

Auslin, Michael. *Pacific Cosmopolitans.* Harvard University Press, 2011.

Bachrack, Stanley D. *The Committee of One Million: "China Lobby" Politics, 1953–1971.* Columbia University Press, 1976.

Barone, Michael. *The Almanac of American Politics.* Washington: National Journal Group, annual.

Bodin, Jean. *Six Books of the Commonwealth.* Oxford: Basil Blackwell, 1955.

Bradley, James. *The Imperial Cruise: A Secret History of Empire.* New York: Little, Brown, 2009.

Brzezinski, Zbigniew. *Power and Principle: Memoirs of the National Security Adviser, 1977–1981.* New York: Farrar, Straus, and Giroux, 1983.

Calder, Kent E. *Embattled Garrisons: Comparative Base Politics and American Globalism.* Princeton University Press, 2007.

———. "Japanese Foreign Economic Policy Formation: Explaining the Reactive State." *World Politics* 40, no. 4 (1988), pp. 517–41.

———. *Pacific Alliance: Reviving U.S.-Japan Relations.* Yale University Press, 2009.

———. "Securing Security through Prosperity: The San Francisco System in Comparative Perspective." *Pacific Review* 17, no. 1 (2004), pp. 135–57.

———. "A Tale of Two Cities: U.S.-Japan Relations in New York and Washington." *Kudan Square,* no. 25 (March 2008), pp. 1–3.

Calder, Kent E., and Roy Hofheinz Jr. *The Eastasia Edge.* New York: Basic Books, 1982.

Calder, Kent E., and Min Ye. *The Making of Northeast Asia.* Stanford University Press, 2010.

Carter, Jimmy. *Keeping Faith: Memoirs of a President.* New York: Bantam, 1982.

Chan, Sucheng. *Asian Americans: An Interpretive History.* New York: Twayne, 1991.

Chang, Gordon H., ed. *Asian Americans and Politics: Perspectives, Experiences, Prospects.* Stanford University Press, 2001.

Chang, Iris. *The Chinese in America.* New York: Penguin, 2003.

Choate, Pat. *Agents of Influence: How Japan Manipulates America's Political and Economic System.* New York: Simon and Schuster, 1990.

Cohen, Warren I. *America's Response to China: A History of Sino-American Relations,* 3rd ed. Columbia University Press, 1990.

Cumings, Bruce. *Dominion from Sea to Sea: Pacific Ascendancy and American Power.* Yale University Press, 2010.

———. *Korea's Place in the Sun: A Modern History.* New York: Norton, 1997.

Dahl, Robert. *Who Governs? Democracy and Power in an American City.* Yale University Press, 1961.

Dulles, Foster Rhea. *America in the Pacific: A Century of Expansion.* Boston: Houghton Mifflin, 1932.

Esthus, Raymond A. *Theodore Roosevelt and Japan.* University of Washington Press, 1966.

Fairbank, John K. *China Perceived: Images and Policies in Chinese-American Relations.* New York: Knopf, 1974.

Frieden, Jeffry A. *Global Capitalism: Its Fall and Rise in the Twentieth Century.* New York: Norton, 2006.

Garver, John W. *The Sino-American Alliance: Nationalist China and American Cold War Strategy in Asia.* Armonk, N.Y.: M. E. Sharpe, 1997.

Gerhard, Ulrike. *Global City Washington, D.C.: Eine politische Stadtgeographie.* Bielefeld: Transcript, 2007.

Gould, Harold A. *Sikhs, Swamis, Students, and Spies: The India Lobby in the United States, 1900–1946.* New Delhi: Sage, 2006.

Griswold, A. Whitney. *The Far Eastern Policy of the United States.* Yale University Press, 1962.

Halberstam, David. *The Powers That Be.* University of Illinois Press, 2000.

Heclo, Hugh. *A Government of Strangers: Executive Politics in Washington.* Brookings, 1977.

Hobbes, Thomas. *Leviathan.* New York: Penguin, 1981.

Hosokawa, Bill. *Nisei: The Quiet Americans,* rev. ed. University Press of Colorado, 2002.

Iguchi, Takeo. *Demystifying Pearl Harbor: A New Perspective from Japan.* Tokyo: I-House, 2010.

International Institute for Strategic Studies. *The Military Balance.* London: International Institute for Strategic Studies, annual.

Iriye, Akira. *Across the Pacific: An Inner History of American–East Asian Relations*, rev. ed. Chicago: Imprint, 1992.

——, ed. *Mutual Images: Essays in American-Japanese Relations*. Harvard University Press, 1975.

Japan Center for International Exchange. *Reinvigorating US-Japan Policy Dialogue and Study*. Tokyo: 2010.

Keohane, Robert. "The Big Influence of Small Allies." *Foreign Policy* 2 (1971), pp. 161–82.

Koehn, Peter H., and Xiao-huang Yin, eds. *The Expanding Role of Chinese Americans in U.S.-China Relations: Transnational Networks and Transpacific Interactions*. Armonk, N.Y.: M. E. Sharpe, 2002.

Koh, Tommy, and Ching Li Lin. *The United States–Singapore Free Trade Agreement: Highlights and Insights*. Singapore: Institute of Policy Studies, 2004.

Kwong, Peter, and Dusanka Miscevic. *Chinese America: The Untold Story of America's Oldest New Community*. New York: New Press, 2005.

LaFeber, Walter. *The Clash: U.S.-Japanese Relations throughout History*. New York: Norton, 1997.

Lampton, David M. *Same Bed, Different Dreams: Managing U.S.-China Relations, 1989–2000*. University of California Press, 2001.

Leifer, Michael. *Singapore's Foreign Policy: Coping with Vulnerability*. London: Routledge, 2000.

Lien, Pei-te, M. Margaret Conway, and Janelle Wong. *The Politics of Asian Americans: Diversity and Community*. New York: Routledge, 2004.

Lim, Eunjung. "Who Is the Strongest in Washington, D.C.? A Comparative Study on the Korean-American Comfort Women Movement and the Japanese American Redress Movement." *International Studies Review* 12, no. 2 (2011), pp. 87–107.

Liu, Xiaohong. *Chinese Ambassadors: The Rise of Diplomatic Professionalism since 1949*. University of Washington Press, 2001.

Mallaby, Sebastian. *The World's Banker: A Story of Failed States, Financial Crises, and the Wealth and Poverty of Nations*. New York: Penguin, 2006.

Mann, James. *About Face: A History of America's Curious Relationship with China, from Nixon to Clinton*. New York: Knopf, 1999.

McGiffert, Carola, ed. *Chinese Images of the United States*. Washington: Center for Strategic and International Studies, 2006.

Mendel, Douglas. *The Politics of Formosan Nationalism*. University of California Press, 1970.

Miller, Hope Riding. *Embassy Row: The Life and Times of Diplomatic Washington*. New York: Holt, Rinehart, and Winston, 1969.

Moon, Chung-in. "Complex Interdependence and Transnational Lobbying: South Korea in the United States." *International Studies Quarterly* 32, no. 1 (1998), pp. 67–89.

Morgenthau, Hans. *Politics among Nations: The Struggle for Power and Peace*. New York: McGraw-Hill, 1948.

Nakanishi, Don T., and James S. Lai, eds. *Asian American Politics: Law, Participation, and Policy.* Lanham, Md.: Rowman and Littlefield, 2003.

Neu, Charles E. *An Uncertain Friendship: Theodore Roosevelt and Japan, 1906–1909.* Harvard University Press, 1967.

Nye, Joseph S., Jr. *The Future of Power.* New York: Public Affairs, 2011.

Peng, Ming-min. *A Taste of Freedom: Memoirs of a Formosan Independence Leader.* New York: Holt, Rinehart, and Winston, 1972.

Porter, Michael E. *The Competitive Advantage of Nations.* New York: Free Press, 1990.

Reckner, James R. *Teddy Roosevelt's Great White Fleet.* Naval Institute Press, 2001.

Roadnight, Andre. *United States Policy towards Indonesia in the Truman and Eisenhower Years.* New York: Palgrave Macmillan, 2002.

Rubinoff, Arthur G., "Changing Perceptions of India in the U.S. Congress," *Asian Affairs: American Review* 28, no. 1 (2001), pp. 37–61.

Sassen, Saskia. *The Global City: New York, London, Tokyo.* 2nd ed. Princeton University Press, 2001.

Saund, D. S. *Congressman from India.* New York: Dutton, 1960.

Shambaugh, David. *Beautiful Imperialist: China Perceives America, 1972–1990.* Princeton University Press, 1991.

———. *China Goes Global: The Partial Power.* Oxford University Press, 2013.

Smith, Hedrick. *The Power Game: How Washington Works.* New York: Random House, 1988.

Smith, James A. *The Idea Brokers: Think Tanks and the Rise of the New Policy Elite.* New York: Free Press, 1991.

Smith, Tony. *Foreign Attachments: The Power of Ethnic Groups in the Making of American Foreign Policy.* Harvard University Press, 2000.

Sohn, Andreas, and Herman Weber. *Hauptstädte und Global Cities an der Schwelle zum 21. Jahrhundert.* Bochum: Dr. D. Winkler, 2008.

Swanberg, W. A. *Luce and His Empire.* New York: Scribner's, 1972.

Takaki, Ronald. *A Different Mirror: A History of Multicultural America.* Boston: Little, Brown, 1993.

Tanaka, Akihiko. *The New Middle Ages: The World System in the 21st Century.* Tokyo: International House of Japan, 2002.

"The Global Cities Index," *Foreign Policy,* annual.

Tucker, Nancy Bernkopf. *Taiwan, Hong Kong, and the United States, 1945–1992: Uncertain Friendships.* New York: Twayne, 1994.

Vogel, Ezra F. *Deng Xiaoping and the Transformation of China.* Harvard University Press, 2011.

Waltz, N. Kenneth. *Theory of International Politics.* Boston: McGraw-Hill, 1979.

Woods, Ngaire. *The Globalizers: The IMF, the World Bank, and Their Borrowers.* Cornell University Press, 2006.

Notes

Introduction

1. Although it was Secretary of State Madeleine Albright who popularized the phrase *indispensable nation*, President Bill Clinton first used it formally, at the United Nations (as Albright later pointed out). See Madeleine Albright, *Madam Secretary: A Memoir* (New York: Miramax, 2003), p. 508.

2. Robert Keohane and Joseph Nye, *Power and Interdependence* (Boston: Little, Brown, 1977).

3. See Akihiko Tanaka, *The New Middle Ages: The World System in the 21st Century* (Tokyo: International House of Japan, 2002).

4. See, for example, Saskia Sassen, *The Global City: New York, London, Tokyo* (Princeton University Press, 2001); Saskia Sassen, "The Global City: Strategic Site/New Frontier," *Seminar*, no. 503 (July 2001) (www.india-seminar.com/semframe.html); and Allen J. Scott, *Global City-Regions: Trends, Theory, Policy* (Oxford University Press, 2001).

5. See Sassen, *The Global City*.

6. The global cities indexes are joint collaborations between A. T. Kearney and the Chicago Council on Global Affairs and published as special reports in *Foreign Policy*. The indexes rank global cities in terms of political engagement but do not analyze the nature of political interactions in global cities or their functional implications for international affairs. See, for example, "The 2010 Global Cities Index," *Foreign Policy* (September/October 2010) (www.foreignpolicy.com/articles/2010/08/11/the_global_cities_index_2010).

7. The concept of realism has been refined in such works as Kenneth N. Waltz, *Theory of International Politics* (Boston: McGraw-Hill, 1979); Robert Gilpin, *War and Change in International Relations* (Cambridge University Press, 1981); and Gideon Rose, "Neoclassical Realism and Theories of Foreign Policy," *World Politics* 51, no. 1 (1999), pp. 144–72. It has been challenged in such works

as Joseph Nye and Robert Keohane, *Power and Interdependence: World Politics in Transition* (Boston: Little, Brown, 1977); and substantially qualified by the "democratic peace" school, beginning with Immanuel Kant, *Perpetual Peace: A Philosophical Essay*, 1795 (www.gutenberg/org/ebooks/26585).

8. Peter B. Evans, Dietrich Rueschemeyer, and Theda Skocpol, *Bringing the State Back In* (Cambridge University Press, 1985).

9. See, for example, Kenneth N. Waltz, *Man, the State, and War: A Theoretical Analysis* (Columbia University Press, 2001), esp. pp. 124–58.

10. See, for example, Leonard Binder, *Crises and Sequences in Political Development* (Princeton University Press, 1971); Stephen D. Krasner, "Approaches to the State: Alternative Conceptions and Historical Dynamics," *Comparative Politics* 16, no. 2 (1984), pp. 223–46; Stephen Skowronek, *Building A New American State: The Expansion of National Administrative Capacities, 1877–1920* (Cambridge University Press, 1982); and Kent E. Calder, *Crisis and Compensation: Public Policy and Political Stability in Japan* (Princeton University Press, 1988).

11. See, for example, Theda Skocpol, *States and Social Revolutions: A Comparative Analysis of France, Russia, and China* (Cambridge University Press, 1979); as opposed to Christopher Hill, *Lenin and the Russian Revolution* (English Universities Press, 1947); or Christopher Hill, *Intellectual Origins of the English Revolution Revision* (Oxford University Press, 1997).

12. Stephen M. Walt, *Taming American Power: The Global Response to U.S. Primacy* (New York: Norton, 2005).

13. On the American empire debate, see, for example, Chalmers A. Johnson, *Blowback: The Costs and Consequences of American Empire* (New York: Metropolitan Books, 2000); Andrew Bacevich, *American Empire: The Realities and Consequences of U.S. Diplomacy* (Harvard University Press, 2002); Niall Ferguson, "Hegemony or Empire?," *Foreign Affairs* 82, no. 5 (2003); and Charles S. Maier, *Among Empires: American Ascendancy and Its Predecessors* (Harvard University Press, 2006). Also see Daniel H. Nexon and Thomas Wright, "What's at Stake in the American Empire Debate," *American Political Science Review* 101, no. 2 (2007), pp. 253–71.

14. See, for example, Joseph S. Nye and John D. Donahue, *Governance in a Globalizing World* (Brookings Institution Press, 2000); as well as Anne-Marie Slaughter, *A New World Order* (Princeton University Press, 2004).

Chapter 1

1. Jean Bodin, *Six Books of the Commonwealth* (Oxford: Basil Blackwell, 1955); Thomas Hobbes, *Leviathan* (New York: Penguin, 1981); Thomas Sabine, *A History of Political Theory*, 4th ed. (Hinsdale, Ill.: Dryden, 1973).

2. Margaret Weir, Ann Shola Orloff, and Theda Skocpol, eds., *The Politics of Social Policy in the United States* (Princeton University Press, 1988).

3. Hans Morgenthau, *Politics among Nations: The Struggle for Power and Peace* (New York: McGraw-Hill, 1948); John J. Mearsheimer, *The Tragedy of Great-Power Politics* (New York: Norton, 2001); and Kenneth N. Waltz, *Theory of International Politics* (Boston: McGraw-Hill, 1979).

4. See for example, J. Friedman, "Reclaiming the Aging Metropolis," *Architecture and Planning,* December 1, 1985, pp. 2–6; Yandri Andru Yamto, "Street Vendors as 'Out of Place' Urban Elements," *Journal of Urban Design* 13, no. 3 (2008), pp. 387–402; X. H. Yuan and others, "Urban Dynamics and Multiple-Objective Programming. A Case Study of Beijing," *Communications in Nonlinear Science and Numerical Simulation* 13, no. 9 (2008), pp. 1998–2017.

5. For a succinct summary of Sassen's thinking on the nonfinancial, communitarian dimension of global cities, see the 2010 interview in Christina Larson, "Swoons over Miami," *Foreign Policy,* October 27, 2010 (www.foreignpolicy. com/articles/2010/08/27/miami_swoon).

6. Saskia Sassen, *The Global City: New York, London, Tokyo* (Princeton University Press, 2001), p. xix.

7. See P. J. Taylor, G. Catalano, and D. R. F. Walter, "Measurement of the World City Network," *Urban Studies* 39, no. 13 (2002), pp. 2367–76; P. J. Taylor, G. Catalano, and D. R. F. Walter, "Exploratory Analysis of the World City Network," *Urban Studies* 39, no. 13 (2002), pp. 2377–94; B. Derudder and others, "Hierarchical Tendencies and Regional Patterns in the World City Network: A Global Urban Analysis of 234 Cities," *Regional Studies* 37, no. 9 (2003), pp. 875–86; Ulrike Gerhard, *Global City Washington, D.C.: Eine politische Stadtgeographie* (Bielefeld: Transcript, 2007); Camilla Elmhorn, *Brussels, A Reflexive World City* (Stockholm: Almqvist and Wiksell, 2001); Andreas Sohn and Herman Weber, *Hauptstädte und Global Cities an der Schwelle zum 21. Jahrhundert* (Bochum: Dr. D. Winkler, 2000).

8. See "The 2008 Global Cities Index," *Foreign Policy* (November/December 2008), p. 70; "The 2010 Global Cities Index," *Foreign Policy* (September/October 2010), p. 124; "The 2012 Global Cities Index" (www.atkearney.com/gbpc/global-cities-index/full-report/-/asset_publisher/yAl1OgZpc1DO/content/2012-global-cities-index/10192).

9. The activist partnership of Michael Bloomberg (New York), Boris Johnson (London), and others made C-40 a global force for change in environmental and transport issues during the 2000s and 2010s. See "Mayor Bloomberg and Siemens Cities CEO Busch solidify partnership," *C-40 Cities,* April 23, 2013.

10. Khanbalik, the capital of Mongol-dominated China, subsequently evolved into Beijing.

11. "The 2012 Global Cities Index" (www.atkearney.com/gbpc/global-cities-index/full-report/-/asset_publisher/yAl1OgZpc1DO/content/2012-global-cities-index/10192). Ratings for business activity and political engagement, represented in figure 1-1 as "global economic center" and "global political influence," respectively, were used in constructing the datapoints in question. The business activity

index includes value of capital markets, number of Fortune Global 500 firms headquartered, and volume of goods passing through the global city in question. Mysore is not included in the index and is included in figure 1-1 for illustrative purposes as a location lacking political-economic influence.

12. Before formal annexation of the Congo by Belgium, it was (from 1885 to 1909) the personal fief of King Leopold II and was known as the Congo Free State. On the history of the Free State, see Ruth M. Slade, *King Leopold's Congo* (Oxford University Press, 1962).

13. James H. Billington, *Fire in the Minds of Men: Origins of the Revolutionary Faith* (New Brunswick, N.J.: Transaction, 1999), p. 309.

14. Ibid., pp. 308–09.

15. In 2007, for example, the Belgium parliament demonstrated its impotence by failing to create a government until nine months after the general election, over tensions between Wallonia and Flanders.

16. On the American empire concept see, for example, Niall Ferguson, *Colossus: The Price of American Empire* (New York: Penguin, 2004); and Charles S. Maier, *Among Empires: American Ascendancy and Its Predecessors* (Harvard University Press, 2006).

17. On this issue, see, for example, Robert Keohane, "The Big Influence of Small Allies," *Foreign Policy* 2 (Spring 1971), pp. 161–82; Tony Smith, *Foreign Attachments: The Power of Ethnic Groups in the Making of American Foreign Policy* (Harvard University Press, 2000).

18. Spain formally ceded them in December 1899 at the Treaty of Paris, which Congress ratified two months later.

19. Stephen Skowronek, *Building a New American State: The Expansion of National Administrative Capacities, 1877–1920* (Cambridge University Press, 1982).

20. Washington's first permanent embassy facilities, those of the United Kingdom, were established in 1866. See Hope Riding Miller, *Embassy Row: The Life and Times of Diplomatic Washington* (New York: Holt, Rinehart, and Winston. 1969), p. 149.

21. Ibid., p. 2.

22. The current street numbering system, based on the quadrant and alphabetical streets, emerged only in 1869. See "Building History Research Guide" (Washington: Historical Society of Washington, D.C., n.d.).

23. The concept is that of Sassen, as noted earlier, denoting the great metropolises of the past. See Sassen, *The Global City*.

24. Carol Gelderman, *Henry Ford: The Wayward Capitalist* (New York: Dial, 1981), p. 325.

25. See ibid., pp. 50–58.

26. Ibid., p. 324. Under NIRA, industries had to create a code of operations to regulate wage and hours. The act also required industries to post signs stating that workers were free to organize collective bargaining.

27. Ibid., p. 324.

28. "Will Use Publicity to Fight 'Open Shop'; Labor Union Conference Decides to Open a Bureau," *New York Times,* February 24, 1921.

29. Paul A. Djupe, Laura R. Olson, and Christopher P. Gilbert, "Sources of Clergy Support for Denominational Lobbying in Washington," *Review of the Religious Research* 47, no. 1 (2005), p. 86.

30. Ibid., p. 86.

31. Ibid., p. 87.

32. "Catholic Relief Services Proposes New World Headquarters in Baltimore City," *Charity Wire,* November 13, 2002 (www.charitywire.com/charity37/04337.html).

33. Christian Relief Services, "2007 Annual Report" (http://crs.org/about/finance/pdf/AR_2007.pdf).

34. Christian Relief Services, "2012 Annual Report," p. 35 (http://crs.org/2012-annual-report/images/PDF/CRS-2012AnnualReport.pdf).

35. Stanley D. Bachrack, *The Committee of One Million: "China Lobby" Politics, 1953–1971* (Columbia University Press, 1976).

36. Svenja Blanke, "Civic Foreign Policy: Human Rights, Faith-Based Groups, and U.S.-Salvadoran Relations in the 1970s," *The Americas* 61, no. 2 (2004), pp. 217–44.

37. Roberto Camagni, "The Economic and Spatial Contradictions," in *Global City-Regions: Trends, Theory, Policy,* edited by Allen J. Scott (Oxford University Press, 2002), pp. 105–06.

38. In December 6, 1921, the Anglo-Irish Treaty was signed, establishing the Irish Free State. It came into force only a year later.

39. *Japan Now,* December 21, 2007.

40. On expanding U.S. government information-processing capabilities, see James Bamford, *The Puzzle Palace: A Report on America's Most Secret Agency* (Boston: Houghton Mifflin, 1982); and "Top Secret America," *Washington Post,* July 19, 20, 21, and December 20, 2010 (http://projects.washingtonpost.com/top-secret-america/).

41. On the impact of technostructure interaction on policy outcomes, see J. Kenneth Galbraith, *The New Industrial State* (Boston: Houghton Mifflin, 1967); and Graham Allison, *Essence of Decision: Explaining the Cuban Missile Crisis* (Boston: Little, Brown, 1971).

42. *West's Encyclopedia of American Law,* 1998, defines *penumbra* as "the rights guaranteed by implication in a constitution or the implied powers of a rule."

43. On the notion of competitive clusters and their importance in generating innovation, see Michael E. Porter, *The Competitive Advantage of Nations* (New York: Free Press, 1990).

44. Department of Justice, Foreign Agents Registration Act (www.fara.gov).

45. See Kent E. Calder, "A Tale of Two Cities: U.S.-Japan Relations in New York and Washington," *Kudan Square,* no. 25 (March 2008), pp. 1–3.

46. See Robert Pear, "Diplomats at Japan's Embassy Worry about Anti-Tokyo Sentiment in U.S.," *New York Times,* November 24, 1989; and Department of Justice, "Report of the Attorney General to Congress of the United States on the Administration of the Foreign Agents Registration Act of 1939, as amended, for the six months ending June 30, 2010" (www.usdoj.gov/criminal/fara/reports/June30-2010.pdf).

47. For a classic picture of this pattern, albeit a hypocritical one, see Pat Choate, *Agents of Influence: How Japan Manipulates America's Political and Economic System* (New York: Simon and Schuster, 1990).

48. Chung-in Moon, "Complex Interdependence and Transnational Lobbying: South Korea in the United States," *International Studies Quarterly* 32, no.1 (1998), p. 82.

49. Ibid., p. 77.

50. Robert Fossaert, "Les villes mondiales, villes du système mondial," *Hérodote,* no. 101, 2e trimestre (Paris: La Découverte, 2001).

51. AIG was nearly 80 percent government owned, and totally subject to dictates from the U.S. Treasury in Washington, following a $182.3 billion bailout in 2008. See "In Shift Wall Street Goes to Washington," *Washington Post,* September 19, 2009.

Chapter 2

1. Thomas J. Carrier, *Images of America: Washington, D.C.—A Historical Walking Tour* (Charleston, S.C.: Arcadia, 1999), p. 7.

2. Ibid., p. 8.

3. For more details on the early history of the Washington area, see U.S. Department of the Interior, National Park Service, "Georgetown Historic District" (www.nps.gov/nr/travel/wash/dc15.htm).

4. Clarence B. Carons, *The Beginning of the Republic: 1775–1825* (Alexandria, Va.: Western Goals Foundation, 1984); and Carrier, *Images of America,* p. 7. The procedural requirement of ratification by nine of thirteen states was met through New Hampshire's accession to the Constitution on June 21, 1788, but the ratification was only formally recognized by the new Congress in December, 1791.

5. Kathryn Allamong Jacob, *Capital Elites: High Society in Washington, D.C., after the Civil War* (Washington: Smithsonian Institution Press, 1995), p. 2. George Washington marched in a parade to promote stable and increased residency in the national capital. See Jacob, *Capital Elites,* p. 5.

6. Hope Riding Miller, *Embassy Row: The Life and Times of Diplomatic Washington* (New York: Holt, Rinehart, and Winston, 1969), p. 1. Of those seven, only four (Great Britain, France, the Netherlands, and Spain) sent ministers to the United States; Portugal and Prussia sent a chargé d'affaires, and Denmark dispatched a consul.

7. Ibid.

8. Ibid., p. 3.

9. Ibid., p. 141.

10. The State Department had eight employees in 1790, ten in 1800, twenty-three in 1830, and forty-two in 1869, not counting overseas personnel. See U.S. Department of State, Office of the Historian, *A History of the United States Department of State, 1789–1996* (Government Printing Office, July 1996) (www.state.gov/www/about_state/history/dephis.html).

11. See British Embassy, Washington, "Embassy History" (http://ukinusa.fco.gov.uk/en/about-us/our-embassy/location-access/embassyhistory).

12. The British Embassy, employing 120 accredited diplomats and over 600 staffers, continues to be one of the largest in Washington and is a fixture at the northern end of Embassy Row, near the U.S. Naval Observatory and the vice president's official residence. Personal communication from British embassy enquiry service, February 12, 2008.

13. The thirty-one-square-mile area that Virginia ceded to the District was returned in 1847, so the Virginia side of the Potomac River was thereafter not part of Washington.

14. U.S. Census Bureau (www.census.gov/population/censusdata/table-26.pdf); NeighborhoodInfo DC (www.neighborhoodinfodc.org/city/nbr_prof_city.html). By 2010 the District of Columbia's population had fallen by a quarter from 1950 levels, to only 601,722; by 2012 the District's estimated population had returned only to 632, 323.

15. Carl Abbott, "Perspectives of Urban Economic Planning: The Case of Washington, D.C., since 1880," *Public Historian* 11, no. 2 (1989), pp. 5–21.

16. U.S. Office of Personnel Management, "Federal Civilian Statistics: Annual Report by Geographical Areas: 1980" (Government Printing Office, 1980).

17. The Interstate Commerce Commission was established in 1887, the Federal Trade Commission began operation in 1915, and the Internal Revenue Service, which was founded in 1862, changed its name to its present form in 1918. See Stephen Skowronek, *Building a New American State: The Expansion of National Administrative Capacities, 1877–1920* (Cambridge University Press, 1982); and Theda Skocpol, *Protecting Soldiers and Mothers: The Political Origins of Social Policy in the United States* (Harvard University Press, 1992).

18. See Max Weber, *Economy and Society: An Outline of Interpretive Sociology,* edited by Guenther Roth and Claus Wittlich (University of California Press, 1978); Max Weber, *The Theory of Social and Economic Organization,* translated

by A. M. Henderson and Talcott Parsons (London: Collier Macmillan, 1947); and Stephen Skowronek, *Building a New American State.*

19. On the general pattern, see Hedrick Smith, *The Power Game: How Washington Works* (New York: Random House, 1988).

20. Pennsylvania Avenue, of course, is the thoroughfare linking the White House with the Capitol.

21. Two of the top-twenty lobbying firms physically remaining on K Street in 2011 were the Washington Group and the Carmen Group; many of the others had left either for logistical reasons or for more space. The redevelopment of Pennsylvania Avenue in the 1990s, and the closure of the segment in front of the White House for security reasons, were two major reasons for the decline of K Street as an actual headquarters for lobbying. See Judy Sarasohu, "More a Symbol than a Street Address," *Washington Post,* April 25, 2006. The Podesta Group (known as Podesta Matton during 2001–06) was founded by Democratic lobbyist Tony Podesta in 1987. Among its major clients are Google, General Dynamics, Walmart, BP, and the Coalition for Affordable Solar Energy. See Dan Beyers, "Post 200," *Washington Post,* December 17, 2012.

22. See, for example, Smith, *The Power Game;* and Pat Choate, *Agents of Influence: How Japan Manipulates America's Political and Economic System* (New York: Simon and Schuster, 1990).

23. "Washington as World News Center," *New York Times,* March 13, 1921. The article lists the first twelve but fails to mention Sweden, which established its embassy in 1912. Pontus Järborg, minister/consul general, embassy of Sweden, e-mail to author, February 15, 2008.

24. For a list of embassies and addresses, see H. P. Caemmerer, *Washington: The National Capital* (Government Printing Office, 1932), p. 453.

25. "A Brief History of the American Red Cross" (www.redcross.org/museum/history/brief.asp).

26. "Will Use Publicity to Fight 'Open Shop': Labor Union Conference Decides to Open a Bureau, Which May Spend a Million," *New York Times,* February 25, 1921.

27. "The Inter-War Years—Peace Movements," *Encyclopedia of American Foreign Relations* (www.americanforeignrelations.com/O-W/Peace-movements-The-interwar-years.html).

28. Susan Zeiger, "Finding a Cure for War: Women's Politics and the Peace Movement in the 1920s," *Journal of Social History* 24, no. 1 (1990), p. 75.

29. The airport's only scheduled direct international flights, however, are to Canada. Dulles airport, Washington's main direct international gateway, was opened in 1962. More than half of National Airport's site was reclaimed from the Potomac River, with the WPA, the PWA, the Army Engineers, and the Public Roads Administration participating. See American Institute of Architects, "A Guide to Washington Architecture, 1791–1957" (New York: Reinhold, 1957), p. 67.

30. U.S. Census Bureau (www.census.gov/population/censusdata/table-16. pdf).

31. U.S. Office of Personnel Management, "Federal Civilian Statistics: Annual Report by Geographical Areas: 1980."

32. Larry Van Dyne, "Foreign Affairs: DC's Best Embassies," *Washingtonian,* February 1, 2008 (www.washingtonian.com/articles/people/6319.html).

33. Miller, *Embassy Row,* pp. 118–19.

34. Ibid., p. 116.

35. Ibid., pp. 120–21.

36. For details, see U.S. Department of State, "Diplomatic List" (Spring 2013) (www.state.gov/s/cpr/rls/dpl/spring 2013/index.htm).

37. In September 1945, just after the end of World War II, the United States had a combined military force on active duty (all services) of 11,858,500. In all, over 16.1 million Americans served in the military during World War II, and over 405,000 died during the struggle, including more than 291,000 battle deaths. See U.S. Department of Veterans Affairs, "America's Wars" (www.va.gov/opa/ publications/factsheets/fs_americas_war).

38. The first occupants of the Pentagon moved in on April 19, 1942, but construction was finally completed only on January 15, 1943. See U.S. Department of Defense, "Pentagon Tours—Facts and Figures: Construction," 2013 (https:// pentagontours.osd.mil/facts-construction.jsp).

39. William Z. Slany, "History of the U.S. Department of State," Historian, Bureau of Public Affairs, Office of the Historian, Department of State, July 1996 (www.state.gov/www/about_state/history/dephis.html).

40. The State Department professional diplomatic corps consists of around 13,800 foreign service officers and 1,500 foreign service specialists.

41. See James Bamford, *The Puzzle Palace* (New York: Penguin, 1982), on the National Security Agency. For a comprehensive, non-classified survey of national security institutions, see "Top Secret America," *Washington Post,* July 10, 2010.

42. Nitze joined Dillon, Read, and Co. in 1929, founded his own firm in 1938, and then returned to Dillon, Read as vice president from 1939 to 1941. On Nitze's career, see Marilyn Berger, "Paul H. Nitze, Missile Treaty Negotiator and Cold War Strategist, Dies at 97," *New York Times,* October 21, 2004 (www. nytimes.com/2004/10/21/politics/21nitze.html).

43. On Nitze's role in the realization of Diego Garcia, see Kent E. Calder, *Embattled Garrisons: Comparative Base Politics and American Globalism* (Princeton University Press, 2007), pp. 184–85.

44. In this capacity, Herter was signatory to (among other major documents) the revised U.S.-Japan Mutual Security Treaty, which provides the legal basis for the U.S.-Japan alliance.

45. In 2011 the two main institutional expressions in these areas at Georgetown were the Center for Eurasian, Russian, and East European Studies (CERES)

and the Edmund A. Walsh School of Foreign Service. For details, see their websites: http://ceres.georgetown.edu and http://sfs.georgetown.edu.

46. See the University of Maryland international programs website: www.international.umd.edu.

47. Defining think tanks is difficult, since they assume substantially different incarnations in different parts of the world. Yet they can be roughly defined functionally as private-sector policy research institutions having both analysis and engagement functions. A precise definition is outside the central concerns of this research, but for purposes of analytical clarity the foregoing should suffice.

48. Although think-tank activities commenced in 1927, Brookings does trace its origins back to 1916, when Robert Brookings and government reforms inspired creation of the Institute for Government Research, "the first private organization devoted to analyzing public-policy issues at the national level." For more details on the early origins of today's Brookings, see the Brookings website: www.brookings.edu/about/History.aspx.

49. The Middle East Institute publishes *The Middle East Journal* and has the largest collection in Washington (outside the Library of Congress) of Middle East source materials in English. MEI was cofounded by Christian Herter, the cofounder of SAIS and later a U.S. secretary of state (1959–61); his cofounder was the distinguished Middle East specialist George Camp Keiser. For more details, consult the MEI website: www.mei.edu.

50. Andrew Denham and Diane Stone, eds., *Think Tank Traditions: Policy Research and the Politics of Ideas* (Manchester University Press, 2004), p. 221.

51. AEI originated in 1943 as the Washington office of the American Enterprise Association, which changed its name to the American Enterprise Institute in 1960. AEI says that this wartime office was "the avant-garde" in the emergence of policy think tanks. See the AEI website: www.aei.org/about/content ID.20031212154735838.default/asp; also see James A. Smith, *The Idea Brokers: Think Tanks and Rise of the New Policy Elite* (New York: Free Press, 1991).

52. Denham and Stone, *Think Tank Traditions*, p. 221; Smith, *The Idea Brokers*, pp. 174–76.

53. P. W. Singer, "Factories to Call Our Own: How to Understand Washington's Idea Industry," *Washingtonian*, August 13, 2010 (www.washingtonian.com/articles/people/16506.html).

54. Japan Center for International Exchange, "Reinvigorating US-Japan Policy Dialogue and Study" (Tokyo: Japan Center for International Exchange, 2010), p. 19. Data from JCIE survey, 2010.

55. For 2012 data for Internal Revenue Service filings, see Hans Gutbrod, "Top 20 Analysis: 2012 TT Data," *On Think Tanks*, July 17, 2013 (http://onthinktanks.org/2013/07/17/now-think-tanks-work-analyzing-budgets/).

56. The budget of France's IFRI, for example, rose from 5 million euros in 1998 to 6 million in 2011 (www.ifri.org/?page=missions_uk). The five largest

Japanese think thanks—JCIE, JIIA, RIPS, IIPS, and the International House of Japan—saw their budgets fall between 1998 and 2008 from $28 million to $18 million. See ibid.

57. In France, for example, government funding at the major think tanks ranged in 2011 from 91 percent at CERI to 86 percent at FJJ (Fondation Jean Jaures), 40 percent at CEPII, and 30 percent at IFRI. See James G. McGann and R. Kent Weaver, eds., *Think Tanks and Civil Society: Catalysts for Ideas and Action* (New Brunswick, N.J.: Transaction, 2009), p. 127.

58. See "2013 Global Go-To Think Tanks Index Report" (University of Pennsylvania). Six other think tanks located all or in part in Washington also ranked in the global top twenty: Council on Foreign Relations (7), Rand Corporation (8), Woodrow Wilson International Center for Scholars (10), Peterson Institute for International Economics (15), Heritage Foundation (17), Cato Institute (18), and American Enterprise Institute (20).

59. On this important structural transformation in the Washington idea industry, which gathered momentum following the Jack Abramoff scandal and passage of the 2007 Honest Leadership and Government Act, see Thomas B. Edsall, "The Unlobbyists," *New York Times,* December 31, 2013.

60. On this partnership, see Hogan Lovells, "Strategic Alliances" (www. hoganlovells.com/strategicalliances).

61. See, for example, Donald E. Abelson, *A Capitol Idea: Think Tanks and U.S. Foreign Policy* (Montreal: McGill-Queens University Press, 2006); and Donald E. Abelson, *Do Think Tanks Matter?* (Montreal: McGill-Queens University Press, 2009).

62. Brookings, Carnegie, CSIS, the Woodrow Wilson Center for Scholars, Peterson Institute, Cato, and AEI are within a mile of 1700 Massachusetts Avenue, N.W. The Heritage Foundation is a bit further away, near Capitol Hill, and the Rand Corporation is in Arlington, Virginia. The Council on Foreign Relations also has a large operation on F Street, N.W., although its headquarters is in New York City.

63. The Constitution specifies a length of ten miles on a side for the District of Columbia (Article 1, Section 8), with the specific boundaries being finalized in 1791. See Hans P. Caemmerer, *Washington: The National Capital* (Government Printing Office, 1932), p. 11. As noted, the thirty-one square miles ceded by Virginia was returned to that state in 1847.

64. See U.S. Census Bureau (www.census.gov/population/censusdata/table-26. pdf).

65. On growth patterns in the Washington metropolitan area, see Paul Mackun and Steven Wilson, "2010 Census Briefs, Population Distribution and Change: 2000 to 2010," U.S. Census Bureau, March, 2011 (www.census.gov/ prod/cen2010/briefs/c2010br-01.pdf); and Marc J. Perry and Paul J. Mackun, "Census 2000 Brief, Population Change and Distribution: 1990 to 2000," U.S. Census Bureau, April 2001 (www.census.gov/prod/2001pubs/c2kbr01-2.pdf).

66. U.S. Bureau of the Census, "Information on U.S. Census Bureau," p. 37 (www.census.gov/prod/2002pubs/censr-4.pdf).

67. See U.S. Bureau of the Census, "2010 Brief," p. 6. The Washington/ Baltimore/Northern Virginia metropolitan area was the fourth most rapidly growing in the country, after Houston, Atlanta, and Dallas–Fort Worth.

68. The Congress was afraid that, should the District face a nuclear attack, any future AEC effectiveness in supporting a counterattack could be crippled. Germantown, Maryland, was both close to Washington and far enough away to comply with the "reasonable dispersal criteria" of a twenty-megaton bomb. The exigencies of a possible nuclear conflict were thus one catalyst for the emergence of metropolitan Washington. See www.er.deo/gov/sc-80/trail/history.htm.

69. American Institute of Architects, "A Guide to Washington Architecture."

70. Bamford, *The Puzzle Palace,* pp. 82, 87. The NSA had around 3,500 employees in the early 1980s.

71. Richard Halloran, "Washington Talk: Military Consultants: A Thriving Industry to Do the Pentagon's Work," *New York Times,* July 14, 1987.

72. Frank Adams, CEO of Geotech, interviewed in Andy Serwer, "Ground Zero Capital of the Net?," *Fortune,* October 9, 2000 (http://money.cnn.com/ magazines/fortune/fortune_archive/2000/10/09/2893909/index.htm).

73. See "Top-Secret Government Organizations by Locations," Top Secret America Series, *Washington Post,* July 20, 2010 (http://projects.washingtonpost. com/top-secret-america/map).

74. Thomas A. Stewart, "The Netplex: It's a New Silicon Valley," *Fortune,* March 7, 1994 (http://money.cnn.com/magazines/fortune/fortune_archive/ 1994/03/07/9043/index.htm).

75. "2012 Top 100 Government Contractors," *Washington Technology,* June 11, 2012 (http://washingtontechnology.com/toplists/top-100-lists/2012.aspx).

76. Alice Lipowicz, "Change Part of Northrop's Growth Strategy," *Washington Technology,* June 1, 2010 (http://washingtontechnology.com/Articles/ 2010/06/01/Top-100-Northrop-Grumman.aspx?p=1); and Peter Pae, "Northrop Grumman Corp. Headquarters Moving to Washington, D.C., Area," *Los Angeles Times,* January 4, 2010 (http://latimesblogs.latimes.com/money_co/2010/01/ northrop-grumman-corp-to-move-to-washington-dc-area.html).

77. Gerald Perrins and Diane Nilsen, "Industry Dynamics in the Washington, D.C., Area: Has a Second Job Core Emerged?," *Monthly Labor Review* 129, no. 12 (2006), p. 9.

78. Loudon County, Virginia, was among the six counties nationwide with a population of 10,000 or more that grew between 75 and 100 percent between 2000 and 2010. See Paul Mackun and Steven Wilson, "2010 Census Briefs, Population Distribution, and Change: 2000 to 2010," U.S. Census Bureau, March 2011 (www.census.gov/prod/cen2010/briefs/c2010br-01pdf). The average per capita incomes of the two leaders in this respect (Loudon County and the City of

Falls Church) were $119,525 and $117,481, respectively. See Tom Van Riper, "America's Richest Counties," *Forbes*, April 25, 2013 (www.forbes.com/sites/tomvanriper/2013/04/25/americas-richest-countries).

79. See U.S. Census Bureau (www.census.gov/popest/counties/COEST2009-08.html).

80. Francesca Levy, "America's Richest Counties," *Forbes*, March 1, 2010 (http://finance.yahoo.com/real-estate/article/108999/americas-richest-counties). These figures are for 2010. There were no figures for counties ranked 11 to 25 in the 2011 Forbes study.

81. Fortune 500 list, *CNN Money*, May 23, 2011 (http://money.cnn.com/magazines/fortune/fortune500/2011/states/VA.html).

82. Gerald E. Connolly, chair, Fairfax County Board of Supervisors, "Letter about Dulles Rail to Federal Transit Administration," at www.fairfaxcounty.gov/news/2008/dulles-rail-letter.htm.

83. "National Top-Secret System: Corporations and Government Organizations," Top Secret America Series, *Washington Post* (http://projects.washingtonpost.com/top-secret-america/map/).

84. Marjorie Censer, "Fort Meade Transforming from Army Base to Cyber City," *Washington Post*, October 11, 2013. In late 2013, Fort Meade had 57,000 employees, up from 33,000 in 2005. There are reportedly six major intelligence offices near the Baltimore-Washington Parkway, in the vicinity of Odenton, close to Patuxent Research Refuge and Fort Meade. Among the six are the Air Force Special Intelligence Detachment and the CI Support Detachment for Military Intelligence. See Top Secret America Series, *Washington Post* (http://projects.washingtonpost.com/top-secret-america/map/).

85. "2010 Washington Technology Top 100 Government Contractors," *Washington Technology*, n.d, (http://washingtontechnology.com/toplists/top-100-lists/2010.aspx?Sort=Rank).

86. Peter Whoriskey, "Soaring View of Tyson's Centers on a Downtown: New Coalition Wants Even More Growth," *Washington Post*, April 22, 2005, p. A-1.

87. Fairfax County Economic Development Authority (www.fairfaxcountyeda.org/publications/fairfax_facts.pdf).

88. U.S. Census Bureau (www.census.gov/population/socdemo/daytime/2000/tab03.csv, 2000).

89. U.S. Census Bureau, "Population 1990, 2000, and 2010."

90. "Forecasts for Tysons Corner to 2050," Report by George Mason University's Regional Center, prepared for Fairfax County (www.fairfaxcounty,gov/dpz/thsonscorner/finalreports/georgemason-forecast-tysons.pdf).

91. Ibid.

92. This congestion is likely to be relieved but not fully eliminated by the Dulles Railway Project and related transit fees. See "Tysons Corner Exodus Is an Early Warning Sign," *Washington, D.C., Examiner*, editorial, November 27,

2007 (www.examiner.com/a-1070308-Tysons_Corner_exodus_is_an_early_warning_sign.html).

93. See www.boozallen/com.

94. See for example Ewen MacAskill, "Edward Snowden: How the Spy Story of the Age Leaked Out," *Guardian,* June 11, 2013 (www.theguardian.com/world/2013/jun/11/edward-snowden-nsa-whistleblower-profile).

95. Working closely with the navy's own planners, Booz consultants developed a special sensor system that could track German U-boats' radio communication and designed a devastatingly effective attack strategy around it. Details of Booz Allen consulting projects are drawn from www.boozallen.com.

96. See www.boozallen.com/capabilities/Industries?industries_articles/658503.

97. Mike H. Rindskopf and Richard Knowles Morris, *Steel Boats, Iron Men: History of the U.S. Submarine Force* (Paducah: Turner), 1994.

98. See www.boozallen.com/about/history.

99. "Booz Allen Hamilton Celebrates the Opening of Its New Office in Abu Dhabi," October 2, 2012 (www.boozallen.com/media-center/press-releases/48399320/bah-celebrates-the-opening-of-its-new-office-in-abu-dhabi); and David E. Sanger and Nicole Perlroth, "After Profits, Contractor Faces the Perils of Cyber-Security," *New York Times,* June 15, 2013.

100. "Booz Allen Hamilton to Support Business and Economic Growth in the Kingdom of Saudi Arabia," February 18, 2013 (www.boozallen.com/media-center/press-release/48399320/booz-allen-to-support-economic-growth-in-saudi-arabia).

101. In 2013, 76 percent of Booz employees had security clearance, and 48 percent had top-security clearances. The Booz network was personified by Vice Chair Mike McConnell, President George W. Bush's director of national intelligence and, before that, director of the NSA. President Obama's director of national intelligence, James Clapper, is also a former Booz executive. See Drake Bennett and Michael Riley, "Booz Allen Knows All, Sees All, Changes All," *Bloomberg Business Week,* June 24, 2013, pp. 73–76.

102. See Thomas Edsall, *The New Politics of Inequality* (New York: Norton, 1984).

103. In 1974 there were 172 subcommittees, compared to 22 full committees, in the House of Representatives. And between 1973 and 1985, the number of congressional staffers jumped from 11,500 to over 24,000. See Smith, *The Power Game,* pp. 24–25.

104. On this sociopolitical transition, see, for example, Martin P. Wattenberg, *The Decline of American Political Parties, 1952–1994* (Harvard University Press, 1996); Robert D. Putnam, *Bowling Alone: The Collapse and Revival of American Community* (New York: Simon and Schuster, 2000).

105. On the transformation during the last two decades of the twentieth century, see David Halberstam, *The Powers That Be* (University of Illinois Press, 2000), pp. xi–xiii, 158–201.

Chapter 3

1. Asia here is considered to be the area from Japan's northeast extremity to the western borders of India, thus excluding Pakistan, Afghanistan, central Asia, and the Middle East, which lack strong historical, cultural, economic, and diplomatic identification with the nations further east. None of those excluded, for example, were members of the East Asia Summit (EAS) in 2010, whereas all those included in our definition of Asia, excepting Australia and New Zealand, were participants in the EAS.

2. The *Empress of China* was the first, landing at Canton on August 28, 1784. The ship spent four months there, trading its cargo of animal skins, cotton, and ginseng for tea, silk, and spice, turning a profit of $30,000 for its sponsors, who included the Philadelphia financier Robert Morris. He was also the superintendent of finance for the Continental Congress and a signer of the Declaration of Independence and the Constitution. See Jonathan Goldstein, *Philadelphia and the China Trade, 1682–1846: Commercial, Cultural, and Attitudinal Effects* (Penn State University Press, 1978).

3. The term *double-bolted land,* directly referring to Japan, is from Herman Melville. See Herman Melville, *Moby Dick* (West Valley City, Utah: Waking Lion Press, 2008), p. 72.

4. On the details, see Walter LaFeber, *The Clash: U.S.-Japanese Relations throughout History* (New York: Norton, 1997).

5. *The Pacific Rivals: A Japanese View of Japanese-American Relations,* by staff of the *Asahi Shimbun* (New York: Weatherhill, 1972), pp. 49–50.

6. Ibid., p. 50.

7. Ibid.

8. On the Japanese response to Perry and his immediate successors, see Peter Duus, editor, *The Japanese Discovery of America: A Brief History with Documents* (Boston: Bedford Books, 1997).

9. Ibid., p. 33.

10. Bruce Cumings, *Dominion from Sea to Sea: Pacific Ascendancy and American Power* (Yale University Press, 2010), pp. 87–88.

11. Ibid., p. 88.

12. The treaty, as Cumings points out, was actually negotiated secretly between Commodore Robert Shufeldt of the U.S. Navy, who considered himself Korea's Commodore Perry, and the Chinese leader Li Hung-chang, thus creating future complexities for U.S.-Korea relations in the minds of the Korean people, as later actions like the Taft-Katsura agreement also did. See ibid., pp. 88–89.

13. Domestically, anti-imperial sentiment remained strong—the Bacon Resolution, granting independence to the Philippines once a stable government was established, was defeated only on a tie-breaking vice presidential vote in 1899. Meanwhile, in the Philippines, a bloody independence struggle that tied down

two-thirds of the U.S. army raged on until 1901. See A. Whitney Griswold, *The Far Eastern Policy of the United States* (Yale University Press, 1962), pp. 3–35.

14. Ibid., p. 35.

15. American advisers like Henry Denison, for example, helped Japan rid itself of the unequal treaties, and American firms built the very first Seoul streetcar lines in the 1890s. See LaFeber, *The Clash;* and Bruce Cumings, *Korea's Place in the Sun: A Modern History* (New York: Norton, 1997).

16. Michael Auslin, *Pacific Cosmopolitans* (Harvard University Press, 2011), pp. 76–82.

17. Among the innovations flowing into Japan from America, soon after the country's opening, were the telegraph and the railway (with Perry's original black ships); baseball; coffee shops; baby carriages; beer factories; motion pictures; photographic slides; milk pasteurization; and the electric motor for Japan's first elevator. See ibid., pp. 56–57.

18. The planters, banding together as the Committee of Safety, were antiroyalist foreigners unwilling to relinquish their considerable power over the local Hawaiian economy and governance. On the details of their uprising, see Ralph S. Kuykendall and A. Grove Day, *Hawaii, A History: From the Polynesian Kingdom to American Commonwealth* (New York: Prentice-Hall, 1949), pp. 174–79.

19. The Open Door notes were transformed into a full-fledged explication of American Far East diplomacy through the Hay circular of July 3, 1900. See Griswold, *The Far Eastern Policy of the United States,* pp. 36–86.

20. That insurrection, viewed in later years as an independence struggle by the Filipinos, cost 200,000 to 700,000 civilian lives, those of 16,000–20,000 insurgents, and 4,165 American military fatalities, from all causes. See Cumings, *Dominion from Sea to Sea,* p. 133. Although largely unknown in the United States, this extended uprising is well remembered in the Philippines, especially among the Moros of Mindanao and among nationalist groups.

21. For his actions, Roosevelt was given the Nobel Peace Prize, the award for which still rests in the Roosevelt Room at the White House.

22. See Griswold, *The Far Eastern Policy of the United States,* p. 4.

23. Alfred Whitney Griswold, *The Far Eastern Policy of the United States* (New York: Harcourt, Brace and Co., 1938).

24. See James Bradley, *The Imperial Cruise: A Secret History of Empire* (New York: Little, Brown, 2009).

25. On the round-the-world voyage of the fleet, and its diplomatic implications, see James R. Reckner, *Teddy Roosevelt's Great White Fleet* (Naval Institute Press, 2001).

26. Raymond A. Esthus, *Theodore Roosevelt and Japan* (University of Washington Press, 1966), pp. 128–228.

27. The cruise was, as Neu points out, originally intended as a means of stimulating popular support for expanded naval appropriations. It also gradually gained other purposes—to make Japan realize that the United States wanted a settlement of the immigration issue and to reassure other English-speaking peoples

of the Pacific in the face of fears of Japanese encroachment, following Tokyo's victory in the Russo-Japanese war. See Charles E. Neu, *An Uncertain Friendship: Theodore Roosevelt and Japan, 1906–1909* (Harvard University Press, 1967), p. 227; and Esthus, *Theodore Roosevelt and Japan,* pp. 266–86.

28. On the Great White Fleet, see Mike McKinley, "The Cruise of the Great White Fleet," Navy Department Library, April 1987 (www.history.navy.mil/library/online/gwf_cruise.htm).

29. Neu, *An Uncertain Friendship,* pp. 150–52.

30. *New York Times,* October 18, 1908, quoted in Neu, *An Uncertain Friendship,* p. 270.

31. The garden party was held at Shinjuku Gyoen, an imperial facility that had only once before been opened to the public, when Togo himself had returned in victory from Tsushima.

32. U.S. Navy Department, *Information Relative to the Voyage of the United States Atlantic Fleet around the World, December 16, 1907, to February 22, 1909* (Government Printing Office, 1910).

33. Neu, *An Uncertain Friendship,* pp. 277–78; and Griswold, *The Far Eastern Policy of the United States,* pp. 122–32.

34. The Taft-Katsura "conversation" was held on July 29, 1905. This understanding affirmed that the United States recognized the Korean peninsula as being within Japan's sphere of influence. Scholars differ on whether to term it an agreement or a pact. Some, indeed, call it instead merely a "frank exchange of views." Both sides of the argument agree, however, that there was at least an understanding that Roosevelt approved Japanese possession of Korea. Taft reportedly voiced his opinion that Japanese control was a logical result of the Russo-Japanese war. This was not the first time that the Americans had expressed support for Japanese ambitions on the Asian continent. Five months previously, Roosevelt informally communicated through Richard Barry and George Kennan Sr. that "Japan must hold Port Arthur and she must hold Korea. Those two points are already settled." In April 1905 Roosevelt also personally spoke with the Japanese minister to Washington, Kogoro Takahiro, reiterating his position on Japanese suzerainty over Korea. See Tyler Dennet, "President Roosevelt's Secret Pact with Japan," *Current History* 21 (1924), pp. 15–21; Raymond A. Esthus, "The Taft-Katsura Agreement—Reality or Myth?," *Journal of Modern History* 31, no. 2 (1959), pp. 46–51; and Johgsuk Chay, "The Taft-Katsura Memorandum Reconsidered," *Pacific Historical Review* 37, no. 3 (1969), pp. 321–26.

35. Yi Song-gye expelled Ming armies and defeated the Koryo in 1392, establishing the Choson dynasty, which sustained Korea's independence until 1910. See Bruce Cumings, *Korea's Place in the Sun: A Modern History* (New York: Norton, 1997), p. 44.

36. See Mark Mason, *American Multinationals and Japan: The Political Economy of Japanese Capital Controls, 1899–1980* (Harvard University Council on East Asian Studies, 1992).

37. See John K. Fairbank, *China Perceived: Images and Policies in Chinese-American Relations* (New York: Knopf, 1974).

38. See, for example, James Thomson, *When China Faced West: American Reformers in Nationalist China* (Harvard University Council on East Asian Studies, 1969); David Shambaugh, *Beautiful Imperialist: China Perceives America, 1972–1990* (Princeton University Press, 1991); and Barbara W. Tuchman, *Stilwell and the American Experience in China, 1911–45* (New York: Macmillan, 1970).

39. For the terminology and concept, see Shambaugh, *Beautiful Imperialist.* Shambaugh, of course, applies the notion to a later period.

40. The combined U.S. military presence in Hawaii and the Philippines—America's two major Pacific possessions—never went beyond 25,000 personnel during the prewar period, one-quarter of the lowest post-1945 levels. See Cumings, *Dominion from Sea to Sea,* p. 150.

41. On the embargo and its regional implications, see Shugang Zhang, *Economic Cold War: The American Embargo against China and the Sino-Soviet Alliance, 1949–1963* (Stanford University Press, 2002).

42. On the details of the system and how it came to be, see Kent E. Calder, "Securing Security through Prosperity: The San Francisco System in Comparative Perspective," *Pacific Review* 17, no. 1 (2004), pp. 135–57; Kent E. Calder, *Pacific Alliance: Reviving U.S.-Japan Relations* (Yale University Press, 2009), pp. 31–66; and Kent E. Calder and Min Ye, *The Making of Northeast Asia* (Stanford University Press, 2010), pp. 57–79.

43. On this broadening pattern and the reasons for it, see Kent E. Calder and Roy Hofheinz Jr., *The Eastasia Edge* (New York: Basic Books, 1982).

44. On the U.S.-China normalization, see Zbigniew Brzezinski, *Power and Principle: Memoirs of the National Security Adviser, 1977–1981* (New York: Farrar, Straus, and Giroux, 1983), pp. 196–233, and pp. 403–25.

45. In 2012 only 17 percent of Chinese exports went to the United States, down from 18 percent in 2010. See International Monetary Fund, data e-library (http://elibrary-data-imf.org).

46. In 2011, for example, the stock of U.S. foreign direct investment in Singapore was $116.6 billion and Singapore's foreign direct investment in the United States was $23.5 billion. U.S. FDI in Hong Kong for 2010 was $54.0 billion, and Hong Kong FDI in the United States was $4.3 billion. See Office of the United States Trade Representative, "Singapore" and "Hong Kong" (www.ustr.gov).

47. Office of the United States Trade Representative, "India" (www.ustr.gov/countries-regions/south-central-asia/ind).

48. James Mann, *About Face: A History of America's Curious Relationship with China, from Nixon to Clinton* (New York: Knopf, 1999), pp. 97–98, 113–14.

49. For the full Pew Global Attitudes data set, see www.pewglobal.org. More than 270,000 interviews in 57 countries have been conducted, as part of the

project's work, since its inception in 2001. Among the major subjects considered have been attitudes toward the U.S. and American foreign policy; globalization; terrorism; and democracy.

Chapter 4

1. Japan established a legation in 1871, with Mori Arinori serving as the first ambassador. See Ivan Hall, *Mori Arinori* (Harvard University Press, 1973), p. 156. China established its Qing Dynasty embassy in Washington, as well as a consulate in San Francisco, in 1878. See Peter H. Koehn and Xiao-huang Yin, eds., *The Expanding Roles of Chinese Americans in U.S.-China Relations: Transnational Networks and Transpacific Interactions* (Armonk, N.Y.: M. E. Sharpe, 2002), p. 5. Thailand established its diplomatic presence in the United States during 1901, as the Siam legation, based in Arlington, Virginia, nearly eight decades after bilateral relations were formally established in 1833. In 1913 the legation moved to Washington. Personal communication with the Thai embassy, February 6, 2008.

2. On the substantial influence of these smaller nations, see Tony Smith, *Foreign Attachments: The Power of Ethnic Groups in the Making of American Foreign Policy* (Harvard University Press, 2000).

3. On the structural problem, see Hugh Heclo, *A Government of Strangers: Executive Politics in Washington* (Brookings, 1977), pp. 88–99.

4. Completed in 1903, the fifty-room Walsh mansion, built by the wealthy owner of Colorado gold mines, is located at 2020 Massachusetts Avenue, N.W., and became the Indonesian Embassy in December 1951. For details on the mansion's history, see www.embassyofindonesia.org/aboutembassy/building.htm.

5. Forty-nine African nations are represented in Washington, compared to twenty-two Latin American and nineteen Asian countries. These figures do not include small island states not geographically or historically identified with a specific world region, such as Nauru and the Seychelles. For details, see U.S. Department of State, *Diplomatic List* (Spring 2013) (www.state.gov/s/cpr/rls/dpl/index.htm).

6. In the spring of 2013 China had 194 accredited officers and attachés on the U.S. diplomatic list, compared to 106 for Japan, 75 for South Korea, 49 for India, 38 for Vietnam, 35 for the Philippines, 27 for Indonesia, and 20 for Singapore. Russia, by comparison, accredited 118, Germany 144, and Britain 120. See U.S. Department of State, *Diplomatic List* (Spring 2013).

7. Over 650 companies from seventy-nine countries, according to this study, lobbied the U.S. federal government during the 1998–2005 period, spending over $620 million. See Julia DiLaura, "Foreign Companies Pay to Influence U.S. Policy," *Center for Public Integrity*, May 20, 2005 (http://projects.publicintegrity.org/lobby/report.aspx?aid=689).

8. Ally Schweitzer, "La Maison Française: A Great Place to Meet Americans," *TBD.com,* January 19, 2011 (www.tbd.com/blogs/tbd-arts/2011/01/la-maison-francaise-7396.html).

9. This is an approach, it should also be noted, that Singapore, as a member of ASEAN, adopts to broaden its appeal, so it is by no means restricted to Europe, although probably it is more common there than in other regions.

10. Twenty-seven EU embassies and nearly thirty American cultural institutions participate in the festival. See Kate Oczypok, "Massive Kids Euro Festival Is No Mere Child's Play," *Washington Diplomat,* October 2, 2012. The French-American Cultural Foundation, formed in 1998, is based in the District. It collaborates actively with la Maison Française to promote binational cultural and intellectual exchanges. It also fundraises for la Maison Française.

11. See Embassy of France, "Francophonie 2013 Raises Its Colors in Washington, D.C.," March 5, 2013 (www.franceintheus.org/spip.php?article4385).

12. Eve Ferguson, "For the Love of France: Francophonie Festival 'Showcase of Countries' Continues," *Prince George's Suite,* 2011 (http://pgsuite.com/stories/2011/03/frenchfest.shtml).

13. For a description of the Woodrow Wilson Center for Scholars, see www.wilsoncenter.org.

14. On the role of think tanks as idea brokers, see James A. Smith, *The Idea Brokers: Think Tanks and the Rise of the New Policy Elite* (New York: Free Press, 1991).

15. The Center for Strategic and International Studies, for example, was founded in 1962. The American Enterprise Institute was founded even earlier, in 1954, but was cash strapped for its first several years. During the early 1970s it had a budget of only $1 million and a staff of 10. By the end of that decade, however, AEI's budget had grown to $8 million and its staff to 125 (www.aei.org/history). The Heritage Foundation was founded in 1973 and also grew rapidly thereafter.

16. The Asia Society also sponsors the Bernard Schwartz Fellows Program, supporting research on business and policy issues in Asia; the International Studies Schools Network, which provides programs for elementary and secondary schools; an annual corporate conference in Asia; and Global Centers to further transpacific dialog in such cities as Hong Kong, Seoul, Manila, Shanghai, and Mumbai.

17. The Pan American Health Organization started as the Pan American Sanitary Bureau, originating from a resolution of the Second International Conference of American States, convened in Mexico in January 1902. That conclave recommended that "a general convention of representatives of the health organizations of the various American republics be convened." The delegates met in Washington over December 2–4, 1902, and established a permanent directing council, which became the current organization. Apart from independent Western Hemisphere nations, the United Kingdom, France, and the Netherlands also participate, as they have a traditional colonial presence in the Americas.

18. On World Bank involvement in early postwar Japanese industrial and infrastructure projects, see Kent E. Calder, *Strategic Capitalism: Private Business and Public Purpose in Japanese Industrial Finance* (Princeton University Press, 1993), pp. 189–91 and pp. 272–73.

19. IBRD is the only agency among the four World Bank Group's agencies (IDA, IFC, MIGA, and IBRD) that has voting shares. These shares reflect, at least in theory, the decisionmaking authority of individual members at those agencies. For more details on World Bank Group governance, see World Bank, "Governance and Public Sector Governance" (http://web.worldbank.org/WBSITE/EXTERNAL/TOPICS/EXTPUBLICSECTORANDGOVERNANCE/0,content MDK:20206128~pagePK:210058~piPK:210062~theSitePK:286305,00.html); Bretton Woods Project, "Analysis of World Bank Voting Reforms Governance Remains Illegitimate and Outdated," April 30, 2010 (www.brettonwoodproject. org/art-566281); and "World Bank President Says Voting Share Change Reflects Developing World's Rise," *People's Daily,* April 26, 2010 (http://english.people daily.com.cn/90001/90777/90856/6962419.html).

20. Among research projects sponsored, see World Bank, *The East Asian Miracle: Economic Growth and Public Policy* (Oxford University Press, 1993). This project was sponsored by the Japanese government.

21. See Devesh Kapur, John P. Lewis, and Richard Webb, eds., *The World Bank: Its First Half Century,* vol. 2 (Brookings, 1997), p. 292; and Mitsuru Misawa, *Current Business and Legal Issues in Japan's Banking and Finance,* 2nd ed. (Singapore: World Scientific, 2011), p. 31. In December 1970 the first yen-denominated, publicly offered bonds were issued by the Asian Development Bank, with the World Bank following seven months later.

22. "World Bank Issues First Chinese Renminbi Bond," World Bank press release, January 4, 2011 (http://treasury.worldbank.org/cmd/htm/FirstChineseRenminbiBond.html?cid=EXTEAPMonth1).

23. The World Bank and the Chinese Export-Import Bank signed a memorandum of understanding in 2007 to provide joint financing on public sector projects, with a focus on Africa.

24. In both 2009 and 2010 China lent more development money than the World Bank. See Geoff Dyer and Jamil Anderlini, "China's Lending Hits New Heights," *Financial Times,* January 17, 2011. Also see Stephanie Ho, "Global Development Aid from China on the Rise," *Voice of America,* January 26, 2011 (www.voanews.com). To read more about Chinese loans and a report by China's State Council Information Office, see Gillian Wong, "China Cites Positive Impact on First Report on Aid," Associated Press, April 21, 2011 (www.msnbc.msn.com/id/42696967/ns/business-eye_on_the_cconomy/42670940).

25. "China Eximbank and World Bank Come Together to Sign Cooperation Memo," World Bank, press release, May 21 2007.

26. Richard McGregor, "World Bank to Work with Chinese in Africa," *Financial Times,* December 19, 2007 (www.ft.com/cms/s/0/047cea58-add3-11dc-9386-0000779fd2ac.html#axzz1KvgoLiHD).

27. The bank has also expressed interest in receiving staff from China Exim Bank at its headquarters in Washington, so that both sides can work more closely and directly with their Africa offices. See Lesley Wroughton, "China's Ex-Im, World Bank to Cooperate on Africa," Reuters, May 21, 2007 (www.reuters.com/article/2007/05/22/usa-china-worldbank-idUSN2136700620070522).

28. Lin defected to China from Taiwan in 1979. He was a captain in the Taiwanese army and reportedly swam from the island of Kinmen to nearby Xiamen. He later obtained a master's degree in Marxist political economy from Beijing University and, subsequently, a Ph.D. in economics—one of the first ever awarded to a Chinese citizen—from the University of Chicago. See Lin's profile on the World Bank website (http://go.worldbank.org/LQ0B2IQ150).

29. The World Bank Institute designs learning programs for development stakeholders. For details, see its website (http://wbi.worldbank.org/wbi/).

30. Min Zhu was deputy governor of the People's Bank of China, China's central bank, before assuming his post at the IMF. He has a Ph.D. from Johns Hopkins University and an MPA from Princeton University's Woodrow Wilson School and has taught economics at Johns Hopkins and Fudan Universities. His position at the IMF is the highest staff position ever occupied by a Chinese citizen there—and follows strong appeals by China and other developing nations for a larger say in the running of the IMF. See IMF profile at www.imf.org/external/np/omd/bios/zm.htm; and "China's Global Profile Increases after Winning Key IMF Position," *Nation* (Thailand), February 26, 2010.

31. International Monetary Fund, "IMF Managing Director Christine Lagarde Proposes Appointment of Mr. David Lipton as First Managing Director and Mr. Min Zhu as Deputy Managing Director," press release, July 12, 2011.

32. International Monetary Fund, "IMF Executive Directors and Voting Power" (www.imf.org/external/np/sec/memdir/eds.htm).

33. Recent IMF projections are that Asia will become the largest global economic region well before 2030. See, for example, Anoop Singh, "Asia Leading the Way," *Finance and Development* 47, no. 2 (2010) (www.fmf.org/external/pubs/ft/fandd/2010/06/singh.htm).

34. Ibid.

Chapter 5

1. Ronald Takaki, *A Different Mirror: A History of Multicultural America* (Boston: Little, Brown, 1993), p. 194.

2. Ibid., p. 195. California was known in Chinese as Gam Saan, or Gold Mountain, throughout the mid-nineteenth century.

3. Ibid., p. 197.

4. Ibid., p. 200.

5. Sucheng Chan, *Asian Americans: An Interpretive History* (New York: Twayne, 1991), pp. 193–94.

6. Ibid., p. 37.

7. From 1907 to 1924 approximately 46,000 Filipino men and 7,000 Filipina women immigrated to Hawaii. See "Filipinos in the Americas," *Ancestors in the Americas,*" Public Broadcasting Studio (www.pbs.org/ancestorsintheamericas/ time_25.html). The first wave of Korean immigration is generally considered to have been between 1903 and 1905, starting with the arrival of 102 Korean laborers in Hawaii on January 13, 1902, aboard the *S.S. Gaelic.* A total of 7,291 Korean laborers immigrated to work in the Hawaiian sugar plantations until Japan forcefully made Korea its protectorate in 1905 and stopped Korean immigration to the United States. See Chan, *Asian Americans,* p. 194; and Ilpyong J. Kim, "A Century of Korean Immigration to the United States: 1903–2003," in *Korean-Americans: Past, Present, and Future,* edited by Ilpyong J. Kim (Elizabeth, N.J.: Hollym), pp. 13–37.

8. In 1894, under the *In re Sato* decision, a Massachusetts circuit court declared that Japanese nationals were ineligible for naturalization. In 1922 *Takao Ozawa v. US* declared Japanese ineligible for naturalized citizenship, with the U..S. Supreme Court upholding the discriminatory naturalization law of the day. In 1923 *United States* v. *Bhagat Singh Thind* declared Asian Indians ineligible for naturalized citizenship.

9. On the Japanese American role in Hawaiian politics, see Bill Hosokawa, *Nisei: The Quiet Americans,* rev. ed. (University Press of Colorado, 2002), pp. 457–72.

10. Only 981 of 160,000 Hawaiians of Japanese extraction were interned or sent to relocation camps in the first weeks of World War II, despite the fact that Hawaii was clearly the most exposed part of American territory to Japanese invasion, as evidenced by the Pearl Harbor attack itself. See ibid., pp. 457–58.

11. Inoue received numerous international awards from Asian countries, including: the Philippine Legion of Honor Award (1993), the Japanese Grand Cordon of the Order of the Rising Sun (2000), the Philippine Bayan Rand Grand Cross Award (2006), the French Legion of Honor award (2007), and the Grand Cordon of the Order of the Paulownia Flowers (2011), Japan's highest decoration conferred upon a foreigner who is not a head of state. For details on these awards, see http://inouye.senate.gov/Awards.cfm.

12. Fong was the first Asian American elected to the Senate as well as the first Chinese American elected to Congress. Spark Matsunaga served as one of Hawaii's first elected representatives, from 1963 to 1977. He subsequently served as senator from Hawaii, from 1977 to 1990. Daniel Kahikina Akaka was elected as representative in 1977, succeeding Spark Matsunaga when Matsunaga moved to the Senate. After serving six terms in the House (1977–88), Akaka became a senator from Hawaii in 1989. Apart from these senators, Patsy Takemoto Mink became the first Asian American woman to serve in Congress, as a representative from Hawaii, 1965–77 and 1990–2002. Patricia Saiki served as a Republican representative (1987–91), and Mazie Hirono, born in Fukushima, Japan, served as a Democratic representative (2007–13); and as senator from 2013. Hirono is also

an executive board member of the Congressional Asian Pacific American Caucus. Hirono is the first elected female senator from Hawaii; the first Asian American woman elected to the Senate, the first Buddhist senator, as well as the first foreign-born woman of Asian ancestry sworn into Congress. See Yonee Koh, "Hirono Becomes First US Senator Born in Japan," *Wall Street Journal,* November 6, 2012.

13. See Chan, *Asian Americans,* pp. 145–65.

14. Population estimates from U.S. Census Bureau, "White House Initiative on Asian American and Pacific Islanders: Key Facts and Figures," press release, April 2010 (www.census.gov/Press-Release/www/releases/archives/population/013733. html).

15. U.S. Census Bureau, "Projections of the Population by Sex, Race, and Hispanic Origin for the United States: 2010 to 2050" (NP2008-T4), table 4.

16. The Chinese, Filipino, Indian, Vietnamese, and Korean communities, in that order, all outnumbered the Japanese in 2010. See U.S. Bureau of the Census, *Statistical Abstract of the United States, 2012.*

17. Between 1980 and 2000 the number of Asian Americans in California law schools quadrupled to 12 percent of the total. Over 11 percent of full-time MBA students in U.S. universities are also now Asian American. See Peter Kwong and Dusanka Miscevic, *Chinese America: The Untold Story of America's Oldest New Community* (New York: New Press, 2005), p. 349.

18. Four of Silicon Valley's top ten high-tech firms in the mid-2000s, generating over $30 billion in revenues, were headed by Chinese American newcomers of this variety. See ibid., p. 350. In 1990 Congress tripled annual quotas for highly skilled professionals and broadened the definition of that H1-B visa category. It created the L-1 visa to facilitate intracorporate transfers to the United States from abroad by U.S. multinational corporations, and introduced the EB-5 (immigrant investor/entrepreneur) and E-1 (trader visa) categories. On these stimuli to skilled immigration from Asia, see ibid., pp. 344–45.

19. On the contemporary meaning of a model minority in a global economy, including critical views of that concept, see Eric Mark Kramer, ed., *The Emerging Monoculture: Assimilation and the "Model Minority"* (Westport, Conn.: Praeger, 2003).

20. From 1942 to 1944, 120,000 people of Japanese descent, 70,000 of whom were U.S. citizens, were forced to relocate to internment camps under President Franklin D. Roosevelt's Executive Order 9066, of February 19, 1942. Exclusion of Japanese Americans from the West Coast continued until December 1944, with the last internment camp being closed on March 20, 1946. For more details, see Commission on Wartime Relocation and Internment of Civilians, *Personal Justice Denied* (1983).

21. On the redress struggle and the extended appropriation process that followed, see Mitchell T. Make, Harry H. L. Kitano, and S. Megan Berthold, *Achieving the Impossible Dream: How Japanese Americans Obtained Redress* (University of Illinois Press, 1999), esp. pp. 200–10.

22. Samoa's representative in the U.S. House of Representatives, Eni Faleoma-vaega, did however serve as chairman of the House East Asian and Pacific Affairs Subcommittee from 2009 to 2011.

23. Asian American Action Fund (www.aaa-fund.org/home.php).

24. See "NAPABA Celebrates Confirmation of Raymond T. Chen to the Federal Circuit," *National Asian Pacific American Bar Association,* press release, August 1, 2013; and Tejinder Singh, "Srinivasan Confirmed as First Asian American Circuit Judge," *India America Today,* May 24, 2013. Goodwin Liu of UC Berkeley's Boalt School of Law was nominated in 2009 by President Barack Obama to the U.S. Court of Appeals for the Ninth Circuit (San Francisco), but his confirmation stalled for over two years in the Senate. See, for example, Bob Egelko, "Senate Panel Again OK's Liu for Appellate Court," *San Francisco Chronicle,* April 8, 2011.

25. See www.usdiplomacy.org/history/service/representative.php#asianamerican.

26. In total, one AAPI senator (Mazie Hirono), ten representatives, and two delegates (American Samoa and Northern Marianas) were elected. Six of these AAPIs were freshmen, and all were Democrats. See Lorraine H. Tong, "Asian Pacific Americans in the US Congress," *Congressional Research Service,* June 12, 2013 (www.fas.org/sgp/crs/misc/97-398.pdf).

27. Quan, the daughter of a restaurant owner, was the first woman and the first Asian American to serve as Oakland's mayor. Hailing from an activist background, she faced difficult political pressures, including ultimately a recall effort, in connection with her handling of the 2011 Occupy Oakland movement. See James Dao, "Oakland's Reins Blister a Mayor Bred on the Other Side of Protest," *New York Times,* December 29, 2011.

28. "Lee's Victory Lifts Asian Hopes in San Francisco," *Japan Times,* November 21, 2011, p. 3. Voter turnout was low, at 39 percent, but heavy in Chinatown, where 80 percent of mail-in ballots were returned.

29. Haley is also the first nonwhite and the first woman to serve as governor of South Carolina and, in 2013, at age forty-one, was the youngest currently serving governor in the United States. See Sean Trende and Josh Kraushaar, *Almanac of American Politics, 2014* (University of Chicago Press, 2013), pp. 1477–79.

30. For more on Asian American leadership in U.S. foreign policy, see Corazon Sandoval Foley, "Asian-Pacific American Trailblazers in Foreign Policy," *State Magazine* (May 2006), pp. 18–19 (www.usdiplomacy.org/downloads/pdf/representative/Foley2006.pdf).

31. Sung Kim, the son of a Korean diplomat, was born in Seoul in 1960, moved to the United States in 1973 with his family, and began serving as U.S. ambassador to Korea on October 13, 2011.

32. See www.usjapancouncil.org.

33. "Indian Americans in New Hampshire," *US-India Political Action Committee* (http://web.archive.org/web/20100427163917/http:/www.usinpac.com/nh/indian_americans_nh.html).

34. According to 2012 census data, 39.7 percent of Indian Americans have a graduate or professional degree, compared with 10.9 percent of the total population. U.S. Census Bureau, "2012 American Community Survey," 2012 (http://factfinder2.census.gov/faces/nav/jsf/pages/searchresults.xhtml?refresh=t).

35. On NCCA activities, see www.myncca.org.

36. "Kamala Harris Wins Attorney General's Race as Steve Cooley Concedes," *Los Angeles Times,* November 24, 2010.

37. Apart from the prominent Japanese American leaders serving on its board of directors, the U.S.-Japan Council also numbers numerous former U.S. ambassadors to Japan, Japanese ambassadors to the United States, and other distinguished citizens of both nations on its board of councilors.

38. Don T. Nakanishi and James S. Lai, eds., *Asian American Politics: Law, Participation, and Policy* (Lanham, Md.: Rowman and Littlefield, 2003), pp. 318–19.

39. Michael Honda served in 2013 as House Democratic senior whip and as a member of the powerful House Appropriations Committee. On his background and struggles to secure apologies from Japan for its wartime actions, see Michael Barone, *The Almanac of American Politics, 2010* (Washington: National Journal Group, 2009), pp. 181–83; and http://honda.house.gov.

40. On the Chinese American transnationals, whose numbers were swelled by congressional expansion of educated-professional immigration quotas in 1990 and by the Chinese Student Protection Act in 1992, see Kwong and Miscevic, *Chinese America,* pp. 343–54.

Chapter 6

1. On the method of similarity and difference and its methodological benefits, see Sidney Verba and Robert O. Keohane, *Designing Social Inquiry: Scientific Inference in Qualitative Research* (Princeton University Press, 1994), p. 168.

2. Hans J. Morgenthau, *Politics among Nations: The Struggle for Power and Peace* (New York: McGraw-Hill, 1993).

3. Robert D. Putnam, "Diplomacy and Domestic Politics: The Logic of Two-Level Games," *International Organization* 42 (Summer 1988), pp. 427–60.

4. Nineteen East, Southeast, and South Asian nations are currently represented in Washington. They are Japan, China, South Korea, Mongolia, the ten nations of the ASEAN, Bangladesh, India, Pakistan, Sri Lanka, and Nepal.

5. Taiwan, to reiterate, is taken up not as a country but as an autonomous subnational part of China, with distinctive and analytically important characteristics.

6. Robert Dahl, *Who Governs? Democracy and Power in an American City* (Yale University Press, 1961).

7. Invitations to deliver these prestigious addresses, the first of which was given by the Marquis de Lafayette, George Washington's comrade in arms, in

1824, are extended by the leaders of the House of Representatives and the Senate and not by the White House.

8. On June 20, 1957, Prime Minster Nobusuke Kishi addressed the U.S. Senate at the invitation of Vice President Richard Nixon, who was also Senate president. On June 22, 1961, Prime Minister Hayato Ikeda similarly addressed Congress. In the congressional archives, two events are both recorded as receptions, rather than meetings, and are apparently the only formal appearances by Japanese leaders before the entire assembled U.S. Congress. See U.S. House of Representatives, History, Arts and Archivists, "House Receptions" (http://history. gov/ installation/ Foreign-Leaders/ House-Receptions).

9. The Foreign Agents Registration Act was enacted in 1938. It requires people acting as agents of foreign principals in a political or quasi-political capacity to make periodic public disclosure of their relationships with their foreign principals. For details, see U.S. Department of Justice, "Foreign Agents Registration Act" (www.fara.gov).

10. For details, see U.S. Department of Justice, "FARA Quick Search" (www. fara.gov/quick-search.html).

11. Ibid.

12

13. Pat Choate, *Agents of Influence: How Japan Manipulates America's Political and Economic System* (New York: Simon and Schuster, 1990), pp. 49–76.

Chapter 7

1. Czarist Russia approached China in expanse only in the mid-seventeenth century, with the two competing as the world's largest nation as the Qing dynasty expanded into Mongolia and Xinjiang. Only by the mid-nineteenth century, after czarist incursions into Central Asia and the conquest of Siberia, were the Russians clearly ascendant. See Benson Bobrick, *East of the Sun: The Epic Conquest and Tragic History of Siberia* (New York: Poseidon, 1992); Warren I. Cohen, *East Asia at the Center: Four Thousand Years of Engagement with the World* (Columbia University Press, 2000); and James A. Millward, *Eurasian Crossroads: A History of Xinjiang* (Columbia University Press, 2007).

2. China had 194 accredited diplomats posted in Washington during March 2013. See U.S. Department of State, *Diplomatic List,* Spring 2013.

3. In August 2013 the USCBC recorded 219 members—down roughly 10 percent from recent years but still substantial. There were at the same time only 37 members of the U.S.-Japan Business Council (www.usjbc.org). For more details on the USCBC, see www.uschina.org; and Kent E. Calder, *Pacific Alliance: Reviving U.S.-Japan Relations* (Yale University Press, 2009), pp. 201–02.

4. On the China-Japan contrast, see Calder, *Pacific Alliance* (2009), p. 201.

5. On the establishment of this important cultural exchange infrastructure for the U.S.-China relationship, see David M. Lampton, *Relationship Restored: Trends in U.S.-China Educational Exchanges, 1978–1984* (Washington: National Academy, 1986).

6. See www.ncuscr.org. In 2011, for example, the USCPF sponsored a public diplomacy roundtable on the outlook in Taiwan as well as educational travel relating to China's minority cultures for congressional staffers to Beijing, western Qinghai province, and Tibet.

7. See www.acls.org/pro-cscc.htm.

8. The China Institute was founded in 1926 by John Dewey, among others, and is the oldest U.S. bicultural organization that focuses on China. See China Institute, *Annual Report,* 2010 (www.chinainstitute.org/pdfs/ChinaInstitute AR_2010.pdf).

9. In October 2013 there were 833 Confucius Institutes in 104 countries, with 339 in the United States. See www.chinesecio.com/m/cio_wci.

10. Zhang Jun, "China Inaugurates Confucius Institute US Center in Washington," Xinhuanet, November 21, 2013 (http://xinhuanet.com).

11. On the structure and activities of the Committee of 100, see the group's website, http://committee100.org.

12. "Wen Makes Proposals to Promote Sino-U.S. Relations," Xinhua News Agency, December 10, 2003.

13. "Press Briefing on the Upcoming Visit of Chinese Vice President Xi Jinping to the United States," White House Office of the Press Secretary, February 10, 2012.

14. In September and October 2011, for example, 300 Chinese and American artists, as part of an arts festival, performed the classical music of both nations, puppet shows, and dance theater (www.kennedy-center.org/programs/festivals/11-12/china).

15. See David Shambaugh. *China Goes Global: The Partial Power* (Oxford University Press, 2013), pp. 207–68.

16. Ibid., p. 227.

17. Charlie Shifflett, "China Daily's US Edition a Hard Sell," *Washington Times Communities,* January 19, 2012.

18. "In D.C., China Builds a News Hub to Polish Its Global Image," *Japan Times,* January 19, 2012, p. 4.

19. From less than $10 billion in 1990, the U.S. trade deficit with China grew to over $273 billion in 2010 and to over $295 billion in 2011. These figures, however, represent total manufacturing cost in Chinese exports, rather than simply value added. See U.S. Census Bureau, "Trade in Goods with China" (www.census.gov/foreign-trade/balance/c5700.html).

20. On the political importance in China of the 1979 Deng visit to Washington, see Ezra Vogel, *Deng Xiaoping and the Transformation of China* (Harvard University Press, 2011), pp. 329, 347.

21. Deng was accompanied in 1979 by China's top news commentator, Zhou Zhongxiang, as well as reporters from all the leading papers and the New China News Agency (Xinhua), with a half-hour program beamed back to China at the end of each day. See ibid., p. 337.

22. I am indebted to a senior official of the U.S. State Department, who held operational responsibility for China affairs, for this informal observation.

23. The Chinese embassy, for example, strongly criticized the "Divine Performing Arts Spectacular" staged at the Kennedy Center on January 26–30, 2011, a program cosponsored by the Falun Dafa Association of Washington, the New Tang Dynasty TV, and the Divine Performing Arts Spectacular. For details on the embassy's objections, see www.china-enbassy.org.

24. James Mann, *About Face: A History of America's Curious Relationship with China, from Nixon to Clinton* (New York: Knopf, 1999).

25. "President Jiang Zemin Visits the United States," *China Daily,* January 7, 2009 (www.chinadaily.com.cn/09chinausrelations/2009-01/07/content_7374465.htm).

26. Chinese embassy officials, for example, meet African World Bank advisers at the embassy to discuss economic and trade cooperation in Africa between China and the World Bank. See "Minister Lu Yongqing Met with World Bank Senior Adviser Celestin Monga" (www.china-embassy.org).

27. See, for example, "Chinese Embassy Hosts 2012 Spring Festival Reception" (www.chinaembassy.org/eng/sghd/events/t900275.htm). The Spring Festival reception, on January 30, 2012, was attended by 700 overseas Chinese, Chinese Americans, and Chinese students resident in the United States.

28. See Zbigniew Brzezinski, *Power and Principle: Memoirs of the National Security Adviser, 1977–1981* (New York: Farrar, Strauss, and Giroux, 1983), p. 54.

29. Clinton attended the 1985 National Day celebrations in Taipei together with Virginia Governor Charles Robb. See James Mann, "How Taiwan Outwitted US Policy," *Los Angeles Times,* June 8, 1995.

30. Jiang Zemin made a state visit to the United States from October 26 to November 3, 1995, and Bill Clinton reciprocated with a state visit to China from June 24 to July 3, 1998.

31. Mary Ann Whitley, "George W. Bush Makes His First Overseas Trip—to China—After Leaving Presidency," *Cleveland Plain Dealer,* April 18, 2009 (http://www.cleveland.com).

32. During early 2008, Obama also condemned Chinese crackdowns on Tibetan Buddhist monks, called on George W. Bush to negotiate with the Dalai Lama, and argued that the United States should keep open the option of boycotting the Beijing Olympics. See "Campaign 2008: Obama and US Policy toward China" (http://cfr.org/experts/world/barack-obama/b11603#10).

33. "China's Fury Building over Obama's New Asia Policy," *Los Angeles Times,* November 21, 2011.

34. See, for example, "Chinese Vice President Xi Jinping's U.S. Visit," *Global Times,* February 15, 2012 (www.globaltimes.cn).

35. Mitt Romney, "How I'll Respond to China's Rising Power," *Wall Street Journal,* February 16, 2012 (http://online.wsj.com/news/articles/SB10001424052 9702048880404577225340763595570).

36. Julie Pace, "Obama, Xi Signal New Start with Palm Springs Meeting," Associated Press, June 9, 2013 (www.huffingtonpost.com/2013/06/09/obama-xi_n_3412312.html).

37. The term *Taiwan* is used throughout this chapter to denote the portion of China currently administered by what is known as the Republic of China, principally located on Taiwan. The usage of this term, like U.S. policy since 1972, does not imply two Chinas—the United States, and indeed officials on both sides of the Taiwan Strait, recognize only one.

38. Currently twenty-three nations, mostly small states in the Caribbean, Central America, and Africa, as well as the Vatican, recognize Taiwan. South Korea dropped relations in 1992, the last Asian nation to do so. Other relatively recent major losses include South Africa in 1998 and Saudi Arabia in 1990. Forty-seven states that recognize the PRC (including the United States) also maintain economic, trade, or cultural relations offices in Taiwan, as the United States also does.

39. J. Michael Cole, "China's Second Artillery Has a New Missile," *Diplomat,* August 7, 2013.

40. The U.S. merchandise trade deficit with the world in 2010 reached $630 billion, with public debt at 59 percent of GDP and a fiscal deficit of over $1.3 trillion. China, with foreign exchange reserves of over $2.6 trillion at the end of 2010, was the largest holder of American public debt, although it remained a large net capital importer at the macroeconomic level.

41. Douglas Mendel, *The Politics of Formosan Nationalism* (University of California Press, 1970).

42. See Catherine Kai-ping Lin, "Taiwan's Overseas Opposition Movement and Grassroots Diplomacy in the United States: The Case of the Formosan Association for Public Affairs," *Journal of Contemporary China* (February 2006), pp. 133–59.

43. Thomas W. Robinson, "America in Taiwan's Post–Cold War Foreign Relations," in *Contemporary Taiwan,* edited by David Shambaugh (Oxford University Press, 1998), pp. 296–317.

44. James Mann, "Congress and Taiwan: Understanding the Bond," in *Making China Policy: Lessons from the Bush and Clinton Administrations,* edited by Ramon H. Myers, Michael Oksenberg, and David Shambaugh (Lanham, Md.: Rowman and Littlefield, 2001), p. 201.

45. The China lobby, for example, succeeded in getting Congress to defeat Truman administration efforts to cut off funding to the KMT during China's civil war. After Chiang's flight to Taiwan, Congress regularly passed resolutions

opposing China's admission to the United Nations and inhibited moves toward relaxing bilateral ties. See ibid. Also see Nancy Bernkopf Tucker, *Taiwan, Hong Kong, and the United States, 1945–1992: Uncertain Friendships* (New York: Twayne, 1994); and Nancy Bernkopf Tucker, *Strait Talk: United States–Taiwan Relations and the Crisis with China* (Harvard University Press, 2009).

46. Mann, *About Face*, pp. 68–73, 83.

47. For details, see Stanley D. Bachrack, *The Committee of One Million: "China Lobby" Politics, 1953–1971* (Columbia University Press, 1976); W. A. Swanberg, *Luce and His Empire* (New York: Scribner's, 1972); and John W. Garver, *The Sino-American Alliance: Nationalist China and American Cold War Strategy in Asia* (Armonk, N.Y.: M. E. Sharpe, 1997). This early China lobby was broadly oriented toward the Republican Party and on delicate terms with most Democrats in Washington.

48. Swanberg, *Luce and His Empire*, pp. 351–56.

49. Ibid., p. 417.

50. Luce, for example, was born in Tengchow, Shandong Province, lived in China to the age of fourteen, and visited frequently thereafter. Apart from powerful support for Chiang Kai-shek, provided in *Time, Life,* and *Fortune,* which he published, Luce collaborated with the *Reader's Digest* and politicians like Senators William Knowland and (at times) Joseph McCarthy to amplify mass support for his pro-Chiang positions. See ibid., especially p. 351.

51. In recent years roughly 10,000 Taiwanese a year have been emigrating to the United States; this is less than a fifth of those from mainland China. There were nearly 4 million Chinese Americans overall by 2010. See "Taiwanese Americans" (http://everyculture.com); and "2011 Statistical Portrait of Asian Americans" (www.aasc.ucla.edu/archives/stats 2011.asp).

52. Jimmy Carter, *Keeping Faith: Memoirs of a President* (New York: Bantam, 1982), p. 187.

53. John Sexton and Zhou Jing, "Former President Carter Hails China-US Relationship," China.Org.Cn, January 12, 2009 (www.china.org.cn).

54. Brzezinski, *Power and Principle,* pp. 223–24.

55. Vogel, *Deng Xiaoping and the Transformation of China,* p. 312.

56. Ibid., p. 316.

57. On the concept of Taiwan as a unique incarnation of China, distinctively faithful to its classic traditions, see Ralph N. Clough, *Island China* (Harvard University Press, 1978).

58. Vogel, *Deng Xiaoping,* p. 480. Chiang Ching-kuo had apparently been awakened in the middle of the night to be told that U.S.-PRC normalization would be announced a few hours later.

59. Mann, *About Face,* p. 95.

60. After announcing the Four Modernizations in late 1978, and normalizing with the United States in January 1979, Deng Xiaoping made an acclaimed visit to Washington and other parts of the United States, which charmed American

legislators and the general public. That visit was followed by intensified U.S.-China political-military cooperation, including intelligence and defense-industrial cooperation, directed against the Soviet Union. Deng also deepened ties with American allies in Japan and Western Europe. On Deng's diplomatic reorientation, which markedly improved Washington's receptivity to China's interests in the nation's capital, see Brzezinski, *Power and Principle,* pp. 401–25; and Vogel, *Deng Xiaoping,* pp. 311–48.

61. See Mann, "Congress and Taiwan," p. 203.

62. One celebrated cause that the subcommittee investigated was the 1984 murder in the United States by Taiwanese intelligence officers of Henry Liu, a Taiwanese émigré who had written a critical biography of Chiang Kai-shek. See ibid.

63. Ibid., p. 204.

64. TECRO-DC in 2011 included a political division, a congressional liaison division, a consular division, an administrative division, a cultural division, an economic division, a science and technology division, a defense liaison division, and a defense procurement division. It also oversaw the twelve offices of the Taipei Economic and Cultural Offices (in Atlanta, Boston, Chicago, Guam, Honolulu, Houston, Kansas City, Los Angeles, Miami, New York, San Francisco, and Seattle). For details on its overall U.S. operations, see www.taiwanembassy.org/US/mp.asp?mp=12.

65. Built in 1888, Twin Oaks is said to have been the site of the first telephone call, involving Alexander Graham Bell himself. It was first rented by the Republic of China in 1937 and then was purchased in 1947 for $450,000. On Twin Oaks and its history, see http://dcist.com/2008/12/rare_look_at_twin_oaks_estate_for_1.php?gallery0Pic=1.

66. Taipei Economic and Cultural Representative Office in the United States, "TECRO Activities," 2013 (www.taiwanembassy.org/us/lp.asp?CtNode=2295&CtUnit=43&BaseDSD=7&mp=12).

67. "US Congressmen Show Support at ROC Centennial Celebration," *Taiwan News,* October 6, 2011. *Double-ten* refers to October 10, the anniversary of the establishment of the Republic of China, although the centennial reception was not actually held on that day.

68. See www.taiwanembassy.org/US/ct.asp?xItem+178656&ct.

69. Pelosi, Speaker of the House of Representatives (2007–11), represents downtown San Francisco, including Taiwan-oriented Chinatown, while Lantos (House of Representatives International Relations Committee chairman, 2007–08) represents Daly City, Pacifica, and the San Mateo area near the San Francisco airport, which is also the home of many Taiwanese immigrants. See Michael Barone, *The Almanac of American Politics, 2006* (Washington: National Journal Group, 2005), pp. 185–89, 197–200.

70. U.S. Representative David Wu (D-Ore.) also served in Congress from 1999 to 2011, before resigning in the face of scandal. See Jeffrey Osborn, "Rep. Wu Resigns amid Sex Scandal," *Northwest Asian Weekly,* July 30, 2011.

71. The church also helped preserve the local Taiwanese dialect, at a time when use of that dialect was restricted on Taiwan, by printing the Bible and hymnals in romanized Taiwanese. See Franklin Ng, *The Taiwanese-Americans* (Westport, Conn.: Greenwood, 1998), p. 93.

72. On Ming-min Peng's career, see his autobiographical account, *A Taste of Freedom: Memoirs of a Formosan Independence Leader* (New York: Holt, Rinehart, and Winston, 1972).

73. Catherine Kai-ping Lin, "Taiwan's Overseas Opposition Movement and Grassroots Diplomacy in the United States: The Case of the Formosan Association for Public Affairs," *Journal of Contemporary China* (February, 2006), p. 144.

74. See http://fapa.org/amin/about_fapa.htm.

75. Mann, "Congress and Taiwan," p. 205.

76. Ibid. Robb was the son-in-law of U.S. President Lyndon Johnson, married to Lynda Bird Johnson.

77. See, for example, "FAPA's Congressional Staff Briefing on ECFA and FTA Today" (http://ataa.us/portal111/index.php?option=com_content&task=view&id=295Gitemid=2).

78. Pell served as a member of a U.S. government team preparing for the military occupation of Taiwan just after World War II. See "Beyond Formosa Betrayed: Toward Truth and Reconciliation in Taiwan" (www.formosafoundation.org).

79. Huntington's research culminated in a major work on comparative democratic evolution. See Samuel P. Huntington, *The Third Wave: Democratization in the Late Twentieth Century* (University of Oklahoma Press, 1992).

80. Between 1989 and 2009, for example, the Chiang Ching-kuo Foundation funded seventy projects at Columbia University, sixty-nine at Harvard, and fifty-three at the University of California–Berkeley, at a cost of over $7 million. On the foundation's history and activities more generally, see www.cckf.org.tw/e-introduce.htm.

81. Daniel Southerland, "Ban on F-16 Sales to Taiwan May End; Bush Move Would Save 3,000 Jobs in Texas, a Prize Election State," *Washington Post,* September 2, 1992.

82. Clinton apparently approved the visit for three reasons: first, he couldn't see a rationale for denying the president of a friendly, democratizing society permission to attend a private function at his alma mater; second, he wanted to avoid complicating an impending congressional fight over most-favored-nation treatment for China; and third, he feared the passage of legislation injurious to Sino-American relations that might flow from a presidential rejection of the Lee visit. On the details, see David M. Lampton, *Same Bed, Different Dreams: Managing U.S.-China Relations, 1989–2000* (University of California Press, 2001), p. 50.

83. Mann, *About Face,* pp. 206–07.

84. In 1994 Lee's KMT government hired Cassidy and Associates for three years to create a more supportive political environment for Taiwan in the United States. According to Stanley Roth, serving on the National Security Council during

the Lee saga, Cassidy did not play a major direct role in persuading Congress to grant Lee a visa, but it nevertheless "helped to generate a political environment that made the issue a very tough call for the administration." See ibid., p. 209.

85. Robinson, "America in Taiwan's Post–Cold War Foreign Relations," p. 301.

86. Mann, *About Face,* p. 208.

87. This legislation, passed by the House of Representatives but not the Senate, would have required the secretary of defense to report by December 1, 1998, on the establishment of a TMD system able to protect Taiwan from ballistic missile attack. See *BMD Monitor,* November 14, 1997.

88. "Foreign Military Sale, TECRO," *DOD Memorandum for Correspondent,* no. 126-M, July 31, 1999.

89. The TSEA passed the House of Representatives on a bipartisan vote of 341-70 but died in 2000 on the Senate legislative calendar. See "Taiwan Security Enhancement Act" (http://thomas.loc.gov/cgi-bin/bdquery/z?d106:HRO1838:@@@R).

90. For more information on the Taiwan Research Institute, see www.tri.org.tw/english.

91. Mann, *About Face,* p. 208.

92. "Office personnel reportedly will focus on promoting Taiwan's entry into international organizations and improving ROC-U.S. ties. The head of the DPP's Washington office will be Legislator Parris Chang." See *Taiwan Journal,* February 24, 1995 (http://taiwanjournal.nat.gov.tw/site/Tj/ct.asp?xItem=12967&CtNode=122).

93. Kerry Dumbaugh, *China-U.S. Relations: Current Issues and Implications for U.S. Policy* (Congressional Research Service, 2009), p. 18.

94. There is however an active association of former members of Congress, which established a congressional study group on Japan in 1993, in cooperation with the East-West Center. It holds periodic roundtable discussions for members and features visiting dignitaries from Japan. For details see http://usafmc.org. A group of current members will reportedly become active in 2014, led by congressman Devin Nunes (R-Calif.).

95. Affiliation was established February 29, 1960. See Tokyo Metropolitan Government, "Sister Cities/States of Tokyo" (www.metro.tokyo.jp/ENGLISH/PROFILE/policy06.htm).

96. See Kent E. Calder, "A Tale of Two Cities: U.S.-Japan Relations in New York and Washington," *Kudan Square,* no. 25 (March 2008), pp. 1–3.

97. The immediate catalyst was the visit of Admiral Ijuin Goro and his two warships, *Tsukuba* and *Chitose,* to New York. On the foundation of the Japan Society in New York, see Michael R. Auslin, *Pacific Cosmopolitans: A Cultural History of U.S.-Japan Relations* (Harvard University Press, 2011), pp. 102–05. This New York–based group was actually the second Japan society to be founded, following that of San Francisco (1905), but New York's rapidly became the most influential.

98. Ibid., p. 109. Arai was also the grandfather of Haru Reischauer, the wife of the future U.S. ambassador to Japan Edwin O. Reischauer.

99. Kent E. Calder, "Securing Security through Prosperity: The San Francisco System in Comparative Perspective," *Pacific Review* 17, no. 1 (2004), pp. 135–57; and Calder, *Pacific Alliance*, pp. 35–37.

100. The ACJ, chaired by *Newsweek* foreign editor Harry Kern, was formally organized in 1947 and was influential in blunting occupation reforms until the occupation ended in 1952 and the ACJ itself was disbanded in 1953. See Harold Schonberger, "The Japan Lobby in American Diplomacy, 1947–1952," *Pacific Historical Review* 46, no. 3 (1977), pp. 327–59; and Robert C. Angel, "Postwar Reconstruction of the Japan Lobby in Washington: The First Fifteen Years," *Japan Forum* 13, no. 1 (2001), pp. 77–90.

101. "The Japanese Embassy," *New York Times,* August 20, 1860 (www.nytimes.com/1860/8/20/news/japanese-embassy).

102. Ivan Parker Hall, *Mori Arinori* (Harvard University Press, 1973), p. 156.

103. One of the most trying early problems was a lack of water supply, due to broken water pipes, regarding which Mori protested to Secretary of State Hamilton Fish in the fall of 1871. Another was the difficulty of attracting attention to U.S.-Japan relations, as the Japanese embassy was being established, due to the high-profile U.S. dispute with Britain over the *Alabama* claims, which threatened war periodically during 1871–72. See ibid., pp. 156–57.

104. The students included Tsuda Umeko, later founder of Japan's first women's college; Kaneko Kentarō, future foreign minister; and Nakae Chōmin, later a distinguished journalist. On the mission and its global accomplishments, see Ian Nish, ed., The *Iwakura Mission in America and Europe: A New Assessment* (London: Routledge Curzon, 1998).

105. Hall, *Mori Arinori*, pp. 160–61, 172.

106. Mori's publications during his ambassadorial tenure include *Life and Resources in America* (1871); *Religious Freedom in Japan* (1872); and *Education in Japan* (1873). See Hall, *Mori Arinori*, p. 156.

107. For this and the following, see ibid., pp. 157–58, 168, 170, 171.

108. Among other such public relations tasks, Mori wrote to dispel rumors of a conservative coup d'etat in Tokyo during the autumn of 1872, performing the remarkably contemporary task of condemning them as "a fabrication concocted in Washington."

109. From 24th Street, the Japanese mission, and then embassy, moved to 1600 Rhode Island Avenue, across the street from the current site of the Reischauer Center for East Asian Studies. In 1931 it moved to its current location at 2520 Massachusetts Avenue, N.W., although only the old ambassador's residence and the east wing buildings existed, according to a Japanese embassy/JICC note of May 4, 2011, to Mariko de Freytas.

110. On this evolution, see Takeo Iguchi, *Demystifying Pearl Harbor: A New Perspective from Japan* (Tokyo: I-House, 2010); Gwen Terasaki, *Bridge to the Sun* (University of North Carolina Press, 1957); and Nomura Kichisaburō, *Beikoku ni tsukaishite—Nichi-Bei Kōshō no Kaikō* [As an envoy to America—Recollections of the U.S.-Japan talks] (Tokyo: Iwanami Shōten, 1946).

111. On Yamamoto and his years in Washington, see Yamamoto Isoroku Kinenkan, *Yamamoto Isoroku Kinenkan Tenji Zuroku* [Records of the Yamamoto Isoroku Memorial Hall] (Nagaoka, Niigata Prefecture: Yamamoto Isoroku Kinenkan, 1999), pp. 14–17; Yamamoto Isoroku, ed., *Yamamoto Isoroku no Keishin* [Yamamoto Isoroku's preparation] (Nagaoka, Niigata Prefecture: Yamamoto Gensui Keigokai, 2010); Hando Kazutoshi, *Yamamoto Isoroku* (Tokyo: Heibonsha, 2007); and Handō Kazutoshi, *Yamamoto Isoroku: Rengo Kantai Shireikan* [Yamamoto Isoroku: Commander of the Combined Fleet] (Tokyo: Bungei Shunjū, 2011).

112. For a detailed, readable history of the cherry tree gift and its implications over the years, see John R. Malott, *Mrs. Taft Plants a Tree: How the Cherry Blossoms Came to Washington* (Washington: Japan America Society, 2012).

113. Japan Economic Institute, "The Who, What, Where of JEI: Mission Statement" (www.jei.org/About JEI/About_JEI.html).

114. Ambassador John R. Malott, JASW's president, at its fiftieth anniversary dinner, December 6, 2007.

115. The JASW's establishment in 1957 came fully half a century after that of the Japan Society in New York (1907). Other early Japan America societies were established in Boston (1904), San Francisco (1905), Los Angeles (1909), Washington State (1920), and Chicago (1930). See Auslin, *Pacific Cosmopolitans,* p. 101.

116. Korea was second, in 1990, with fifty-one registered agents, followed by Taiwan with thirty-eight, India with thirteen, and Singapore and Indonesia, with seven each. See Department of Justice, "Foreign Agents Registration Act" (www.fara.gov).

117. The chair was established through the support of Toyota Motor Corp., which also contributed generously to the Reischauer Center. The U.S.-Japan Foundation was established by the Japan Shipbuilding Industry Foundation in 1980, followed in 1985 by the Matsushita Foundation and the Hitachi Foundation.

118. Japan America Society, "Public Affairs Dinner" (www.us-japan.org/dc/annualdinner.php).

119. See www.jcaw.org/english/index.jtml.

120. The expressed purpose of the council was to create a better political climate that would help ease the trade frictions that dominated the 1980s, by promoting "good corporate citizenship." The council sponsored seminars on improving community relations, understanding affirmative action, and coordinating contributions by Japanese companies to minority groups and civic causes. Japan's Ministry of Finance ruled that contributions from corporate headquarters in Japan to U.S. nonprofit organizations would be nontaxable, provided that such contributions were funneled through the Council for Better Investment or similar organizations. See Nancy R. London, *Japanese Corporate Philanthropy* (Oxford University Press, 1991), pp. 107, 125.

121. Department of Justice, Foreign Registration Act data (www.fara.gov).

122. See http://congressional.proquest.com.

123. Between 2000 and the end of 2009 there were 25,648 *New York Times* articles that mentioned Japan, compared to 52,082 articles during the decade of the 1980s. See ProQuest content-analysis data, http://search.proquest.com/hnp newyorktimes?accountid=11752.

124. Japan Center for International Exchange, *Reinvigorating U.S.-Japan Policy Dialogue and Study* (Tokyo: 2010), p. 22.

125. In 2002, six members also visited, including Senator Paul Sarbanes (D-Md.). Representative Brian Baird (D-Wash.) visited in 2003 and Representative Rick Boucher (D-Va.) in 2007. See Japan Center for International Exchange, "U.S.-Japan Parliamentary Exchange Program" (www.jcie.or.jp/pep/exchange/index.html); and Japan Center for International Exchange, *U.S.-Japan Parliamentary Exchange Program: 28th Congressional Delegation to Japan, February 20–24, 2011* (www.jcie.or.jp/pep/exchange/us/28.html).

126. "Abe, U.S. Senator Concur on Need to Bolster Alliance," *Japan Times,* August 15, 2013.

127. In 1997, 102 congressional staffers visited Japan, but only 24 in 2009. In contrast, 93 visited China in the latter year. See Japan Center, *Reinvigorating U.S.-Japan Policy Dialogue and Study,* p. 49.

128. Ibid. Japanese Diet delegations to the United States numbered seven in 2001, seven in 2004, three in 2006, and three in 2013.

129. The combined budgets of Washington's five leading policy institutes (AEI, Brookings, CFR, CSIS, and IIE) more than doubled, from $79 million in 1998 to $199 million in 2008. See Japan Center, *Reinvigorating U.S.-Japan Policy Dialogue and Study,* p. 19.

130. Ibid., p. 13. In 2012, for example, both the Brookings Institution and the Carnegie Endowment for International Peace, two of the top think tanks in the world, established active Japan programs.

131. "Mireya Solís Named Philip Knight Chair in Japan Studies at Brookings" (www.brookings.edu/about/media-relations/news-releases/2012/0905-solis).

132. Japan Center for International Exchange, *Reinvigorating U.S.-Japan Policy Dialogue and Study,* p. 13.

133. The five universities were Tokyo, Kyōto, Waseda, Keio, and Ritsumeikan. The group had expanded by 2013, adding three more universities: Doshisha, Kyūshū, and Tsukuba. On the organization and activities of the Research Institute, see www.us-jpri.org.

134. The property on which the Japanese embassy stands was acquired in 1930. Until the postwar period, the operations of the embassy were housed in a building next to the current chancery (the *kyūkan*), which is still used occasionally for receptions and seminars.

135. Both communities are relatively stable in size. The Japanese community in Washington rose from 882 in 2000 to 913 in 2009, while that in New York rose from 48,517 to 54,718. Data are number of Japanese citizens registered as locally resident with the Japanese embassy in Washington or the Japanese Consulate General in New York City.

136. On the structure and functioning of the Japanese embassy in Washington, see Agawa Naoyuki, *Massachusetts Dōri 2520 Banchi* [2520 Massachusetts Avenue] (Tokyo: Kōdansha, 2006).

137. Japan in 2013 had consular representation in Anchorage, Atlanta, Boston, Chicago, Denver, Detroit, Hagatna (Guam), Honolulu, Houston, Los Angeles, Miami, Nashville, New York City, Portland, San Francisco, and Seattle. See www.us-emb-japan.go.jp.

138. JICC director Itō Misako, interview by Mariko de Freytas, July 2, 2008.

139. *Sumie* are traditional Japanese ink and wash brush paintings. *Obon* is the traditional Buddhist custom of honoring the departed spirits of ancestors, centering on a three-day festival during late July or mid-August.

140. Shiori Okazaki, "Celebrating the Embassy Adoption Program at the Ambassador's Residence," *Japan Now*, December 21, 2007 (www.us.emb-japan. go.jp/jicc/EJN_vol3_no12.htm).

141. Susan Laszewski, "Composing a Bigger Picture: Music, Art, and the Embassy Adoption Program," *Japan Now*, February 21, 2012 (www.us.emb-japan. go.jp/jicc/japan-now/EJN_vol8_no3.htm#Article4).

142. Douglas McGray, "Japan's Gross National Cool," *Foreign Policy*, May/June, 2009.

143. Otacon is a fan convention focusing on East Asian popular culture (especially anime, manga, music, and film). The name derives from the Japanese word *otaku* and the English word *convention*. Katsucon is a similar fan convention for anime and manga enthusiasts. See Katsucon information (2008@Anime.com and www.animecons.com/events/info-shtml/1326).

144. On this challenge, see for example Agawa, *Massachusetts Dōri 2520 Banchi;* and Komori Yoshihisa's articles on "Iza!," *Sankei Shimbun*'s blog site.

145. Agawa, *Massachusetts Dōri*, p. 84.

146. Long-time Japan Foundation director Hiroaki Fujii made this critique, cited by Agawa. See ibid., p. 42.

147. Japan Bowl brings U.S. high school students knowledgeable about Japan to Washington for a competition regarding factual knowledge about Japan; it is sponsored by the Japan America Society of Washington and held during the Cherry Blossom Festival. The funding difficulty, Agawa emphasizes, lies in Tokyo rather than the embassy, and the Japan Foundation ultimately agreed to contribute half of the funds required to implement the Japanese-language advanced placement program in 2004. See ibid., pp. 141–42.

148. Since November 2012 an online interactive web magazine, *Discuss Japan: Japan Foreign Policy Forum,* has assumed some of *Japan Echo*'s functions, at reduced cost to the Japanese government, but the international visibility of this successor publication is much reduced for some important constituencies, since the print version was discontinued. The new online forum is accessible at www. japan policy forum.jp/en/.

149. Agawa, *Massachusetts Dōri*, pp. 200–04.

150. Ibid., pp. 214, 248, and 266.

151. Yoshihisa Komori, "Nihon no Gaikokan wa Naze Kaigai Chūzai ga Mijikai no ka?" [Why are the overseas tours of diplomats so short?], *Iza B Ban*, May 31, 2008 (http://komoriy.iza.ne.jp/blog/entry/592672).

152. Recent vice ministers posted to Washington include Sasae, Kuriyama, and Yanai, as well as Saitō Kunihiko, Murata Ryōhei, and Matsunaga Nobuo. See Komori Yoshihisa, *Bōkoku no Nihon Taishikan* [The Japanese embassy of a defeated country] (Tokyo: Shōgakkan, 2002), pp. 112–13.

153. Ambassador Fujisaki Ichirō, for example, is the son of a Foreign Ministry official, as Ambassadors Yanai and Kuriyama also were, and a great-grandson of Prime Minister Itō Hirobumi, one of the key leaders of the Meiji Restoration. His predecessor, Tōgō Fumihiko, ambassador to Washington from 1975 to 1980, married Tōgō Ise, the daughter of former Foreign Minister Tōgō Shigenori, adopted the Tōgō name, and thus entered the Tōgō family, in accordance with Japanese custom.

154. Ambassador Fujisaki's wife, for example, is the daughter of Kashiwagi Yūsuke, former vice minister of finance for international affairs, while his predecessor's wife was the daughter of a distinguished diplomat.

155. See Japan-America Society of Washington, "Public Affairs Dinner" (www.us-japan-org/dc/annualdinner.php).

156. In early 2011 the JCAW had around 110 corporate/organizational members and 104 individual members, drawn from the Washington area business community and associated groups. See the JCAW website (www.jcaw.org).

157. JCAW (www.jcaw.org/English/index.html).

158. See www.jcaw.org/news/local/old/2005/carefund.html. JCAW played a particularly important role in preparations for the 2012 centennial commemoration of the original cherry tree gift, sponsoring a major review by young scholars of the U.S.-Japan bilateral relationship as a whole.

159. See www.jcaw.org.

160. For details, see www.spfusa-org.

161. See www.jcaw.org/news/local/old/2005/carefund.html. Also see the website of the Japanese American Care Fund (http://jacarefund.org/aboutus.html). The fund is based in Annandale, Virginia.

162. Consulate-General of Japan in Los Angeles, "Japanese Americans and Japan" (www.la.us.emb-japan.go.jp/e_web/e_w06_htm).

163. U.S.-Japan Council, "2010 Japanese American Leadership Delegation," 2010 (www.usjapancouncil.org/2010_Japanese_American_leadership_delegation).

164. U.S.-Japan Council, "Japanese American Leadership Delegation" (www.usjapancouncil.org/programs/program/JALD).

165. U.S. Japan Council, "USJC Japan Week 2013," 2013 (www.usjapancouncil.org/p/japan_symposium).

166. On activities of the U.S.-Japan Council, see www.usjapancouncil.org/about.html.

167. See www.jacl.org/documents/Article%20-%20Ambassador%20of%20Japan%20Hosts%20Reception%20for%20JA's.pdf.

168. U.S.-Japan Council, "2010 U.S.-Japan Council Annual Conference," September 20, 2010 (www.usjapancouncil.org/programs/program/2010_Annual_Conference).

169. U.S.-Japan Council, "Annual Conference" (www.usjapancouncil.org/programs/program/annual-conference).

170. See, for example, Lisa Curtis and Devin Stewart, "Reflections on the Japan-U.S. Leadership Network Program, Fall, 2007," *Japan Now,* February 25, 2008 (www.us.emb-japan-go.jp/jicc/JapanNow/EJN_vol4_no3.htm).

171. First Lady Lady Bird Johnson, on behalf of the United States, accepted 3,800 more cherry trees from Japan. See the National Cherry Blossom Festival website (www.nationalcherryblossomfestival.org).

172. Ibid.

173. The National Gallery featured the vivid, naturalistic animal and flower paintings of Itō Jakuchu (1716–1800), part of the private Japanese Imperial collection, which had previously only been exhibited once before at the Jotenkaku Museum in the Shōkokuji monastery in 2007. The exhibition ran for nearly a month before and after the Cherry Blossom Festival centennial celebration. Ken Johnson, "Teeming with Transcendent Life," *New York Times,* March 29, 2012 (www.nytimes.com/2012/03/30/arts/design/colorful-realm-works-by-ito-jakuchu-at-national-gallery.html?_r=0). For details, see the National Gallery website, www.nga.gov/exhibitions/jakuchuinfo.shtm. The Smithsonian's Sackler Gallery featured classic Japanese wood-block prints, "Hokusai: Thirty-six Views of Mount Fuji," which ran from March 24 to June 17, 2012. For details, see www.si.edu/Exhibitions/Details/Hokusai-Thiry-six-Views-of-Mouht-Fuji-4768.

174. See the Tomodachi Initiative website, 2012/content/uploads/2012/04/TOMODACHI2012Report_E_Website.pdf.

175. U.S.-Japan Council, "Tomodachi Initiative, 2013" (http://usjapantomodachi.org).

176. In this chapter, the term *Korea* is used interchangeably with *South Korea.*

177. Data from U.S. Central Intelligence Agency, *World Fact Book.*

178. Bruce Klingner, "Supporting Our South Korean Ally and Enhancing Defense Cooperation," *Heritage,* web memo 1859 on Asia, March 18, 2008 (www.heritage.org).

179. The KORUS free trade agreement negotiations were announced on February 2, 2006, and were concluded on April 1, 2007. The treaty was first signed on June 30, 2007, with a renegotiated version signed in early December 2010. See "US, South Korea Sign Landmark Free Trade Agreement," Agence France-Presse, December 5, 2010.

180. "Korea's National Assembly Ratifies KORUS FTA," *Arirang,* November 2011.

181. By 2011 the United States had bilateral free trade agreements with eighteen countries, including Australia, Chile, Canada, Peru, and Mexico, and in the Asia Pacific region, Korea and Singapore. It was also in negotiations on a regional, Asia Pacific trade agreement, with the objective of shaping a high-standard, broad-based regional pact.

182. John Kie-chiang Oh and Bonni Bongwan Cho Oh, *The Korean Embassy in America* (Elizabeth, N.J.: Hollym International Corporation, 2003), p. 20.

183. The Korean National Association, led by An Ch'angho, was founded in Hawaii in 1920 and published two newspapers. See ibid., p. 74.

184. Ibid., p. 31.

185. Do Je-Hae, "1919 Independence Movement Had Global Implications," *Korea Times*, February 27, 2009.

186. Chang Lee Wook served as Korean ambassador to the United States in the historic October 1960 to June 1961 period, right after the fall of the Syngman Rhee regime. Both before and after his ambassadorship, Ambassador Chang worked for the Hungsadan (Young Korean Academy), an important Korean patriotic organization that emphasized leadership training of young Korean leaders. It was founded in 1913 in San Francisco. See Oh and Oh, *The Korean Embassy in America*, p. 74.

187. Chang Myun later served as both vice president and prime minister of Korea. He was head of government following President Syngman Rhee's resignation in 1960, serving for about a year.

188. The Korean embassy included four diplomats in 1950, twenty-two in 1962, and twenty-eight in 1966. In 1990 the embassy chancery, at 2450 Massachusetts Avenue, N.W., was purchased and the embassy expanded significantly. It included sixty-nine diplomats in 2000 and seventy-five by 2013, together with over seventy clerical or administrative personnel. See Oh and Oh, *The Korean Embassy in America*; and U.S. Department of State, *Diplomatic List*.

189. Chung-in Moon, "Complex Interdependence and Transnational Lobbying: South Korea in the United States," *International Studies Quarterly* 32, no. 1 (1988), p. 73.

190. There were allegations in Korea that President Park Chung Hee in 1970 had ordered this massive campaign to win support for South Korea from senators and representatives through lavish entertainment and substantial cash gifts. See Chong-Ki Choi, "American-Korean Diplomatic Relations, 1961–1982," in *U.S.-Korean Relations, 1882–1982*, edited by Tae-Hwan Kwak and others (Seoul: Kyungnam University Institute for Far Eastern Studies, 1982), p. 109.

191. On Tongsun Park's activities and the related Koreagate scandal, see Robert B. Boettcher, *Gifts of Deceit: Sun Myung Moon, Tongsun Park, and the Korean Scandal* (New York: Holt, Rinehart, and Winston, 1980).

192. Ibid.

193. On the delicacy of U.S.-Korean relations under Carter, see Don Oberdorfer, *The Two Koreas: A Contemporary History*, rev. ed. (New York: Basic Books, 2001), pp. 84–108.

194. Moon, "Complex Interdependence and Transnational Lobbying," p. 75. For sources for this paragraph, see also pp. 74, 76, 77.

195. The number of Korean students in the United States rose from 49,000 in 2001 to over 72,000 in 2013. There are now over 150 Korean students in the United States for every 100,000 Korean citizens. Only Chinese and Indian students outnumber Korean students in the United States. See East-West Center, *Korea Matters for America*, p. 12.

196. KORUS House was, for example, the venue on December 15, 2009, for an awards ceremony for the Korean War veterans' appreciation essay contest, which recognizes the sacrifice made by Korean War veterans. The contest was open to all U.S. elementary, middle school, and high school students.

197. On the King Sejong Institute, see http://eng.sejonghakdang.org.

198. The Federation of Korean Industries can be thought of as a consortium of *chaebol* groups and is very similar to Japan's Keidanren. The Korea International Trade Association is a privately owned nonprofit organization established in 1946. It is one of Korea's largest umbrella economic organizations and is focused on international trade. It has more than 80,000 member firms, including LG, Samsung, and Hyundai.

199. Japan in 1957 established the U.S.-Japan Trade Council, later to become the Japan Economic Institute, affiliated with the Japanese Foreign Ministry. The council provided useful economic information to the Washington policy community for three decades and nurtured such distinguished economists as Edward Lincoln and Arthur Alexander.

200. Among KEI's programs oriented toward agenda setting in U.S.-Korea relations are Congressional Roundtables, the Opinion Leaders' Seminar, National Assembly orientations, the Academic Paper Series, Korean American Day, Academic Symposia, and the Korea Club. See Korea Economic Institute, "Promoting Dialogue and Understanding between the United States and Korea" (keia.org).

201. One especially active member of Congress is Mark Kirk (R-Ill.), who has a large Korean American constituency. Representative Kirk chairs the Korea-U.S. Internship Exchange Program run by the Meridian International Center. The program sends Korean and American college students to each other's countries as interns, to learn about the other nation's legislative processes. See www.kirk forsenate.com?pageid=1020.

202. Ambassador Lee holds a master's degree from Johns Hopkins School of Advanced International Studies, and Ambassador Han holds a Ph.D. from Harvard University.

203. On September 23, 2013, for example, nearly two thousand guests attended a dinner reception and concert at the Kennedy Center, celebrating the alliance, at the Korean ambassador's invitation, following a Capitol Hill reception cohosted also by the Congressional Caucus on Korea, and a glittering dinner hosted earlier in the year by the Asan Institute for Policy Studies.

204. KORUS passed the U.S. Congress on October 12, 2011, by 278-151 in the House of Representatives and 83-15 in the Senate. It then passed Korea's National Assembly on November 22, 2011, by 151-157. See Victor Cha, "The US-ROK Free Trade Agreement," *Center for Strategic and International Studies,* October 13, 2011 (http://csis.org/publication/us-rok-free-trade-agreement); and Kyle Horseman, "KORUS FTA Ratification in Korean National Assembly," *Northern Kentucky International Trade Association,* November 23, 2011 (http:// nkita.wordpress.com/2011/11/23/korus_fta_ratified/).

205. The ambassadors' dialogue, unique to U.S.-Korea relations, involves joint presentations by the U.S. ambassador to Korea and the Korean ambassador to the United States at a variety of U.S. locations. It has continued annually, with only a few exceptions, since 1992. For details, see www.keia.org.

206. Among other activities, the ambassadors were briefed by energy industry officials in Houston, observed brain surgery by a leading Korean American neurosurgeon, and participated in a private briefing at the U.S. Pacific Command. See www.keia.org/kei-events-ambassadors-dialogue.

207. According to the survey, there were 1.73 million self-identified Korean Americans in 2011 (http://factfinder.census.gov).

208. The Korean American Voters' Council, formed in the wake of the 1992 Los Angeles riots, has been conducting an active voter registration program since 1995 and a broad program of education for Korean Americans on U.S. laws and the American political system since 2000. On the activities of the council, see http://kavc.org.

209. "Korean Americans Demonstrate 'to Protect Dokdo,'" *Munhwa Ilbo,* July 17, 2008 (www.munhwa.com/news/view.html?no=2008071701070432112020).

210. The first comfort women resolution was proposed in 1997 by Representative William Lipinsky. Subsequent attempts to introduce such resolutions were made in 2000, 2001, 2003, 2005, and 2006. In September 2006 the House Committee on Foreign Affairs unanimously passed the resolution, but it was not introduced into the full House. In January 2007 the resolution was introduced again by Representative Michael Honda (D-Calif.). On the history of the comfort women issue, see Cheah Wui Ling, "Walking the Long Road in Solidarity and Hope: Study of the 'Comfort Women' Movement's Deployment of Human Rights Discourse," *Harvard Human Rights Journal* 22, no. 1 (2008), pp. 32–107.

211. For a detailed analytical chronicle of the comfort women controversy in Washington, see Eunjung Lim, "Who Is Strongest in Washington? A Comparative Study on the Korean-American Comfort Women Movement and the Japanese American Redress Movement," *International Studies Review* 12, no. 2 (2011), pp. 87–107.

212. The comfort women issue was first brought to the attention of the House of Representatives by Representative Lane Evans (D-Ill.). He submitted the resolution three times, beginning in 1999. In September, 2006, his last effort passed the

House International Relations Committee. On September 22, 2006, twenty-five cosponsors, including Mike Honda, urged House Speaker Dennis Hastert to bring the resolution to the floor before the session adjourned. Hastert declined their request, however, and the resolution was automatically erased from the House calendar for the next congressional session.

213. The Lantos tea event was also attended by ranking House International Relations Committee member Ileana Ross-Lehtinen, Japanese Ambassador Ryozo Kato, Deputy Chief of Mission Akitaka Saiki, and Urban Institute President Robert Reischauer; it was cosponsored by the Reischauer Center for East Asian Studies at SAIS.

214. Dong-suk Kim, executive director of KAVC; Ok-cha Soh, president of the Washington Coalition on the Comfort Women Issue; Moon-hyung Lee, the cochair of the Washington Coalition; and In-Hoe Huh, a veteran organizer, were among these leaders.

215. Through Amnesty International, for example, the activists were able to secure community service advertising, while the Japanese conservatives reportedly paid $10,000 for their ill-fated *Washington Post* ad.

216. The bureau proposed to reclassify them from Tok Island (Korea) to Liancourt Rocks (status undefined). See "Korean Librarian Halts Library of Congress Move on Dokdo," *Chosun Ilbo,* July 17, 2008 (http://english.chosun.com/site/data/html_dir/2008/07/17/2008071761008.html).

217. Ibid. Hana Kim was conscious of the seemingly obscure terminological change and was in an authoritative position to pronounce on it, as she was concurrently chairing the North American Council on East Asian Libraries.

218. "South Korea, US Reach Deal on Free-Trade Agreement," *Korea Herald,* December 4, 2010.

Chapter 8

1. In July 2013 India's population was estimated at 1.22 billion. Although this is less than China's 1.35 billion, India's population is increasing significantly faster (1.28 percent annually, compared to China's 0.46 percent). This difference in estimated growth is due principally to the lower median age of India's population (26.7 years, compared to China's 36.3 years). For comparative statistics, see Central Intelligence Agency, *World Fact Book.*

2. All figures are from ibid. India's real economic growth rate for 2012 was 6.5 percent; for 2011, it was 7.7 percent.

3. Harold A. Gould, *Sikhs, Swamis, Students, and Spies: The India Lobby in the United States, 1900–1946* (New Delhi: Sage, 2006), p. 98.

4. On the Luce-Celler Act, see ibid., pp. 393–431. The India League of America, based in New York, was founded by the U.S. activist Lajpat Rai in 1917. However, by 1939 membership had dwindled to twelve. J. J. Singh became its president

in 1940 and revitalized the league into a major lobbying and publicity force. Anup Singh and Syud Hossain founded the National Committee for India's Freedom in Washington in 1939. Singh founded the India Chamber of Commerce at Nehru's request in 1938 to establish trade with the United States. For this and the following, see Gould, *Sikhs, Swamis, Students, and Spies,* pp. 261–326, 313, 98.

5. See D. S. Saund, *Congressman from India* (New York: Dutton, 1960), chap. 4 (www.saund.org/dalipsaund/cfi/chapter4.html).

6. Saund, born in Chajulwadi, Punjab, emigrated to the United States through Ellis Island. He obtained a Ph.D. (1924) in mathematics from the University of California, Berkeley, before becoming a farmer in Imperial County, California. He was naturalized in 1949 and held a seat in the U.S. Congress from 1957 to 1963. On Saund's career, see ibid.

7. See Joseph M. Grieco, "Between Dependency and Autonomy: India's Experience with the International Computer Industry," *International Organization* 36, no. 3 (1982); and Dennis J. Encarnation, *Dislodging Multinationals: India's Strategy in Comparative Perspective* (Cornell University Press, 1989). The Indian government's persistent demands during 1966–78 for a share in IBM India ownership and control led to IBM's withdrawal from India in 1978.

8. "Indian-Americans Lobby Washington," NewsRoom, *USINPAC,* November 1, 2010 (www.usinpac.com/index.php?option=com_content&view=article&id=6 72:indian-americans-lobby-washington&catid=35:media-coverages&Itemid=79).

9. "Members of Congressional Caucus on India and Indian Americans," *USINPAC,* November, 2008 (www.usinpac.com/track-congress/house-caucus. html). In addition to the caucus, thirty-seven senators are also members of the Friends of India.

10. The Friends of India was cochaired by Senators Hillary Clinton (D-N.Y.) and John Cornyn (R-Texas).

11. "Indian-Americans Lobby Washington," NewsRoom, *USINPAC,* November 1, 2010 (www.usinpac.com/index.php?option=com_content&view=article&id=6 72:indian-americans-lobby-washington&catid=35:media-coverages&Itemid=79).

12. The American India Foundation is today the largest diaspora philanthropy organization focused on India based in the United States. It has benefited over a million people by investing in 115 Indian NGOs, focusing on employment, health care, and education. For details, see www.aifoundation.org.

13. Arthur G. Rubinoff, "The Diaspora as a Factor in US-India Relations," *Asian Affairs* 32, no. 3 (2005), p. 175.

14. Lalit K. Jha, "White House to Have India Desk at National Security Council," *Business Standard,* July 2, 2009. India is only the second country, after Russia, to be handled separately by a senior director.

15. McDermott's legislation was modeled after the U.S.-Japan Legislative Exchange Program, which he also chaired following its inception in the early 1990s.

16. Chidanand Rajghatta, "Obamas to Host Diwali Bash," *Times of India TNN,* October 15, 2009 (http://articles.timesofindia.indiatimes.com/2009-10-15/ india/28096778_1_kal-penn-barack-obama-kalpen-modi).

17. Chidanand Rajghatta, "Obama Seeks Light and Knowledge from Diwali," *Times of India TNN,* October 15, 2009 (http://articles.timesofindia. indiatimes.com/2009-10-15/us/28111796_1_indian-americans-indian-festival-asian-americans).

18. On the details, see Lavanya Ramanathan, "Kennedy Center's India Festival Puts on a Maximum Display," *Washington Post,* February 24, 2011.

19. See Aaron Terrazas and Cristina Batog, "Indian Immigrants in the United States," *Migration Policy Institute,* June 2010 (www.migrationinformation.org/usfocus/display.cfm?ID=785); and "ACS Demographic and Housing 2012 American Community Survey 1-Year Estimates," U.S. Census Bureau, 2010 (http://factfinder2.census.gov/faces/tableservices/jsf/pages/productview.xhtml?pid=DEC_10_DP_DPDP1&prodType=table).

20. Terrazas and Batog, "Indian Immigrants in the United States."

21. Ibid.

22. In the 2012–13 academic year, 96,754 students from India were studying in the United States, and 235,597 from China. See Institute of International Education, "Fact Sheets by Country: 2012" (www.iie.org/Research-and-Publications/Open-Doors/Data/Fact-Sheets-by-Country/2012).

23. Jason Richwine, "Indian Americans: The New Model Minority," Forbes.com, February 24, 2009 (www.forbes.com/2009/02/24/bobby-jindal-indian-americans-opinions-contributors_immigrants_minority.html).

24. Terrazas and Batog, "Indian Immigrants in the United States."

25. Manjeet Kripalani, "India's Whiz Kids: Inside the Indian Institutes of Technology's Star Factory," *Business Week,* November 25, 1998 (www.businessweek.com/1998/49/b3607011.htm).

26. Abhishek Pandey and others, "India's Transformation to Knowledge-Based Economy: Evolving Role of the Indian Diaspora," *Evalueserve,* July 21, 2004 (http://info.worldbank.org/etools/docs/library/152386/abhishek.pdf).

27. Terrazas and Batog, "Indian Immigrants in the United States"; and Jeanne Batalova and Monica Whatley, "Indian Immigrants in the United States," Migration Policy Institute, August 2013 (www.migrationinformation.org/USfocus/display.cfm?ID=962).

28. "Obama Names Yet Another Indian American to Key Post," *Times of India,* April 11, 2011 (http://m.timesofindia.com/PDATOI/articleshow/7944799.cms).

29. In 1991 U.S. foreign direct investment in India totaled only $11 million, for example. By 2006, however, it had risen to $737 million—and to more than $1.9 billion by March 2010. See Kingshuk Chatterjee, "It's Economics, Stupid," *Financial Express,* May 12, 2008.

30. In 2009 Indian outsourcing exports reached $47 billion, with 60 percent going to the Americas. India was the largest outsourcing nation in the world, capturing over half of the global market. See "India," Sourcingline, February 19, 2012 (www.sourcingline.com).

31. Established in 1988, NASSCOM is a nonprofit corporation promoting sustainable growth for the industry.

32. "NASSCOM Prepares for US Lobbying," *Outsource,* July 7, 2010; and "NASSCOM to Launch Campaign on Local Hiring in the US," *India Times,* October 25, 2010.

33. "Indian-Americans Lobby Washington," NewsRoom, *USINPAC,* November 1, 2010 (www.usinpac.com/index.php?option=com_content&view=article&id=6 72:indian-americans-lobby-washington&catid=35:media-coverages&Itemid=79).

34. Mira Kamdar, *Planet India: How the Fastest-Growing Democracy Is Transforming America and the World* (New York: Scribner's, 2007), p. 35.

35. Kamdar, *Planet India,* p. 35. The Ministry of Overseas Affairs, and with it the embassy, also strengthens ties with Indian Americans through its Know India and Study India programs, both of which are open principally to individuals of Indian origin. The embassy website is also linked directly to India's Overseas Facilitation Centre, which publishes materials directed at those in the diaspora interested in business opportunities in India. See www.oifc.in/Resources/ Publications.

36. The Indian embassy includes a representative of the Indian Space Research Organization; air, military, and naval attachés; a science counselor; and a Community Affairs Department, which handles liaison with the Indian American community.

37. In addition to appearances on Capitol Hill and speeches across the United States, Ambassador Chandra had a statue of Mahatma Gandhi, the pacifist Indian nationalist leader widely admired in the United States, erected in front of the Indian embassy. It was dedicated by the presidents of both India and the United States in May 2000.

38. In 2010 the embassy helped coordinate the visit of Finance Minister Pranab Mukherjee to Washington for the IMF-World Bank semiannual meetings; it also hosted the visit of Prime Minister Manmohan Singh for the Nuclear Security Summit. Ambassador Shankar spoke at George Washington University's Ambassador's Forum, at the annual roundtable of the U.S. Center for Naval Analysis and the National Maritime Foundation of India, and at the Baltimore Council on Foreign Affairs. She also hosted a cultural program and reception to celebrate the Islamic holiday of Eid-ul-Fitr. Foreign Secretary Nirupama Rao spoke at Harvard University; Minister of Finance Pranab Mukherjee spoke at the Woodrow Wilson Center; and National Security Adviser Shivshankar Menon spoke at the Carnegie Endowment. See www.indianembassy.org.

39. "US Imposes Sanctions on India," *CNN,* May 13, 1998 (www.cnn.com/ WORLD/asiapcf/9805/13/india.us/index.html).

40. Ex-Im Bank loans and guarantees of roughly $500 million, OPIC insurance of $10.2 billion, and U.S. aid of over $142 million were affected; World Bank loans of $1.5 billion were called into question. On the details, see James M. Zimmerman, "U.S. Sanctions against India; Arms Export Control Act; Impact

on Exports," *FindLaw for Legal Professionals* (http://library.findlaw.com/1998/May/13/127144.html).

41. See "Pokhran—The Intelligence Failure," *Global Security* (www.globalsecurity.org/wmd/world/india/pokharan-intell.htm).

42. Among the key members of Congress Chandra saw were Benjamin Gilman (R-N.Y.), chair of the House International Relations Committee; Bill McCollum (R-Fla.), chair of the Republican Policy Committee; and Frank Pallone (D-N.J.), chair of the Caucus on Indian Americans and India. See "Ambassador Naresh Chandra's Meeting with US Congressmen on India's Nuclear Tests," May 22, 1998 (www.indianembassy.org/prdetail1428/ambassador-naresh-chandra"s-meeting-with us).

43. Naresh Chandra, "The Most Challenging Period in Life," *the-south-asian. com,* December 2000 (www.the-south-asian.com/dec2000/Naresh%20Chandra. htm).

44. Ibid., p. 2.

45. Pallone, who displayed no particular interest in either American foreign policy or the Indian American community until the early 1990s, rapidly became a key figure in congressional relations with India and the Indian American community, filling a political vacuum left by the defeat, due to redistricting in 1992, of Steve Solarz, long-time principal congressional contact of Indian Americans. See "Confrontation and Retreat: The U.S. Congress and the South Asian Nuclear Tests," *Arms Control Today,* January/February, 2000 (www.armscontrol.org/print/605), pp. 6–7.

46. Pallone, also vice chair of the Native American Caucus and cochair of the Congressional Caucus on Armenian Issues, received this award in 2002. See *Telegraph* (Calcutta), January 12, 2004 (www.telegraphindia.com).

47. These amendments, passed by Congress in October 1998 (Brownback Amendment, or India-Pakistan Relief Act) and October 1999 (Brownback II), gave the president discretion to waive sanctions against nonnuclear nations testing nuclear weapons.

48. Gadbaw retired from GE in February 2008, although he continued to be active in U.S.-Asian business-government relations as a board member of the National Bureau of Asian Research, cochair of the U.S.-China Legal Cooperation Fund (USCLCF), and in other capacities. See "Michael Gadbaw" (www. partnersglobal.org).

49. "Ambassador Naresh Chandra Meets Members of India Interest Group," *India News,* October 1, 1999 (www.indianembassy.org).

50. Chidanand Rajghatta, "Dan Burton Drops Anti-India Plea," *Indian Express,* September 19, 1998 (www.indianexpress.com).

51. President Bill Clinton visited India March 20–25, 2000, announcing $2 billion in financial support for U.S. exports to India through the Export-Import Bank and other conciliatory measures. In September 2000 Indian Prime Minister Vajpayee visited Washington, addressing a joint session of Congress and urging

closer economic and political ties between the two countries. For a useful chronology of developments following the Indian nuclear tests, see "US v. India: Nuclear Weapons Proliferation," *Case Studies in Sanctions and Terrorism* (Washington: Peterson Institute for International Economics, 2011) (www.iie.com/research/topics/sanctions/india.cfm).

52. "Joint Statement between George W. Bush and Prime Minister Manmohan Singh," White House Office of the Press Secretary, July 18, 2005 (http://georgewbush-whitehouse.archives.gov/news/releases/2005/07/200050718-6.html).

53. Speech by Representative Edward Markey, September 26, 2008 (www.youtube.com/watch?v=YF8TTXCeIAM).

54. Statement of Senator Daniel Akaka, October 1, 2008 (http://akaka.senate.gov/press-releases.cfm?method=releases.view&id=a5beaf6d-f7a0-45ff-be81-fc6a523c2c35).

55. "India Gets NSG Waiver, Manmohan Calls It 'Historic Deal,'" *Express India,* September 6, 2008 (www.expressindia.com/latest-news/Nuclear-deal-India-gets-NSG-waiver-at-Vienna/358098).

56. The left, led by the communists, contended that the agreement was a crucial step "to lock India into U.S. global strategic designs." Meanwhile, the right, led by the nationalist and traditionally pro-U.S. Bharatiya Janata Party, argued that the deal would "promote external interference in India's nuclear program, and eventually cap its nuclear arsenal." See Praful Bidwai, "Nuke Deal with US Draws Domestic Opposition," Inter Press Service, August 13, 2007 (www.ipsnews.net).

57. See, for example, the comments of George W. Bush on signing the U.S.-India civilian nuclear agreement, reported on Channel News Asia, October 9, 2008 (www.channelnewsasia.com.stories/afp_asiapacific/view/381390/1/html). Also see the parallel comments of Indian External Affairs Minister Pranab Mukherjee on working with the United States on building a knowledge society, in "Nuclear Deal Set to Boost US-India Ties," *Energy Daily,* October 5, 2008.

58. Ronen Sen, "US-India Civilian Nuclear Agreement and Beyond," University of California, San Diego School of International Relations and Pacific Studies, January 16, 2007 (http://irps.ucsd.edu/media-center/events/eents_2010090715555.htm); Ronen Sen at George Washington University: "India Committed to Indo-US Nuclear Deal, says Ronen Sen," Rediff India Abroad, March 13 2008 (www.rediff.com/news/2008/mar/13ndeal.htm); at Yale: "Ronen Sen to Give Keynote for Yale Symposium on U.S.-India Strategic Relations," Yale Office of Public Affairs, March 29, 2007 (http://opac.yale.edu/news/article.aspx?id=2441); at University of Pennvania: Aziz Haniffa, "India Must Break through Insularity of the Past: Ronen Sen," Rediff India Abroad, April 23, 2008 (www.rediff.com/news/2008/mar/13ndeal.htm); and at the 26th annual convention of the American Association of Physicians of Indian origin: Aziz Haniffa, "N-Deal Will Be Consummated, Ronen Sen Tells AAPI," Rediff India Abroad, July 1, 2008 (www.rediff.com/news/2008/jul/01ndeal1.htm).

59. The embassy paid BGR $700,000 for its services, over the period September 2005 to August 2006. Foreign Agents Registration Act filing 5430, August 29, 2005 (www.fara.gov/docs/5430-Exhibit-AB-20050912-21.pdf).

60. Blackwill, a career foreign service officer, served as ambassador to India (2001–03) and subsequently as national security council deputy for Iraq (2003–04), before joining the lobbying firm Barbour, Griffith, and Rogers in November 2004.

61. Foreign Agents Registration Act filing 5435.

62. On the council, see http://www.usibc.com.

63. "Emissary Capital Business Report," January 16, 2009 (www.emissary capital.com/docs/ECBR01162009.pdf).

64. "Founder's Note," *Business Leasing and Finance News,* April 2007 (www.pattonboggsblfn.com/blfn_2007_04/?past=yes).

65. Patton Boggs initial six-month contract was reportedly worth $350,000. See Foreign Agents Registration Act filing 2165.

66. "Chamber Launches Massive Grassroots Effort to Win Congressional Approval of US-India Nuclear Deal," March 10, 2006 (www.uschamber.com/press/releases/2006/march/chamber-launches-massive-grassroots-effort-win-congressional-approval-us-i).

67. The CII reportedly spent more than $500,000 to arrange trips to India for nineteen members of Congress and fifty-eight staff members. See Farah Stockman, "Trade Plan Would Allow Nuclear Sales to India," *Boston Globe,* July 3, 2006.

68. This BGR lobbying contract was reportedly in the amount of $520,000 for 2005. See "Lobbying Spending Database: Confederation of Indian Industry, 2005," *Open Secrets* (www.opensecrets.org/lobby/clientsum.php?id=F3372&year=2005).

69. "On Brink of Collapse, AIG Lobbied for India Nuke Deal (Really!)," *AlterNet,* October 25, 2008 (www.alternet.org/world/104547/on_brink_of_collapse,_aig_lobbied_for_india_nuke_deal_%28really!%29/coments?page=entire).

70. Michael Forsythe and Veena Trehan, "US Pro-India Groups Out in Full Force," *Standard,* July 18, 2006.

71. "US-India Nuclear Cooperation" (www.usinpac.com/index.php?option=com_content&view=article&id=567&Itemid=302).

72. "Indian Americans Lobby with NRIs for India-US Nuke Deal" (www.usinpac.com).

73. Suman Guha Mozumder, "AJC Throws Weight behind Nuclear Deal," *Indians Abroad,* May 26, 2006.

74. In 2008 the Indian outsourcing industry had revenues of $11 billion annually and employed over 700,000 people. Roughly 60 percent of sales were in the United States. See "India's Outsourcing Revenue to Hit $50 billion," *Financial Express,* September 29, 2008.

75. Sharon Otterman, "Trade: Outsourcing Jobs," Council on Foreign Relations, February 20, 2004 (www.cfr.org/pakistan/trade-outsourcing-jobs/p7749).

76. John C. McCarthy, "3.3 Million US Services Jobs to Go Offshore," Tech strategy research brief (Washington: Forrester Research, 2002); and Saritha Rai, "India Sees Backlash Fading over Boom in Outsourcing," *New York Times,* July 14, 2004 (www.nytimes.com/2004/07/14/business/worldbusiness/14infosys. html).

77. Government Accountability Office, "Report to Congressional Requesters: International Trade: Current Government Data Provide Limited Insight into Offshoring of Services," September 2004 (www.oecd.org/dataoecd/3/32/35542215. pdf).

78. On the evolution of the outsourcing controversy in U.S. politics, see www. nytimes.com/2004/07/14/business/woridbusiness/14infosys.html.

79. Rai, "India Sees Backlash Fading."

80. David J. Karl, "America's New Anti-India Backlash," *Business Week,* May 13, 2010 (www.businessweek.com/blobalbiz/content/may2010/gb20100513_ 405539.htm).

81. "India Inc. Happy about Defeat of Antioutsourcing Bill in U.S.," *Economic Times,* September 30, 2010.

82. The additional fees are expected to cost the Indian information technology outsourcing sector $250 million, although the resulting markup to their American clients is uncertain. See "Border Security Bill Discriminatory: India to US," *Times of India,* August 20, 2010 (http://timesofindia.indiatimes.com/india/Border-security-bill-discriminatory-India-to-US/articleshow/6367131.cms).

83. Yashwant Raj, "Indian IT Majors Face US Visa Fee Heat," *Hindustan Times,* December 24, 2010 (www.hindustantimes.com/Indian-IT-majors-face-US-visa-fee-heat/Article1-642119.aspx).

84. "Gillibrand, Schumer: New Momentum for 9/11 Health Bill," Senator Kirsten Gillibrand, December 19, 2010 (http://gillibrand.senate.gov/newsroom/ press/release?id=768CDBOC-7259-4762-8BF8-2CF11E1EBC27).

85. Indira Kannan, "It's Going to Come Back and Hurt Us," *Business Standard,* August 12, 2010.

86. Surabhi Agarwal and Asit Ranjan Mishra, "India Objects to New US Bill on Higher Visa Fees," *Live Mint,* December 23, 2010 (www.livemint. com/2010/12/23221912/India-objets-to-new-US-Bill-o.html).

87. Dana Bash and Jennifer Liberto, "Bill on Outsourced Jobs Fails Senate Test," *CNN Money,* September 28, 2010 (http://money.cnn.com/2010/09/28/ news/economy/Outsource_jobs_bill_dead/).

88. Global Mobility and Immigration Practice Group, "First Responders Health Act Funded by Extension of Increased Application Fees for L and H-1B Visas," January 10, 2011 (www.globalimmigrationcounsel.com/2011/01/articles/ us-immigration/first-responders-health-act-funded-by-extension-of-increased-application-fees-for-l-and-h1b-visas/).

89. Agarwal and Mishra, "India Objects to New US Bill."

90. International Institute for Strategic Studies, *The Military Balance, 2012* (London : Institute for Strategic Studies, 2012).

91. In the first three months of 2013, for example, bilateral trade between the United States and Burma totaled $90 million. In 2012 bilateral trade totaled $65.7 million. See U.S. Census Bureau, "Trade in Goods with Burma," August 2013 (www.census.gov/foreign-trade/balance/c5460.html).

92. This publication follows the convention of the U.S. government, which traditionally uses the names Burma and Rangoon, although local government usage is now Myanmar.

93. Ambassador Burton Levin left his post on September 30, 1990, and Ambassador Derek Mitchell presented his credentials on July 6, 2012. Burma did not downgrade its representation to chargé d'affairs in Washington until 2004. Ambassador Than Swe was the first person to assume the post since 2004, when Lynn Myaing served as the seventeenth Burmese ambassador to the United States.

94. In 1988 Ronald Reagan suspended U.S. aid to Burma, imposed an arms embargo, and introduced a range of economic sanctions. Under the next three U.S. presidents these measures were reinforced through three laws and four presidential directives. See Michael F. Martin, "U.S. Sanctions on Burma" (Congressional Research Service, 2011).

95. U.S. Department of State, *Diplomatic List* (Spring/Summer 2012). This expanded to fifteen by the spring of 2013.

96. Leon T. Hadar, "Sanctions against Burma: A Failure on All Fronts," *Trade Policy Analysis,* March 26, 1998.

97. For pronouncements by Thein Sein, see Anne Gearan, "Burma's Thein Sein Says Military 'Will Always Have a Special Place' in Government," *Washington Post,* May 19, 2013; and Ashish Kumar Sen, "Myanmar President Pledges to Press Ahead with Reforms," *Washington Times,* May 20, 2013. For Aung San Suu Kyi, see Sen, "Myanmar President Pledges to Press Ahead"; Anne Gearan, "Aung San Suu Kyi Urges Easing of U.S. Sanctions on Burma," *Washington Post,* September 19, 2012; and Mark Magnier, "Burma's Suu Kyi Says She's Aiming for the Top," *Washington Post,* June 6, 2013.

98. See David Steinberg, "Analyzing the Prospects for Change in Myanmar," interview by Keith W. Rabin, KWR International, October 26, 2011 (www. kwrintl.com/library/2011/steinberginterview.html).

99. See "Text of Broadcast by Dulles of His Report to the Nation on His Trip to Far East," *New York Times,* March 9, 1955 (http://select.nytimes.com/gst/abstract.html?res=F10F15FE3E5C1B7B93CBA91788D85F418585F9).

100. See U.S. General Accounting Office, "Drug Control Enforcement Efforts in Burma Are Not Effective" (GAO/Nmained SIAD-89-197, 1989).

101. "Myanmar and World Bank Sign Deal to Clear Old Debt," *New York Times,* January 27, 2013.

102. SLORC ruled Burma from 1988 to 1997, when it was succeeded by the State Peace and Development Council, which was dissolved by President Thein

Sein in 2011. Both SLORC and the SPDC were essentially military juntas, ruling through collective leadership.

103. U.S. nonmilitary aid amounting to $12.3 million (including $7 million in development assistance, $5 million in antinarcotic support, and $260,000 in military training funds) was suspended on September 23, 1988. More significantly, a week later Japan suspended its economic assistance, totaling $300 million a year. See Martin, "U.S. Sanctions on Burma"; and Susan Banki, "Contested Regimes, Aid Flows, and Refugee Flows: The Case of Burma," *Journal of Current Southeast Asian Affairs* 28, no. 2 (2009), pp. 47–73. Also see Office of the President, "Memorandum on Amendments to the Generalized System of Preferences," April 13, 1989 (www.presidency.ucsb.edu'ws'index/[j[?[od=16924/).

104. For a transcript of the hearings, see U.S. House of Representatives Committee on Foreign Affairs, Subcommittee on Human Rights and International Organizations, "Crackdown in Burma: Suppression of the Democracy Movement and Violations of Human Rights," hearing, September 13, 1989, Serial 26-305 (Government Printing Office, 1990).

105. David Serchuk, "Burma's Billionaire," *Forbes Asia* 3, no. 7 (2007), pp. 68–60.

106. Zarny Mann, "Burmese Exile Government Dissolves after 22 Years," *Irrawaddy*, September 14, 2012.

107. McConnell's passionate support of Burma sanctions has often puzzled casual Capitol Hill observers, given his conservative Republicanism and vocal opposition to cutting financial ties with China. His position on Burma sanctions reportedly had its roots in his desire to punish the SLORC regime for its collaboration in the heroin trade. He also reportedly wanted to oust SLORC because he feared that China's arms sales to Burma were cementing a Sino-Burmese alliance contrary to U.S. strategic interests. See Kevin Danaher and Jason Mark, *Insurrection: Citizen Challenges to Corporate Power* (New York: Routledge, 2003), p. 196.

108. See Toshihiro Kudo and Fumiharu Mieno, "Trade, Foreign Investment, and Myanmar's Economic Development during the Transition to an Open Economy," Discussion Paper 116 (Tokyo: Institute of Developing Economies, August 2007), p. 26; and Martin, "US Sanctions on Burma."

109. Ken Silverstein, "Their Man in Washington: Undercover with D.C.s Lobbyists for Hire," *Harper's*, 315, no. 1886 (2007), pp. 53–61.

110. "Burma's Image Problem Is a Moneymaker for US Lobbyists," *Washington Post*, February 24, 1998.

111. On the deaths, see Soubhik Ronnie Saha, "Working through Ambiguity: International NGOs in Myanmar" (Harvard University Hauser Center for Non-Profit Organizations, 2011), p. 8. For a prescient view of later developments, see Richard P. Cronin, "Burma's Suffering: Will a Horrific Tragedy Become a Change-Forcing Event?," *PacNet*, May 20, 2008.

112. Saha, "Working through Ambiguity," p. 8.

113. Kurt M. Campbell, "US Policy toward Burma," special briefing, U.S. Department of State, September 28, 2009.

114. Asia Society Burma Policy Task Force, "Current Realities and Future Possibilities in Burma/Myanmar: Options for U.S. Policy" (New York: Asia Society, 2010). Amartya Sen is a professor of economics at Harvard and Nobel Prize Laureate; Thomas Pickering is vice chair of Hills and Company and a former U.S. undersecretary of state for political affairs. Donald Emmerson is director of the Southeast Asia Forum at Stanford University; Frances Zwenig, former chief of staff to Senator John Kerry, was counselor of the US-ASEAN Business Council at the time of the report. Maureen Aung-Thwin is director of the Burma Project at the Open Society Institute.

115. See also Priscilla Clapp and Suzanne DiMaggio, "Advancing Myanmar's Transition: A Way Forward for U.S. Policy" (New York: Asia Society, 2012).

116. "Aung San Suu Kyi and Hillary Clinton Address Asia Society in D.C.," Asia Society blog, September 18, 2012 (http://asiasociety.org/blog/asia/photos-aung-san-suu-kyi-and-hillary-clinton-address-asia-society-dc#1).

117. See Ernest Bower and others, "CSIS Myanmar Trip Report" (http://csis.org/files/publication/120911_MyanmarTripReport.pdf). On the September 2012 Myanmar conference at CSIS, held just before Aung San Suu Kyi's visit, see http://csis.org/publication/csis-myanmar-trip-report.

118. Kurt Campbell had been executive vice president of CSIS until entering the Obama administration, while Derek Mitchell had been director of the Southeast Asia program.

119. This figure includes some multiyear programs. Actual annual allocations were $29.04 million for 2011 and $33.05 million for 2012. See Organization for Economic Cooperation and Development, "Query Wizard for International Development Statistics," 2012 ed. (http://stats.oecd.org/qwids).

120. See, for example, Antoni Slodkowski, "How Japan Inc Stole a March in Myanmar," Reuters Special Report, October 2, 2012; and Lex Rieffel and James W. Fox, "Too Much, Too Soon? The Dilemma of Foreign Aid to Myanmar/Burma," Nathan Associates, March 2013 (www.nathaninc.com/news/too-much-too-soon-foreign-aid-and-myanmar).

121. Indonesian President Susilo Bambang Yudhoyono and Representative Diaz-Balart also made this observation. See Yudhoyono, "Indonesia: Regional Role, Global Reach" (www2.lse.ac.uk/publicEvents/pdf/20090331_Bambang Yudhoyono.pdf); and Diaz-Balart, "Providing for Consideration of H.R. 1886, Pakistan Enduring Assistance and Cooperation Enhancement Act of 2009, and Providing for Consideration of H.R. 2410, Foreign Relations Authorization Act, Fiscal Years 2010 and 2011," *Congressional Record* 155, no. 86, June 10, 2009, pp. H6421–29 (www.gpo.gov/fdsys/pkg/CREC-2009-06-10/html/CREC-2009-06-10-pt1-PgH6421-2.htm).

122. Ann Marie Murphy, "US Gives a Long Overdue Nod to Indonesia," *Asia Times,* March 18, 2009 (www.atimes.com/atimes/Southeast_Asia/KC18Ae02.html).

123. During the 2000–09 period there were 35,195 articles about China; 25,648 about Japan; 17,929 about India; 14,715 about Korea; and 4,796 about

Indonesia. Derived from *New York Times* content analysis, using Proquest and employing search terms that included country names, polit*, and econom*.

124. Analysis by Mariko de Freytas based on *New York Times* articles published between 2000 and 2009.

125. Andre Roadnight, *United States Policy toward Indonesia in the Truman and Eisenhower Years* (New York: Palgrave-Macmillan, 2002), p. 183.

126. On the Bandung Summit, see George McTurnan Kahin, *The Asia-African Conference: Bandung, Indonesia, April, 1955* (Cornell University Press, 1956); and Richard Wright, *The Color Curtain: A Report on the Bandung Conference* (New York: World Publishing, 1956).

127. Roadnight, *United States Policy,* pp. 181–82.

128. *Konfrontasi* was Sukarno's term for political-military opposition, through undeclared warfare, to the creation of Malaysia. See J. A. C. Mackie, *Konfrontasi: The Indonesia-Malaysia Dispute, 1963–1966* (Oxford University Press, 1974).

129. The United States figures more importantly in Indonesia's trade picture than the converse, being Indonesia's sixth-largest import partner in 2013, but what likely matters most in Washington, especially on Capitol Hill, is America's role as an exporter.

130. See Foreign Agents Registration Act (www.fara.gov). As of November 1, 2013, FARA data indicated that Indonesia had no foreign registrants.

131. See "Obama Cancellation Accepted by Australia and Indonesia," *BBC News,* March 19, 2010; and Donny Syofyon, "Obama's Postponed Visit: Blessing in Disguise," *Jakarta Post,* June 9, 2010.

132. On the East Timor massacres, see Geoffrey Robinson, "East Timor Crimes against Humanity," University of California–Los Angeles, July, 2003 (http://www.etan.org/etanpdf/2006/CAVR/12-Annexe1-East-Timor-1999-Geoffrey Robinson.pdf).

133. Yenni Djahidin, "Ed Masters: A Loyal Friend in Washington," *Jakarta Post,* 2009 (www.thejakartapost.com/news/2009/01/30/ed-masters-a-loyalfriend-washington.html).

134. Michael Barone, *The Almanac of American Politics,* 2010 ed. (Washington: National Journal Group, 2009), pp. 392–94.

135. Ibid., p. 560.

136. On Senator Leahy's activities, see http://leahy.senate.gov.

137. Senator Patrick Leahy has spoken out about and introduced legislation on a broad range of Indonesia-related issues, including East Timor atrocities (2001–02), restriction on military assistance to Indonesia (2002), human trafficking (2005), the untimely death of Indonesian human rights defenders such as Munir Said Thalib (2006), and protecting Indonesian rain forests and ecosystems (2008–09). See http://leahy.senate.gov.

138. Senator Leahy opposed the resumption of military aid to Indonesia in 2002 due to the alleged involvement of the Indonesian army in drug smuggling, prostitution, human trafficking, and illegal logging. See "America and Indonesia: Good

Friends or Bad Company?" (www.cdi.org). For details on restoration of military ties in November 2005, see Glenn Kessler, "Military Ties to Indonesia Resume Too Soon for Some," *Washington Post,* November 23, 2005 (www.washington post.com/wp-dyn/content/article/2005/11/22/AR2005112201751.html).

139. Susilo Bambang Yudhoyono, "Indonesia and America: A 21st Century Partnership" (Washington: USINDO, 2008).

140. "U.S.-Indonesia Joint Declaration on Comprehensive Partnership," November 9, 2010 (www.america.gov/st/texttrans-english/2010/November/201 01109102136suO.2631146html).

141. "Mobile Money Initiative and the US-Indonesia Comprehensive Partnership," November 18, 2011 (www.state.gov/r/pa/prs/ps/2011/11/177384.htm).

142. Dino Djalal, who served as his president's personal spokesman for six years before arriving in Washington, brought many communications strengths to his post, including long experience with North America. He first came to Washington as a teenager in 1979, when his father, Hasjim Djalal, served as the embassy deputy chief of mission. He attended McLean High School in Virginia, later graduating from Carleton University (B.A.) and Simon Fraser University (M.A.) in Canada, before earning a Ph.D. at the London School of Economics. On Djalal's career and accomplishments, see Larry Luxner, "Indonesia's Ambassador Embodies Ambitions of His Emerging Nation," *Washington Diplomat* 18, no. 11 (2011), pp. 15–17, 22.

143. Fortuitously, the event was held on the same day as the annual Smithsonian Folklife Festival and the Dalai Lama's "Talk on World Peace." See "Around the Mall: Today's Events at the Folklife Festival," July 9, 2011 (http://blogs.smithsonianmag.com/aroundthemall/2011/07/july-9-todays-events-at-the-folklife-festival/).

144. On the details of the event, see *Washington Post,* July 10, 2011.

145. For reports of the event, see "In the Bamboo Shaking Business, Indonesians Have the Edge," *Indonesia Creative Hub,* July 15, 2011 (http://indonesia creativehub.org./in-the-bamboo-shaking); and Jessica Goldstein, "Indonesia Fest in D.C. Aims for Record in Mass Performance on Traditional Angklung Instrument," *Washington Post,* July 8, 2011. Also see www.embassyofindonesia.org/indonesianfestival/.

146. One postponement was due to health care reform legislation and the second due to the BP oil spill. The visit, however, when it finally happened, was considered successful. On the details, see Chico Harlan, "Obama's Visit to Indonesia Mixes Pride with a Dose of Reality," *Washington Post,* November 8, 2010.

147. Roberta Rampton, "Obama to Visit Asia Next Month to Discuss Economy, Security," Reuters, September 13, 2013 (www.reuters.com/article/2013/09/13/us-usa-obama-asiidUSBRE98C0TS20130913).

148. Larry Luxner, "Indonesian Envoy Steps Down in Long-Shot Bid for President," *Washington Diplomat* 18, no. 1 (2013), pp. 11–13.

149. See I. M. Destler, "Country Expertise and U.S. Foreign Policymaking: The Case of Japan," *Pacific Community,* July 1974, pp. 546–64.

150. The Indonesian embassy has been in the former mansion of Colorado gold-mining magnate Thomas Walsh since 1951. Walsh hosted many prominent early-twentieth-century visitors there, including Alice Roosevelt and King Albert of Belgium. The last private sale of the Hope Diamond was also negotiated there. See www.embassyofIndonesia.org.

151. Central Intelligence Agency, *World Factbook,* 2013–14 edition.

152. Foreign Agents Registration Act (www.fara.gov).

153. On the notion of a virtual state applied to Singapore, see Richard Rosecrance, "The Rise of the Virtual State," *Foreign Affairs* 75, no. 4 (1996), pp. 45–61.

154. On the distinctive Singapore model of bilateral defense cooperation, including Luke AFB training exercises, see Kent E. Calder, *Embattled Garrisons: Comparative Base Politics and American Globalism* (Princeton University Press, 2007), pp. 60–62, 236–37.

155. On the details, see Calder, *Embattled Garrisons,* pp. 147–48. Clark Field was, at the time of its closing, the largest U.S. airbase outside the United States and had been operated continuously by U.S. forces since 1903, except during the Japanese occupation. On the Philippine Senate's rejection of the base agreement, it is notable that the constitution of 1987 already forbade foreign military bases not governed by a formal treaty. Article 18, section 25, provides that "after the expiration in 1991 of the Agreement between the Republic of the Philippines and the United States of America concerning Military Bases, foreign military bases, troops, or facilities shall not be allowed in the Philippines except under a treaty duly concurred in by the Senate and when the Congress so requires, ratified by a majority of the votes cast by the people in a national referendum held for that purpose, and recognized as a treaty by the other contracting State."

156. Emma Chanlett-Avery, *Singapore: Background and U.S. Relations* (Washington: Congressional Research Service, January 7, 2005) (www.policyarchive.org/handle/10207/bitstreams/3347.pdf).

157. Tommy Koh served in 2013 as ambassador-at-large of the Singapore Foreign Ministry, special adviser of the Institute of Policy Studies, and chairman of the SymAsia Foundation of Credit Suisse. He served previously as the ambassador to the United States (1984–90) and as the permanent representative to the United Nations (1968–71 and 1974–84). Koh has a law degree from Harvard University and a Ph.D. from Cambridge University. He was chief negotiator for the U.S.–Singapore Free Trade Agreement from 2000 to 2003. On Koh's career, see http://law.nus.edu.sg.

158. U.S. Department of State, *Diplomatic List,* Spring 2013.

159. Ambassador Chan's Ph.D. thesis, awarded by the University of Singapore in 1974, was titled "The Dynamics of One-Party Dominance: A Study of Five Singapore Constituencies."

160. These include Singapore's National Book Award in 1978 for *The Dynamics of One-Party Dominance: The PAP at the Grassroots* (Singapore University Press, 1976) and a second National Book Award in 1986 for *A Sensation*

of Independence: A Political Biography of David Marshall (Oxford University Press, 1984).

161. In 2011 Ambassador Roble Olhaye of Djibouti was the longest serving, having been accredited to Washington since 1988. See U.S. Department of State, "Diplomatic List: Order of Precedence and Date of Presentation of Credentials" (www.state.gov/s/cpr/rls/dpl/29710.htm).

162. Ashok Kumar Mirpuri began his appointment as Singapore's ambassador to the United States in July 2012. He had served previously as ambassador to Indonesia (2006–12), high commissioner to Malaysia (2002–06), and high commissioner to Australia (2000–02). Apart from his Harvard experience, Mirpuri also has a master's degree from SOAS. For further details, see Embassy of the Republic of Singapore, "About the Ambassador," 2012 (www.mfa.gov.sg/content/mfa/overseasmission/washington/about_the_embassy/about_the_ambassador.html).

163. See Tommy Koh and Chang Li Lin, *The United States–Singapore Free Trade Agreement: Highlights and Insights* (Singapore: Institute of Policy Studies, 2004), p. 171.

164. On embassy events, see www.mfa.gov.sg/washington.

165. Temasek hired Weber Shandwick to do media monitoring and outreach; to contact U.S.-based companies, think tanks, organizations, and individuals; and to provide strategic counsel and analysis of federal and congressional actions. In 2009 Quinn, Gillespie, and Associates lobbied for CFIUS approval for Rio Tinto and Chinalco on behalf of Singapore's Shining Prospect Pte, which wanted to have the Australian-Chinese partnership approved by Congress. The partners were ultimately approved by CFIUS. "Foreign Lobbying Influence Tracker: Country Singapore, Client Shining Prospect Pte," ProPublica and Sunlight Foundation, March 2011 (http://foreignlobbying.org/client/Shining%20Prospect%20Pte.%20Ltd./). In 2008 Lee Kuan Yew's family sued the *Wall Street Journal* for defamation against the Singapore judiciary. The Singapore Economic Development Board, closely related to the Singapore government, hired Daniel J. Edelman, Inc., to provide media counsel. See "Singapore Strikes Again," *Wall Street Journal,* November 29, 2008 (http://online.wsj.com/article/SB12279198931176553.html); and "New Charges by Singapore against the Wall Street Journal," *Asia Sentinel,* March 17, 2009 (www.asiasentinel.com/politics/new-charges-by-singapore-against-the-wall-street-journal).

166. On Singapore International Water Week, see www.siww.com.sg/.

167. For a detailed study of the U.S.-Singapore free trade agreement and its implications, see Koh and Lin, *United States–Singapore Free Trade Agreement.*

168. The USSFTA Implementation Act (H.R. 2739) passed the House of Representatives on July 24, 2003, and was passed a week later by the Senate. The act was then signed by President George W. Bush in September 2003, three months after he signed the free trade agreement with Goh. See "USA-Singapore," SICE—the Organization of American States' Foreign Trade Information System (www.sice.oas.org/TPD/USA_SGP/USASGP_e.ASP).

169. Koh and Lin, *The United States–Singapore Free Trade Agreement*, p. 165.

170. Ibid., p. 171.

171. Ambassador Chan, for example, met personally with 353 of 435 members of the House of Representatives or their staff, and 78 of 100 Senators or their staff, in the course of the FTA effort. See Chang Li Lin, "Eight Lessons from the U.S.-Singapore FTA," Third World Network (www.twnside.org.sg).

172. Koh and Lin, *The United States–Singapore Free Trade Agreement*, p. 166.

173. Ibid., p. 168.

174. For the text of the support letter, see Ministry of Foreign Affairs in Singapore (http://app.mfa.gov.sg/pr/read_content.asp?View,1611). Although there may have been some hyperbole in their statement, Singapore was the eleventh-largest trading partner of the United States in 2001, with bilateral trade amounting to over $40 billion. Singapore also played host to more than 1,500 American companies and was home to more than 17,000 Americans—mostly employees of major U.S. multinationals—statistics that were not lost on members of Congress.

175. Press release, embassy of Singapore (http://app.mfa.gov.sg/pr/read_content.asp?view,1611).

176. Koh and Chang, *The United States–Singapore Free Trade Agreement*, p. 166.

177. Ibid., p. 167.

Chapter 9

1. See Stephen Skowronek, *Building A New American State: The Expansion of National Administrative Capacities, 1877–1920* (Cambridge University Press, 1982).

2. See, for example, Arthur M. Schlesinger Jr., *The Age of Jackson* (Boston: Little, Brown, 1945), p. 126; and Alexis de Tocqueville, *Democracy in America*, trans. Richard D. Heffner (New York: Penguin, 2003), p. 10. Jackson's notorious presidential inaugural reception, with backwoodsmen knocking over punch bowls, smashing glasses, and tramping in muddy boots on White House tables, was a conspicuous example.

3. Schlesinger, *The Age of Jackson*.

4. Tocqueville, *Democracy in America*, pp. 72–76.

5. The phrase is from a classified, March 1944, British Foreign Office study, "The Essentials of an American Policy," cited in C. Ball, *The Debatable Alliance: An Essay in Anglo-American Relations* (Oxford University Press, 1964), p. 7.

6. See Stephen M. Walt, *Taming American Power: The Global Response to U.S. Primacy* (New York: Norton, 2005).

7. For a concise, authoritative treatment of globalization and its political-economic implications, see Jeffrey A. Frieden, *Global Capitalism: Its Fall and Rise in the Twentieth Century* (New York: Norton, 2006), pp. 339–412.

8. For this and the following paragraphs, see ibid., pp. 343, 379, 380, 381.

9. The estimated value of the world's outstanding bonds, equities, and banking assets reached $150.1 trillion in 2001 and $190.4 trillion in 2006. See U.S. Treasury Department, "Cross-Border Capital Flows and Foreign Exchange Activity" (www.treasury.gov/sesource-center/iteraction/exchange-rate-politicies/Documents/Dec-2007/Appendix1).

10. In 1998 global turnover in the foreign exchange market was estimated by the Bank of International Settlements at $1.65 trillion, followed by $1.42 trillion (2001), $1.95 trillion (2004), and $3.21 trillion (2007). See ibid.

11. On economic, social, and political developments of the 1970s related to globalization, see Niall Ferguson and others, eds., *The Shock of the Global: The 1970s in Perspective* (Harvard University Press, 2010).

12. On this trend, see Raymond Vernon, *Sovereignty at Bay: The Multinational Spread of U.S. Enterprises* (New York: Basic Books, 1971); Raymond Vernon, *Storm over the Multinationals: The Real Issues* (Harvard University Press, 1977); and Daniel A. Yergin and Joseph Stanislaw, *The Commanding Heights: The Battle for the World Economy* (New York: Touchstone, 1998).

13. Chongqing in China, for example, shows this tendency. See Emilie Frenkiel, "From Scholar to Official: Cui Zhiyuan and Chongqing City's Local Experimental Policy," *Booksandideas.net,* December 6, 2010 (www.booksandideas.net/IMG/pdf/20101206_Cui_Zhiyuan_EN.pdf).

14. See Anne-Marie Slaughter, *A New World Order* (Princeton University Press, 2004); and Anne-Marie Slaughter, "America's Edge: Power in the Networked Century," *Foreign Affairs* 88, no. 1 (2009), pp. 94–113.

15. Ngaire Woods, *The Globalizers: The IMF, the World Bank, and Their Borrowers* (Cornell University Press, 2006), pp. 6–7.

16. From April 2011 an Egyptian international civil servant, Nemat Shafik, previously at the World Bank, also served as a third IMF deputy managing director. For further details on the IMF's top management structure, see the IMF website (www.imf.org/external/np/omd/bios/mns.htm).

17. On this point, see Joseph E. Stiglitz, *Globalization and Its Discontents* (New York: Norton, 2003), pp. 195–213. Stiglitz served as chief economist of the World Bank during the Asian financial crisis and its aftermath (1997–2000).

18. The current World Bank president, David Kim, is a medical doctor who previously served as president of Dartmouth College. His immediate predecessor, Robert Zoellick, was U.S. trade representative in the George W. Bush administration. Zoellick's predecessor, Paul Wolfowitz, had been deputy secretary of defense. Former Secretary of Defense Robert McNamara also served for thirteen years (1968–81) as World Bank president.

19. Woods, *The Globalizers*, p. 35.

20. See Stiglitz, *Globalization and Its Discontents*.

21. David D. Driscoll, "The IMF and the World Bank: How Do They Differ?," International Monetary Fund website (www.imf.org/external/pubs/ft/exrp/differ/differ.htm#a8).

22. As noted, World Bank veteran Nemat Shafik was appointed one of three IMF deputy managing directors.

23. Woods, *The Globalizers,* p. 3.

24. See Michael E. Porter, "Clusters and the New Economics of Competition," *Harvard Business Review,* November/December, 1998, pp. 77–90; and Michael E. Porter, *The Competitive Advantage of Nations* (New York: Free Press, 1990).

25. On the statistical details, see Central Intelligence Agency, *World Fact Book.*

26. See, for example, Kent E. Calder, "Japanese Foreign Economic Policy Formation: Explaining the Reactive State," *World Politics* 40, no. 4 (1988), pp. 517–41.

Chapter 10

1. Michael E. Porter, *The Competitive Advantage of Nations* (New York: Free Press, 1990).

2. Robert Dahl, *Who Governs? Democracy and Power in an American City* (Yale University Press, 1961).

3. See Michael Leifer, *Singapore's Foreign Policy: Coping with Vulnerability* (London: Routledge, 2000); and Richard N. Rosecrance, *The Rise of the Virtual State: Wealth and Power in the Coming Century* (New York: Basic Books, 1999).

4. See, for example, Benjamin Weiser, "A New York Prosecutor with Worldwide Reach," *New York Times,* March 27, 2010 on the Southern District Court and the drug trade. Also see Saskia Sassen, *The Global City: New York, London, Tokyo,* 2nd ed. (Princeton University Press, 2001).

5. For a pioneering effort at this sort of comparative subnational analysis, see the 2009 APSA panel, "The Global Political City and International Affairs," including Kent E. Calder, "Washington, D.C. as a Global Political City"; Mariko de Freytas, "Comparative Global Political Cities: Brussels and Paris"; Eunjung Lim, "New York as a Global Political City"; and Min Ye, "Beijing as an International Metropolis."

Index

355